Labour Law and Industrial Relations in Canada

Labour Law and Industrial Relations in Canada

by
Prof. H. W. Arthurs
Prof. D. D. Carter
Prof. H. J. Glasbeek

This book was originally published as a monograph in the International Encyclopaedia for Labour Law and Industrial Relations

1981

KLUWER
DEVENTER/BOSTON/LONDON/FRANKFURT/ANTWERP

BUTTERWORTHS
TORONTO/VANCOUVER/LONDON/SEATTLE

Distribution in Canada and the USA

Butterworths and Co. Ltd.
2265 Midland Avenue
Scarborough, Ontario
Canada M1P 4S1

Cover design: Pieter J. van der Sman

Library of Congress Cataloging in Publication Data

Arthurs, Harry W.   1933-
Labour Law and Industrial Relations in Canada
Originally published as a monograph in the International Encyclopaedia for Labour Law and
Industrial Relations.
Bibliography: p.
1. Labor laws and legislation – Canada.
2. Industrial relations – Canada. I. Carter, D. D., joint author. II. Glasbeek, H. J., joint author.
III. Title.
KE3109.A76   344.71'01   80-22468

ISBN 90 312 0139 1 (Kluwer) 0-409-81184-X (Butterworths)

D/1981/2664/15

© 1981, Kluwer, Deventer, The Netherlands

Foreword

This text is one of a collection of national monographs which have appeared under the aegis of the International Encyclopaedia for Labour Law and Industrial Relations. The Encyclopaedia, taken as a whole, will provide intellectual stimulus and a wealth of detailed information for scholars and practitioners seeking a comparative and transnational perspective on problems of labour law and industrial relations. However, it is a reference publication, rather than one which is likely to be within easy reach of those who seek knowledge about their own domestic system.

Because no broad, up-to-date general survey of Canadian labour law presently exists the authors, with the co-operation of the editor-in-chief, Professor R. Blanpain, and the publisher, Messrs. Kluwer, have decided to make this Canadian monograph available as a separate volume. We hope that it will provide advocates and administrators, management and labour, and especially students, with an overview of all aspects of Canadian labour law, and, to some extent, of its social, economic and political context.

At the same time, we urge readers to regard this work as the starting point for their reading, rather than as a final destination. The law of labour is becoming, for better or worse, infinitely and regressively complex. We do not claim that we have been able to reproduce each detail of the law as it stood at the moment we laid down our pens (roughly August, 1979) let alone to foretell subsequent developments with infallible accuracy.

H. W. Arthurs
D. D. Carter
H. J. Glasbeek

Table of Contents

Table of Contents

Part I. The Individual Employment Relationship 53

Table of Contents

Table of Contents

Table of Contents

Table of Contents

List of Abbreviations

LAW REPORTS AND PERIODICALS
Can. Bar Rev.	– Canadian Bar Review
C.L.L.C.	– Canadian Labour Law Cases
C.L.L.R.	– Canadian Labour Law Reporter
C.L.R.B.R.	– Canadian Labour Relations Boards Reports
D.L.R.	– Dominion Law Reports
L.A.C.	– Labour Arbitration Cases
O.L.R.B.Rep.	– Ontario Labour Relations Board Monthly Report
O.R.	– Ontario Reports
Rel.Ind.	– Relations Industrielles
U.B.C.L.R.	– University of British Columbia Law Review
U. of T.L.J.	– University of Toronto Law Journal

STATUTES
S.C.	– Statutes of Canada
R.S.C.	– Revised Statutes of Canada
S.B.C.	– Statutes of British Columbia
R.S.B.C.	– Revised Statutes of British Columbia
S.O.	– Statutes of Ontario
R.S.O.	– Revised Statutes of Ontario
S.Q.	– Statutes of Quebec
R.S.Q.	– Revised Statutes of Quebec
S.N.S.	– Statutes of Nova Scotia
S.S.	– Statutes of Saskatchewan

LABOUR RELATIONS BOARD AND COURTS
B.C.L.R.B.	– British Columbia Labour Relations Board
C.L.R.B.	– Canada Labour Relations Board
O.L.R.B.	– Ontario Labour Relations Board
Q.L.C.	– Quebec Labour Court
S.L.R.B.	– Saskatchewan Labour Relations Board
Alta. S.C.	– Alberta Supreme Court
B.C.S.C.	– British Columbia Supreme Court
B.C.C.A.	– British Columbia Court of Appeal
Fed.C.A.	– Federal Court of Appeal

List of Abbreviations

N.B.S.C., App.Div.	– New Brunswick Supreme Court, Appeal Division
Ont.C.A.	– Ontario Court of Appeal
Ont.Div.Ct.	– Ontario Divisional Court
Ont.H.C.	– Ontario High Court
P.C.	– Judicial Committee of Privy Council
Q.S.C.	– Quebec Superior Court
S.C.C.	– Supreme Court of Canada

Introduction

I. General Observations

1. To speak of the Canadian system of labour law, however defined, is in a sense to mislead. In effect, there are at least eleven functioning labour relations systems in Canada, embracing the ten provinces and the federal (national) sphere. Each of these systems, moreover, is in large measure regulated by a statute which governs labour relations in the private sector generally. But often, as well, special provision is made for one sector of the labour market, such as construction, or even a single major undertaking, such as the development of a new energy resource. And almost always, special legislation deals with labour relations in the civil service, and with various private sector and municipal activities which are perceived to be of special concern to the public.

Nor is this list exhaustive: common law (or, in Quebec, civil law) principles play an important role, especially in relation to the rules of industrial conflict, as does the federal criminal law; administrative and judicial pronouncements are of vital importance in the authoritative interpretation of all aspects of law; and labour law necessarily intersects with other aspects of the general legal system.

Finally, to a greater or lesser extent, most aspects of Canadian labour law presuppose that employers, employees and unions, at the level of the individual enterprise or, occasionally of local labour markets in a particular industry, will generate their own 'law' through formal agreements and informal understandings and customs.

2. The picture, then, is one of great complexity and diversity. The problem of the editors is to present this picture in a way which simplifies it, yet remains accurate. We have tried to do this by identifying common policy themes and typical legal solutions, and recording significant departures. We have generally looked to the four jurisdictions of Quebec, Ontario, British Columbia and the national government, both because they embrace the largest numbers of workers, and because they offer interesting comparisons and contrasts. Reference is made to the law of other jurisdictions where unusual provisions exist. Unfortunately, we can do no more than sketch in the 'law' of the parties themselves, but we try to do so at least where its absence would make the formal system incomprehensible. This selective approach, we trust, will accurately and sufficiently inform the foreign, or non-expert Canadian reader. But we do not intend that our work should be regarded as a definitive text for domestic, professional consumption.

II. General Background Information

§1. GEOGRAPHIC SETTING

A. Size

3. In terms of land mass, Canada is the second largest country in the world. However, its rather sparse population of only some 23 millions is widely dispersed across its enormous land mass (each province having one or two principal cities) except for a dense area of settlement in the highly industrialized crescent which reaches from Montreal through Toronto, along the northern and western shores of Lake Ontario to the Niagara frontier with the United States.

B. Boundaries

4. Canada is bounded on the east and west by the Atlantic and Pacific oceans, respectively. It shares its northern border in the Arctic with the Soviet Union, and its southern border, along 49° latitude and the Great Lakes – St. Lawrence river system, with the United States. Its extended and open frontier with the United States has had important historic and contemporary influences on Canadian economic, social and political development. Its boundary with the Soviet Union and its address to both Europe and Asia are also facts of profound geo-political significance.

C. Transportation and communications

5. The pattern of settlement and population distribution have made east–west communications a matter of vital national concern. There is a heavy dependency on railways for moving wheat and other natural resources from the middle of the continent to the oceans and inland seas for export, but also for purposes of domestic trade. An east–west pipeline also exists for the purposes of moving gas and oil from production fields on the western plains to major users, primarily in the industrial east-central region. Roads, rivers and canals complement the railways and pipelines.

Establishment and maintenance of east–west transportation and communications has been an important national priority. However, the natural, easier and shorter communication routes running north–south have helped to promote continental integration between Canada and its much larger neighbour to the south, the United States.

The tension between an east–west Canadian orientation and a north–south continental connection, dominates debate over national transportation, economic, finance and cultural policies.

D. Physical resources

6. From earliest times, there has been a considerable dependence on the great natural endowment of the country – principally wheat, timber and minerals, and more recently oil and gas – which has been largely destined for export rather than domestic consumption. Development of a modern industrial economy has been impeded not merely by the relatively small and scattered population, and problems of east–west transportation, but as well by the high degree of foreign ownership, principally by United States and multi-national firms. Attempts to reverse this pattern are to some extent inhibited by difficulties of accumulating domestic capital and of interrupting existing patterns of ownership and development without losing the benefits of foreign investment. However, initially in the east and more recently in the west, considerable pressure has developed to use natural resources as the base for domestic primary and secondary industries. This has exacerbated regional rivalries especially between the resource-rich western provinces and the more highly industrialized eastern provinces, Ontario and Quebec.

§2. GOVERNMENTAL STRUCTURE

A. The Constitution[1]

7. Canadian constitutional principles are essentially derived from the United Kingdom. To a significant extent, therefore, they are either found in historical British texts or subsist merely in unwritten conventions. However, the British inheritance has been modified by Canadian constitutional convention, and certain important legislative texts of specific Canadian significance.

1. See generally P. Hogg, *Constitutional Law of Canada* (Toronto 1977).

8. The most important of these texts is the British North America Act of 1867 which establishes the Canadian federation, allocating powers to the federal and provincial governments, partly defining the rights of linguistic minorities, and identifying certain major governmental institutions. This Act was passed by the United Kingdom parliament and is still subject to amendment by that parliament, although the United Kingdom will obviously act only in a formal sense and in response to a Canadian request. Political realities are such, however, that there is great difficulty in securing consensus within Canada as between the federal and provincial governments for constitutional amendment (even for an amendment which would establish a purely Canadian amending procedure).

9. Other important constitutional documents include legislation by which

19

various territories were joined to the original federation, by which federal and provincial governments have organized elections and their respective public services, and by which protection is secured for civil and minority rights. Particularly significant in this latter respect is the Canadian Bill of Rights, adopted in 1960, by which the federal government undertook to limit its own legislative authority to the extent necessary to secure respect for certain fundamental libertarian principles.[1] However, like all other legislation, the Canadian Bill of Rights is subject to amendment or repeal by parliament which thus remains the ultimate arbiter of the rights of citizens.

1. Canadian Bill of Rights, S.C. 1960, c.44.

B. Federalism

10. The British North America Act, as amended and judicially interpreted, creates a federal state comprising ten provinces and two territories with limited local autonomy.

11. To the federal government is theoretically assigned the responsibility for 'peace, order and good government', as well as residual authority over all matters not falling within exclusive provincial competence, including national defence, inter-provincial and international trade and communications, criminal law, fiscal matters and a comprehensive taxing power. However, provincial authority, nominally limited to 'matters of a purely local and private nature' and 'civil rights within the province', has been expanded through a process of judicial interpretation to embrace many of the concerns of modern social and economic legislation.[1]

1. See *infra*, c.V, §1, for an analysis of constitutional jurisdiction over labour relations.

12. As a practical matter, there exists something of a constitutional stalemate between apparently broad federal powers, especially powers of taxation, and provincial assertion of responsibility for costly programmes of social welfare and for regulation of economic activity (such as collective bargaining) which obviously affects the national economy. This stalemate has tended to be resolved through formally negotiated schemes of inter-provincial co-operation and revenue sharing, or by informal understandings. A recent Supreme Court decision, however, sustained the constitutional right of the federal government to respond to the 'emergency' of double-digit inflation, by establishing a system of wage and price controls, overriding normal collective bargaining procedures under provincial legislation.

13. But the major issue for Canadian federalism has been the emergence of strong regional pressures, and particularly of a genuine separatist movement in Quebec. These, in turn, have produced demands for formal redefinition, and perhaps even dissolution, of the Canadian federation.

C. Formal structure

1. The legislative power

14. The formal head of the federal government is the Governor-General (and of the provincial government, the Lieutenant Governor) representing the Queen of the United Kingdom who is also Queen of Canada. However, the real head of government is the federal Prime Minister (or the provincial Premier) who, in the parliamentary tradition, enjoys the support of a majority of members in the federal parliament (or provincial legislatures).

15. The federal parliament is bicameral. The lower house, the House of Commons, like the provincial legislatures (which are unicameral), is elected by universal suffrage, almost exclusively in single member constituencies. The upper house, the Senate, with limited powers, comprises members appointed by the federal government, on a basis which ensures regional representation.

2. The executive

16. The Prime Minister (or provincial Premier) is by constitutional convention leader of the largest party. He forms a cabinet from amongst the elected members of his own party, or any other party which formally agrees to participate in the government. Cabinet ministers are occasionally appointed from the non-elective Senate at the federal level, but are otherwise expected to seek and secure election as soon as possible after appointment. The maximum term of office for a government is five years, but the Prime Minister may seek earlier dissolution and a new electoral mandate; in fact the usual term of office is about four years. Most federal and provincial governments have enjoyed clear majorities, often successively renewed for extended periods of time. However, there have been a few instances of formal coalitions and, more recently, minority governments dependent upon the tacit and informal support of one or more rival parties.

17. The cabinet not only controls the legislative process, but it also directs the activities of the civil service. The civil service is, almost entirely, recruited to permanent government service up to and including the most senior administrative officials. Thus, the civil service is expected to survive intact any changes in government, although ministers have small personal staffs and may recruit key senior people into the civil service on a permanent or temporary basis, especially in policy-sensitive roles.

In theory, the civil service is responsive to policy laid down by the government in legislation or through cabinet orders. In practice, the civil service obviously has a great influence on both the formation and implementation of policy.

3. Administrative agencies

18. Much modern legislation is administered neither by the ministries of government, nor by the courts, but rather by specialized and expert administrative tribunals. These are, typically, established by statute and often operate (as for example in labour relations) with a high degree of autonomy from executive interference. By statute or practice, they are reasonably – not entirely – immune from changes in government although not, of course, from explicit changes in legislation.

19. The powers and prestige of such tribunals varies greatly. Some perform relatively low-level routine tasks; some are responsible for major sectors of public policy, including the elaboration of specific rules within very general lines laid down by legislation, and other tasks of investigation, adjudication, and enforcement. Their pervasive presence can be attributed to a desire to secure expertise, informality and flexibility in the administration of modern social and economic legislation.

20. Although probably not constitutionally required, the right to seek judicial review is generally afforded persons dissatisfied with the action of an administrative tribunal. This review usually does not involve an appeal on the merits, but rather is limited to questions of conformity to the mandate conferred upon the administrative agency by parliament, and adherence to fair procedures.

4. The judiciary and legal system

21. Except for Quebec, the law in all Canadian jurisdictions is rooted in the traditions of the English common law, with an overlay of legislation passed by the competent authority, parliament or the provincial legislature. Quebec private law is based on French civil law notions, incorporated into the Quebec Civil Code; in other respects (particularly as regards commercial affairs and administrative law) Quebec law resembles that of the other jurisdictions.

22. Appeals from the courts of all jurisdictions, including Quebec, may ultimately be taken to the Supreme Court of Canada, which has a discretionary jurisdiction to entertain the appeal, or to leave unreviewed the decision of the province's highest court. Thus, the Supreme Court of Canada has the final word in all common or civil law controversies, in the interpretation of all federal and provincial statutes, and in the adjudication of constitutional disputes.

23. Typically, the superior courts of the provinces are organized into trial and appellate divisions, all of whose judges (along with those of the Supreme Court of Canada) are appointed by the federal government. In addition, there are minor and specialized courts in various provinces whose judges are provincial appointees, while a federal trial and appellate court (below the Supreme Court of Canada) has exclusive competence in certain specialized areas under federal jurisdiction, including the review of decisions of federal administrative tribunals.

24. There is an historic prejudice, perhaps now receding, against the establishment of specialized courts. The role played by such courts in other countries is, in Canada, largely discharged by administrative tribunals.

§3. INFORMAL POLITICAL STRUCTURES

25. There are three major political parties in Canada – Liberals, Conservatives and the labour-affiliated New Democratic Party. While the first two of these parties have always dominated the federal parliamentary process, the N.D.P. has formed several provincial governments, as has the Social Credit (a minor conservative party), and various other regional parties. Principal amongst those is the Parti Quebecois – a social democratic party committed to the separation of Quebec from Canada – which assumed office in Quebec in 1976.

The two major national parties, indeed almost all parties which have enjoyed recent electoral success, are essentially centrist. They draw upon regional, ethnic or religious blocs, to some extent, but seek to make broad, 'consensus' appeals to the entire electorate.

The N.D.P. (and, in Quebec, the Parti Quebecois) differs slightly in espousing a social democratic philosophy. The N.D.P. enjoys formal affiliation with the labour movement (but does not receive the automatic allegiance of its members) while the P.Q. has the informal support of many Quebec unions. However, neither N.D.P. nor P.Q. governments have moved far from the general trend of Canadian labour legislation, although introducing various legislative reforms and occasionally adopting somewhat more pro-labour positions in particular disputes.

§4. POLITICAL CULTURE

26. Cutting across formal and traditional organizations and loyalties are important themes which dominate Canadian political life.

27. Nationalism and regionalism are both important factors in the Canadian political calculus. Nationalism, on the one hand, has sought to foster a Canadian identity, to resist or turn back foreign (United States) penetration of the Canadian economy and Canadian cultural life, and to rally all segments of the population around the theme of national unity.

28. Regionalism, historically strong but quiescent in the post-war period, has recently revived. For the western and Atlantic regions, the concern is essentially to obtain a 'fair share' of the benefits of a national economy, which is perceived to be dominated by the central provinces of Ontario and Quebec. For Quebec, in turn, regionalism fuelled by similar concerns is compounded by a desire for autonomy based on the distinctive French language, history, culture and ethnic roots of the majority (80%) of its population. But even within the regions, within the individual provinces, there exist tensions between the centre and the periphery. Both nationalism and regionalism influence government policies, business decisions, and patterns of union organization.

29. To some extent associated with the theme of regionalism is that of populism, which tends to manifest itself in a dislike of elites, experts and bureaucracies – which, in turn, are perceived to reside at the centre rather than the periphery. Populism, of both the left and right, has had some influence on political developments in the western provinces and Quebec. However, it does not appear to have fundamentally affected the structure of Canadian political decision-making or administration.

30. While occasionally important at a rhetorical level, the issue of public *versus* private control of the economy does not produce deep divisions amongst the major political parties. It has long been accepted in practice, if not in theory, that Canada's is a mixed economy, and that the government has an important role in it. Whether this role should be to dominate or direct private enterprise, to stimulate and support it, or merely to curb and repair its worst effects, is essentially the range of available political options. All of the major parties advocate all of these measures, although in varying proportions at various moments.

31. In the post-war period, the single national political debate of direct relevance to the conduct of labour relations resulted from the sudden imposition, in October, 1975, of pervasive anti-inflation measures at the federal level, which had the effect of limiting maximum salary increases which could be gained through collective bargaining. This measure provoked an unprecedented and only modestly successful 'National Day of Protest', a one day work stoppage called by the labour movement. The termination of the anti-inflation programme in 1978, has helped to restore the relative consensus amongst the national political parties on labour relations issues.

32. Finally, as in most developed countries, political debate has increasingly focused in Canada on the quality of life. This debate embraces such diverse concerns as protection of the natural environment, the status, growth and relationship of the diverse ethnic groups which comprise the 'Canadian mosaic', and the effects of demography, urbanization and modern communications upon education, family life, social values and social welfare systems.

§5. THE PEOPLE OF CANADA

A. Generally

33. The outstanding characteristic of Canada, a new country, is its ethnic diversity. The Francophone population, largely derived from the original French colonial settlement, comprises about 28 per cent of the population and is located almost entirely in Quebec or on its boundaries in adjacent provinces. Relatively small and isolated Francophone communities exist elsewhere across the country.

34. In the balance of the population United Kingdom ancestries predominate, but 'other' ethnic elements exist in very great numbers. The latter originally settled in the western agricultural communities, but since World War I have tended to concentrate in the largest urban centres. Large Mediterranean and central European immigrant groups have been complemented by recent arrivals from the Caribbean, the Indian sub-continent, and southeast Asia. All of these groups have been encouraged to maintain their cultural integrity through newspapers, and cultural and social organizations.

35. Relatively small, but recently resurgent, communities of native peoples are scattered across the country and exist in some concentration in the two northern territories.

B. The work force

36. The Canadian population embraces the skills, professions and talents required by a modern economy. The general educational system is relatively strong, although technical and managerial training have only recently been developed. Traditionally, it is immigrants who have made up deficiencies in both the skilled, and especially the unskilled, labour force.

37. However, Canada has also experienced a persistent unemployment level of well over 5 per cent, and recently of 8–9 per cent, and probably will continue to do so. This situation is attributable both to demographic trends – a bulge in the birth rate from 1945 to 1960 – and to unsettled internal and international business conditions. The problem is endemically severe in the depressed Atlantic provinces and in Quebec.

38. While there is free movement of labour amongst the provinces, and indeed considerable internal migration, there has never been a coherent national manpower policy embracing both immigration and the internal redeployment of labour. Amongst the obstacles to such a policy are the constitutional and political limits of federal power, linguistic and social barriers to movement, and the cost of movement attributable to distance. What have emerged, instead, have been various schemes for regional development designed to provide employment in areas of economic depression. These too have foundered to some extent because of disparaties of natural endowment, distances from markets, problems of capital accumulation and the existence of established patterns of trading and production across the country.

39. In common with most industrialized countries, Canada has experienced a considerable re-allocation of jobs within the employed labour force. The percentage of workers employed in agriculture has dropped steadily (to about 5.2 per cent in 1975) while the proportion of those engaged in service industries has expanded greatly (to 34.2 per cent).

C. Income distribution

40. Canada is one of the world's richest countries. However, while spared the most extreme disparaties of wealth and poverty, it can hardly be said that Canada is an egalitarian society.

Apart from the effects of progressive taxation (at a maximum marginal rate of about 62 per cent) and of transfer payments through the social welfare system, there exists no programme of income equalization or of guaranteed minimum incomes, except at a rudimentary level.

41. Despite some fluctuations, ironically most favourable during the period of anti-inflation controls, the percentage of the gross national product attributable to the labour sector has grown relatively slowly (46.1 per cent in 1939, to 48.7 per cent in 1955 to 55.1 per cent in 1975). Within the labour sector there has probably been some relative improvement in the position of workers in service occupations, especially in the public sector, in recent years.

42. In heavily unionized sectors, gains secured through collective bargaining have tended to be adopted by non-union firms seeking to avoid unionization. It is therefore difficult to assess the extent to which unionized workers enjoy any advantage in relation to wages and working conditions. This difficulty is compounded by the highly decentralized and diversified pattern of collective negotiations in Canada in most industries.

D. Union membership

43. Union membership in Canada for some time hovered about 33 per cent of the non-agricultural work force, a plateau reached after a low point in the depression years of the 1930's, as a result of rapid advances during the war years and the immediate post-war period. Recent increases in union membership in the public sector especially have now raised this figure to over 38 per cent.

44. Concentrations of union membership are found in particular industries –

mining, construction, petro-chemical, transport and communications, steel, and manufacturing (especially in larger establishments). The fast-growing 'white collar' service sector of the labour market, however, has been traditionally difficult for unions to penetrate. Their only substantial successes in this field have been amongst government employees who only recently have been permitted to be, and have become, highly organized.

III. General Notions and Special Definitions

§1. 'LABOUR LAW' DEFINED

45. Canadian labour law, as is characteristic of most aspects of law in systems derived from the common law, lacks precise definition of either its general boundaries or its specific concepts and institutions. However, most lawyers, legal academics and lay practitioners who use the term 'labour law' refer to the system of rules governing collective relations amongst management, trade unions, their members, and the institutions involved in such relations.

46. This emphasis upon collective relations is significant in view of the fact that most Canadian workers are employed under a regime of individual contracts, rather than collectively-bargained terms. It suggests, first, that legal and other professionals have been preoccupied with the collective, largely to the exclusion of the individual. Perhaps the explanation for this lies in the relative financial attractions of professional work in relation to group interests. Second, it suggests that there is an affinity between the collective and 'law' which, impliedly, does not exist between the individual and 'law'. This affinity approximately reflects reality: although individuals may have enjoyed contractual rights in theory, in practice they secured effective legal protection only with the advent of the collective regime. Third, to the extent that 'law' represents a social good, an aspiration for which to strive, it would seem that the collective is regarded as normatively preferable to the individual.

47. At the same time, the reluctance – now, perhaps, changing – to address the legal position of individual workers has led to the relative underdevelopment of legal scholarship and representational skills and resources in matters which are vitally important to the majority of Canadians who are not union members. In their relations with their employers, individual workers are governed by the rules of contract, sometimes embraced by the term 'employment law'. But their employers are, in turn, bound by statutes and regulations relating to minimum wages, benefits and working conditions, occupational health and safety standards, and prohibitions against discrimination. These rules, emanating from government, are sometimes generically grouped as 'employment standards legislation'. And, providing protection both for workers and others who encounter financial disaster, there is a system of 'social security legislation' embracing pensions, unemployment insurance, public health care, and other welfare payments.

There is no logical reason why 'labour law' should not embrace employment law, labour standards legislation, and social security, as well as the law of collective relationships – especially because of the interaction and overlap amongst these systems. But relatively little progress has been made in their functional and conceptual integration. This monograph, while focussing upon collective 'labour law' will also deal extensively with individual 'employment law' and, to a lesser extent, with 'labour standards legislation'; 'social security' will be dealt with only peripherally.

48. Finally, although labour policies in the public sector have come, in recent years, increasingly to resemble those in the private sector, they will not be dealt with in this work. Accordingly, no attempt will be made to explore either the special public sector adaptations of general private sector policies, or the influence of public sector models upon the private sector.

§2. GENERAL NOTIONS OF COLLECTIVE LABOUR LAW

49. Canadian labour law, in the collective sphere, draws heavily upon that of the United States. Workers enjoy a statutorily protected right to organize for collective bargaining. Their bargaining representative, selected by a majority of the workers in an appropriate bargaining constituency, may require the employer to bargain in good faith, with a view to concluding a collective agreement binding on all employees. And if no agreement is negotiated, the employees may have recourse to a strike, or the employer to a lockout, as a bargaining sanction.

50. The primary feature of English common law which has survived in the collective sphere is the use of ordinary private law principles to regulate industrial conflict, although this is now giving way to new, specially designed, legislative rules. To some extent, English common law principles also dominate the field of individual 'employment law'. In both cases, integration between the common law and the modern collective labour legislation has been difficult to accomplish.

51. Two distinctively Canadian features of collective labour law are both concerned with reducing industrial conflict. No strikes are permitted while a collective agreement is in effect (arbitration being required instead) or, after the expiry of the agreement, until extensive peacekeeping procedures have been exhausted.

§3. DEFINITIONS

1. General

52. The following terms are widely used in discussions of labour law in Canada. However, they are not terms of art which have precise definitions,

except to the extent that particular statutes in which they appear lay down such definitions. And even such statutory definitions generally have an overlay of judicial or administrative interpretation.

2. Arbitration

53. Arbitration is a process of independent, third party adjudication. The 'third party' may be a single neutral individual selected by agreement of the parties (or in default of such agreement, by a government agency) or a tripartite body similarly selected, but comprising, as well as the neutral, equal numbers of partisan nominees. 'Rights arbitration' (or 'grievance arbitration') refers to the adjudication of disputes relating to alleged violations of a collective agreement. It is the most widespread method of deciding such disputes, and is the sole method legislatively prescribed in most jurisdictions. 'Interest arbitration' refers to the adjudication of terms of a collective agreement when the parties are unable to agree upon its (re)negotiation. Interest arbitration is legislatively compelled in a few key industries and occupations, but the parties seldom voluntarily opt for interest arbitration and the abandonment of the right to strike or lockout which otherwise resolves such disputes.

3. Bargaining units

54. A bargaining unit is the constituency, defined by the labour relations board or agreed upon by the parties, within which collective bargaining occurs. The bargaining unit may embrace workers sharing a single craft (a 'craft unit') or those whose common denominator is participation in a particular operation, plant or industry (an 'industrial unit'). In either case, the bargaining unit must be 'appropriate for collective bargaining', i.e. the workers must have a common interest in the outcome of negotiations. All workers within a bargaining unit have the right to participate in the selection of the bargaining agent, the union which will represent the bargaining unit, but once selected, the bargaining agent has the exclusive right to speak for all present and future employees in the bargaining unit.

4. Boycott

55. A boycott is the abstention from dealing with an employer, or from handling goods destined for or produced by him, in aid of collective bargaining (or other) demands by those organizing the boycott.

5. Certification

56. Certification is the process by which the Labour Relations Board determines that a trade union is entitled to act as the exclusive bargaining agent of employees in a bargaining unit. Entitlement normally depends upon majority support, as demonstrated by either a secret ballot vote in favour of, or membership in, the trade union. Occasionally, absent such majority support, a union may nonetheless be certified if the employer has improperly interfered in its attempts to organize.

6. Collective agreement

57. A collective agreement is a document recording the terms and conditions of employment and the rights and duties of the employer, trade union and employees in a bargaining unit. In almost all Canadian jurisdictions, it is legally enforceable only through arbitration procedures initiated by the employer or the trade union, and is deemed to contain certain statutory provisions – a minimum term of one year, the prohibition of strikes and lockouts during that term, and a requirement for the submission of all disputes concerning its interpretation or alleged violation to arbitration.

7. Collective bargaining

58. Collective bargaining is the process whereby an employer and a trade union seek to negotiate a collective agreement. In almost all jurisdictions, this process must be undertaken 'in good faith' and requires 'every reasonable effort to make a collective agreement'.

8. Conciliation

59. Conciliation is a process of non-coercive, third party intervention designed to assist parties in resolving differences. In many Canadian jurisdictions, conciliation must be attempted before the parties are legally free to break off negotiations, or to have recourse to economic sanctions. Historically, conciliation was undertaken by *ad hoc* tripartite boards whose findings were made public. Today, this process has largely been replaced by one employing professional mediators who work with the parties on an informal, confidential basis, and seldom make normative reports.

9. Employee/Employer

60. The relationship of employer and employee subsists when one of several different tests (laid down by a legislature, court or Labour Relations Board) are met: (a) the employer has the right to direct the manner of execution of work of the employee, or (b) the employee is a member of the employer's enterprise or organization, or (c) the various incidents of their relationship place the em-

ployee in a position of economic dependence upon the employer, such that he could profit from participation in collective bargaining. In some Canadian jurisdictions, this latter category is legislatively enlarged by the inclusion of 'dependent contractors' who have some of the characteristics of independent entrepreneurs, but who ultimately exhibit the requisite degree of economic dependence. Only 'employees' have the right to engage in collective bargaining under most labour legislation, and only 'employees' can claim the benefit of most protective labour legislation.

10. Employers' associations

61. An employer's association is an organization of employers formed for the purposes of collective bargaining with trade unions. In some Canadian provinces, such associations may be 'accredited', a process analogous to 'certification' for trade unions, and thus gain certain legal rights to speak authoritatively for their members.

11. Labour relations board

62. Labour relations boards are administrative agencies, established by statute, to regulate the relationship between employers and trade unions. In most jurisdictions, the membership of the labour relations board is tripartite, embracing labour, management and neutral members. Either by statute or tradition, members enjoy some security of tenure, and inevitably independence of decision. While their precise jurisdictions vary, all have power to determine disputes relating to union certification and to remedy unfair labour practices; some also have power to deal with violations of collective agreements and to curb illegal strikes, lockouts and picketing. Orders of a labour relations board are enforceable in the regular courts as orders of those courts. They are also, typically, subject to limited judicial review by the courts.

12. Lockout

63. A 'lockout' may be either (a) the refusal by an employer to continue to employ employees, in order to interfere with their right to engage in trade union activities, or (b) a temporary economic sanction imposed by an employer, the analogue to a strike, in order to pressure a trade union to accede to his collective bargaining demands.

13. Management

64. 'Management' embraces those individuals in a firm who have effective direction of the work of other employees. Members of management are pre-

cluded from participating in the organization of trade unions by other employees, and except in a few jurisdictions, may not themselves form trade unions.

14. Mediation

65. 'Mediation' and 'conciliation' are often used interchangeably, although in some jurisdictions, they denote slightly different methods of intervention to promote dispute settlement.

15. Picketing

66. Picketing is a tactic for pressuring an employer involved in a labour dispute. It customarily advertises the existence of a dispute by means of the attendance of workers carrying signs or distributing leaflets. Picketing may be intended as an appeal to the public for support, to employees to maintain their solidarity, or to other workers to decline employment or to refuse to enter the employer's premises.

16. Strike

67. A strike is the concerted cessation of work by employees. By statutory extension, the term may also include various forms of partial cessation, including a slowdown.

17. Trade union

68. A trade union is an organization of employees formed for purposes that include the regulation of relations between employers and employees.

18. Unfair labour practices

69. Unfair labour practices are illegal tactics by an employer or a trade union which interfere with the right of employees to organize in the trade union of their own choice, to enjoy representation by that trade union for collective bargaining purposes, or otherwise involve violation of the prohibitions of the Labour Relations Act.

19. Union security

70. Union Security provisions in a collective agreement are intended to

protect the union's institutional arrangements. Minimal arrangements may provide for a 'voluntary dues checkoff', a commitment by the employer to deduct from the pay of each consenting employee, and remit to the union, union dues. The 'Rand formula', or 'agency shop', requires the employer to deduct dues, or a sum in lieu thereof, from the pay of all employees, in recognition of the union's obligation to bargain for all. Other arrangements may require union membership as a condition of continuing employment ('union shop') or of initially securing employment ('closed shop').

20. Voluntary recognition

71. In lieu of certification, a union may gain the right to act as an exclusive bargaining agent if the employer voluntarily agrees to recognize its status.

§4. EXPLANATION OF REFERENCES

72. Each Canadian province, as well as the national government, has enacted a general statute regulating private sector labour relations. These are variously entitled 'Labour Relations Acts', 'Labour Codes' or 'Trade Union Acts', and are referred to in footnotes by the name of the jurisdiction only, e.g. 'Manitoba, s.72'. The following is a complete list of these statutes. (In each case, reference is made to the latest comprehensive enactment, or to its most recent decennial consolidation. Reference to subsequent amendments is provided in footnotes to the text, where appropriate.)

> Canada Labour Code, R.S.C. 1970, c.L–1, as am. R.S.C. 1970
> (1st Supp.) c.22; R.S.C. 1970 (2nd Supp.) c.17.
> Alberta Labour Act, S.A. 1973, c.33.
> Labour Code of British Columbia, S.B.C. 1973 (2nd Sess.) c.122.
> Manitoba Labour Relations Act, C.C.S.M., c.L10.
> New Brunswick Industrial Relations Act, R.S.N.B. 1973, c.I–4.
> Newfoundland Labour Relations Act, S.N. 1977, c.64.
> Nova Scotia Trade Union Act, S.N.S. 1972, c.19.
> Ontario Labour Relations Act, R.S.O. 1970, c.232.
> Prince Edward Island Labour Act, R.S.P.E.I. 1974, c.L–1.
> Quebec Labour Code, R.S.Q. 1964, c.141.
> Saskatchewan Trade Union Act, R.S.S. 1978, c.T–17.

All other statutes are referred to by title, year of latest consolidation, revision or relevant amendment, and chapter number, *e.g.* Rights of Labour Act, R[evised] S[tatutes] of O[ntario], c.416.

References to cases in footnotes are to the following series of reports:

> D.L.R.   – Dominion Law Reports
> O.R.   – Ontario Reports

S.C.R.   – Supreme Court Reports
C.L.R.B.R. – Canada Labour Relations Board Reports
C.L.L.C   – Canadian Labour Law Cases
O.L.R.B.   – Ontario Labour Relations Board Reports
L.A.C.   – Labour Arbitration Cases

IV. The Canadian Labour Movement

73. The beginnings of the Canadian labour movement antedate the establishment of the Canadian Confederation in 1867. As early as 1794 employees of the North West Fur Trading Company went on strike for higher wages. However, only with the introduction of industry at the beginning of the nineteenth century was a true labour movement begun. Journeymen and craftsmen in the few urban areas, particularly in the building, printing, clothing and shoe trades, began to organize for the purpose of mutual aid and protection and to achieve by united action such objectives as the ten hour day, higher wages and better working conditions. In 1830, for example, the journeymen shoemakers in Toronto went on strike against 'scanty wages . . . beds of straw . . . and tyrranical oppression'. The union movement grew slowly before 1840 owing to depression and labour surpluses but gained momentum in the years prior to Confederation, a period which was further characterized by the affiliation of Canadian unions with their British and American counterparts. This growth brought unionism into collision with the law.

74. Union organizers were subject to prosecution for the common law crime of conspiracy. The freedom of workers to associate and to alter conditions of work was restricted by legislation modelled upon the English Combinations Act of 1800, such as the Nova Scotia statute of 1816, which prohibited unlawful meetings and combinations for the purpose of regulating wages. Union organizational activities were interdicted as well. In the old Province of Canada, the Master and Servant Act declared the persuasion of labourers 'to confederate for demanding extravagant or high wages' to be unlawful. The common law prohibition against restraint of the course of free trade also affected the civil status of unions. As a result of common law prohibitions, the trade unions were unable to use the courts to enforce any contractual rights they may have achieved, or to protect their property.

75. In the years following Confederation, labour began to develop a new assertiveness and unity. Local labour councils sprang up in the cities and in 1873, representatives of thirty-five unions formed the first central labour council, the Canadian Labour Union. The C.L.U. resolved to promote union membership, to bring unorganized workers into the C.L.U., and to provide financial assistance to striking unions. Realizing that efforts in these directions would be in vain in view of the existing state of the law, it resolved further to:

> . . . agitate such questions as may be for the benefit of the working classes, in order that we may obtain the enactment of such measures by

the Dominion or local legislatures as will be beneficial to us, and win the repeal of all oppressive laws now existing. [Canadian Labour Union, Proceedings, Sept., 1873.]

This organization petered out in 1877, but it must be credited with arousing in government an awareness of the grievances and aspirations of this segment of the electorate.

76. The 1870's were, indeed, the turning point in the use of criminal sanctions to inhibit trade unionism. The legislative response to labour organization evolved from one of repression to one of tolerance as restraints on the right of association were lifted and the sphere of legitimate activity was expanded by amendments to the criminal law. In part, this reflected the evolution of English law, in part, local political realities. Popular working class support for the nine hour day movement in 1872, and public reaction against the arrest of the strike committee of the Toronto Typographical Union on conspiracy charges, moved Parliament to undertake far reaching reforms. Trade unions were encouraged to register under a new Trade Unions Act, and thereby to escape the taint of illegality which the common law had assigned them as 'conspiracies in restraint of trade.' The Criminal Law Amendment Act of the same year legalized all strikes except those in which the means employed were calculated to coerce the employer or to prevent him carrying on his business. Further amendments in 1875 and 1876 narrowed the definition of criminal conspiracy for the purposes of trade combinations to the performance of acts expressly punishable by law. In 1890, the refusal to work with a workman or for an employer was expressly legalized. By the end of the nineteenth century, the doctrine of criminal conspiracy had ceased to be of practical significance in relation to ordinary labour–management disputes,[1] although it has become, and remains, a central theme in relation to the regulation of business competition.[2]

1. Now Criminal Code, R.S.C. 1970, c.C–34, ss. 423, 425.
2. The Combines Investigation Act, R.S.C. 1970, c.C–23, as am. S.C.1974–1975–1976, c.76, outlaws conspiracies to suppress competition in the supply of goods and services. Labour union activities are expressly protected by s.4, C. Backhouse, *Labour Unions and Anti-Combines Policy* (1976) 14 Osgoode Hall L.J. 113.

77. Another significant development of the 1870's was the definition of the permissible limits of picketing, or 'watching and besetting' as it is called in the Criminal Code. From the outset, violent and coercive conduct was outlawed, while the peaceful communication of appeals was permitted. However, when the Criminal Code of 1892 was enacted, the peaceful picketing proviso was omitted. Until it was restored in 1934,[1] the courts tended to deal severely with all forms of picketing, no matter how innocuous.

1. Now Criminal Code, s.381(2).

78. If the 1870's were a period of legal reform and advance for the cause of trade unionism, the next two decades were to represent a considerable setback. The 'long' depression (mid-1870's to mid-1890's), and the growth of manufacturing on an industrial scale, combined to create abysmal working conditions

and nullify the bargaining power of the individual employee. By 1889, as the report of the Royal Commission on the Relations of Capital and Labour disclosed, employers deemed it their prerogative to discipline workers by administering beatings, by imprisonment and by fines; factories were often unsanitary; employees were required to sign agreements to work on religious holidays; the 60 hour week prevailed, and the penalty for joining a union was dismissal and blacklisting. These practices stimulated the growth of unionism in the worst years of the depression, and led to the establishment of the Trades and Labour Congress of Canada and the more militant Knights of Labour. By the end of the century, then, it was becoming clear that the repeal of criminal prohibitions against unionism did not automatically place labour organizations on an equal footing with employers. Moreover, industrial conflict was potentially disruptive to the emerging economy of the country.

79. As unions grew in size and in solidarity, and as the consequences of their conflicts with employers began to involve the interests of large segments of the public, the need arose for third party intervention in disputes of this nature. Thus began a series of experiments in provincial legislation designed to secure industrial peace. By and large, this legislation involved key certain areas of employment – typically, coal mines, railways and public utilities – and sought to resolve labour–management controversies by either conciliation or arbitration. Much of this legislation, as well, became operative only with the consent of both parties – a condition which usually led the stronger party to refuse consent.

80. Experimentation at the provincial level led to the enactment of three federal statutes, the Conciliation Act of 1900, the Railway Labour Disputes Act of 1903, and the Conciliation and Labour Act of 1906. These statutes were ultimately consolidated in the Industrial Disputes Investigation Act of 1907,[1] whose principal features remain vestigially visible in Canadian labour legislation down to the present time: the availability of conciliation upon either the request of the parties, or at the initiative of the Minister of Labour; the use of tripartite boards of conciliation with extensive investigatory powers; and the issuance of a normative, but non-binding, report identifying the issues and proposing their proper resolution; and, as a quite conscious decision, avoidance of the use of compulsory and binding interest arbitration.

    1. S.C. 1907, c.20.

81. While the legislation did not finally resolve the basic issues of labour–management relations, and was further weakened by constitutional attack,[1] it at least implied certain policy judgments which were later to mature in modern collective bargaining legislation. These were recognition of the legitimacy of collective bargaining itself, of the possibility that strikes might result, and of the propriety of even-handed government intervention to assist in the establishment of a permanent, bilateral relationship.

    1. In 1925, in *Toronto Electric Commissioners* v. *Snider*, [1925] A.C. 396, the Privy Council confined the operation of the Act to industries within the federal sphere. However, most provinces soon passed enabling statutes extending the reach of the statute.

82. The first third of the twentieth century witnessed Canada's coming-of-age as an industrial nation. Foreign investment attracted by extensive natural resources provided the capital required to stimulate economic growth while immigration opened up the West, swelled the unskilled labour force and created larger domestic markets for industry. Between 1901 and 1915 capital investment in Canadian manufacturing quadrupled and, as the capital requirements of industrial enterprises expanded, this commodity became organized increasingly along corporate lines. In these same years, the number of workers employed in manufacturing rose from 340,000 to 600,000. Labour organization grew even more dramatically, especially during World War I, as union membership swelled from 50,000 in 1901 to 175,000 in 1915 to 250,000 in 1919. Unions grew more militant, too, as the number of workers involved in strikes grew from 43,000 in 1912 to 150,000 in 1919.

83. However, this period proved something of a false dawn for trade unions. Throughout, the unity of the labour movement was imperilled by controversies over international versus national unionism, over the issue of social reform versus higher wages as prime union objectives, over organization of unskilled industrial workers versus organization of skilled craftsmen. Schismatic labour organizations were formed.[1] The Winnipeg General Strike of 1919 plunged the entire city into chaos, halting virtually all work, including essential services, until suppressed by the intervention of the federal authorities. And substantial segments of the industrial work force remained unorganized. Not surprisingly, wages and working conditions improved only slightly in the 1920's and became substantially worse during the depression years of the 1930's. With great unemployment, the bargaining position of the individual worker became desperate, and the power of the unions (together with their membership) declined dramatically.

1. See generally Abella, *Nationalism, Communism, and Canadian Labour* (Toronto, 1973).

84. Throughout these two decades, the federal legislation – the 1907 Industrial Disputes Investigation Act – had limited impact. The fundamental problem of industrial relations remained the gross disparity of bargaining power as between employers and employed. Given this disparity, employers could ultimately afford to ignore conciliation efforts, to disregard concessions sought, and occasionally secured, by workers in favourable market conditions, and even to make it impossible for workers to bargain collectively. Workers who joined unions were threatened with discharge and then fired; they were easily replaced from the ranks of the unemployed. When unions were formed, employers simply refused to deal with them. And when strikes occurred, either to secure union recognition or for better conditions, employers were almost always able to replace the strikers and to outlast them in any endurance contest.

85. Increasingly, in the 1930's, industrial strife began to centre on the very basic issue of whether workers would be prevented from associating together for purposes of collective bargaining – not by legislation as in the early days, but by the harsh economic realities. As this issue was being thrashed out on picketlines and street corners throughout North America, unions and employers both began to resort increasingly to coercive and violent tactics. Added to the debilitating effects of the depression, this industrial warfare was doubly damaging.

86. A landmark of profound significance occurred in 1935, when the U.S. Congress passed the National Labour Relations Act (also called the 'Wagner Act' after its sponsor, Sen. Wagner of New York). This statute explicitly recognized the right of employees to belong to the trade union of their choice and to participate in the process of collective bargaining through that union. To make effective these rights, the statute forbade certain unfair labour practices commonly practised by employers to thwart unionization, and imposed upon employers the duty to bargain in good faith with the union selected by their employees.

87. Similar legislation was not to come to Canada for almost a decade. In the interim, particularly with the example of the Wagner Act before them, Canadian unionists continued to struggle for the basic right of association and for the fruits which could be won through the practice of collective bargaining. Perhaps the most dramatic episode in this struggle came in 1937 when the Premier of Ontario threatened to use the provincial police to end a strike at the General Motors plant in Oshawa where the company refused to recognize the newly-organized United Automobile Workers. This threat, in turn, precipitated both a cabinet crisis and considerable public protest. In the end, a facesaving compromise emerged in which the union gained some of its demands, but not formal recognition. The incident, however, was regarded as a moral victory for industrial unionism, and a spur to further organization.

88. From the mid-1930's onwards the pace of change quickened. Between 1935 and 1937, for example, union membership increased from 280,000 to 383,000. By 1942, membership stood at 578,000, and by 1947, it had reached 912,000. In part, this development reflected the general economic recovery of the country, and particularly the manpower shortage created by World War II. In part, too, the expansion of trade unionism took place under the umbrella of increasingly favourable legislation.

89. Beginning in 1937, both federal and provincial governments began to move towards the position expressed in the American Wagner Act. In 1939, the federal Criminal Code was amended to prohibit discrimination or discharge of workers because of their union activities.[1] During the period 1937–1942, a number of provinces and the federal government enacted statutes or regulations which announced the basic right of association and declared public policy to be in favour of collective bargaining. However, these statutes were either declaratory or enforceable only through criminal prosecution. None of them resembled their progenitor, the Wagner Act, in providing an administrative tribunal whose function it was to police the provisions of the statute, and particularly to test by secret ballot, or other means, the desire of employees to be represented by a trade union.

1. Now Criminal Code, R.S.C. 1970, c.C–34, s.382.

90. As the basic issues of union representation and collective bargaining continued to cause industrial strife, with strikes of miners and steelworkers disrupting war production, the need to move to an American-style statute became increasingly obvious. In 1943, Ontario became the first jurisdiction to adopt a full-fledged collective bargaining statute, although its enforcement was entrusted to the Ontario Labour Court (a division of the High Court of Justice), rather than to an administrative board. Experience under the Ontario statute was short-lived, as the federal government preempted the field of collective bargaining in 1944 by enacting P.C. 1003, regulations made under the War Measures Act, which covered virtually all significant industry and economic activity. The federal regulations established the Canada Labour Relations Board and brought the regime of collective bargaining within the reach of virtually all Canadian workers. Following the repeal of the federal war-time regulations in 1948, virtually all provinces (and the federal government) adopted Wagner-style labour relations statutes, covering all employees in the private sector.

91. Following World War II, the Canadian labour movement continued to grow. Organized workers constituted 27.9 per cent of the total non-agricultural paid work force in 1946 by 1958, the figure was 34.2 per cent. During the period 1959–1964, however, unions experienced a reversal of their previous potential for growth, falling to a low of 29.4 per cent in 1964, but later regained momentum. In 1971, organized workers constituted 33.3 per cent of the work force. In 1977 union membership stood at 3,149,000, which represented 38.2 per cent of the work force.

92. The strength of the unions is concentrated in a few important areas of the economy. The following table[1] shows the heavy concentration of union mem-

Industry	Actual Membership in 1976 (1,000's)	As a Percent of all Paid Workers in Industry
All Industries	3,141.9	35.2
Agriculture	3.0	2.1
Forestry	32.2	48.8
Fishing and trapping	3.0	42.9
Mining	60.4	41.6
Manufacturing	866.2	45.1
Construction	304.2	56.3
Transportation, communication and other utilities	440.1	54.9
Trade	131.8	8.8
Finance	9.2	1.9
Services	753.8	32.2
Public administration	436.4	63.7

bership in sectors such as construction, transportation and utilities and the public sector, and the relative low level of membership in the rapidly-expanding financial, service and trade sectors.

1. Source: Woods & Kumar (eds.), *The Current Industrial Relations Scene in Canada* (Kingston, 1977).

93. Institutional reorganization has accompanied overall union growth since the 1930's. The conservative Trades and Labour Congress of Canada (T.L.C.) had largely concentrated upon the organization of workers on a craft-by-craft basis, thus largely ignoring unskilled and semi-skilled employees in mass-production industry. Its constituent unions were largely affiliated with international unions who were associated with the American Federation of Labour (A.F.L.). In the late 1930's a new, more vigorous, and less restrictive, philosophy of 'industrial' organization soon produced the Congress of Industrial Organizations (C.I.O.) in the United States and the Canadian Congress of Labour (C.C.L.) in Canada. Competition between the A.F.L.–T.L.C. and the C.I.O.–C.C.L. persisted for almost 20 years, and counterpoised not only two approaches to organization, but also the 'business' unionism of the older group and the broader social and political objectives of the newer. Finally, in an effort to end this rivalry, merger movements on both sides of the border produced the A.F.L.–C.I.O. and the unified Canadian Labour Congress (C.L.C.). The only major group of unions outside of the C.L.C. are those affiliated with the Confederation of National Trade Unions and the Congress of Democratic Trade Unions, both Quebec-based organizations. A small grouping of purely Canadian unions has also emerged, the Confederation of Canadian Unions.

94. In the 1960's efforts to bring labour unions into politics (which had begun as early as 1870) culminated in the affiliation of many labour organizations with the New Democratic Party. In the post-war period, too, government began to recognize organized labour as a factor of importance in the community, frequently consulting with the C.L.C. and C.N.T.U. on issues of national economic policy, and other matters of general interest to the trade union movement. Most importantly, collective bargaining has been accepted throughout the country, and by many of the largest employers, as a legitimate (if not altogether affirmative) public policy.

95. But all has not been well for the Canadian labour movement. Although its membership has expanded dramatically in absolute terms over the past generation, the fact remains that labour unions have failed – except in one or two areas – to significantly increase the proportion of workers who are members. Membership has stabilized at about one-third of those eligible for unionization in the private sector. The movement is continuing to enjoy only limited success in organizing the rapidly-growing clerical and technical occupations. Only in public administration, where 92 per cent of office workers are now unionized, have unions claimed dramatic advances. Due almost exclusively to these public sector advances, 37 per cent of all office workers were covered by collective agreements in 1976, more than double the percentage covered a decade earlier. Within the area of private sector white collar employment, the banks have been a particular focus of recent organizational efforts. About 150,000 unorganized employees work for these financial institutions, but despite favourable legal interpretations, by mid-1978, only some 38 local branch banks had been organized.

96. Political issues have reappeared on the primary agenda of the labour movement. In 1944, the first C.C.F. (social democratic) provincial government was elected in Saskatchewan, and it promptly enacted an advanced labour relations statute. In the 1970's, the New Democratic Party, which had succeeded the C.C.F., elected provincial governments in British Columbia and Manitoba. These governments also enacted reforming labour legislation. But such legislation did not succeed in cementing the bonds between the political and collective bargaining wings of the labour movement, at least in part because of differences over the appropriate degree of government intervention into the collective bargaining process, although for other reasons as well.

97. However, the catalyzing event which appears to have propelled Canadian labour into more concerted political activity was the introduction by the federal government, in 1975, of an Anti-Inflation Act,[1] a primary component of which was a rigid system of wage controls. Labour's response to this perceived attack on its freedom of action was largely ineffective: a withdrawal from consultation and cooperation with the government, a one day general strike (Day of Protest) on October 14, 1976, and a short-lived campaign for tripartitism. Finally, in the 1979 federal election, after the expiry of the wage control programme, the Canadian Labour Congress announced its intention to work in active support of the New Democratic Party. Prior to 1979, labour support for the N.D.P. had been sporadic, uneven, and dependent upon the sympathies of local unions. The formal affiliation of the C.L.C. with N.D.P. had hitherto produced few initiatives to actually translate support in principle into a sizeable number of labour votes. In 1979, the C.L.C. finally attempted to deliver those votes, but its efforts were only marginally effective, if at all. Whether the experience of 1979 will stimulate or discourage future political activity remains to be seen.

1. Anti-Inflation Act, S.C. 1974–75–76, c.75.

98. Finally, questions of internal structure and external international affiliation, which have plagued the Canadian labour movement since its inception, have by no means been resolved.[1]

1. See *infra*.

99. Job satisfaction and enrichment have become increasingly matters of concern both within and beyond the labour movement; attention has been focused especially on restive, young workers. But some dissenting voices disparage this concern, arguing that 'job fulfillment' is a middle-class ideal and that work has never been and never will be particularly creative for most employees. The issue is seen as the imposition of middle-class values on other

strata of society and as a means of avoiding the hard economic issues of increased monetary benefits and more leisure time.

100. The Canadian literature is neither extensive nor comprehensive enough to draw any hard conclusions. Job satisfaction has not yet surfaced as a major issue in collective bargaining. Yet rank-and-file discontent has manifested itself in wildcat strikes and rejection of agreements. It is difficult to know whether this represents another aspect of general societal discontent or deep dissatisfaction with union leadership, and if the latter, whether over their unresponsiveness to deep-rooted psychic needs or their inability to deliver more money, leisure and security for their constituents.

101. The Canadian labour movement has travelled a long and difficult road since it was first, formally established, as the Canadian Labour Union, in 1873. Its future as an effective force in the economic, political and social affairs of Canada seems assured. Yet the complexity, and apparent intractability, of the problems confronting the country as a whole virtually guarantee that its aspirations will inevitably outstrip its achievements.

V. The Role of Government Institutions in the Shaping and Administration of Labour Law and Industrial Relations Policy

§1. CONSTITUTIONAL BACKGROUND

102. In theory, there are no constitutional limits to government action (or inaction) in the field of labour law and industrial relations. The only constitutional challenge available is that the impugned legislation has not been passed by the appropriate level of government – either the federal government or the provinces.

103. Jurisdiction over industrial relations is divided between the two levels of government on the basis of the nature of the activity involved. The federal government has jurisdiction over interprovincial and international trade, transportation and communications, defence-related industries (*e.g.* uranium), a few other anomalous industries and, of course, industrial relations in the federal public service. Only about ten per cent of Canadian private sector employees fall under federal jurisdiction. All others, embracing those who work in all major manufacturing sectors, mining and other natural resource industries (other than uranium mining), construction, service industries etc. fall within provincial jurisdiction.

104. However, some collective bargaining relationships have emerged which do not conform to the demarcation of constitutional responsibilities. For example, local trucking comes under provincial jurisdiction and interprovincial and inter-national trucking comes under federal, but collective bargaining in the trucking industry has sometimes embraced trucking of both sorts. In such

42

situations, the division of constitutional responsibility has often created difficulties which can be resolved only by intergovernmental co-operation.

105. The federal government, however, has several potentially important possibilities for expansion of its present, secondary role in industrial relations. First, although the term has not been given a generous interpretation, courts have held that when the activity of an enterprise is 'necessarily incidental' to a federal undertaking, federal labour legislation governs.[1] Second, although again the matter is somewhat unclear and conservatively stated, the courts have conceded that the federal government enjoys power to deal with a national economic crisis, such as inflation, by enacting legislation which overrides otherwise valid provincial collective bargaining statutes. In a recent decision, the Supreme Court of Canada sustained the federal Anti-Inflation Act on this basis.[2]

Third, perhaps most importantly, the federal government can exert leadership and exercise moral suasion by the way it conducts labour relations within its own jurisdiction. Indeed, it did this by using its broad wartime powers to launch the first nationwide collective bargaining scheme in 1944, again by enacting in 1967 an advanced statute which introduced collective bargaining in the federal public service, in 1968 by sponsoring the far-reaching Task Force on Labour Relations which, in turn, laid the groundwork for substantial changes in both federal and provincial collective bargaining legislation, and most recently, in 1977, by according individual workers within its jurisdiction a statutory right to adjudication in the event of unjust dismissal.

1. See *e.g. Letter Carriers* v. *C.U.P.W.* (1973) 40 D.L.R. (3d) 105(S.C.C.) (private trucking firm under contract to post office to collect mail held to come under federal jurisdiction, although also involved in local operations).
2. *Re Anti-Inflation Act* [1976] 2 S.C.R. 373.

106. Two further constraints of a quasi-constitutional nature may be mentioned. First, as a matter of general constitutional law, federal legislation which 'occupies the field' has been held to pre-empt provincial legislation directed to the same end. However, although the federal government has enacted valid legislation regulating federal elections, a provincial statute limiting union political activity in both provincial and federal elections has been upheld.[1] Similarly, although the federal Criminal Code generally deals with matters of public order, and has specific provisions relating to picketing, provincial authority over labour (and other) demonstrations has been upheld, and there is little doubt that the provinces' attempt to regulate picketing by administrative, civil and quasi-criminal sanctions are likewise valid.[2]

1. *Oil Workers* v. *Imperial Oil*, (1963) 41 D.L.R. (2d) 1 (S.C.C.).
2. *A.G. Canada* v. *Dupond*, (1978) 84 D.L.R. (3d) 420 (S.C.C.).

107. A further possible limitation on federal action is the *Canadian Bill of Rights* which prevails over ordinary federal statutes, unless express provision is made to the contrary. An attempt to use the Bill of Rights to strike down federal legislation which allegedly interfered with freedom of association was unsuccessful.[1] This possibility, however, remains open in appropriate future cases.

1. *Swait* v. *Maritime Trustees*, (1966) 61 D.L.R. (2d) 317 (Que. C.A.).

§2. THE ROLE OF GOVERNMENT INSTITUTIONS

A. The legislature

108. The federal parliament and provincial legislatures have plenary authority to shape Canadian labour law within their respective constitutional spheres. If fully exercised, legislative power can displace ordinary rules of civil or common law, preclude judicial review, and authorize or limit administrative and tribunal action.

But legislative power is not unconstrained. Labour law is politically-charged: extreme measures may bring unwanted consequences. Labour law is complex: it has ramifications for many parts of the legal system which must be carefully considered. And for these reasons labour law legislation tends to be episodic and piecemeal: it tends to receive low legislative priority, and when new statutes are enacted, they are often anticipated by considerable study and consultation, not to say by changes in actual behaviour.

Nonetheless, it remains true to say that the legislature is the most important single influence in the development of Canadian labour law.

B. The courts

1. The superior courts

(a) Appellate courts

109. At the apex of the judicial system is the Supreme Court of Canada. It has a discretionary jurisdiction to accept appeals from all other federal or provincial appellate courts, and its interpretations of the constitution and of legislation, and decisions on matters of civil or common law, have authoritative effect across the country. Consequently, its impact on the development of labour law is potentially great.

110. Each province also has a general appellate court, usually referred to as the 'Court of Appeal', whose decisions on all matters are final, unless appealed successfully to the Supreme Court of Canada. Usually, these courts are not involved in matters of labour law until they have been litigated at a lower level. However, the Federal Court of Appeal (which unlike the provincial appellate courts has a limited jurisdiction in relation to certain federal matters) does have the primary obligation of reviewing the decisions of various federal labour tribunals.

(b) The trial courts

111. Each province has a general trial court, variously named 'the Supreme Court', 'the High Court', or the Court of Queen's Bench'. (There is also a federal Trial Court, but its role in labour law is insignificant.) These provincial courts have a residual jurisdiction to decide all controversies, whether under federal or provincial law, not expressly assigned elsewhere. They play a major role in shaping labour law in two areas.

112. First, ordinary lawsuits involving principles of common or civil law are normally brought in these courts. These include the enforcement of individual employment contracts, and claims for damages or injunctions arising out of industrial action. Litigation amongst union members, or relating to union property, is also found in these courts.

113. Second, decisions of labour tribunals operating under provincial law are usually subject to review by, and enforcement proceedings in, the provincial trial courts. (In Ontario, a special Divisional Court, comprising three High Court judges, is assigned the task of review.)

114. Thus, whether exercising original or reviewing jurisdiction, the provincial trial courts, in theory, have the power to shape the development of labour law in virtually all matters of significance. This power is, however, limited by several constraints. First, legislatures have increasingly confined the role of the courts by assigning responsibility for industrial action to labour relations boards, and by expressly forbidding the courts to review various tribunal decisions. Second, the costs, formality and delays of conventional litigation create some disincentives to the use of these courts in labour matters. And third, perhaps aware of the first two matters, the courts themselves are developing procedural rules and substantive doctrines which somewhat limit their role in labour law.

2. The lower courts

115. The provinces are authorized to establish minor courts of civil and criminal jurisdiction. These play some role in labour law, although largely in its ongoing administration rather than in the adumbration of broad principles, or in the announcement of authoritative interpretations, functions reserved to the superior trial, and especially appellate, courts.

116. 'Small Claims Courts' deal with most claims for unpaid wages. Lower criminal courts, variously named, deal with prosecutions for violations of the federal Criminal Code (e.g. by violent conduct during a strike) or of federal or provincial labour legislation. However, such prosecutions are relatively rare. Only Quebec has a special Labour Court/*Tribunal du travail*, whose principal function is enforcement of the Labour Code.

C. The executive

1. The cabinet

117. In any parliamentary system, the Cabinet as a whole is ultimately responsible for the development, enactment and administration of legislation. This is particularly true in such a politically sensitive area as labour policy. Thus, the Cabinet will carefully vet legislative proposals originating in the ministries and, on occasion, even decide whether to intervene *ad hoc* in a dispute with high public visibility. Moreover, the Cabinet will play a mediative role amongst the various ministries concerned with labour matters.

118. Subject to Cabinet control, the ministries themselves are charged with both the origination and review of policies, and their daily execution. The distribution of responsibility amongst the ministries concerned with labour matters differs from jurisdiction to jurisdiction.

2. The ministry of labour

119. Typically the Ministry of Labour has the main responsibility for collective bargaining policy, although administration and enforcement of the general private-sector labour relations statute is almost inevitably undertaken by an independent labour relations board.

In addition, the Ministry of Labour may be responsible for such matters as manpower policy, human rights legislation, occupational health and safety, trade licensing and training, some forms of social insurance, and legislation regarding individual (as distinct from collective) employment rights.

3. The ministry of justice or of the attorney general

120. In almost all Canadian jurisdictions, the chief legal minister is responsible for drafting legislation, including labour legislation, and for undertaking court proceedings on behalf of the government. These functions may be undertaken in close co-operation with the relevant ministry, or even delegated to the department in question.

4. Other ministries

121. No consistent pattern exists by which labour relations-related responsibilities are distributed amongst other ministries. At the federal level, for example, the Ministry of Finance is responsible for anti-inflation initiatives, including wage and price controls, the Ministry of Manpower and Immigration for manpower policies, the Ministry of National Health and Welfare for some employment-related schemes of social insurance, etc. In some provinces,

46

responsibility for anti-discrimination legislation may be vested in the Attorney-General or another minister, while responsibility for occupational health and safety, trade training and licensing may be assigned elsewhere.

D. The labour relations board

122. In every Canadian jurisdiction, except Quebec, the private-sector labour relations statute establishes a labour relations board which is charged with administering and enforcing the statute in relation to union certification, unfair labour practices, and in some cases, industrial conflict and regulation of internal union affairs. In Quebec, such functions are divided between a Labour Court/*Tribunal du travail* and departmental officials called commissioners/ *commissaires*.

In British Columbia, the labour relations board has reached its fullest flowering and enjoys plenary independent authority as well over conciliation, strikes, picketing and grievance arbitration, *inter alia*. Other labour relations boards enjoy some, but not all, of these responsibilities.

123. The organization and membership of the labour relations board varies from jurisdiction to jurisdiction. In some provinces, the board has tripartite membership, *i.e.* a presiding officer who is a neutral, and equal numbers of management and labour representatives. However, the Canada Labour Relations Board and those of some other provinces, comprises neutral members only.

124. Labour relations boards have at their disposal sizeable supporting staffs. The staff is, typically, used to make inquiries concerning facts which will determine union bargaining rights, but also to investigate and seek amicably to dispose of complaints made under the act against employers or unions. Some labour relations boards also control a staff of employees whose function it is to conciliate interest disputes.

125. While much of the noncontentious business of the boards is disposed of through informal processes of investigation, or *pro forma* disposition by the board itself, a certain number of cases are inevitably submitted for formal adjudication. Following adjudication, most labour relations boards enjoy the power to make remedial orders in order to secure compliance with statutory policies. These orders are, typically, registrable in, and enforceable as orders of, the superior courts.

In almost all jurisdictions, violation of the governing labour relations statute, or board orders, is also a quasi-criminal offence. However, prosecution is usually possible only with the prior consent of the board, which is loathe to give consent except in egregious cases. Indeed, neither unions nor employers evince much interest in criminal prosecution, and the criminal courts are seldom involved in labour relations matters.

VI. Sources of Labour Law

§1. Methods of Legal Analysis

126. As a practical matter, the vast bulk of disputes which may arise between an employer and his employees or their union are settled bilaterally, and not always in accordance with legal norms. The predominant influence in such settlements is the desire to preserve an amicable and mutually profitable relationship.

127. However, if such settlement proves impossible, and recourse to law is necessary, the courts almost inevitably have the last word. In certain areas, they possess original jurisdiction to decide issues of constitutional or private law in labour relations; otherwise, they may possess power to review or hear appeals from legal decisions in other forums. In the latter case, however, whether because of the limited scope of review, or as a result of diffidence about intervention, or – by far the most important factor – because the parties choose not to resort to courts – the 'law' of other forums is, in fact, of primary importance. This is significant because the procedures of dispute resolution, the norms of decision-making, the modes of reasoning, the methods of proof, and the remedial powers of these other forums may often differ considerably from those of the courts.

§2. Common Law

A. General

128. In the absence of legislation, common law governs wherever the courts choose to intervene. There are several areas of importance where the court has, in fact, intervened in labour law.

B. Tort

129. The law of industrial conflict (in all provinces except British Columbia) is in essence tort law. The legality of strikes and picketing is measured by general doctrines of civil liability, although it must be said that the development of these doctrines was largely influenced by the fact that they evolved in the context of industrial relations controversies; indeed, they are relatively seldom employed elsewhere. Damages, and especially injunctions, are the remedies sought from the courts usually to restrain illegal strikes, picketing or boycotting.

C. Contract

130. Contract law is the primary source of law governing relationships between non-unionized workers and their employers, although the existence of a formal contract is, in fact, relatively rare amongst ordinary employees. The extent to which the advent of a regime of collective bargaining displaces the common law of contract is a matter of considerable controversy. So too is the question of whether common law contract principles are relevant to the interpretation and enforcement of collective agreements by arbitrators.

The relationship amongst union members is, in part, also viewed as a contractual matter, the 'contract' being the union constitution.

D. Property

131. Property law is occasionally relevant insofar as an employer asserts his rights as a property owner vis-a-vis a union or his employees. For example, he may complain that union organizers have trespassed on his property, or that picketing is conducted in such a way as to interfere with access to property. Property law may also govern disputes among union members over the ownership of union assets.

E. Judicial review of administrative decisions and arbitration awards

132. To the extent that such rules are not explicitly provided by statute, common law principles govern the procedures by which courts review the decisions of administrative tribunals and of arbitrators, and the scope of such review.

§3. LEGISLATION

133. Legislation is supreme over all other legal sources, displaces common law to the extent it explicitly or implicitly can be read as doing so, and also defines the power of administrative tribunals. However, legislation must inevitably be interpreted and the role of the courts, particularly in reviewing the decisions of administrative tribunals, but also in determining the continued survival of common law principles, limits the practical extent of legislative supremacy.

At times, the courts have been highly interventionist, disputing the interpretations of labour legislation adopted by administrative tribunals. Legislatures have responded, on occasion, either by limiting or entirely eliminating judicial review, or by enacting amendments expressly restoring the original administrative interpretation.

However, legislation remains the most important source of law in labour relations. Even the law of industrial conflict, historically rooted in common law tort doctrines, is increasingly intertwined with legislation. Indeed, in British Columbia, although to a lesser extent elsewhere, legislation has almost entirely displaced the common law of industrial conflict.

§4. SUBORDINATE LEGISLATION

134. Often, legislation lays down broad lines of policy, leaving details to be worked out over a period of time, especially in the light of changing circumstances, or where technical or scientific matters are at issue. Where these details of regulation are required to be given legal force, the governing statute generally provides for the enactment of 'subordinate legislation' by the responsible department or administrative agency, subject usually to (formal) approval of the Cabinet. Examples of such subordinate legislation include the procedural rules of the labour relations board, health and safety standards in particular industries, and levels of benefits and standards of entitlement in social security schemes.

§5. ADMINISTRATIVE DECISION-MAKING

135. Labour relations boards have developed an extensive jurisprudence of decisions made by them in interpretation of the labour relations act and its subordinate procedural rules. These decisions, which are contained in various series of reports, are extremely important in understanding the actual operation of the legislation, and often involve significant declarations of policy, especially where legislation is itself couched in general terms. These decisions are subject to judicial review, although the scope of review has been statutorily narrowed in some jurisdictions, and review is almost entirely foreclosed in British Columbia.

A labour relations board may also announce, through a published policy statement not made in the context of a specific case, that it intends to exercise (or has exercised) its decision-making discretion in a particular manner. Such announcements enable the parties to conduct themselves in a manner consistent with the board's policy.

A labour relations board is, however, not legally bound by its own prior decisions or announced policies. Nonetheless, it will generally adhere to such precedents until it is demonstrated that they were erroneous, or have become obsolete.

§6. COLLECTIVE AGREEMENTS

136. Collective agreements are a primary source of law which defines the rights of unions and employers who are parties to the agreement, and of the employees governed by them. They are often documents of considerable length and complexity, and deal with such matters as the wages to be paid for various jobs, working conditions, the assignment of work, 'fringe benefits' such as pensions, insurance, paid vacations and holidays (over the statutory minimum), and the prerogatives of the employer and union. Of overriding significance are clauses – whose inclusion is typically required by statute – providing for the recognition of the union as the exclusive bargaining agent of the employees, requiring the submission of all disputes during the term of the agreement to arbitration, and prohibiting strikes and lock-outs for the duration of the agreement. Occasionally required by statute, but almost inevitably included by agreement of the parties, is a clause which stipulates that an employee may not be disciplined or discharged except for 'just cause'.

137. Disputes over the meaning of the collective agreement are generally not justiciable in common law courts. In all Canadian jurisdictions, parties to a collective agreement are either compelled or permitted to submit their disputes over the application, interpretation or alleged violation of a collective agreement to arbitration. In some provinces, notably British Columbia, the parties have the additional option of submitting their dispute to the labour relations board, which may either resolve it through mediation, itself adjudicate the matter, or remit it to arbitration.

138. In most jurisdictions, the awards of arbitrators are subject to judicial review, generally on grounds of procedural impropriety, or because the arbitrator has exceeded his powers or has assigned meaning to the language of the agreement it cannot (in the court's view) reasonably bear. As a practical matter, the possibility of judicial review allows the court to require arbitrators to adhere fairly closely to a common law contractual approach. Departures from such an approach are most likely to succeed if they are explicitly licensed by the agreement itself, or, as in British Columbia, by governing legislation which directs arbitrators to decide cases according to 'principles consistent with the industrial relations policy of [the British Columbia Labour Code]' and 'not . . . a strict legal interpretation of the issue in dispute'.

139. Awards of arbitrators are published, and tend to be cited as persuasive (but not binding) authority by other arbitrators. However, it is ultimately the language of the agreement which governs the award provided it is sufficiently clear and unequivocal.

§7. Industrial Custom and Practice

140. Although in fact many features of the ongoing relationship between a union and employer, or between an employer and his individual, non-organized employees, is governed by custom and practice, custom and practice are not generally *per se* enforceable in arbitration, labour relations board or court proceedings (unless, of course, they are expressly or impliedly given binding effect by language in the collective agreement or contract of employment).

However, to the extent that they can be proved to, noted by, or lie within the expert knowledge of, an arbitrator or labour relations board, industrial custom and practice may serve several important functions. They may supplement and help to give meaning to general language in a collective agreement. They may illuminate or help to determine the credibility of contentious evidence. And they may, especially, guide the parties in the bilateral resolution of their differences, before they seek adjudication by a third party.

Processes of daily administration of an employment relationship not only adhere to, but obviously in turn generate, informal practices, customs and understandings. The 'web of rules' thus produced is part of the true law of the workplace, and is as functionally significant as if it were legally binding.

§8. BIBLIOGRAPHY

D. J. M. Brown and D. M. Beatty, Canadian Labour Arbitration (Canada Law Book: Toronto, 1977)

Canadian Industrial Relations, The Report of the Task Force on Labour Relations (H. D. Woods, Chairman, 1968) (and 23 published studies)

A. W. R. Carrothers, Collective Bargaining Law in Canada (Butterworths: Toronto, 1965

J. H. Crispo, The Canadian Industrial Relations System (Toronto: McGraw-Hill, 1978)

P. Cutler, Code du travail du Québec annoté-comparé (Livres Toundra: Montreal, rev. ed., 1976) (English or French)

S. M. A. Hameed, Canadian Industrial Relations (Butterworths: Toronto, 1975)

D. Harris, Wrongful Dismissal (DeBoo: Toronto, 1978)

S. Jamieson, Industrial Relations in Canada (Macmillan: Toronto, 2nd ed., 1974)

Labour Relations Law Casebook Group, Labour Relations Law (Queen's U.I.R. Centre: Kingston, 3rd ed., 1980)

F. Morin, Rapports collectifs du travail au Québec (Editions Thèmis: Montreal, 1978)

E. E. Palmer, Collective Agreement Arbitration in Canada (Butterworths: Toronto, 1978)

J. Sack and M. Levinson, Ontario Labour Relations Board Practice (Butterworths: Toronto, 1973, with Supplement, 1977)

H. D. Woods, S. Ostry, M. A. Zaidi, Labour Policy and Labour Economics in Canada (Macmillan: Toronto, 2nd ed., 1973)

Part I. The Individual Employment Relationship

Chapter I. Definitions and Concepts

141. Before turning to the core of the material to be dealt with in the two chapters of this Part, attention must be drawn to the fact that, in Canada, there is no overriding theory which unifies the doctrines governing employment contracts made between individuals and those made between employers and unions, that is, collective agreements. The individual contract of employment law is inherited from England and modified to be made applicable to Canadian conditions. The collective bargaining regime is indigenous and, although often the same semantics seem to be used when it is legally analysed, many of the assumptions of the common law have been abandoned or, at least, perceptibly changed. From a doctrinal point of view, the accommodation between the two regimes has not been worked out with precision. In this Part, the individual contract of employment is the focus. It is to be remembered however that, even though the law relating to this aspect of labour relations has a role to play when collective bargaining law governs the relationship between employers and employees, it will not necessarily be the same role, either theoretically or functionally.

§1. The Central Place of the Contract of Employment

A. The ubiquity of the concept

142. The term contract of employment denotes an essential concept in labour law. There must be a relationship recognized by law to be one of contract between an employer and an employee before any of the incidents of labour law will be applicable. This is so whether the labour law sought to be applied relates to the making, administering or enforcing of agreements between employers and trade unions, or to the exercise of rights and imposition of obligations arising out of long established rules of custom or the common law in respect of working conditions, or to the rights arising under legislation dealing with working conditions. It is so, even though some of the legislation, such as workers' compensation statutes, refers to 'workers' rather than 'employees' in describing its scope and it is so when a statute defines 'employee' for its own limited purposes. The interpretation of such statutory provisions has been to require the establishment of a contract of employment whatever the terminology used to describe the persons covered by them,[1] unless there is a specific legislative direction to the contrary.[2]

1. *E.g. Re The Employment Relationship* (1974) 1 W.C.R. 127 (Workmen's Compensation Board of B.C.), 'workmen' interpreted; *Re Telegram Publishing* (1973) 3 L.A.C. (2d) 175 (Carter), 'employee' in Employment Standards Act, R.S.O. 1970, c.147 interpreted.
2. In many jurisdictions the collective bargaining legislation specifically provides that persons who otherwise would not be treated as employees by the law of the contract of employment should be treated as such for the purposes of collective bargaining law; *e.g.* Saskatchewan, s.2; British Columbia, s.1(1); Ontario, s.1(1) (ga).

B. Working definition

143. The contract of employment is, in simple terms, an agreement by one party, the employee, to serve the other party, the employer, the consideration being remuneration for those services. It will readily be seen that this is a widesweeping description. It includes many relationships which in other jurisdictions might be classified separately.

144. The common law of Canada makes no distinction in principle between *probationary* and *temporary* employees and other employees. In as much as collective bargaining and legislative provisions create special duties, rights and obligations in respect of probationary and temporary employees, this has no effect on the legal classification of such employees. Similarly, although there was once some doubt, persons who work for the government are considered to have contracts of employment with the Crown, even though many of the terms and conditions of employment are dictated by statute and are not the result of contract negotiations.[1] Again, sometimes persons are spoken of as 'office' holders. Whatever special meaning attached to that term, today it has no special magic in labour law. An 'office' holder will be classified as an employee on the basis of the same principles which apply to persons who do not hold an 'office'. Being an 'office' holder may have other implications such as, for instance, bearing the burden of special obligations if the 'office' is that of a director of a corporation, or of not being able to claim certain expenditures against earned income as a taxpayer, but such incidents are not germane to legal classification.[2]

1. See *Reilly* v. *R.*, [1932] S.C.R. 597 at 600, per Orde, J.; S. A. de Smith, *Constitutional and Administrative Law* (London, 1971) 198–200.
2. Statutes in respect of companies usually define 'officer' as including presidents, directors, secretaries, treasurers, general managers. *E.g.* The Business Corporations Act, R.S.O. 1970, c.53, s.1(1)19. For the purposes of the Income Tax Act, S.C. 1970–71–72, c.63, s.48(1) defines 'officers' as persons who have been appointed to have ascertained incomes, *e.g.* judges.

145. On the other hand, there are many relationships which apparently fall within the scope of the contract of employment as described but which are not categorized as employment relationships for the purposes of labour law. Much will depend on the weight given to certain aspects of the context in which the services rendered for remuneration are given. This issue is explored in §2.

146. Note also that many persons who do render services in a way which would normally qualify them as employees are specifically excluded from the operation of statutes which purport to govern employment relationships. Typically, collective bargaining statutes exempt persons who may be termed 'professionals' such as doctors, lawyers, dentists, and the like from their operation. Also they often do not apply to other persons who work under contracts of employment such as agricultural or domestic workers or to members of the police force, firefighters or teachers. Frequently, other statutory schemes create special industrial relations' systems for such groups. It is impossible to catalogue the great number of special legislative schemes here, but a perusal of the sections relating to coverage in the basic collection bargaining legislation will indicate whether or not such special legislation exists.

147. Finally, many persons who are legally classified as working under contracts of employment are excluded from statutes which provide that employees shall be paid a prescribed minimum wage, shall not be paid more than a prescribed period of notice of vacation, etc. Typically, such employees include domestic, agricultural and horticultural workers. Again, a compilation is impractical in this work, but the basic standard statutes to which reference will be made below ought to be consulted.

C. Apprenticeships

148. Apprentices form a special category of employees worthy of separate treatment. An apprenticeship may have to be served as a condition of admission to an occupational field. Once it was common for an apprentice not to receive any remuneration apart from this instruction and supervision and support and maintenance. Today, the apprentice receives, like other employees, remuneration. Because of the special nature of this contract of employment, many of the incidents normally associated with the contract of employment – to be considered below – do not apply as a matter of common law. In particular, unless there is a covenant or a contract to the contrary, misconduct on the part of the apprentice does not permit an employer to terminate the contract. Neglect, intoxication, incompetence, disobedience of orders will not normally provide grounds for dismissal. Termination of the contract, without a custom or covenant to the contrary, is to be by mutual consent. If an apprenticeship is wrongfully terminated, the apprentice may sue for damages for the remuneration for the amount of time which the apprenticeship still had to run (subject to the duty to mitigate such loss by accepting other employment) and also, in appropriate cases, for the value of injured future prospects.[1]

In all jurisdictions there are statutes governing apprenticeships.[2] They create Boards empowered to make recommendations, and/or regulations, in respect of specified occupations, which govern the requirements of training, impose duties on employers to instruct, require registration of apprenticeship agreements; they may provide for a system of granting proficiency certificates and even specify some conditions of employment.

1. *Dunk* v. *George Waller*, [1970] 2 A11 E.R. 630(C.A.).
2. *E.g.* Apprenticeship and Training Development Act, S.B.C. 1977, c.65; The Apprenticeship and Tradesmen's Qualifications Act, S.M. 1972, c.45; Manpower Vocational Training and Qualification Act, S.Q. 1969, c.51; The Apprenticeship and Tradesmen's Qualification Act, R.S.O. 1970, c.24.

D. The service characteristic

149. As described, the contract of employment is an agreement to render services in return for remuneration. The significance of this lies in the fact that the employee is, as the language suggests, in a position where most of the onerous obligations under the contract will be imposed on her/him. Thus, while it is true that, for the purposes of legal classification, the relationship is one of ordinary contract, (that is, an enforceable agreement entered into on a voluntary basis by the two parties), it differs from such an ordinary contract in that one party will be assumed to have accepted more burdensome duties of performance than the other. On a strictly analytical basis this is not a valid distinction between a contract of employment and other kinds of contracts. After all, an employee is free to negotiate terms which would diminish his obligation to serve. The reality is otherwise. The need for collective bargaining arises out of this reality. Further, where collective bargaining does not occur, legislatures will step in to ensure that employees are guaranteed certain minimal conditions, regardless of tneir strength to obtain these by free contract negotiations. To return: the essence of the contract of employment being the rendering of services, such contracts will, by implication, impose obligations of a special kind on the employee. These implied obligations will be discussed below. Note that today we eschew the language of master and servant which used to describe these relationships because it implies a relationship between superiors and inferiors. The modern terminology of contract of employment suggests a freedom and equality which better reflects our aspirations. But the language of master and servant is useful because it explains the existence of many of the incidents of the contract of employment. They stem from the duty to serve: obedience, co-operation, good faith and fidelity from the employee are to be expected. They would not be considered integral to the relationship if employment was regarded as just another contractual arrangement. One would expect the corresponding employer obligations to relate to the provision of an appropriate environment for the rendering of services. Additional obligations do not flow naturally from the contract of employment. It is proper, therefore, to underline the importance of the characteristic of service.

§2. Distinguishing the Contract of Employment from Other Contracts
    to Provide Service

A. The need to distinguish

150. It has been seen that a determination of whether or not there is a
contract of employment is crucial to the issue of the applicability of collective
bargaining legislation, minimum conditions' statutes, workers' compensation
law and the incidents attached to the contract of employment. It is also vital to
such questions as to whether or not social welfare benefits are obtainable and as
to whether or not claims of expenditures may be made against taxable income.
In addition, the attribution of vicarious liability for the acts of another may
depend on the existence of a contract of employment between the defendant
and the wrongful actor.

B. Relationships which need to be distinguished

151. There are several contractual relationships which, on their face, bear a
close resemblance to contracts of employment in that they too are contracts to
provide services for a fee. First, there is the *independent contractor* agreement.
This is traditionally described as being a contract with a person who agrees to
perform tasks to produce a particular result. The notion is that *how* the result is
produced is a matter within the performer's discretion. Secondly, the *agency*
agreement is to be kept separate from the contract of employment. The salient
differentiating feature is that an agent brings his principal into contractual
relations with others. The agent is usually given power to use his judgment and
discretion as to how to bring this about. It is self-evident that it will be very
difficult to distinguish independent contractors and agents from each other
and, more importantly, from employees, because services are rendered for
consideration in all of these relationships. It has been suggested that employees
are persons who work under a contract of service whereas independent contractors and agents work under a contract for services.[1] But this seems merely
to restate the problem in a different way; it does not resolve it.

1. *E.g. Cassidy* v. *Ministry of Health*, [1951] 1 All E.R. 574(C.A.).

152. Other relationships which need to be differentiated from the employment one include *bailment*, *partnership* and *landlord and tenant*. Typically, in a
bailment for hire, chattels are left with a bailee. He is often entitled to use the
chattel for some specific purpose in return for the payment of money, often
periodically payable. The question of whether or not such a relationship is in
fact a contract of employment will arise where the use of the chattel by the
bailee is alleged to be for the benefit of the owner-bailor of the chattel. The hire
of a car might be such a situation.

153. A partnership is the carrying on of business by two or more people for profit. It is sometimes the case that, although the relationship is said to be a partnership, it is more fairly characterized as a contract of employment because it involves the rendering of services by one party to another for remuneration.

154. The last group of relationships which it is necessary to discuss here is that of landlord and tenant. An issue may arise where a person who is unquestionably an employee occupies a dwelling of his employer and the question is whether or not landlord and tenant law applies to such occupation. The difficulty then will not be whether or not such occupation can be distinguished from a contract of employment, but rather whether or not the occupation is primarily to further the employer's interest in which case the employee will not be a tenant for landlord and tenant law. Here the question is whether the character of the employment is such that it prevents the employee from claiming another status under law. This problem, being different in kind, will not be treated again in this work.

C. The criteria used to make the distinctions

155. As has been noted, the most important characteristic of the contract of employment is that it is a contract of service. To differentiate it from other relationships concerned with the rendering of service, the nature of the service becomes crucial. Reference here is not being made to the tasks which are to be performed, product to be produced or result to be reached. Rather the emphasis is on the essence of the relationship: does it more closely approximate one in which the person performing the task is a servant vis-a-vis the hiring entrepreneur rather than an equal, contracting person operating his own business in much the same way as the hiring entrepreneur? Linedrawing will necessarily be imprecise. It can be shown that the original concept of master and servant (with its attendant notions that to be a servant was to be legally classified as having a status in society with duties, rights, obligations and privileges which were not negotiable) still pervades legal thinking when the determination of whether or not a relationship is a contract of employment is to be made. Master and servant law assumed that the master had control over the servant. The test of control is of great importance today when deciding whether or not a contract of employment exists. But the notion of control is itself an elusive one. When society was much less industrialized than it is now, it was practical to assume that, in the much smaller and simpler enterprises which then existed, the master was the servant's equal in his understanding of the task to be performed. Under such conditions the control test was applicable. The court could look at whether or not the alleged servant had any real discretion as to what he was asked to do and as to how to do it. If the answer was that he possessed such discretion, no master and servant relationship would exist. The utility of this test diminished as the mode of organization of enterprises and technical developments made it increasingly less likely that the employer would have any skill or competence in, or experience of, the many tasks which had to be performed in daily operations. The test of control over the way tasks are to be performed is still, however, useful. Where the degree of the supervision makes it clear that the working person does not have the power to exercise any discretion in mode of performance nor to delegate his duties, there will be an employment relationship.[1] These inquiries are, therefore, still made in the cases. Other criteria of this kind include the ownership of the tools used. If the person for whom the work is to be done supplies the tools, this may be taken as an indication that the performer is an employee rather than an independent contractor who is self-employed. But, while complete control over the mode of production indicates the existence of a contract of employment, incomplete control over how the work is to be done, or ownership of the tools by the performer of the work, does not mean that there is no contract of employment. The courts, acknowledging the new modes of organization in enterprise, have sought alternative and complementary tests. Hence, the use of a formulation which distinguishes between a contract of service or a contract for service came to be employed to permit the courts to look at other criteria than the mechanistic one of control over the mode of carrying out tasks. But such formulations do not provide precise guidelines. A variant which has been offered is the organization test: to determine whether or not a person is an employee is to depend on a judgment as to whether the person is part and parcel of the organization.[2] By definition, this includes a lot of people who are not strictly controlled in the mode of carrying out their tasks, permitting doctors, professional people of all kinds, skilled craftspeople, etc., to be treated as employees. But, once again, this test provides no real means of differentiating people who have contracts of employment from persons who are self-employed. A formula much in use in Canada is that offered by Lord Wright in *Montreal* v. *Montreal Locomotive Works*:[3]

> In earlier cases a single test, such as the presence of absence of control, was often relied on to determine whether the case was one of master and servant . . . In the more complex conditions of modern industry, more complicated tests have often to be applied. It has been suggested that a fourfold test would in some cases be more appropriate, a complex involving (1) control; (2) ownership of the tools; (3) chance of profit; (4) risk of loss.

1. A classic statement is found in *Performing Right Society* v. *Mitchell and Booker*, [1924] 1 K.B. 762, at 767, per McCardie, J.
2. *Bank voor Handel en Scheepvaart N.V.* v. *Slatford*, [1952] 2 All E.R. 956, at 971, per Denning, L. J. (C.A.).
3. [1947] 1 D.L.R. 161 at 169(P.C.).

D. Application of the criteria

156. No useful purpose would be served by cataloguing decisions on the question of whether or not a contract of employment existed. The tests used are different in kind and each requires a weighing of facts, while leaving much discretion to the judges as to the significance of the various facts to be considered. Further, courts and/or boards are not duty bound to use one test rather than any other and are likely to use aspects of all. But some feeling for the flavour of decision-making may be gained by considering a few examples. A court, using the control test fairly rigidly, found that salesmen were servants. They worked on commission and could choose their own routes, subject to veto by the hirer, who also had the right to stipulate which merchandise to push, how to keep books of account and who required full-time devotion to the sale of its goods.[1]

Drivers of mobile canteens who worked under not very different conditions were held to be independent contractors on an appeal from a determination under an Employment Standards Act. This was done even though the appeal board noted that many of the circumstances of the relationship indicated an employment contract. The test apparently used was the four-fold one from *Montreal Locomotive Works* set out above.[2] A court applied a mixed test to determine the status of a painter who had worked under a contract of employment with his hirer prior to the creation of the relationship in question. He performed the same tasks, but he could do them whenever he felt like it. He had to provide his own transport. He was held to be an employee rather than an independent contractor.[3] But people who manage general stores held under franchises, have been held to be employees for the purpose of minimum standards' legislation, even though their earnings were tied to profits and they had a good deal of discretion in the day-to-day running of the store. Factors which influenced those decisions to go as they did included the nature of the right of selection and termination of the store operators by the franchisors, the contractual requirement to take a certain amount of stock, etc.[4] Two final examples: a court held a 13-year-old newsboy who collected and delivered papers for which he was remunerated on the basis of number delivered to be an independent contractor. Crucial to the decision seemed to be the fact that the boy had a choice as to which method he used to deliver the papers: on foot, by bicycle, by wagon or by motor vehicle. He also was to seek new subscribers and customers for his route.[5] A very strict adherence to the control test seems to have governed the decision. Contrast this with a case in which persons, known as district circulation managers for a newspaper, were held to be employees. They contracted with and supervised carriers; they assumed responsibility for the wholesale value of the newspaper they accepted for distribution. Their remuneration was held to be a guaranteed lump sum although the agreement had tied remuneration to the value of the newspapers sold. The expenses of running the district managers' offices were shared by them with the newspaper owners. These factors were evaluated in light of the *Montreal Locomotive Works'* test, and led to the determination that there was a contract of employment between the district managers and the newspaper.[6]

1. *Wright* v. *Jeffrey*, [1937] 1 D.L.R. 227 (Ont.C.A.).
2. *Re Appeal, Employment Standards; Gil's Lunch Service Limited*, Oct. 1970 (Frank G. Harrington).
3. *Armstrong* v. *Mac's Milk*, (1975) 7 O.R. (2d) 478 (Ont.H.C.).
4. *E.g. Becker Milk*, (1973) 1 L.A.C. (2d) 337 (Carter).
5. *Wm. Elliott* v. *Preston and Bartholomew*, [1957] O.W.N. 205 (Ont.C.C.).
6. *Telegram Publishing*, (1973) 3 L.A.C. (2d) 175 (Carter).

E. Significance of the context as a criterion

157. As has been seen, the cases arise, in the main, in two large areas. One, where a person who has rendered services seeks to have some of the guaranteed benefits of minimum standards' legislation apply to him. The other is where a person other than the one who actually inflicted injury is being sought to be made responsible vicariously for the injury-causing action. The nature of these cases and the seemingly agreed-upon notion that employers cannot be expected to exercise the same amount of control over their employees as they could in times gone by, have influenced decision-makers to look more towards tests such as the 'Montreal Locomotive Works' one than the control ones. The minimum standards' legislation is designed to ensure certain terms and conditions which society has determined are the bare minima which must obtain in the work place for those employees in the work force who are in poor contractual bargaining positions. The central notions behind vicarious liability are to be discussed below but they seem to be, (i) that those who profit from work done at their behest should bear the cost of harm inflicted on strangers by the profit-earning operation and, (ii) that the injured strangers should have a means of redress available against someone economically capable of compensating them. In both sets of situations, important social objectives could be undermined by a restrictive reading of the definition of the contract of employment. Given the existence of those social objectives, the decision-makers have – often subconsciously – increasingly been swayed by questions such as: Is this person claiming the benefits of minimum standards legislation the kind of person who needs such help? Is it proper that the cost of this accident should be borne by a person who has no contact with a profit-making enterprise? Arguably such an approach is legally perverse because it tackles the question of whether or not an employment relationship exists from the viewpoint of what social benefit can be gained from such a characterization rather than from the perspective of what more or less established legal indicia suggest the relationship is in law. The latter approach is the one our common law methodology demands and decision-makers have, for the most part, not openly advocated the former approach. What is suggested here is that the 'social benefit' formulation, whilst not explicitly used, may well provide a useful means of predicting the outcome of cases in which any number of conflicting criteria can be used by courts and boards when making a decision. There is some indication that the 'social benefit' approach may gain ground. As was noted above, collective bargaining legislation frequently allows persons who are not, by the use of one or more of the established common law tests employees, to form trade unions for the purpose of bargaining. This is done to give persons who could benefit from such bargaining (that is, make gains not achievable by contract-making as independent contractors or self-employed business persons), an opportunity to do so. The notion that to classify persons as employees because this will aid them in attaining an economic position of sufficiency, regardless of their initial desires or perceptions, is thus already explicitly accepted in some aspects of labour law.[1] The notion may be of some assistance in applying the elastic rules relating to the determination of the existence of a contract of employment.

1. The very descriptive term 'dependent contractor' is sometimes used to denote who these people are. See H. W. Arthurs, The Dependent Contractor: A study of the Legal Problems of Countervailing Power, (1965) 16 U.T.L.J. 89.

F. Who is the employer?

158. There are some other situations which give rise to the question of whether or not a contract of employment exists. One of these is where a person who is unquestionably an employee under a contract with employer A is sent to B to do some work and, while he does this, causes injury. There could be an issue as to whether A or B should be held vicariously responsible for the damage caused. Circumstances in which employees are lent in this way can vary a great deal, but there are some which recur more often than others in the reported decisions. They include the lending of vehicle drivers, crane operators, seamen to operate charter vessels and doctors from one hospital to another. The courts have traditionally approached the question by asking in whose employ the servant was at the time he inflicted injury.

159. The task facing the courts in these kinds of cases is complicated by the fact there there often is a contract between employer A and B, setting out the conditions of the lending of A's employee and/or equipment. Although such a contract is of itself not dispositive of the question of who the employer is, even if the contract states that, say B, shall be the employer for certain purposes and time,[1] the terms of the contract may affect the determination. This will be so because they may specify the amount of control which A and B shall have, who is to pay for what aspects of the servant's remuneration and other such indicia of the existence of an employment relationship. Thus much will depend on the facts of the particular case, but some general observations can be offered to aid in prediction of the outcome of such cases.

1. *Mersey Docks and Harbour Board* v. *Coggins & Griffith*, [1947] A.C.1 (H.L.).

160. The same developments in jurisprudence which were noted above, from adherence to a restricted notion of control to the use of an approach which recognizes the modes of organization of modern enterprise, can be recognized. Early on, there was a readiness by the courts to say that B had become the responsible employer where most of the direction as to how the work was to be done was given by B.[1] But, more recently, the courts have held that the original employer, usually referred to as the general employer, has a very heavy burden to discharge in order to prove that a transfer has taken place to the borrowing employer, referred to as the temporary employer.[2] It seems that part of this shift in emphasis is due to the fact that many of the borrowed employees are not subject to control in the carrying out of their tasks, being highly skilled. Thus, the courts have come to look to such criteria as: who can actually dismiss the employee, who is the real paymaster, for what length of time is the borrowed service to continue, etc.? Such questions will, more frequently than not, lead to the conclusion that the lending employer has remained the responsible employer.

1. *Canadian Northern Transfer* v. *Toronto Storage*, (1924) 55 O.L.R. 352 (Ont.C.A.): *A.H. Bull* v. *West African Shipping Agency and Lighterage*, [1927] A.C. 686 (P.C.); *Donovan* v. *Laing, Wharton and Down Construction Syndicate*, [1893] 1 Q.B. 629 (C.A.).
2. *Mersey Docks and Harbour* v. *Coggins, Supra*; *McKee* v. *Dumas*, (1976) 12 O.R. (2d) 670, (Ont.C.A.).

161. To establish an employment relationship there must be a contract between identifiable individuals. Difficult questions may arise because it is not clear who the actual employer is when services are rendered for the benefit of a number of associated businesses. An enterprise may, for reasons such as limiting commercial liability, minimizing the incidence of taxation, enhancing efficiency by, say, separating storage from distribution in its operations, etc., organize itself so that several separate legal entities are created, although the business is, in functional terms, one. Workers may be asked to do work for several of the legal entities. At common law, one of these entities will have to be capable of being classified as an employer before the incidents of the contract of employment will be applicable.[1] Such a determination will have to be made on the basis of such tests as control, ownership of tools, the four-fold test of *Montreal Locomotive Works*, and so forth. As the question will seldom be a burning one unless an employee, claiming applicability of minimum standards' legislation, is met with the argument that he has failed to prove that the respondent is his employer, some jurisdictions have ensured that their minimum standards' legislation shall have its intended scope by copying a feature of collective bargaining legislation. That kind of statutory scheme provides that related activities, businesses or undertaking may be treated as one employer for the purpose of collective bargaining. Similar provisions appear in some of the minimum standards' statutes,[2] overcoming the conceptual difficulty the common law has in tinkering with notions of individual contracting-making and the piercing of corporate veils.

1. *Holland* v. *Saltair Beach Resort*, (1951) 1 W.W.R. (N.S.) 816 (B.C.C.A.).
2. *E.g.* Alberta, s.20; The Employment Standards Act, R.S.M. 1970, c.E110, as am. S.M. 1972, c.50, s.34.1(5) (in respect of maternity leave only); Labour Standards Code, S.N.S. 1972, c.10, s.9; The Employment Standards Act, S.O. 1974, c.112, s.12.

162. In the same vein, a problem could arise when an employer sells his business: who will be responsible for existing obligations to the employee? Frequently, of course, the matter will be controlled by the contract between the seller and buyer of the business. But it may not be. Further, there may be occasions where the employee will not want to bring an action against the seller of the business because of the financial difficulties of the seller. Again, some jurisdictions have copied collective bargaining legislation. There it is provided that unions, faced with a change of ownership of an undertaking with which they have an agreement about working conditions will, in given circumstances, have that agreement continue to operate vis-a-vis the successor owner. Some

63

minimum standards' statutes have similar provisions to ensure the continuation of availability of benefits to employees.[1]

1. *E.g.* Alberta s.21; Employment Standards Act, R.S.M. 1970, c.E110, as am. S.M. 1972 c.52, s.34.1(7); Nova Scotia, s.10; Ontario, s.55; An Act Respecting Labour Standards, S.Q. 1979 (not proclaimed in force as of, July 1979), s.97; The Labour Standards Act, R.S.S. 1978, c.L–1, s.83.

163. Sometimes a claim will be made that a person who ran a one-person company was an employee of that company. This is possible because a company is a juristic person separate and distinct from the incorporators. The problem is most likely to arise where dependents wish to make a workers' compensation benefit claim or the like. In such a case there can be no argument that the person is under the control of the company as to either what work can be done or how it ought to be done. On the basis of such a test, the director/ worker cannot claim an employment relationship. It is also difficult to succeed on the basis that the relationship is one of such dependency that there is in fact an employment relationship. This latter argument would fly in the face of the fact that the company was formed to serve the needs of the director/worker. Yet such a person may well be classified as an employee if the context warrants, once again highlighting the fact that the semantic tests used by decision-makers may not be as important as the felt need to satisfy unstated policy objectives. Thus, in one such case, the Privy Council refused to pierce the corporate veil and held that the one-man company was the employer of the one man who had formed it, had appointed himself as a life long director of it and had then employed himself as a servant. The need of a widow and children were thus met (as well as those of an arbitrary company law rule).[1] In a very similar case, the chairman of a workers' compensation board held that the failure to register the one-man company as an employer under the scheme (as well as not seeking protection as a sole proprietor), showed that the intent of the guiding soul of the company was to avoid having to pay premiums under the scheme. Such an attitude was seen as leading to an undermining of this socially beneficial compensation scheme. Thus, it would be dysfunctional to now permit dependents to collect compensation on the basis that the deceased had been an employee. It would mean that a business man had obtained free insurance, because the normal rule of the scheme did not punish an employee for the employer's failure to pay premiums would have been applied to benefit a person who should not, whatever his classification would have been for other purposes, be regarded as an employee under this statute.[2] That is, a contrary position to that adopted by the Privy Council in respect of the corporate veil and the existence of an employment relationship was taken because different purposes were sought to be served.

1. *Lee* v. *Lee's Air Farming*, [1960] 3 All E.R. 420 (P.C.).
2. *Re A One-Man Company*, (1975) 2 W.C.R. 41 (Workmen's Compensation Board of B.C.).

§3. FORMATION OF CONTRACTS OF EMPLOYMENT

A. Types of contract of employment

164. A contract of employment is, in some respects, similar to other kinds of contracts. That is, it is a voluntarily-entered into agreement, between two capable parties, with an intention to create legal relations. There will have been an offer of certain terms and an acceptance thereof, and consideration must be proved before the contract can be enforced. All these criteria must be met. They are usually very easy to establish where an employment relationship is alleged to exist. But there is at least one significant difference between a contract of employment and other contracts. In the ordinary contract, even one which provides for a fixed period of duration, performance will terminate the contract. A contract of employment is, typically, one of indefinite duration which terminates upon appropriate notice being given.

165. It was common for English courts to read a contract of employment of indefinite duration as being a yearly contract, that is, a contract for at least one year certain. The effect of this was that it could not be terminated until that year had elapsed. Should the yearly hiring continue beyond the first year, without any express arrangements being made by the parties, the employment would be considered a yearly one. This was known as the *presumption of yearly hiring*. It was always a weak presumption, one which could be easily rebutted by, say, showing that the method of payment of wages had reference to a different time period than a year. The presumption had its origins in a society whose economic base, being primarily agricultural, was markedly different to our present one. Indeed, at a time when the presumption of yearly hiring was still part of the formal statement of the rules relating to employment relationships, society was changing so fast that a number of courts had already begun not to treat contracts of indefinite duration as yearly contracts.[1] As early as 1898, the Supreme Court of Canada rejected the notion that the presumption of a yearly hiring was a rule of law. It held that the nature of the contract had to be deduced from surrounding facts, not by presumption of law.[2] It was not until 1969 that an English Court of Appeal finally stated that in England the presumption of yearly hiring was no longer effective.[3]

1. M. R. Freedland, *The Contract of Employment* (Oxford, 1976) 143–146.
2. *Bain v. Anderson and Anderson Furniture*, (1898) 28 S.C.R. 481.
3. *Richardson v. Koefod*, [1969] 3 All E.R. 1264 (C.A.).

166. Once the presumption of yearly hiring is not applied to a contract of employment of indefinite duration, the question arises as to how such a contract is to be treated. One tendency has been to regard it as a periodic hiring, the length of the period being ascertained by reference to the incidents of the contract, especially the method of payment of wages. For example, an indefinite hiring in which wages are paid on a monthly basis could be treated as hiring for a month, which is renewed every month for a month. But the notion that employment contracts are of this nature is at a variance with the common understanding of both employers and employees, namely that the relationship is a continuing one. Accordingly, the prevailing and better view is that such contracts are to be treated as being of indefinite duration, terminable by reasonable notice. We will return, later, to the nature of reasonable notice but it suffices to note that the method of payment of wages is a significant factor.

167. It is also possible to have a contract of employment for a fixed term. Under such a contract the relationship cannot be ended by either party until the specified period expires, unless the conduct of one of the parties is such as to amount to a repudiation of the contract. Not every provision for a fixed term will characterize the contract as being one which cannot be ended by the giving of reasonable notice. The particular circumstances of the contract, including the express provision for a fixed term, will be weighed.

B. The requirement of writing

168. The contract of employment may be formed in the same way as all other contracts: the parties may write down the terms of their agreement, they may merely express their agreement orally, or the relationship can be inferred as having been created by the conduct of the parties. The latter is very common. Typically, an employee will commence work and obey the employer's commands, as well as receive certain benefits. On the other hand, contracts of employment concerned with managerial-type employees will often be in writing. The law does not require that they should be so unless they are to last for a term longer than a year. Where contracts are entered into on the basis that they are not to be completed within the space of one year, the seventeenth-century English Statute of Fraud's[1] Canadian equivalents[2] must be satisfied. These requirements are that the agreement must be in writing, or some memorandum or note of it must exist, before an action can be brought on it. Further, the party who is made a defendant to the action must have signed the agreement, memorandum or note; the plaintiff need not be a signatory. Where a memorandum or note is relied upon, it need not be in a particular form. The signed minutes of a company's books or a letter from a principal to an agent accepting the terms negotiated by that agent, may satisfy the Statute. But the memorandum or note must contain the material terms of the agreement. What is material is a question of fact but, at the very least, there must be an indication of the essence of the bargain between the parties and the condition in respect of which the action is brought must be in writing. Note here that failure to comply with the writing requirements does not render the contract void, merely a particular term or terms unenforceable.

1. Statute of Frauds, (1677) 29 Car. II, c.3.
2. *E.g.* The Statute of Frauds, R.S.O. 1970, c.444; Statute of Frauds, R.S.N.B. 1973, c.S–14; Statute of Frauds, R.S.N.S. 1967, c.290.

169. The notion behind the Statute of Frauds was that parties in a dispute about an agreement should not be in a position where they had to rely on differing and fading memories, making it easy to perjure themselves about the terms of the agreement. Those dangers increase as the length of the contractual relationship increases. Binding the parties to what they had written down made some sense but the mechanism used was crude. For example, the resolution of a dispute which takes place a day after entering an agreement which was to last for more than a year hardly requires protection against failing memories. Or, conversely, a dispute about an agreement which was not, at the time of entering, meant to last for as long as a year, but which had continued for much longer, could be enforced regardless of the lack of writing which supposedly protects against defective memory and the possibility of perjury. Further, the Statute of Frauds frequently has the very opposite effect to its intended one. More often than not the party relying on the failure of writing is a defendant who seeks to escape the obligations he has taken on under the agreement. Such a defendant will not have to say that he has not agreed to the term with which he is now charged, but merely that it is not contained in writing signed by him. Inevitably, the courts' disapproval of the Statute of Frauds led to the development of many means to avoid its literal application. Some of these included: (i) inroads on the parole evidence rule which theoretically forbids the use of parole evidence to complement evidence which must be in writing and (ii) the reading in of implied terms into a memorandum or note, thus amplifying the ambit of the available writing. A detailed discussion of these judicial tools of avoidance is out of place here; attention must be reserved for the reading given to the Statute of Frauds in the particular context of contracts of employment. It is a narrow one. Such contracts are read as not being caught by the Statute, (that is, to be enforced they do not require writing) if either party's obligations under the agreement can be performed within one year of entering into the agreement, even if the agreement stipulates that it was to last longer than one year. All that needs to be shown is that it is possible, regardless of the parties' intentions, that one party's obligations may be discharged within one year.[1] Thus, even if the contracts of employment is said to be for the life of the employee, the contract will not need to meet the requirements of the Statute of Frauds because the employee might die within a year of entering into such an agreement.[2] Similarly, a contract of indefinite duration does not have to meet the Statute of Frauds criteria to be enforceable because, as was noted above, it can be terminated by reasonable notice (provided the reasonable notice in the particular case does not exceed one year).[3] This is of particular importance now that the presumption of yearly hiring is a thing of the past. It seems as if the only contracts of employment which have to be in writing for the purposes of enforcement are those which are specifically stated to be for more than one year and where performance by neither party can be discharged within a year. It has been held in England that, when such a rare case arises, the contract must be in writing even though one of the terms of the contract says that it could be terminated by notice within one year.[4] This seems a strange view of the law, one which ought not to be followed in Canada.

1. *Cemco Electrical Manufacturing* v. *Von Snellenberg*, [1947] S.C.R. 121; *Mott* v. *Trott*, [1943] S.C.R. 256.

2. *Campbell* v. *Business Fleets*, [1954] O.R. 87 (C.A.); *Cemco supra* note 1.
3. *Harvard* v. *Freeholders Oil*, (1952) 6 W.W.R. (N.S.) 413 (Sask. Q.B.); *Dalimore* v. *Canada Permanent Trust*; [1947] O.W.N. 682 (H.C.).
4. *Dobson* v. *Collis*, (1856) 1 H. & N. 81; *Hanau* v. *Ehrlich*, [1912] A.C. 39 (H.L.).

170. The Western provinces of Canada have similar legislative provisions to those of the Statute of Frauds in respect of the contract of employment. They are found in specialized statutes, that is, statutes not dealing with all of the incidents of the contract of employment.[1] This has raised the question of whether or not the requirement of writing applied to terms other than those covered by the particular statute. In one Saskatchewan case it was held that the requirement of writing should be so restricted, but the Saskatchewan Act was amended to overcome this defect.[2] The other statutes, however, are still in the form which gave rise to the judicial decision in Saskatchewan. Another aspect of these statutes is that they are phrased differently from the Statute of Frauds. The latter requires writing whenever the contract is not to be performed within the space of one year; the Western statutes demand writing where a contract is to last longer than one year, no matter when it commences. This could make for different application.

1. Master and Servant Act, R.S.B.C. 1960, c.234, s.5(4); The Masters and Servants Act, R.S.A. 1970, c.228, s.3(2); The Wages Recovery Act, R.S.S. 1965, c.296, s.4; The Wages Recovery Act, R.S.M. 1970, c.W–10, s.3(1).
2. *Edwards* v. *Grosser & Glass*, [1936] 3 W.W.R. 670 (Sask. C.A.).

171. It is important to note that to hold that a plaintiff cannot succeed because there is no adequate writing does not necessarily mean that the plaintiff fails altogether. For instance, an employee may still recover wages for work proved to have been performed (even though s/he cannot prove the terms of the agreement relating to wages by reference to the agreement), by way of the remedy of *quantum meruit*. This will be discussed below.

172. Some special relations are required to be in writing by statute, not because of their duration but because their contents have been considered to be worthy of particular attention. Reference has already been made to apprenticeship contracts. No list of special cases is being offered here, but note that frequently teachers' contracts are required to be in writing.[1] As we shall see below, in some instances statutes will provide that certain terms of the contract must be reduced to writing after the contract has been entered into, notably in situations where the calculation of remuneration has to be accounted for and where the conditions relating to safety have to be revealed.

1. The Education Act, S.O. 1974, c.109, s.224(2), which provides that where there is no written memorandum of the agreement, a contract embodying the terms and conditions contained in the form of contract prescribed for a full-time teacher will be assumed to regulate the contract. See also: The Public Schools Act, R.S.M. 1970, c.P.–250, s.281 (1); The School Act, R.S.S. 1965, c.184, s.225 (temporary teachers only); The School Act, R.S.A. 1970, c.329, s.74(4).

C. Capacity to contract

1. Minors

173. All adults have the same capacity to enter into contracts of employment, subject to what is discussed below, about the rules relating to immigrants. But minors or infants, that is, persons below the age of 18, have attracted special rules. The first thing to note is that a contract entered into between an adult and an infant is not enforceable unless the contract (i) provides goods and services which can be classified as 'necessaries' at law (food, clothing, and lodging, which are suitable to the infant's station in life and required at the time when they are tendered),[1] (ii) is, on the whole, beneficial to the infant. It was held long ago that contracts of apprenticeship and employment were, *prima facie* to be regarded as being of the second kind, viz., contracts which on the whole benefitted the infant.[2] Of course, certain adverse provisions in such a contract might render it disadvantageous to the infant and, hence, not binding on him.[3]

1. *Chapple* v. *Cooper*, (1844) 153 E.R. 105 (Exch.).
2. *De Francesco* v. *Barnum*, [1886–90] All E.R. Rep. 414 (Ch.).
3. *Olsen* v. *Corry*, [1936] 3; All E.R. 241, (K.B.).

174. It is clear that the special rules relating to the enforceability of infant contracts were the result of the perceived need to protect people of tender years from being exploited. It is equally clear that the judicial reasoning that contracts of service were on the whole beneficial to infants created a risk that minors could be taken advantage of by employers. The abuses of child labour have been well documented and, as a result, modern legislatures have limited the capacity of infants to enter into employment relationships. The statutes are too numerous to list and differ so much in detail that only a general picture can be presented. Typically, they define 'child' as a person of a particular age or less, and 'adolescent' or 'young person' as a person of an age less than 18 but older than a 'child'. They go on to prohibit employment for each grouping in certain industries altogether, in other occupations they permit employment only where certain conditions are satisfied so that the work will not interfere with school attendance, and effort; permission of the parents may have to be obtained; the work must be adjudged, by the appropriate ministry, not to be dangerous to the physical well-being of the child, the work must not be performed at certain hours (usually not between midnight and early morning, sometimes not in the early evening), unless there is special parental permission; the work must not be a hazard to the mental well-being of the child, by say, being associated with 'morally' unattractive behaviour (as in the business of hotel keeping, entertainment, and the running of licensed premises). A common exception to prohibitions in respect of child employment is found in employment in a family undertaking.

2. *Migrants*

175. As was the case with respect to minors, migrants are people whose status affects their right to enter into employment relations. The federal *Immigration Act* 1976, which came into effect on April 10, 1978, has specific provisions aimed at dovetailing immigration objectives with employment policies. Accordingly, it has special rules about persons who are not Canadian citizens or permanent residents of Canada and who seek employment in Canada. The Act eschews discrimination against them on the basis of race, nationality or place of origin, but it has regard to the employment prospects of such persons and of the effect of such employment on Canadian citizens' and permanent residents' prospects for employment. Immigrants must therefore obtain an employment authorization before they will be given the necessary visa permitting them to enter the country. Typically, an employer will have determined that he has a need for a particular worker or group of workers who are not presently Canadian citizens or permanent residents. The employer may have been contracted by such prospective employees or have decided that the skills he requires can only be found outside Canada. Once the employer has made a decision to employ such a person or persons, he must provide information to an immigration officer which enables that officer to consider whether or not (i) the employer has made reasonable efforts to hire citizens or permanent residents, (ii) the job offered is a good one in the sense that the conditions of employment are ones which would be acceptable to Canadian citizens and permanent residents. The immigration officer is to consult with the National Employment Services office in the pertinent geographical area when making these assessments. The National Employment Service operates as a manpower office.

176. If an employment authorization is given, it is valid only for the specified duration of the employment relationship. Should this or any aspect of the job description, terms and conditions change during that time, a new application for an employment authorization must be made. Failure to do so may result in deportation and this and any other violations of the Immigration Act will be grounds for refusing future employment authorization. A burden has been put on employers to make all reasonable inquiries to ensure that they do not hire anyone who is not a Canadian citizen or a permanent resident and does not have a valid employment authorization.

177. Another aspect of the law relating to immigration which shows its integration with employment law is that no employment authorization may be granted to workers whose employment will affect the settlement of a labour dispute at the intended place of employment or the employment of a disputant.

178. There are exemptions to the need for an employment authorization. They include diplomats, sports' teams, certain entertainers, foreign representatives, trade representatives of foreign countries, companies' and unions' employees who come for less than 90 days, and other such special cases.

3. Collective agreements as a restraint on capacity to contract

179. If employees' conditions of work are governed by a collective agreement, the employer and his employees cannot enter into agreements to change such conditions, unless the collective agreement provides to the contrary. This underscores the difference made to the employment relationship when it comes to be governed by the collective bargaining regime. Whereas the legal capacity to enter into and to vary contracts is unlimited outside this sphere. employees are restricted in their right to negotiate as individuals once collective agreement-making has taken place. This restriction of capacity to contract is justified on the basis that a greater advantage for many can be obtained by not permitting individuals to undermine the solidarity of collective action.

D. Purpose of contract

180. As in all other contract situations, a contract of employment otherwise validly formed, may be held to be unenforceable or even void if the purpose of entering into the relationship was to engage in conduct which offends public policy, such as when it contravenes the criminal law, a statutory provision or the rules governing restraint of trade, or where the contract offends public morality.[1] What effect the particular offence against public policy has on the contract depends on the nature of the conduct and on whether or not it can be severed from the remainder of the contract, permitting the remainder a life of its own. Brief reference to the principles of severance in respect of the restraint of trade doctrine will be made below.

1. *E.g. Dann* v. *Curzon*, (1911) 104 L.T. 66 (K.B.).

181. It remains to note that it may be that contracts, which on their face are employment ones, may be held to be void if the obligations on the apparent employee go far beyond those which may be required of a servant. A contract of slavery is apparently not enforceable. But it is far from clear when the imposed obligations will lead courts to say that the alleged contract of employment is unenforceable. The only attempt at propounding a test came in a nineteenth-century case in which the issue was not directly before the court. The following formulation was offered:

> The law of *England* allows a man to contract for his labour, or allows him to place himself in the service of a master, but it does not allow him to attach to his contracts of service any servile incidents – any elements of servitude as distinguished from service.[1]

It is worthwhile keeping this notion in mind when reading Chapter II which considers the nature and scope of obligations of employees.

1. *Davies* v. *Davies*, (1887) 36 Ch. D. 359 at 393, per Bowen, L. J. (C.A.). The passage was also cited with approval, but again by way of an aside, in *Horwood* v. *Millar's Timber & Trading*, [1917] 1 K.B. 305 (C.A.).

E. Requirements of fairness in formation of contracts of employment

1. The human rights statutes

182. The essence of the employment relationship being that it is a freely negotiated contract, it follows that employers and employees are free to determine with whom they will form such a relationship. The economic reality is that this gives the employer a great advantage: complete freedom in the selection of employees, in normal market conditions, will, for the most part, benefit employers in the bargaining game. The freedom to select has been restricted to a considerable extent by legislative support for the countervailing policy of preventing a variety of discriminatory practices.

183. Every legislature has enacted human rights legislation.[1] Such statutes proscribe discriminatory conduct of various kinds, especially in relation to hiring and during employment. Each jurisdiction's statute must therefore be examined for the precise scope of prohibitions. It is impractical to cover anything but the more basic aspects of the enactments. All of the statutes prohibit discrimination on the basis of race, national origin (sometimes termed ethnic origin or origin of ancestry), colour and religion (sometimes referred to as creed). Discrimination on the basis of sex and marital status is not permitted, nor is discrimination on the basis of age allowed. The age groups which are protected (by not permitting an employer to take account of age in his hiring or dealing with employees) vary from jurisdiction to jurisdiction, with the most common providing protection to persons between the ages of 40/45 to 65. In addition to these commonly specified grounds there are noteworthy special heads of non-discrimination in various provinces. Manitoba, New Brunswick, Nova Scotia, Prince Edward Island and the federal jurisdiction prohibit discrimination on the basis of a physical handicap and on the basis of a person's association with another person of a particular race, creed, national origin, etc.; British Columbia does not permit discrimination against a person who has been convicted of a criminal charge unless certain conditions are met;[2] political belief is a proscribed ground of discrimination in British Columbia, Newfoundland, Prince Edward Island and Quebec; Newfoundland bars discrimination on the basis of social origin, a term as yet undefined.[3]

1. Canadian Human Rights Act, S.C. 1976–77, c.33; The Individual's Rights Protection Act, S.A. 1972, c.2; Human Rights Code of British Columbia Act, S.B.C. 1973 (Second session) c.119; The Human Rights Act, S. M. 1974, c.65; Human Rights Code, R.S.N.B. 1970, c.262, Human Rights Act, R.S.N.B. 1973, c.H–11; The Newfoundland Human Rights Code, R.S.N. 1970, c.262; Human Rights Act, S.N.S. 1969, c.11; The Ontario Human Rights Code, R.S.O. 1970, c.318; Human Rights Act, S.P.E.I. 1975, c.72; Charter of Human Rights and Freedoms, S.Q. 1975, c.6; The Saskatchewan Human Rights Commission Act, R.S.S. 1978, c.S–25; The Fair Employment Practices Act. R.S.S. 1978, c.F–3, the latter two were consolidated in the Saskatchewan Human Rights Code, s.5 1979, c.S–24.1.
2. Usually a pardon is required, but in British Columbia, a conviction with no relation to occupation is a proscribed ground.
3. British Columbia proscribes all discrimination unless it is for an acceptable cause. It then enumerates as practices which will never be acceptable causes the traditional proscribed

grounds of discrimination. But this formulation clearly permits a much larger range of practices to be restrained. Human rights' boards have responded inventively to this challenge and have added at least nine new bases for holding conduct discriminatory, including the categories of training, spousal occupation, appearance (long hair), homosexuality (which is not usually subsumed under sex), and physical stature (an employer who would not employ people below 5'6").

184. There are exceptions to the law on discrimination. For our purposes the most important ones are (i), that discrimination may be allowed where there is a bona fide occupational need to hire someone on a basis which otherwise would be discriminatory and (ii), the permission granted to non-profit organizations whose major objective is to further the interests of a particular religion, ethnic group, or the like, to discriminate to this end.[1]

1. In some jurisdictions, any educational non-profit organization may be exempt from the legislation, *e.g.* Nova Scotia, Ontario, Prince Edward Island.

185. Typically the operation of human rights legislation requires the lodging of a complaint with a commission set up under the statute. The commission will then despatch an investigating officer and/or conciliator. Sometimes the commission is empowered to initiate such an investigation without receiving a complaint. The officer will make a report (usually to the pertinent Minister), unless a settlement is effected. Where that report indicates that there are grounds for believing that proscribed discrimination has occurred, a board or tribunal[1] may be set up. The carriage of the hearing of the matter before such a board or tribunal may be left to the complainant in some cases, to the commission itself in others.[2] The board or the tribunal may have a variety of powers: to make an order to end a discriminatory practice and/or award compensation and damages for emotional distress caused by the discrimination. Such an order may be given effect by registering it in an appropriate superior court, giving it the standing of a judgment and making it enforceable as such. In some cases, the board or tribunal may merely make a recommendation leaving it to the commission to make an order, and in Alberta, by leaving it to the appropriate ministry to determine whether the steps leading to enforcement will be taken. In addition, contraventions of human rights legislation are offences in respect of which criminal prosecutions may be launched, although this means of enforcement is seldom employed, particularly because a Minister's consent has to be obtained and this makes such a route unattractive. There are not all that many hearings before boards or tribunals considering the great number of potential situations in which prohibited practices might occur. But this does not mean that the existence of the legislation is unimportant. To the contrary, its educational effect is very significant and may well have led, in the employment field, to a much greater awareness of the need to provide equality of opportunity than existed before.[3]

1. In Saskatchewan, the commission itself may hold the hearing.
2. *E.g.* Ontario, where also any person can lay a complaint, not just a person who alleges that s/he is a victim of discrimination.
3. There are other statutes proscribing discrimination in employment. Of particular importance are the Fair Wages and Hours of Labour Act, R.S.C. 1970, c.L–3 (requires federal government contractors to stipulate non-discriminatory practices in their dealings with sub-

contractors); The Unemployment Insurance Act, S.C. 1970–71–72, c.48 (requires non-discriminatory practices in placement of people). In addition, collective bargaining legislation proscribes discriminatory practices by employers and unions whose practices could vitally affect employment opportunities because of the creation of a closed shop or modification thereof.

186. In as much as employers are not free to select employees by reference to criteria which offend human rights legislation, the advertising and posting of vacancies must comply with such legislation. Sometimes it is provided directly that the publishers of the invitation to treat (as advertisements and postings are usually treated as a matter of law) may not publish discriminatory material. Certainly all the human rights statutes but Alberta's proscribe discrimination by employment agencies. Further such employment agencies are often regulated directly by legislation which also proscribes discriminatory practices.

2. Investigation and testing

187. It has been noted that employers will be exempted from the operation of human rights legislation if the basis for the discrimination which they practice is related to a bona fide occupational requirement. In determining whether or not an applicant is qualified for a position, the employer might make inquiries into a person's background and/or ask the applicant to submit himself to a test. In Manitoba, the right of an employer to make pre-employment investigations is fettered by a statute, requiring that an employee who is to be investigated must be given notice of that fact and that only certain types of information may be sought.[1] In other jurisdictions, prospective employees are protected from such potential invasions of their privacy in a rather fragmented way. Thus, protection against some practices could come from human rights legislation, from special statutes relating to the storage of computer data, or from the obligations of confidence imposed by the law of contract and/or tort on potential informants.

1. The Personal Investigations Act, S.M. 1971, c.23.

188. In relation to testing, there is as yet no equivalent of the American jurisprudence in Canada. There it has become established that employers may not use tests which are not solely oriented towards determining whether potential employees have the capacity and qualification for the position, nor tests which are culture-biased in such a manner that they permit discrimination on otherwise proscribed bases under the guise of being occupational qualifications' tests. If such jurisprudence is to be developed in Canada, it will most likely fall to imaginative boards appointed under human rights legislation to take the initiative.

3. Employment agencies

189. An industry has grown up in which agents undertake to put employers

in touch with employees for the purposes of entering into contracts of employment. Such agencies may be acting, as a matter of law, as either the agents of the
prospective employer or employees. They may bind their principles if they
were acting within their ostensible authority. As they are thus in a position to
discriminate in relation to employment on proscribed grounds, they have been
made subject to the human rights statutes in all provinces except Alberta. In
addition, because they are also in a position to take what is deemed to be
unacceptable advantage of persons' lack of information about the labour
market, some of the provinces have passed statutes directly regulating the
conduct of employment agencies.[1] The usual form of regulation is to require
that the agency must apply for an operating license. The licencees are normally
not permitted to charge employees for services rendered. An assumption
seems to have been made that the employer should bear the burden of this cost
of enterprise.[2] The charging of a fee to employees leads to fines and, possibly,
loss of licence to operate.[3] In addition to such controls, the agencies may be
required to keep records and to provide employees referred to employers with
pertinent information about the nature of the employment.[4]

1. The Employment Agencies Act, R.S.A. 1970, c.123; Employment Agencies Act, R.S.B.C.
1960, c.127; The Employment Services Act, R.S.M. 1970, c.E100, Employment Agencies
Act, R.S.N.S. 1954, c.82; Employment Agencies Act, R.S.O., 1970, c.146; The Employment
Agencies Act, R.S.S. 1965, c.297.
2. In Ontario, a regulated, small fee may be charged to employees.
3. In Manitoba, a fee paid by an employee is recoverable by way of civil action.
4. See *e.g.* Ontario.

4. *Fair practices and collective bargaining*

190. The practices in respect of fairness in hiring have to conform with the
principles set out above, even when the employer and employees have entered
into a collective agreement. In addition, the union, which as a matter of law is
one of the parties to the collective agreement, may have insisted on inserting
clauses in the collective agreement which bolster its security. Typically, a union
may have inserted a clause requiring that only union members should be hired,
or that anyone hired must become a union member within 30 days of joining
the bargaining unit or, at the very least, that non-union member employees
should pay union dues. Such clauses will limit the hiring freedom of the
employer, an inhibition which is accepted by the collective bargaining schemes
because of the importance they place on the policy of promoting union formation and stability. But, having put the unions in a position where they can, and
do, directly affect employment prospects, unions have been made subject to
rules of the same nature as are found in human rights legislation, as well as
other constraints. This will be discussed in greater detail below.

Chapter II. Rights and Duties of the Parties to the Employment Relationship

§1. THE ROOTS OF SUCH RIGHTS AND DUTIES

191. The terms of any contract may be expressly spelt out provided by statute or they may be implied by a court. When the court imply terms they may do so on the basis that an officious bystander, watching the parties enter into the contract, would have have said: 'Of course, they meant to include a provision to this or that effect'.[1] This is the way that the courts insert terms which they believe will be fair to both parties. It also allows them to insert terms which lead to commercial efficiency because this, it will be assumed, is consonant with what the parties would have understood to be the underpinning of the agreement. To this general approach two previously mentioned special features of the contract of employment dictate particular modifications: (i) the contract of employment, even though it is usually terminable by notice, is one which the parties intend to be a continuing one, and (ii) it is a contract of service. These aspects of the contract of employment cause the courts to imply terms into contracts of employment as a matter of law, in addition to the use of their general power to imply terms arising out of the particular fact situation before them. Because the first feature is not usually emphasized in analysis, whereas the second one – the need to serve – is, the rights and obligations which, as a matter of law, will be said to arise from a contract of employment tend to focus on the obligations of the employee and the correlative rights of the employer. But some of the obligations of the employer can best be explained by fastening on the continuing nature of the contract. This aspect of the contract of employment leads some commentators to categorize it as a contract of mutual co-operation which gives rise to legal rights and duties. But this phraseology does not explain why the more onerous of the obligations are imposed on employees rather than on employers.

    1. See *Shirlaw* v. *Southern Foundries (1926) Ltd*, [1939] 2 K.B. 206 at 227, per Mackinnon, L. J. (C.A.), *aff'd.* [1940] A.C. 701(H.L.).

§2. THE EMPLOYER'S DUTIES AND OBLIGATIONS

A. The duty to pay remuneration

1. The foundation of the duty

192. As has been noted, the essence of the contract of employment is that the employee is to render services in return for remuneration. In many cases, the contract itself will specifically provide that remuneration must be paid, the amount which is to be paid, how it is to be paid, and so forth. Where there is no expression of such terms they will be implied if the circumstances of the relationship are such that they indicate an understanding by both parties that there should be payment for the services. It may seem strange to put the proposition in this form, but courts have held that where there is no express agreement to pay remuneration and the circumstances surrounding the agreement are ambiguous, there ought to be no implication that wages are due. The doubt about the parties' understanding of the bargain usually arises in cases where the employer provides board and lodging and other such benefits to a person who renders services, or where the parties cohabit or are related in some way.[1]

1. *Reeve* v. *Reeve*, (1858) 1 F. & F. 280 (N.P.); *Bradshaw* v. *Hayward*, (1842) Car. & M.591(N.P.) *R.* v. *Inhabitants of Sow*, (1817) 1 B. & Ald. 178, *Osborn* v. *Guy's Hospital (Governors)*, (1726) 2 Stra. 728.

193. It follows that if the parties have explicitly agreed that the employer shall have discretion as to whether or not there shall be payment for the services, there will be no enforceable contractual obligation to pay remuneration. Such arrangements are rare and are sometimes termed engagements of honour to differentiate them from contracts of employment.[1] But it does not follow that if there is no enforceable contract of employment in existence there will be no obligation to pay remuneration to a person who has rendered services. There may be a variety of reasons for the unenforceability of a contract. To take but one, refer to para. 168 in which it was noted that a failure to comply with the requirement of writing necessitated by the Canadian Statutes of Frauds or equivalents, might lead to unenforceability. Another such situation might arise where there had been a fundamental mistake by the parties in respect of the bargain they thought they had struck. In such circumstances, services might well have been rendered on the basis that the contract was an enforceable one. Remuneration may then be ordered by the courts on a *quantum meruit* basis. Although there is some confusion in analysis about the origin and scope of this remedy,[2] the best view is that it is a remedy based on general restitutionary principles. The calculation of the remuneration to be paid by way of *quantum meruit* is done on the basis of inferences drawn from the circumstances of the parties' understandings and agreements. The awarding of pay on the basis of *quantum meruit* thus involves the same exercise as is involved in implying a term into a valid contract, although analytically it is a different process. Note that the notion of *quantum meruit* may also be employed to award remuneration for services rendered when an employer's conduct is of such a kind that the employee is entitled to treat it as a repudiation of the contract and accordingly to exercise his right to rescind it. If the contract is not rescinded, the employee must seek compensation under the contract and a differing means of calculating the sum due will be used, frequently leading to a very different result.[3] The nature of the right of the employer and the employee to sue under the contract will be discussed below.

1. *E.g. Loftus* v. *Roberts*, (1902) 18 T.L.R. 532(C.A.). Sometimes the problem arises in situations where the employer, in addition to the agreed-to remuneration, promises to pay more. The question then becomes whether or not a new contract has been entered into; if it has not, there will be no obligation to pay the extra remuneration, it merely being a promise of

honour; *Stilk* v. *Myrick*, (1809) 170 E.R. 1168(N.P.) *Hartley* v. *Ponsonby*, (1857) 119 E.R. 1471; *Powell* v. *Braun*, [1954] 1 All E.R. 484(C.A.).
2. One of the arguments is that *quantum meruit* is available where there is a contract on foot. See *Way* v. *Latilla*, [1937] 3 All E.R. 759.
3. *Planché* v. *Colburn*, (1831) 8 Bing. 14.

2. When the obligation to pay matures

194. The agreement may expressly provide when remuneration shall be paid and it might be that the parties agree that there shall be payment before services have been rendered. Failing such an express term, it has been the common law view that remuneration is payable in arrears. It will be paid at the end of agreed-upon periods. Such agreement may, of course, be implied. If such a period is not completed at the time of termination of the contract of employment for reasons other than a breach of contract by the employer, at common law there will be no obligation to pay for the incompleted period of service.[1] But legislation may have alleviated this potential problem in some provinces. Various statutes provide that wages must be paid at fixed intervals or shorter ones. Further, it is enacted that if a contract is terminated, the employer must, within a given time span, pay all wages due to the employee.[2] Theoretically, a question remains: are all wages due upon termination the wages which would be due if the common law applied, that is, wages due for completed periods only? In practice, it is not a major problem. It is likely that employers accept an obligation to pay for all services rendered, regardless of whether or not remuneration is thus paid for incomplete periods. Further, contracts usually terminate upon the giving of reasonable notice. Reasonable notice, more often than not, will be a complete pay period.

1. *Cutter* v. *Powell*, (1795) 101 E.R. 573.
2. The Alberta Labour Act; Payment of Wages Act, S.B.C. 1962, c.45; The Employment Standards Act, R.S.M. 1970, c–E110; Minimum Wage Act, R.S.N.B. 1973, c.M–13; The Labour Standards Act, S.N. 1977, c.52; Minimum Wage Act, S.N.S. 1964, C.7.

195. Sometimes, regardless of the periods at the end of which remuneration is to be paid (by dint of legislation or as a result of the apparent agreement of the parties), a contract may be read as being one which requires a certain amount of service to be given before any contractual obligation to pay remuneration arises. Typically, this will be the case in services to be rendered by a seaman or by a worker hired to bring in the harvest.[1] The courts' appreciation of custom in the undertaking and of the understanding of the parties will control the outcome of such cases. Suffice it is to say that it will be rare in modern times to read a contract as one which requires performance in its entirety before remuneration for services rendered has to be paid.

1. *Cutter* v. *Powell*, *supra*; *La Plante* v. *Kinnon*, (1915) 8 W.W.R. 332 (Sask.S.C.); *Abramoff* v. *Podratz*, [1920] 2 W.W.R. 6 (Sask.C.A.).

3. The effect of illness

196. Because the contract of employment is one of rendering services, it follows that where an employee becomes so ill that he becomes incapable of doing any work at all or, at least, not for a protracted period, the contract will have been frustrated. This will be considered again when termination of the contract of employment is discussed in paras. 271–274.

197. Where an illness is of a temporary duration, the courts have treated the contract as continuing. Further, they have permitted recovery of wages for such periods of illness, even though no work was done by the employee. In one case, the Supreme Court of Canada justified the recovery of wages for an employee who had not rendered services during a temporary illness on the basis that common humanity required such an approach.[1] Analytically it would seem sounder to rationalize the obligation to pay employees during temporary periods of illness on the basis that the employee does not warrant his good health and that as long as he is willing to render the services due under the contract of employment there is no breach of contract disentitling him from remuneration.[2] Hence, the stress on the temporary nature of the illness; should the employer be forced to hire a substitute to perform the necessary work because of the length of absence of the willing and ill employee, the obligation to pay may well have ended.

1. *Dartmouth Ferry Commission* v. *Marks*, (1903–4) 34 S.C.R. 366 (S.C.C.).
2. *Cuckson* v. *Stones*, (1859) 120 E.R. 902 (K.B.), *Marrison* v. *Bell*, [1939] 2 K.B. 187 (C.A.) *Orman* v. *Saville Sportswear*, [1960] 3 All E.R. 105 (Q.B.).

198. The parties may, and usually do, agree that there shall be remuneration paid during absences due to illness. Such agreements stipulate that a certain number of sick days will be allowed to an employee per year. Sometimes the sick leave plan is cumulative. That is, unused sick days are added (sometimes at the rate of one and a half days for each day not used) until a maximum period of continuous sick leave is reached. When the plan is not a cumulative one, sick leave entitlement not used during the prescribed period (usually a year) is lost. An employee entitled to paid sick leave may be fully or partially remunerated. Occasionally the plan provides that the employee has to undergo a waiting period before sickness payments begin. These may then be retroactive to the date of the commencement of absence. If the sick leave agreement is of the indemnity insurance kind, the waiting period is nearly always written in and is often quite long. Under such schemes, the employer and/or employee contribute to the purchase of an insurance plan to obtain coverage for either long or short term illness. A maximum period of entitlement to benefit is usually prescribed. The entitlement is usually a proportion of weekly earnings, tailored in some way to ensure that the total amounts recovered from the sick leave plan and other benefit schemes do not exceed normal earnings. Note at this point that there are legislative schemes providing disability pensions and that workers forced to be absent from work by illness may get workers' compensation or unemployment insurance benefits. The nature of these schemes will be discussed below.

199. It is of interest, perhaps, to note that it is conceivable that an employee would be better off by relying on his common law right of remuneration during a temporary illness than by relying on an agreed-upon number of sick days under a sick leave plan. It is likely, however, that, where there is such an agreed-upon entitlement to sick leave pay, courts would read down the common law entitlement to coincide with such agreed-upon terms.

4. Form of remuneration

200. When we speak of remuneration today, we automatically think of monetary payments. But it is, of course, possible to pay in other ways, for instance, by providing employees with goods, lodging, stocks, shares and the like. Indeed, this mode of payment led to abuses in the nineteenth century. Employers paid employees by giving them goods, but cheated them by overvaluing these goods; or they paid them with vouchers which entitled them to buy goods from the employer; or arranged with innkeepers that wages should be paid at the inn, tempting the workers to spend a larger portion of their wages on drink than they otherwise might, etc. These means came to be termed as payment in 'truck' and necessitated the enactment of Truck Acts. These have modern equivalents in Canada and are of two kinds. They either protect all workers or only those who are within the scope of minimum employment standards' statutes. The protection afforded is to require that all payments are to be in cash or by cheque. Deductions made from wages by the employer for the purchase of shares, options and the like in the employing company are not permissible. Where the employee agrees to it, it is permitted to make deductions for payments to charities, for insurance schemes, for union dues or plans which benefit the employee.

5. Legislative standards in respect of remuneration

(a) Minimum wage legislation

201. All jurisdictions have enacted minimum wage legislation.[1] The variations are many but there are some common features. Typically, a board or commission is created which has power to make general or specific orders. These orders will prescribe that no employee within its scope is to earn less than a particular hourly rate for work done. A general order will regulate all the employees covered by the empowering legislation; a specific order will be aimed at workers in one or more particular industries. In some jurisdictions, the board merely recommends and orders are issued by the Lieutenant-Governor in Council;[2] in others, the board makes recommendations to the Lieutenant-Governor in Council who may then authorize the board to make an

order;[3] in others, the Lieutenant-Governor in Council will set minimum wages
by regulation.[4]

1. Canada, Part III; Alberta, Division 2; Minimum Wage Act, R.S.B.C. 1960, c–230; The
Employment Standards Act, R.S.M. 1970, c.E110, Part II; Minimum Wage Act, R.S.N.B.
1973, c–M–13; The Labour Standards Act, S.N. 1977, c.52, Part IV; Labour Standards Code,
S.N.S. 1972, c.10, s.46–52; The Employment Standards Act, S.O. 1974, c.112, Part V; Prince
Edward Island Labour Act, Part III; Minimum Wage Act, R.S.Q. 1964, c. 144; The Labour
Standards Act, R.S.S. 1978, c.L–1, Part II.
2. Newfoundland.
3. Prince Edward Island, Quebec, Saskatchewan.
4. Ontario.

202. Although the kinds of employees covered by the various statutes differ
from province to province, they nearly always exclude domestic servants and
various classes of agricultural workers. Also specifically excluded may be
members of the family of the employer, some professional employees, and
employees in industries which in the particular jurisdiction require special
economic treatment, *e.g.*, fishing, timber. Students working part-time or sea-
sonally, or employees in recreational camps, are often excluded or have special
rates apply to them. Minimum wages are set on the basis of an hourly rate. It is
common to prescribe that where workers work less than three (or in some cases
four) hours they shall nonetheless be paid a minimum of three hours' (or four
hours') wages. Employers may be exempted from paying the standard
minimum wages to handicapped people. There are also differentiations in rates
depending on age. Typically a rate is set for adults and for persons under 17 or
18 years of age. Often salespersons are specifically covered by minimum wage
regulations, even where their wages are calculated on a commission basis.
Frequently there are specific provisions which exclude gratuities from the
definition of wages, thus ensuring that people in service industries are paid the
minimum rate by their employers. A common provision is that the value of
board and lodging which is provided by an employer may not be calculated as
being part of the minimum remuneration which must be paid unless the
minimum wage legislation specifically permits a certain part of the due wage to
be so paid or authorization is obtained from the appropriate agency or Minister. Such provisions are, in effect, exemptions from the protection afforded
against payment in truck. See para. 200.

203. In addition, safeguards for employees are provided by requiring that
contracts for public works done for the government must stipulate that fair
wages[1] or in some cases, at least minimum wage rates,[2] be paid to employees.

1. Public Construction Fair Wages Act, S.B.C. 1976, c.45; Fair Wages and Hours of Labour
Act, R.S.N.B. 1973, c.F–2; The Government Contracts Hours and Wages Act, R.S.O. 1970,
c.194; Regulations under Fair Wage Resolution, Sask. O.C. 301/44.
2. The Construction Industry Wages Act, R.S.M. 1970, c.C190.

(b) Equal pay legislation

204. Consonant with the principles evinced in human rights legislation, all
jurisdictions provide that there should be no differentiation in rates of pay on

the basis of sex.[1] Sometimes the provisions are found in the minimum standards statute, sometimes in the human rights statute. The process and remedies will vary accordingly. Where the minimum standards statute operates, the Director will have a complaint investigated, a settlement attempted and/or an order made. Such an order may include, in addition to providing for payment making up for the proved discrimination in respect of wages, a fine. There may be provision for bringing an action in a civil court. Where the human rights legislation applies, the process described above will apply. Sometimes the minimum standards and the human rights legislation (by implication, perhaps) may both proscribe discrimination in pay on the basis of sex. The usual rule is that where proceedings have been commenced under the human rights statute, no action may be initiated under the minimum standards one. Another common provision is that the recovery of wages due because of sex discrimination is limited to 12 months of pay.

1. Canada, Part III, Division II–1; Canadian Human Rights Act, S.C. 1976–77, c. 33, s.11; The Individual's Rights Protection Act, S.A. 1972, c.2, s.6; Human Rights Code of British Columbia, S.B.C. 1973 (Second session), c.119, s.6; The Employment Standards Act, R.S.M. 1970, c.E110, Part IV; The Newfoundland Human Rights Code, R.S.N. 1970, c.262, s.10; Labour Standards Code, S.N.S. 1972, c.10, s.55; The Employment Standards Act, S.O. 1974, c.112, Part IX; Human Rights Act, S.P.E.I. 1975, c.72, s.7; Charter of Human Rights and Freedoms, S.Q. 1975, c.6, s.19; The Labour Standards Act, R.S.S. 1978, c.L–1, Part III.

205. Although the principle underlying equal pay seems uncontroversial, its effectuation has not been easy. The language of the governing statute may be vital. Thus, when the ruling statutes provided that there was to be no differentiation in rates for males and females doing identical or substantially identical work, it was held that relatively slight variation in duties and services permitted the employer to use different wage rates for employees.[1] Most statutes now provide that there should be equal pay where the same work is done by male and female employees in the same place of employment. The same work will be deemed to be done where the duties to be performed require the exercise of similar skill, the use of equal effort and the acceptance of equal responsibility.[2] Although this formulation could be read as requiring identical duties to be performed, it has not been so read by either courts or other decision-makers. It has been explicitly reasoned that there is no need to show that identical work is being done by male and females.[3] In one case it was decided that the fact that female orderlies could only deal with female patients and male orderlies only with male patients did not permit the employer to differentiate in pay between females and males.[4] The employer had argued that, even though equal skill, effort and acceptance of responsibility were required from all employees, they were not doing the same work in the same place. Equal pay proponents can draw some comfort from the court's interpretation, but the facts of the case point to a problem which the language of the statutory provisions does not overcome. It is the ghetto problem. Some work is only done, as a matter of industrial practice, by females. When that happens it is possible to set wage rates without having to worry about what men doing comparable work earn. Consequently, there is much support for the notion that the statutes ought to provide that there should be equal pay for work of equal value. Presumably, if the productivity of women in ghettoized work is of the same value to an employer as work done by men in his employ, equal rates ought to be offered, other things being equal. The difficulty with giving this principle practical scope is manifest. Thus, the federal Human Rights Act, after providing that there should be equal pay for males and females doing work of equal value, goes on to say that in assessing the value of work performed the criterion to be applied is the composite of skill, effort and responsibility required in the performance of the work.[5] This formula necessitates the similar inquiry which other statutes mandate and does not solve the ghetto problem without more.

1. *Re Harris and Bell Canada*, (1975) 58 D.L.R. (3d) 610 (Fed.C.A.)
2. The Newfoundland Human Rights Code, R.S.N. 1970, c.262, s.10; Labour Standards Code, S.N.S. 1972, c.10, s.55; The Employment Standards Act, S.O. 1974, c.112, s.33; Human Rights Act, S.P.E.I. 1975, c.72, s.7; The Labour Standards Act, R.S.S. 1978, c.L–1, s.17.
3. *R* v. *Howard Ex p. Munipality of Metro Toronto*, [1970] 3 O.R. 555 (C.A.)
4. *Board of Governors of Riverdale Hospital*, (1973) 73 C.L.L.C. para 14,174 (Ont.C.A.).
5. Canadian Human Rights Act, S.C. 1976–77, c.33, s.11; see Equal Wage Guidelines, SI/78–155, gazetted September 27, 1978, which spell out in detail how skills, efforts and acceptance of responsibility ought to be assessed.

206. It was noted above that equal pay for work requiring similar skill, effort and responsibility is only mandated when all other things are equal. Discrimination in wage rates is always permitted, despite similarities in skill, effort and responsibility, where a seniority system requires it, or a merit system has been agreed upon, or a payment by quantity produced system exists or where the discrimination can otherwise be shown not to be based on the criterion of sex.

6. Important benefits related to remuneration

(a) Unemployment insurance

207. The power to enact legislation with respect to unemployment insurance has, since 1940, rested with the federal legislature. That power to legislate has been implemented.[1] The scheme created is complex and can only be described in outline.

1. Unemployment Insurance Act, S.C. 1970–71–72, c.48.

208. Persons who lose their jobs are entitled to receive unemployment benefits. The amounts of those benefits and the periods for which they are payable are laid out in the statute. Entitlement to benefits depends, principally, on the length of employment prior to becoming unemployed.

209. To raise revenue for the scheme, a tripartite contributory scheme has been devised. All employees who do not fall into a classification known as 'excepted employment' will have deductions made from their earnings. There is a ceiling on the maximum amount of earnings which are subject to such deductions. At the moment, the ceiling is $265. per week. These deductions from the employee's insurable earnings are known as premiums. At the time of writing, the annual rate of premiums for employees is 1.35 per cent, that is, $1.35 on every $100 of insurable earnings.

210. Employers also contribute to the scheme. Employers' contributions are presently calculated on the basis that they are to be 1.4 times the employees' premium rate. Where an employer has privately provided for a wage scheme whereby employees will be indemnified for loss of wages due to illness or pregnancy, the employer may have the premiums payable to the unemployment insurance fund reduced on the basis that the unemployment benefits which would otherwise have been payable are reduced. Finally, the government contributes to the fund. Its contributions, which are drawn from general revenue, are to cover those benefits which are termed extended benefits.

211. The kinds of benefits available under the scheme fall into two main categories, initial and extended benefits. In addition, there is provision for regional extended benefits. An employee who claims benefits must show that he has been an insured (that is, contributing) employee for a specified period prior to becoming unemployed. At the time of writing, an employee must show a minimum attachment to a job of 10–14 weeks prior to making a claim for unemployment. Claimants are entitled to one week of initial benefits for every week of insured employment up to 25 weeks. This is known as the initial benefit. It they remain unemployed beyond this period they are entitled to extended benefits. This permits one week of benefits for every two weeks of insured employment over 26 weeks. Finally, because of the varied labour market in Canada, benefits over and above initial and extended benefits are made available. If the regional employment (region being defined) rises above a particular percentage of the labour force, benefits may be payable in that region for a maximum of 32 weeks beyond initial and extended benefits. But no matter how much theoretical entitlement has been accrued, no person can get more than 50 weeks of paid benefits in a 52-week period. There are special entitlement provisions for pregnant women who have had at least 10 weeks of insurable employment prior to the week of expected confinement. Payment of benefits is flexible enough to permit women to choose when to retire from the work force.

212. There is generally a two-week waiting period before benefits are payable. The amount of benefits paid is 60 per cent of the average weekly pay of the claimant during the qualifying period up to the ceiling of insurable earnings.

213. A claimant is not entitled to unemployment benefits if he does not show that he is ready, able and willing to take suitable employment. He can furnish evidence of his readiness to return to work by showing that he is making reasonable effort to find employment. The claimant may be asked to register with the governmental or private placement agencies. The claimant is given a span of time in which to search for a job compatible with his training and experience. After such a reasonable period, he may be asked to reduce his expectation in respect of both congeniality and pay.

214. The unemployment insurance scheme is to some extent integrated with collective bargaining schemes by disallowing claims made by persons whose employment is attributable to a labour dispute at the place where he was employed. This disentitlement is removed if the former employee accepts a job elsewhere, intending not to return to his former employment. He can then receive benefits for the period of his unemployment. He may also be so entitled where he can show that he did not finance or was directly involved in the dispute which led to the interruption of work. Difficult questions arise as to what is a labour dispute, how long it is, what direct involvement is, and the like.

215. Claimants will also not get benefits for the periods of unemployment during which they were imprisoned for an offence or were out of Canada. Note also that, unless a pregnant woman is able to bring herself within the specific provisions relating to maternity leave, she cannot claim compensation as if she were an insured worker asking for the basic benefits available under the scheme.

216. In addition to being totally disentitled in certain circumstances, claimants may be disqualified for specified periods of time, that is, their benefits, although accrued, are withheld. This may occur where a claimant fails, due to his own actions or lack thereof, from seeking re-employment in the expected manner. It could also happen where an employee lost his employment because he left it without a good reason or was dismissed because of his misconduct. At the moment, the period of disqualification is not to exceed six weeks following the waiting period which must elapse before receiving the initial benefits. For the purposes of calculating the length of benefit entitlement of such a disqualified claimant, benefits shall be deemed to have been paid for the first six weeks.

217. The raising of revenue for the scheme comes under the jurisdiction of the federal Minister for National Revenue. He therefore makes decisions as to who is to pay premiums and determines the amount of earnings of persons who are covered by the Act. Accordingly, decisions have to be made as to whether there is an appropriate employment relationship, that is, a contract of service. These decisions usually do not have to be made unless there is a dispute between the main administrative agency, the Canada Employment and Immigration Commission, the employers and employees concerned. Where there is a dispute, the Commission or such persons may apply to the Minister for a dispositive determination. There is an appeal from the Minister's decision to an umpire. Umpires are appointed from among the judges of the Federal Court, and of the superior and county courts of the provinces. A further appeal may be taken to a body known as the Pension Appeal Board on any question concerned with whether or not there is employment under a contract of service.

218. The Employment and Immigrant Commission deals with the claims made for benefits. It accordingly makes decisions as to entitlement, including assessing the time of insured employment, whether the claimant is disentitled because of, say, his unwillingness to accept employment, his absence from the country, or participation in a labour dispute, whether and for how long the claimant should be disqualified because his loss of job is due to misconduct, and so forth. The Commission is a Crown Corporation and is tripartite in nature. All members are appointed by the Governor in Council. One is named as chairman and chief executive. One is selected after consultation with employer organizations, the other after consultations with employee organizations. Many offices throughout the land carry out the functions of the Commission.

(b) Pension plans

219. Manifestly, provision for income after termination of one's working life is a major concern of employed persons. There are both public and private schemes of arrangements, which seek to provide such security.

Canada Pension Plan

220. This is a contributory, earnings-related scheme. The first $1,300 of each person's annual earnings are exempted from the calculation of contributions. On earnings above that amount, up to a specified ceiling, the employee has to contribute 1.8 per cent of those earnings to the Plan. His employer has to make a matching contribution of 1.8 per cent of the operative earnings of his employees. The employer makes the appropriate deductions and returns them (together with income tax and unemployment insurance contributions) to the Minister of Revenue. These contributions are calculated to render a specified benefit upon retirement. Thus a portion of the year's maximum pensionable earnings (those earnings subject to contribution) will be payable upon retirement, or age 65 if the employee continues to work beyond that age. The year's maximum pensionable earnings are adjusted annually by reference to a cost-of-living index. Thus, both contributions and benefits rise or fall with cost-of-living changes.

221. The Plan applies to nearly all workers. Self-employed persons earning no more than $1,300 are exempt. If their earnings are more than that, they are to pay the combined contributions of employers and employees, that is, 3.6 of their total earnings. Some employed persons are excepted employees under the Plan: migratory workers who do not spend at least 25 working days a year with the same employer or who do not earn at least $250 per year from the same employer; casual workers (*e.g.* baby sitters, lawn cutters); provincial and foreign government employees unless their employers agree that they should be covered by the federal Plan; exchange teachers and persons employed by their spouses, as well as people belonging to religious orders which have taken a vow of poverty are excepted from the operation of the Plan.

222. Where a contributor becomes disabled to the extent that he is unable to become regularly employed, a disability pension will be paid to the contributor who has made contributions for a specified period. The Plan also provides for a survivor's pension. This means that the spouse of a pensioner is entitled to receive the pension if he survives the original contributor unless the contributor dies within one year of the marriage having taken place and the Minister is not satisfied that the contributor was not at the time of his marriage in such a state of health as to lead to the belief that he would be alive one year after the marriage. Survivor pensions cease to be paid upon the death of the survivor or remarriage. Where the subsequent marriage ends, the original survivor's pension may be reinstituted (or the pension which is payable because of the death of the later spouse, if that is how the marriage ended).

223. A contributor's pension rights are fully portable as he moves from employment to employment. Note that to avoid harsh results because of irregularity in employment or low payment circumstances, benefits are calculated on the basis that the average earnings of a contributor can be computed by permitting the contributor to dropout of the data base 15 per cent of the months of lowest average monthly earnings.

224. Finally, it is to be noted that initially there was some doubt as to whether the federal legislature could pass legislation with respect to retirement income of survivors and disabled persons. This was eventually taken care of by amendment to s. 94A of the *British North America Act.* This left intact the provincial jurisdiction of the provinces to legislate with respect to pensions. Quebec has taken advantage of this. Initially it was not satisfied with the proposed Canada Pension Plan because of its perceived incapacity to provide supplementary benefits. It had instituted its own scheme. It continues to do so. This scheme is now, in all essentials, the same as the federal scheme described above.

Old Age Security Pension
225. Everyone who has resided in Canada for 40 years after reaching the age of 18 is entitled to a full benefit under this pension plan upon reaching 65. Any one with lesser residence will get a pro-rated amount. This pension is payable as a flat rate, regardless of income or wealth of the recipient. It can only be received for 6 months if the recipient lives out of Canada unless he has resided in Canada for at least 20 years after the age of 18. The amount payable is adjusted in line with quarterly fluctuations in the Consumer Price Index.

226. To supplement the Old Age Security when some people were ineligible for Canada or Quebec Pension Plan benefits, the Guaranteed Income Supplement was instituted. Today, all persons in receipt of the Old Age Security Pension are eligible for a Guaranteed Income Supplement. It is an additional amount allowed if the income of the applicant justifies it. That is, it is a means-tested pension.

227. Another supplement to the Old Age Security Pension is the Spouse's Allowance. It guarantees to one-pensioner couples (that is, where one spouse is of the age 60–64), the income that two pensioners couples would receive by way of the Old Age Security plus Guaranteed Income Supplement. Both the Guaranteed Income Supplement and Spouse's Allowance are reduced if the recipients earn income above a certain amount.

228. It is here apposite to note that in addition to these federal government programmes, the provinces have set out to guarantee basic incomes to the elderly. The variety of the programmes prevents a detailed discussion here.

Private pension plans

229. About 40 per cent of the work force is covered by private sector plans. They are most commonly found in the collective bargaining section of the economy. They may consist of employee, employer or employer-employee contributions to a fund. The variety of plans is great, being tailored to the particular profiles and aspirations of distinct groups. Thus, there is the money purchase plan in which the contributions are predetermined but the retirement income is directly related to the profitability of the investment. A profit sharing plan is one in which the contributions are made by the employer on the basis of a percentage of the employer's profits. The retirement income of an employee is calculated on a points system based on his years of service and earnings. A flat benefit plan is one which guarantees an income of an amount based on so many dollars per month of service or some such equivalent. Typically, the employer is the sole contributor and his contributions vary with the profile of his work force. Unit benefit plans are the most common. Under these the benefit payable varies with the employee's earnings. Typically both the employee and the employer make contributions, the employee's contributions being certain, the employer's varying with the benefits which become payable. These benefits are calculated by taking a percentage of the employee's earnings (usually around 2 per cent), multiplying this by the number of years of service and multiplying this by an earnings' base (last year's earnings, average of last five years, average of lifetime earnings, etc.).

·230. The funds created are administered by insurance or trust companies, sometimes banks, specialized pension counsellors, or, increasingly, the employers themselves. There is some concern over the adequacy of the plans. In particular, the plans usually provide that employees must remain with a particular employer for a particular time before they become entitled to benefits. The mobility of an employee may thus deny him pension rights. This is aggravated by the fact that, because of the plans' emphasis on being tailored to the needs of a particular bargaining unit, they are seldom portable from one employer to another, even in the same industry. This is ameliorated somewhat by legislation. Many of the provinces have provisions which stipulate that an employee's pension rights shall be vested after 10 years of service and the reaching of age 45. This means that the pension rights cannot be lost after that time. A plan can provide for shorter periods and some do. Further, such legislation typically provides that an employee cannot take out his contributions after vesting. They are said to be locked-in. If an employee leaves before his pension benefits have vested, the legislation typically provides that he is entitled to a return of whatever contributions he made plus interest. The employer contributions, however, are not returnable even though they could be classified as deferred wages. The legislation also prescribes that employees are to be informed of their rights and interests in the employer plans, puts conditions on how pension funds may be invested in order to maintain solvency and also dictates how the assets of a pension plan are to be distributed when it is wound up.[1]

1. *The Pension Benefits Act*. S.A. 1966, c.69; *The Pension Benefits Act*, S.M. 1975, c.38; *The Pension Benefits Act*, S.N.S. 1975, c.14; *The Pension Benefits Act*, R.S.O. 1970, c.342; *Supplemental Pension Plans Act*, S.Q. 1965, c.25; *The Pension Benefits Act*, S.S. 1967, c.67.

231. Finally, it is to be noted that private sector pension plans are seldom fully indexed to fluctuations in the cost-of-living. In an inflationary age, this sharply diminishes the value of benefits received, no matter how calculated.

B. The duty to provide work

232. Unless the contract is one determinable at will, the parties may only end it by giving appropriate notice or by properly treating a breach of the contract by the other party as one which repudiates the contract. Thus, when an employer for some reason does not want work done, a question may arise as to whether or not he can both insist that the contract continue on foot and not provide work to be performed by the employee. At common law, the starting point is that an employer is under no duty to provide work. If no attempt is made to end the contract, the employer remains under an obligation to pay the non-working employee the agreed-upon remuneration.[1] There are two major modifications of this general doctrine. The nature of some contracts is such that the employer will be required to provide work. This will be so where the employee's remuneration depends on the number of things he makes or sells. In such cases the employer may be required to provide that amount of work which will enable the employee to earn the average level of remuneration he had earned when work was being made available. In contracts which provide that a piece-worker or commission employee is to receive a guaranteed minimum wage, the employer need only provide sufficient work to permit the guaranteed amount to be earned, rather than an amount equivalent to a higher average. When there is no such guaranteed minimum income a question arises as to whether or not the statutory minimum wage rates provide a limit to the employer's obligation to provide work. Another kind of situation in which the employer will be required to provide work is where the employee claims that at least as real a benefit of the contract as remuneration is the publicity and experience which performance will bestow on him. Typical of such claims are those of actors or managers in particular trades. The courts have, on occasion, held that in such cases the employer has a duty to provide work.[2]

1. *Driscoll* v. *Australian Royal Mail Steam Navigation*, (1859) 1 F. & F. 458 (N.P.); *Collier* v. *Sunday Referee Publishing*, [1940] 2 K.B. 647.
2. *Marbe* v. *George Edwardes (Daly's Theatre)*, [1928] 1 K.B. 269 (C.A.) (actor), *Hall* v. *British Essence*, (1946) 62 T.L.R. 542 (managing director).

233. The reason that the employer is under a duty to pay an employee, even though he does not require him to work, is that it would be a very one-sided contract if the employer had no obligation to provide work or to pay wages while the employee had to remain available and willing to perform. The courts have suggested that the contract would lack mutuality. But if the surrounding circumstances are such that an inference can be drawn that the parties had agreed that the employer could refuse both to provide work and to pay if certain contingencies materialized, then normal contract interpretation permits a suspension – as opposed to a termination – of the contract. Although in *Devonald* v. *Rosser*[1] it was held that the employer had a heavy burden to discharge when seeking to prove that a custom neither to provide work nor to pay wages existed when the suspension of the contract was due to lack of orders for the employer's goods, the courts have found in favour of employers who have not provided work nor paid wages where production was halted because machinery needed repair and where safety conditions warranted it.[2] It may well be that in Canada the employer's right to suspend the contract of employment will be considered a normal inference to be drawn from the circumstances of employment relationships and that the common law principles set out above, although intact, have little application. Certainly this may be so when a collective agreement governs the relationship between the parties.

1. [1906] 2 K.B. 728 (C.A.).
2. *Browning* v. *Crumlin Valley Collieries*, [1926] 1 K.B. 522 and the cases cited therein.

234. Collective agreements frequently provide how lay-offs are to be regulated. Lay-offs are temporary suspensions of the employment relationship. Elaborate seniority provisions are brought into play, seeking to guarantee as much job security as possible to the most senior employees when the employer determines that he will not provide work to the same extent as before. This is so common place that minimum standards' legislation does not require termination notice to be given where there is a lay-off of a certain duration and kind. Clearly the principle that an employer must pay remuneration or else terminate the relationship when not providing work is customarily modified by express agreement.

235. Similarly, where the parties to a collective agreement agree that the employer may (provided that he does not discriminate between employees) reduce the number of working hours, such a reduction, which results in less work being provided, may take place without imposing an obligation to pay remuneration for anything but the hours actually worked. Where the agreement has no such express provisions, arbitrators have still held that reduction of the hours worked will permit the employer to pay only for the hours worked. To overcome the notion that this offends the common law, it may be argued that grievance arbitrators, who have developed the collective agreement jurisprudence and who are very familiar with industrial customs, have regarded employees working under collective agreements as hourly employees. If this is so, no violence is done to the legal doctrine by permitting the employer to reduce the amount of work available by an hourly dimunition and paying accordingly. But, conceptually, this is not very satisfying . It is difficult to think of employees who have obtained the security which goes with a collective agreement as being as insecure as hourly employees. Further, the minimum standards' legislation provides for a minimum period of notice which must be given to all employees who have worked for longer than three months. Such provisions negate the notion that, with some rare exceptions, any employees are hired by the hour. Perhaps it would be best to argue that the precepts of the common law of employment relating to the duty to provide work just simply do not apply when collective bargaining has taken place.

236. It has already been noted that there are some occupations in which the opportunity to perform is the essence of the contract and where, therefore, a failure to provide work will be a breach of contract (para. 232).

237. In similar vein, it may be that a failure to provide work of the calibre that an employee had a right to expect will be deemed to be such an insult that an employee will be entitled to claim that he has been wrongfully dismissed[1] and to obtain the appropriate relief.[2] In this light, note that there has been at least one case in which it has been suggested by a court that a failure to provide work, even though the employer remains willing to pay, is a breach of the contract of employment because an employee's dignity is seriously undermined by denying him an opportunity to play a productive role in the enterprise.[3] This precept has not found a following as yet, but it is of some interest in view of the widespread attention alienation in the workplace is attracting amongst industrial relations' experts.

1. *E.g. Re Rubel Bronze and Metal and Vos*, [1918] 1 K.B. 315.
2. Para. 297.
3. *Langston* v. *A.U.E.W.*, [1974] I.C.R. 180 at 190, per Lord Denning but the point was considered doubtful in *Langston* v. *A.U.E.W.* (*No. 2*), [1974] I.C.R. 510 at 522 (an appeal to the Industrial Court from the original decision).

C. Responsibility for the employee's conduct

1. Master's tort theory

238. There are basically two ways in which an employer can be made responsible for the acts of his employees which cause harm to others. Firstly, he may be held liable to redress the damage because he is adjudged to be personally at fault. That is, the employer is said to owe a duty of care to the injured party, which duty is breached because he should have prevented a situation arising in which the employee could inflict injury.[1] When this argument is relied on, the so-called 'Master's tort theory' is being espoused. The justification for this approach is that although the employer has a need to act which can only be implemented through others, he cannot delegate his duty to take care. By and large this theoretical approach is not adopted by the courts.[2] Where it is, it leaves much discretion to the courts as to when a duty is of a non-delegable kind. This problem is exacerbated by the fact that there is no rationale for imposing a duty on the employer rather than the actor. If judicial discretion is to be exercised it is always helpful to have a principled reason for exercising it one way rather than another. On this basis, the second theory for holding the employer responsible for the conduct of his employees is that he is to be made liable for the acts of others not because they were, in effect, his acts but rather because it is socially useful to make him vicariously liable. Most plaintiffs will, as a matter of practicality, not care on which theoretical basis an employer is held responsible, but it will make a difference where the employee would not have been liable to the plaintiff. When this occurs, the master's tort theory is manifestly more useful to the plaintiff as the employer may still be in breach of a non-delegable duty of care.[3]

1. *Twine* v. *Bean's Express*, [1946] 1 All E.R. 202.
2. *Co-operators Insurance Assoc.* v. *Kearney*, (1965) 48 D.L.R. (2d) 1 (S.C.C.).
3. *Broom* v. *Morgan*, [1953] 1 Q.B. 597 (C.A.).

2. Vicarious liability

239. The notion that the employer should be responsible for the tortious acts of his employees is, at first glance, an anomaly in the law of torts. It is so because it is normally deemed to be necessary to establish that a defendant was at fault before he may be held liable to compensate an accident victim. To attribute the fault of an employee to the employer strikes a jarring note. But, the concept of liability without fault is not unknown to the law.[1] Justification for holding an employer vicariously liable has to be found. Several are available. One is that the employer has control over his employees. This being so he ought to be responsible for their conduct while under his control. In as much as this implies that the acts of the employee are really the acts of the employer, this is but another version of the master's tort theory. But, if the employer is held liable, even though he was not in any way careless in the way that he chose his employees, organized their work, supervised their activity, etc., the liability must be based on the notion that, because the employer is in control, he is the person who must be saddled with taking precautions to avoid harm to others. That is, it is not enough to engage competent employees and the like: strangers are entitled to hold the employer responsible for tortious conduct of his employees which affect them because the employer is in a better position to prevent such faulty conduct than anyone else. Associated with this reasoning are other lines of argument. For one, it appears reasonable that a person who benefits from an activity which creates risk should be held responsible when that risk materializes. The argument thus is that an employer benefits directly from the labour of others, unlike the rest of society which also benefits but does so indirectly. The employer is therefore an appropriate person to bear the cost. This is in nature different from another rationale underpinning vicarious liability: economic efficiency may require the redistribution of the loss caused by the enterprise of the employer and the employer is much better-situated to spread the loss than any other person in the causal chain. The employer, through insurance and market position will be enabled to spread the loss if the enterprise is efficient. In addition, the victim is assured of finding a defendant who is capable of paying. Moreover, the plaintiff is relieved of what would otherwise be serious evidentiary problems. He will more easily be able to prove an employee responsible than an employer.[2] Amongst these rationala for holding employers vicariously liable, none predominates. The co-existence of these various raisons d'être for the doctrine has led to some rather unclear guidelines as to when an employer will be held vicariously liable.

1. *E.g.* the Rule in *Rylands* v. *Fletcher* is often cited as an illustration, even though in practice it may be doubted that it operates as a no-fault doctrine.
2. See generally, P. Atiyah, *Vicarious Liability in the Law of Torts* (London, 1967).

240. An employer will be held vicariously liable for the tortious conduct of his employees and agents if they were acting within the scope of their employment. This formulation is obviously wider than one which would limit liability to tortious acts committed when the employee was complying with the mode of performance demanded by the employer. That is, the employer may be vicariously liable even for unauthorized means of carrying out the work. It will readily be seen that this runs counter to the notion that employers are made vicariously responsible because of their right to control. The rule can be harmonized, however, with the other rationala for vicarious liability viz., that the direct reaper of benefits should pay, and/or economic efficiency requires the best loss distributor to pay. Nonetheless, because the courts are not clear as to what is a proper basis for founding vicarious liability, there are endless battles about whether or not the employee was on a frolic of his own when the injury was inflicted,[1] or about whether or not the fact that the employer had actually prohibited the particular conduct which caused the injury precluded a finding of vicarious responsibility,[2] or about whether or not intentional wrongdoing by an employee can render an employer vicariously liable,[3] etc. In this work, no more can be done to indicate that these problems exist and that their resolution depends on which of the justifications for the doctrine of vicarious liability a particular court favours.

1. *E.g. Hall* v. *Halifax Transfer*, (1959) 18 D.L.R. (2d) 115 (N.S.S.C.); *Bamert* v. *Parks*, (1965) 50 D.L.R. (2d) 313 (Ont.C.C.); *Hamilton* v. *Farmers'*, [1953] 3 D.L.R. 382 (N.S.S.C.).
2. *Hamilton* v. *Farmers'*, *ibid*.
3. *Sheppard Publishing* v. *Press Publishing*, (1905) 10 O.L.R. 243 (D.C.); *Griggs* v. *Southside Hotel*, [1947] 4 D.L.R. 49 (Ont.C.A.); *Lloyd* v. *Grace Smith*, [1912] A.C. 716 (H.L.); *R* v. *Levy Bros.*, (1961) 26 D.L.R. (2d) 760 (S.C.C.).

241. It will have been noted above that the basis for vicarious liability was expressed in terms of liability for the conduct of employees and agents. The word agent encompasses both employees and independent contractors in as much as agency denotes a contract to have work performed by another. Where such work is done in a representative capacity, it is appropriate, as a matter of linguistic convenience, to refer to the performer as an employee or an agent, whereas if the performer can be classified as a principal in his own right, it is best to describe him as an independent contractor. As between an employee and an agent, it is customary to reserve the term agent for those representatives who are employed on a casual rather than a continuous basis.

242. It will readily be seen that this categorization lacks in precision. The determination of whether or not a person acts as a principal rather than as a representative involves the analysis discussed above. When the purpose of categorization is to decide whether an employer ought to be made vicariously liable, the underlying justifications for the existence of the doctrine will play a determining role. Thus, whereas it was once thought that an employer could only be held liable for the tortious acts of an independent contractor where the tort to be performed was inherently ultra-dangerous,[1] the physical diminution of control over enterprise and the attendant devaluation of the control test led to an ever increasing approximation in treatment of employees and independent contractors. Thus the initial starting position has been modified and employers may be held vicariously liable for the conduct of independent contractors in an increasing number of circumstances: hospitals are often held responsible for work performed by consulting medical practitioners;[2] occupiers will be responsible to some lawful entrants on their land who are injured by independent contractors working on that land;[3] most importantly, employers will be held responsible for not providing a safe system of work or for not ensuring compliance with statutory safety standards.[4] Such duties are said to be non-delegable. Manifestly, the increased scope of vicarious liability in respect of independent contractors reflects the augmented importance of the rationale that (i) the reaper of profits should bear the cost and (ii) loss-distribution principles dictate a finding of vicarious responsibility. As these principles are imprecise in scope, it follows that there will still be many occasions where an employer will be permitted to say that an independent contractor should, as a principal, be the sole person to bear the burden of causing harm.[5] In such cases, the courts will justify their decision by reasoning that the employer's duty was a delegable one and that it had been properly delegated.

1. *Honeywill and Stein* v. *Larkin Bros.*, [1934] 1 K.B. 191 (C.A.); *City of St. John* v. *Donald*, [1926] 2 D.L.R. 185 (S.C.C.); *Savage* v. *Wilby*, [1954] 3 D.L.R. 204 (S.C.C.); *Holinaty* v. *Hawkins and Neilsens' Maintenance*, (1966) 52 D.L.R. (2d) 289 (Ont.C.A.).
2. *Yepremian* v. *Scarborough General Hospital*, (1978) 6 C.C.L.T. 81 (Ont.S.C.) but contrast *Hôpital Notre-Dame de L'Espérence* v. *Laurent*, [1978] 1 S.C.R. 605, in which it was held that the hospital was not liable for the acts of a consultant surgeon, *semble* because the hospital exercised no control over the performance of the work.
3. *Francis* v. *Cockrell*, (1870) 5 Q.B. 501 (Exch.).
4. *Wilsons & Clyde Coal* v. *English*, [1938] A.C. 57 (H.L.).
5. *Davie* v. *New Merton Board Mills*, [1959] A.C. 604 (H.L.).

D. Duty to provide a safe work environment

1. The common law duty

243. As indicated in section C, the doctrine of vicarious liability makes employers liable for the acts of their employees which cause harm to strangers and for the conduct of independent contractors who cause harm to the employer's employees. But the courts had refused to make employers responsible for injuries caused to their employees by fellow-employees. The contract of employment was interpreted as including a term implied by law that employees agreed to run the risk of injury due to the acts of fellow-employees. This was the common employment doctrine. It was eventually repealed by statute. In the meanwhile, the courts came to realize the harshness of the doctrine and, in typical common law fashion, developed a tool to overcome the problem without having to disavow the existing law. They simply held that an employer had a positive legal duty to all his employees to provide a safe system of work. This duty is spelt out as requiring an obligation (i) to provide competent fellow workmen (ii) to provide safe tools, machinery and equipment, (iii) to provide a safe place of work and safe access to that place of work and (iv) to provide a safe system of working.[1] These being the employer's personal responsibilities, they cannot be delegated to competent managers. Similarly, the hiring of independent contractors ought not to discharge these duties of employers, although, as we have seen, reliance on others may sometimes permit the employer to claim that they have discharged their obligations.[2]

1. *Wilson v. Tyneside Window Cleaning*, [1958] 2 Q.B. 110 (C.A.); *Wilsons and Clyde Coal v. English*, [1938] A.C. 367 (H.L.); *Marshment v. Borgstrom*, [1942] S.C.R. 374.
2. *Davie v. New Merton Board Mills*, *supra*.

2. Workers' compensation legislation

244. There is relatively little jurisprudence in Canada relating to the employer's implied duty to provide a safe work environment because, from early on in this century, statutory schemes of workers' compensation schemes have replaced judicial sections for damages as a recovery mechanism. All provinces have such statutes and they provide that workers shall be compensated for personal injuries arising out of, or incurred in the course of, their employment. The amounts paid are 75 per cent of the worker's earnings, not exceeding a specified amount. Where the worker has been permanently disabled, there may be an award up to 75 per cent of the worker's previous earnings, the amount awarded depending on the extent of the disablement. Where the disablement is slight, the award may be made by way of paying a lump sum. Otherwise, a monthly pension is awarded. Where the worker has died as a result of a work-related accident, a lump sum is payable to the dependents for funeral expenses and the like. A monthly pension will also be paid to the dependents. The rate of all benefits may change over time.[1] One of the obvious

95

advantages of schemes of this nature is that it is possible to review the conditions of the worker frequently. The injured worker is to be provided with all medical and therapeutic aid, hospitalization expenses and rehabilitative care.

1. In British Columbia the rates are tied to the Consumer Price Index; in Quebec, to the Quebec Pension Index. Elsewhere, they are changed by order or legislation.

245. Diseases arising out of working conditions are also compensable, but on a much less universal scale. Although details differ, in general the statutes provide that certain diseases are compensable if it can be shown that the worker was employed in a particular industry at a relevant time. That is, schedules in the statutes list a number of diseases and go on to say that there is a presumption that the suffering of such a disease is compensable if the worker was employed in a scheduled industry. In some provinces, the worker must have been so employed at any time in the twelve months previous to the manifestation of the disabling disease,[1] in others there is no time limit.[2] Where the disease complained of is not listed in such a schedule, the burden is on the worker-applicant to show that the disease is work-related.

1. Alberta, British Columbia, New Brunswick, Nova Scotia, Prince Edward Island and Quebec.
2. Newfoundland, Ontario and Saskatchewan.

246. The schemes are funded on a collective basis. The industries covered by the statutes are grouped by types, the relevant employers paying into a collective fund for their industry groups. The sum levied from each employer is calculated on the basis of the estimated payroll for the coming year. The Workers' Compensation Board (as the administrative agency running the scheme is usually called) calculates the contribution rate on the basis of the known hazard in a particular group of industries. At the end of the year, an accounting is done to re-adjust the rate based on actual payroll and actual accident-rates. An advantage that the schemes bestow is that the Boards can adjust for particularly hazardous enterprises in a group. There is also power to provide for preventive regulation and there ought to be an incentive for employers to co-operate in such efforts. But it is fair to assert that the preventive efforts of the schemes have seldom been pushed very far. In the main, they have consisted of setting up advisory bodies, mainly comprised by appropriate employers, which publicize obvious safety problems.

247. The statutory schemes thus provide compensation without workers having to establish that their employers or fellow employees were at fault, although an employee may be denied compensation if it is found that the injury was caused by his serious misconduct and the injury was not serious. A majority of the statutory schemes provide that certain excluded employers (listed in Part II of the appropriate statutes) are liable to compensate their employees on a negligence basis. That is, such employees must establish fault.[1] By generally removing fault notions, the compensation schemes have reduced a source of controversy, but areas of dispute remain. The questions of whether the injury

arose out of or in the course of employment, whether the disease is a compensable one, the extent of disability, etc. are all potentially contentious issues.

1. The employee must prove a defect in the machinery, faulty process organization or injury caused by the negligence of the employer or of those for whom he is responsible. The employee's own negligence may bar his cause of action or diminish the amount of damages recoverable.

248. In Ontario and Quebec, large governmental-type operations, such as railways, federal telephone companies, steamship companies and the like are exempted from paying into the workers' compensation's Accident Fund, but participate in the scheme by contributing to its administrative cost. Their employees are paid compensation by the Workmen's Compensation Board on the same basis as all other covered employees.

3. Developing occupational health and safety legislation

249. It was noted in the foregoing paragraphs that, even though the Workers' Compensation statutes empower the various Boards to make provision for safer working conditions, they have, on the whole, not used this power extensively. There has always been a plethora of particular and general statutes prescribing safety standards and norms. Many of these are still intact. They tend to be rather rudimentary. Some merely list industries and prescribe practices which are designed to avoid accidents in those industries.[1] Some give the appropriate ministry power to legislate in respect of safety and occupational disease prevention.[2] In either case, inspectorates are created with enforcement powers. Enforcement, on the whole, has been minimal. More recently, in line with a growing awareness of the dangers posed to workers by the use of toxic substances in manufacturing processes, omnibus-type legislation has been enacted. The most far-reaching legislation is to be found in the federal jurisdiction, Ontario, Saskatchewan and Manitoba.[3] These statutes provide for the imposition of a set of obligations on both employers and employees in order to attain certain standards of safety in the work environment. Usually, there is provision for regulations to be passed after appropriate recommendations by an agency created for this purpose. The agency will be given the task of evaluating the feasibility of imposing safety standards in the work place. It is given research facilities. The amount of money given in this respect is of the utmost importance in view of the difficulties inherent in setting appropriate exposure levels to the thousands of chemical substances in use in manufacturing. The agency is aided by an inspectorate which not only has the task to enforce the existing standards, but also has to report on the need for more regulation or deregulation. The enforcement process involves consultation with the employers and employees, the making of recommendations, the possible imposition of fines and, where there is immediate danger, ordering the cessation of work until the premises comply with essential safety standards. As well, these statutory schemes seek to improve the safety of the work environment by placing an onus on employers and employees directly. This is done by providing for joint employer-employee safety committees. In some jurisdictions, the appropriate Minister is given power to appoint committees comprised by an equal number of employer and employee representatives where he deems it desirable, in others it is mandated that, where the workforce exceeds a certain number,[4] a joint committee of this kind must be appointed. Committees of this kind must make inspections regularly, may make joint recommendations, call inspectors where needed or where no agreement as to appropriate action can be reached. Employers are under an obligation to make available information as to levels of exposures of particular workers, new substances introduced into the plant, medical advice respecting employees, etc.

1. *E.g.* Industrial Safety Act, R.S.N.S. 1967, c.141.
2. *E.g.* Occupational Safety Act, S.N.B. 1976, c.0–0.1.
3. Canada, Part IV; The Workplace Safety and Health Act, S.M. 1976, c.63; The Occupational Health and Safety Act, 1978 S.O. 1978, c.83; The Occupational Health Act, S.S. 1972, c.86.
4. *E.g.* Ontario.

250. In addition, where workers have a reasonable apprehension of danger, they are entitled to refuse to work until the situation is remedied. Where a supervisor feels that the worker's fear is misplaced, the joint committee (or a safety representative who may be appointed in lieu of such a committee in some cases) may be asked to adjudicate. A worker is not to be disciplined where his belief is adjudged to be reasonable. When he refuses to accept the work, he may be asked to take on other equivalent work. It is an open question as yet as to whether or not he will be considered disciplined if the remuneration rate is less for this other task than the one in respect of which he is normally employed. It may be noted that, at common law, it was always open for an employee to refuse work in unsafe conditions. But such a worker, not supported by a legislative scheme of the kind described, ran a great risk: if his refusal was thought unreasonable by a court, there was no question but that the employer could dismiss such an employee. Further, even if it was a reasonable refusal, it was considerably easier for an employer to rid himself of such a troublesome worker. This note about the practical improvement of the worker's lot draws attention to the fact that employees are free to bargain about safety in the work environment and all the schemes permit such agreement-making, provided that the terms are at least equal in their provision for safety to the legislative schemes. For instance, they must provide for joint committees with, at least, the same powers of inspection, access to information and right to make recommendations as the legislatively-mandated committees have.

251. The efficacy of these elaborate schemes are still not established. Much will depend on the political will supporting the work of the agencies which are to set standards. Much depends on economic circumstances. These will dictate whether a standard can be imposed in view of the effect on the competitive position of an industry or people within it.

§3. THE EMPLOYEE'S DUTIES AND OBLIGATIONS

A. Introduction

252. Duties and obligations may be imposed because they are explicitly agreed to by the parties. They may also be implied. At this stage, note once again that the essence of the relationship is that it is primarily a contract of service, although it has elements which make it look like a contract of mutual co-operation. Consequently, duties and obligations have come to be imposed on employees by implying them as a matter of law and these duties and obligations reflect the reality of the relationship.

253. Broadly, the duties and obligations imposed on employees by implication of law fall into two categories. On the one hand, there is the duty to obey and duty to use appropriate skill and care; on the other hand, there is the duty of good faith. Manifestly, these categories overlap, but the nature of particular obligations which employees must honour is most easily perceived by referring them to one of these two discrete categories. Further, the two categories are distinct in one important aspect, despite the potential for overlap. Thus: the duties and obligations which will be discussed under the heading of good faith may require that an employee be held in breach of such duties and obligations where that breach causes damage to the employer after the contract has terminated or even that an employee comply with his duty of good faith after the contract has run its course. The duties to obey or to use appropriate skill and care can have no such post-contractual scope.

254. Where an employee is in breach of an express or implied duty, the employer may have a cause of action in damages in respect of the loss occasioned or have a right to dismiss the employee from his service.

B. The duty to obey

255. There are certain orders of an employer which an employee may refuse to carry out with impunity. These include commands to do something which is illegal and those which would jeopardize the physical well-being of the employee if obeyed. As to the latter, the right to refuse an order to do unsafe work has already been discussed in para. 250. As pointed out there, recent statutes have made it somewhat easier for a worker to take such a stand. In addition, if an employer requires an employee to carry out his duties in an area where he is endangered because say, his political or religious beliefs are anathema in the region, the employee is entitled to refuse to accept such an assignment.[1] It is interesting, however, that if the employee can merely show that it is awkward for him to go to a particular place because of a language difficulty and because the local authorities do not like him, the employer will be entitled to summarily dismiss such an employee. The argument is that, as long as there is no personal danger, the employee has to obey the employer's order.[2] That is, the duty to obey truly reflects the notion that the relationship is one of service.

1. *Ottoman Bank* v. *Chakarian*, [1930] A.C. 277 (P.C.).
2. *Bouzourou* v. *Ottoman Bank*, [1930] A.C. 271 (P.C.).

256. Disobedience of an order will not automatically give the employer the right to dismiss an employee. The disobedience must be wilful. The meaning of wilfullness has not been clearly spelt out in the case law. It seems to require more than an intent to disobey the employer's command, although once this was a view expressed by the courts.[1] The term, as used in modern times, appears to connote some deliberate design or purpose to derogate from one's duty.[2] To pinpoint the nature of the intent required further is fraught with difficulty. It may well be easier to classify a disobedience as being one which offends the duty imposed by law when it is accompanied by behaviour which can be described as insolent. This was the case in *Markey* v. *Port Weller Dry Docks*,[3] in which the employee not only refused to obey instructions but justified his conduct to his supervisor by telling him that he was incompetent, challenging him to a trade test and suggesting that, to prove who was more rational, they should both be examined by a psychiatrist. The employee indicated that he, the employee, would come out 'the better'. In such a case, it is readily apparent that the reason for the disobedience was wilfulness rather than any other basis. (Note that, apart from the disobedience, insolence itself may give the employer a right of discipline against an employee. This will be discussed below.) This kind of disobedience can easily be differentiated from those cases in which the refusal to abide by an order can be attributed to a reasonable misunderstanding about the nature of his duties by the employee.[4]

1. *Turner* v. *Mason*, (1845) 153 E.R. 411, *Clouston* v. *Corry*, [1906] A.C. 122 (P.C.).
2. *Bist* v. *London and South Western Railway*, [1907] A.C. 209 at 211, 213–14 (H.L.); *George* v. *Glasgow Coal*, [1909] A.C. 123 at 128–29 (H.L.).
3. [1974] 4 O.R. (2d) 12 (C.C.).
4. *Walker* v. *Booth Fisheries*, (1922) 21 O.W.N. 395 (C.A.) (reasonable belief that employer would have wanted goods shipped in the absence of grounds to know that cheque given by purchaser had been dishonoured).

257. In as much as the contract of employment requires an employee to perform certain kinds of services, it precludes the employer from making demands on that employee which are not incidental to the agreed-upon area of performance. Where the terms of the contract are relatively specific, the scope of orders which require obedience will be comparatively easy to delimit. This is more likely to occur where the agreement imposing the employer's duties is a collective agreement than where an individual contract of employment does so. But in either circumstance, there will be room for controversy. Oft-raised questions include such issues as to whether it is part and parcel of a secretary's duties to make and get coffee for the employer, to file driver's license applications, and the like. More serious, perhaps, are those cases in which an employer changes production processes and asks an employee to take on a new task or to work different days and/or hours. In all these cases, much will depend on how the question of prerogative of management is approached. At one end of the spectrum is the notion that, unless the employer's order is way out of line with any explicit or implicit term of the agreement, the order ought to be seen as reasonable and ought to be obeyed. At the other end of that spectrum is the notion that unless the task required to be done has been agreed to be within the employer's right to demand, the order can be disobeyed with impunity. As the employee disputing the scope of an employer's authority is at risk, it is not surprising that these issues are most likely to crop up when the protection of a collective bargaining scheme is available. In that context the imposition of discipline by employers may be challenged by a trade union which has an intrinsic interest in making explicit the boundaries of the prerogative of management. In this regard note that, where the common law principles prevail, and the employer requires an employee to do different work, or to work a different shift or the like, the employee's claim that he is entitled to be given specific tasks at specific times, is not aided by the fact that, failing an agreement to the contrary, the employer is under no duty to provide work. See para. 232.

Duty to obey commands to work for a particular period – the statutes
258. A particular problem raised in this context is the reasonableness of an employer's demand that an employee work a certain number of hours. In the absence of a specific term in the contract or an established custom, given that the essential nature of the employment relationship is that it is a contract of service, there seems to be no *a priori* logical barrier to the number of hours on any one day or to the number of days per week an employer can require an employee to work. The not so long ago battles for the 10-hour and then 8-hour days are testimony to that proposition. But customs and conventions now exist. Significantly, they are bolstered by statutory limitations on this aspect of the prerogative of management. All jurisdictions[1] provide for a maximum number of hours per week an employee may be required to work. The actual number specified varies from jurisdiction to jurisdiction. Under the federal, Manitoba and Saskatchewan statutes it is 40 hours per week; in British Columbia, Newfoundland (except for assistants in shops and the like) and Quebec it is 44 hours per week; in New Brunswick, Nova Scotia, Ontario and Prince Edward Island it is 48 hours per week. There are also variations according to the industrial groupings and special rules may apply when young employees (usually 16 or less) are engaged. The maximum number of hours may be exceeded where an emergency has been created by a breakdown in the plant or like catastrophe. In addition, extra hours may be worked where a permit is obtained from the appropriate Director or Board under the relevant legislation. The number of additional hours for which such a permit may be obtained is itself limited and in some jurisdictions, for instance, Ontario, the acquiescence of the employee or his agent (usually a trade union) must be obtained in addition to a permit before extra hours can be demanded. When hours over and above the prescribed maximum are to be worked (or sometimes a lesser number of specified hours), the statutes provide that special rates of pay, usually one-

and-a-half times the ordinary rate, are to be paid. Note that when a collective agreement regulates the relationship, it is likely to provide how overtime is to be allotted. This is of some interest because it indicates that whereas legislative intervention was seen as necessary to prevent otherwise legal exploitation of employees in poor bargaining positions, extra work may be attractive to employees who are not subject to oppression.

1. Alberta, Part 3, Division 1; Hours of Work Act, R.S.B.C. 1960, c.182; Fair Wages and Hours of Labour Act, R.S.C. 1970, c.L–3; Canada, Part III; Minimum Employment Standards Act, R.S.N.B. 1973, c.M–12; Fair Wages and Hours of Labour Act, R.S.N.B. 1973, c.F–2; The Labour Standards Act, S.N. 1977, c.52, Part III; Labour Standards Code, S.N.S. 1972, c.10, ss. 58–63; The Employment Standards Act, S.O. 1974, c.112, Part IV; Prince Edward Island, s.63, Board Order No. 2–78, No. EC 89/478 gazetted Nov. 11, 1978; Hours of Work Act, R.S.Q. 1941, c.165, Ordinance No. 4 1972, s. 5, Ordinance No. 9, 1970, s.5, Minimum Wage Commission Ordinance No. 13, 1976, s.5; The Labour Standards Act, R.S.S. 1978, c.L–1, Part 1.

259. The statutes also provide that when the nature of the enterprise makes it logical to do so, a compressed work week may be allowed. The statutes as well as providing for a maximum number of hours which may be demanded per week, also specify the maximum number of hours which may be worked on any one day and the amount of time which must elapse between shifts. This compressed week arrangement is a modification of these rules. So also is the frequently found provision that, because of the nature of the enterprise, the requirement that no more than a certain number of hours may be worked in one week may be met by permitting the aggregate number of hours over, say, two weeks to be halved. This gives an employer flexibility where necessary without allowing employees to work more than the desirable number of hours over the long haul.

260. An addendum must be made to this catalogue of how, in respect of lawful commands relating to amount of work, the employer's right has been limited by statutes. It is that in all jurisdictions there is a prohibition on work on the Lord's Day. Exceptions to this on the basis that emergencies or the special nature of the enterprise requires it, exist.

C. The duty to exercise skill and care

261. It was once thought that the failure by an employee to exercise adequate skill and care entitled the employer to discipline an employee without more. This, of course, meant instant dismissal without notice. The basis for this rule was that the employee, by accepting employment, had held out that he had the skill and competence to do the job.[1] This rationale is not consonant with modern employment conditions. As between the employer and a potential employee the former is in the best position to assess the requirement of skill and capacities necessary to the work to be performed. Further, even if the employee has the requisite skills when hired, quickly changing technological processes and inability of the employee to adopt to these may result in 'faultless' incapacity of the employee. To hold fast to the old rule under these circumstances, except where the employee expressly holds out that he has a special kind of expertise, would be unwarrantedly draconic. This reasoning is in line with the arguments canvassed in respect of the duty to obey by which it was shown that, for disobedience to permit discipline, it has to be wilful and/or insolent. Reasonable refusal is not enough. Similarly, lack of adequate skill by an employee who is doing his best no longer permits discipline. This attitude is reflected in statutes which provide for minimum standards in respect of termination of employment. As we shall see below, minimum periods of notice are required by legislation. The right to dismiss without notice is explicitly reserved but may only be used where there is a finding of wilful misconduct.[2] In at least one case, a Referee has held that 'it is axiomatic that mere inefficiency on the job is not sufficient to constitute wilful misconduct, unless the inefficiency is so extreme that a reasonable person could only conclude that it ceased to be mere inefficiency but rather became a calculated course of action deliberately aimed at harming the employer by disrupting the normal business production at the place of employment or being so reckless in one's action that such a result would naturally follow.'[3] (Of course, an employee's lack of exercise of adequate skill and care can lead to dismissal after appropriate notice.)

1. *Harmer* v. *Cornelius*, (1858) 5 C.B. (N.S.) 236 at 247.
2. *E.g.* The Employment Standards Act, S.O. 1974, c.112, s.40; But note at this point Canada, s.61.5, which prevents termination of employees without just cause.
3. *Re: Reid Industries*, 6 December 1975 Ontario (McNish).

262. As a matter of law, the above does not signify that the employee's implied duty to exercise skill and care is of no import. Apart from the moral suasion it gives an employer when demanding better effort from employees, it also gives a potential tool of great menace. It will be remembered that an employer may be held vicariously responsible for the conduct of an employee acting within the scope of his authority. As was seen, the dominant justifications for this doctrine are that the employer (i) is the best loss distributor and (ii) ought to pay costs incurred as a consequence of seeking profits. If the employer is held vicariously liable on this basis rather than that the conduct of the employee in fact constitutes a tort by the employer, the employer is in a position to argue that he is entitled to be indemnified by his employee's lack of skill and care which led to the injury in respect of which the employer has been held vicariously liable. The argument is based squarely on the notion that there is a duty owed to the employer to use adequate skill and care. The House of Lords upheld this line of reasoning in the rather infamous decision in *Lister* v. *Romford Ice and Cold Storage.*[1] There the employer's insurer was permitted to exercise its right of subrogation against its insured employer's employee who had, by his neglect, caused injury for which the employer had been held vicariously liable. The outcry was predictably great and English insurance companies entered into a 'gentlemen's agreement' not to pursue their legal right of subrogation in cases of this kind. Although there are no instances of similar travesties in Canada, the decision in *Lister* v. *Romford Ice* has been treated as good law.[2]

1. [1957] A.C. 555 (H.L.). Note that, even though the employee may be within the scope of

his authority, the misconduct which accordingly makes the employer vicariously liable may not take place in a context in which the employee is required to exercise the skill and care for which he has been hired; see *Harvey* v. *R. G. O'Dell*, [1958] 2 Q.B. 78.
2. *McKee* v. *Dumas*, (1976) 8 O.R. (2d) 229, 240–41 (Ont. HC.) (overruled on a different basis, (1976) 70 D.L.R. (3d) 70 (Ont. C.A.); see the dissenting judgment of Cartwright, J., in *Co-operations Insurance* v. *Kearney*, (1964) 48 D.L.R. (2d) 1 (S.C.C.).

D. The duty of good faith and fidelity

263. The phraseology itself suggests that this duty implied by law into the contract of employment has more to do with notions of service than co-operation. The duty is not to injure the employer by conduct which amounts to an abuse of the trust reposed in the employee. This requires an examination of what that trust is.

1. Trade secrets

264. An employee is only bound to serve his employer for the time they have agreed that services shall be rendered. Therefore, what the employee does in his own time is of no concern to the employer. Otherwise, it has been judicially said, the employee of modern days would be placed 'in a position little, if at all, better than the villein of former times'.[1] But there are some activities which an employee will not be permitted to engage in, even though he is acting on non-employer's time. Thus, in *Hivac* v. *Park Royal Scientific Instruments*,[2] employees who aided a rival employer in his competition with the plaintiff-employer by giving him their services and know-how were held to be in breach of their contract of employment.

1. *Sheppard Publishing* v. *Harkins*, (1905) 9 O.L.R. 504 at 508, per Anglin, J. (D.C.), delivering the judgment of the court.
2. [1946] 2 All E.R. 350.

265. The issue in *Hivac, supra* was that the employees were using information obtained during their employment to benefit a rival. They would also be in breach of their duty of good faith or fidelity if they consciously and surreptitiously made use of their employer's time, secret processes, connections or the like to advantage themselves. The classic illustration is one in which the defendant employee milkman compiled a list of customer's from his employer's order book. Shortly after this he left his master's employment, and used the list in setting up his own business. He was forced to pay damages to his former employer and to return the list of customers.[1] Obviously, the breach of good faith would occur whether the employee took a physical list or merely committed it to memory. What is of significance is whether the essence of the employer's business was such that divulging of a confidence amounted to a breach of good faith.[2]

1. *Robb* v. *Green*, [1895] 2 Q.B. 315; *Wessex Dairies* v. *Smith*, [1935] 2 K.B. 80 (C.A.).
2. *Polyresins* v. *Stein-Hall*, (1972) 25 D.L.R. (3d) 152 (Ont. H.C.).

266. What it turns on, then, is whether or not the employee makes wrongful use of a trade secret. It is very difficult to define a trade secret. It may be a formula, special material, list or process. It is essential that the employer wishes the secret to be kept and only shares it with those employees in whom it is necessary to confide.[1] It is different from a copyrighted or patented idea in that anyone who comes by the confidential information or trade secret without in any way relying on the original possessor's knowledge nor on that of those employees entrusted with it, is entitled to use it in any way he likes.[2] One of the indicia to determine an employer's right to successfully obtain judicial protection is whether or not the divulged information was such that no other competitor in the field would be able to make the product or render the services without possession of the information. As it is not necessary that the subject-matter of the trade secret be capable of being copyrighted or patented, it need not be completely original information, process or material.[3] Where competitors do not need knowledge of the trade secret to compete and/or the information about it is freely available, the plaintiff-employer will not get protection, nor will, in all likelihood, his employee be held to be in breach of the duty of good faith if he divulges information.[4]

1. *Herbert Morris* v. *Saxelby*, [1916] 1 A.C. 688 (H.L.); *Gibbons* v. *Drew Chemical*, (1973) 8 C.P.R. (2d) 105 (B.C.S.C.).
2. *R. I. Crain* v. *Ashton*, [1949] O.R. 303, *aff'd.* [1950] O.R. 62 (C.A.).
3. *Int'l. Tools* v. *Kollar*, [1968] 67 D.L.R. (2d) 386 (Ont. C.A.).
4. *Cooperheat* v. *Slater*, (1974) 13 C.P.R. (2d) 25 (H.C.).

267. It will be apparent that, in addition to relying on the implied duty of good faith, employers can have terms inserted into the contract of employment which explicitly prevent employees from divulging information and/or to use it for their own, or for other people's benefit. Such restraint of trade clauses have to be read in the normal contractual way. That is, they must be reasonable from the point of view of both contracting parties and the public.[1] The question of whether it is reasonable from the parties' point of view tends to be resolved on the bases discussed above: the assumptions about the duty of good faith, the existence of a trade secret and its competitive significance.

1. *Nordenfelt* v. *Maxim Nordenfelt Guns and Ammunition*, [1894] A.C. 535 (H.L.).

268. The underlying rationale for these intertwined areas of the law of contract is that the courts are eager to promote enterprise. Those who have gained a competitive advantage by their endeavour and initiative should not lose it to competitors who have not exerted such efforts. When an employee, who owes a duty of fidelity, threatens loss of competitive advantage, it is not surprising that the original employer will be protected by giving him actions against his employee (or ex-employee), and against the unmeritorious competitor. But, when an employee uses skill and knowledge gained during his employment for his own ends, the question is more difficult. The courts are now faced with the fact that, in their zeal to promote initiative and enterprise, they may inhibit enterprising conduct. A delicate balance thus has to be struck between skill and knowledge acquired in the normal course of employment and skill and knowledge specifically classifiable as a trade secret and not usable by the employee, except for his employer's benefit. A more slippery formula is hard to imagine. One judge was moved to say that the 'answer may be one of degree, defying precise formulation, and . . . a particular case can only be considered on its merits'.[1]

1. Per Brightman J., *United Sterling* v. *Felton & Mannion*, [1974] R.P.C. 162 at 170; *Alberts* v. *Mountjoy*, (1977) 16 O.R. (2d) 682 (H.C.); *Consolidated Textiles* v. *Corneiller*, (1975) 18 C.P.R. (2d) 1 at 9, per Addy, J. (Fed.T.C.).

2. Inventions

269. Implicit in the discussion of the duty of good faith so far has been that whatever an employee does by way of obtaining benefits, he does for the employer. Accordingly, an employee can be made to account to the employer for profits he has made when using information, materials, processes rightfully belonging to the employer.[1] Again, as the employee's enterprise must also be protected, the employee will not have to give up profits he made when acting on his own time, relying on his own skills, knowledge, materials, etc.[2] A particularly difficult application of this principle is related to inventions. The basic doctrine seems to be that an invention by an employee makes him the beneficial owner of it. But where there is an explicit term in the contract to the contrary, or where vesting the benefit of the invention in the employee would be inconsistent with his duty of good faith, the invention will belong to the employer. When will it be inconsistent with the duty of good faith for the employee to retain the benefit of the invention? Where the employee is employed to invent, the duty of good faith will make the employer the rightful owner of any invention. Where it is not clear that this was part and parcel of the employment understanding, the surrounding circumstances will have to be examined. Facts such as when and where the invention was made, whose materials were used, the level of employment of the particular employee in relation to the invention, will all be pertinent.[3] The English House of Lords has held that it is an implied term of the contract of employment that an employee is a trustee for his employer of any invention made in the course of his duty as an employee, unless such an implied term is displaced by a contrary agreement having legal effect.[4] Although this is a different verbal formulation, at least one Canadian court has held that it invokes the same consideration as does the first-stated test.[5]

1. *William R. Barnes* v. *MacKenzie*, [1973] 2 O.R. 511 (H.C.).
2. *Jones* v. *Linde British Refrigeration*, (1901) 2 O.L.R. 428 (C.A.); *Sheppard Publishing* v. *Harkins*, (1905) 9 O.L.R. 504 (D.C.).
3. *Fine Industrial Commodities* v. *Powling*, (1954) 71 R.P.C. 253.
4. *Sterling Engineering* v. *Patchett*, [1955] 1 All E.R. 369.
5. *W. J. Gage* v. *Sugden*, (1967) 62 D.L.R. (2d) 671 (Ont.H.C.).

§4. Termination of Employment

270. The general rules of contract apply to the termination of contracts of employment. Thus a contract of employment may be terminated according to the terms relating thereto in the contract, by mutual agreement, by performance, by frustration, death of one of the parties, by the sale of the business, by bankruptcy and by retirement. Some of these matters will be specifically discussed. As usual, the common law principles have been modified by minimum standards legislation.

A. Frustration

271. A contract will be terminated as a result of frustration when it has become impossible of performance because of a supervening event which is fortuitous and unforeseeable. A standard example is the case of a plant which has been burnt down, making work impossible. But the event which allegedly frustrates the contract by rendering it impossible of performance must not have been the result of the conduct of the party seeking to rely on the frustration argument.[1]

1. *Re Dennis Ryan – Review of an Order of an Employment Standards Officer,* – 24 March 1977 (Pilcher – Referee).

272. The question of whether or not a contract has been rendered impossible of performance is a question of fact. No hard and fast rule can be formulated. In some cases, the special nature of the contract may permit characterizing temporary incapacity by one of the parties as frustration of the contract. Typically, this will be so where the employees are skilled artists. In *Poussard* v. *Speirs & Pond*[1] there was an engagement of an opera singer for three months. Due to illness she could not rehearse, nor appear on the first three nights of actual performances. The contract was held to be frustrated by her illness.[2] Where the relationship is not of this kind, the question for a court or board to answer is whether or not the supervening event has created a fundamentally different situation from that which existed at the outset of the contract. In one case, a person who was ill for two years of a five-year engagement was held to have had his employment wrongfully terminated by an employer who relied on frustration to treat the contract as ended. In that case medical advice had been given to the effect that the employee would recover.[3] In another case, where similar medical advice was given, the employer was held to have rightfully treated the contract as terminated when the employee, in fact, was incapacitated for the whole period of projected employment and then died.[4]

1. (1876) 1 Q.B.D. 410.
2. Contrast *Loates* v. *Maple,* (1903) 88 L.T. 288 (K.B.) (3-year contract for jockey; incapacitated for two months; no frustration).
3. *Storey* v. *Fulham Steel Works,* (1907) 24 T.L.R. 89 (C.A.).
4. *Dartmouth Ferry Commission* v. *Marks,* (1904) 34 S.C.R. 366.

273. There are statutory provisions which make it clear that absence due to pregnancy shall not operate to frustrate a contract. Typically, employees who have been employed for at least twelve months are to give notice of the fact that they wish to take maternity leave. They may take a certain number of weeks (most often 17), to commence a specified number of weeks prior to confinement; a given period of time after confinement may form part of the leave. The employee shall be entitled to return to her job without suffering adverse effects if she claims such leave. The employer may, if performance at work is adversely affected by the employee's condition, insist that maternity leave be taken. A leave of absence may be granted even if the employee does not give appropriate notice if, after (usually) two weeks of leaving work she provides evidence that she has left work because of her pregnancy and shows that the expected confinement date falls within the statutory time span.[1]

1. *E.g.* Canada, Part III, Div. V.1; The Employment Standards Act, S.O. 1974, c.112, Part XI.

274. When a contract of employment is frustrated it terminates at the time that the contract becomes impossible of performance. No requirement of notice has to be satisfied, not even the statutory ones which are to be discussed below. Finally, note that where illness incapacitates employees but not to the point of frustration, the right to be paid wages during that period of illness or incapacity is determined on the bases discussed above.

B. Death

275. As the contract of employment is a personal one, death of either party terminates the contract. Death does not extinguish the parties' rights which had vested at the point such as, say, the right to wages.

C. Bankruptcy

276. Unless the contract of employment depended on the personal attributes and characteristics of the parties, there is nothing about the bankruptcy of either party which, per se, leads to termination of the contract.[1] Bankruptcy may often give rise to frustration and, if this is so, the contract will be terminated. Where an act of bankruptcy occurs, a breach of a contract may ensue, giving rise to an action for damages. Note that bankruptcy law has an effect on the capacity of employees to recover arrears of wages. There are rules, interlocking with common law and minimum standards legislation, which govern the priority given to employees as creditors of a bankrupt employer.

1. *Thomas* v. *Williams*, (1834) 110 E.R. 1369 (employer bankruptcy); *Bailey* v. *Thurston*, [1903] 1 K.B. 137 (C.A.).

277. The winding-up of a company, similarly, does not lead to the termination of the contract of employment. It is treated as a breach of contract, giving rise to an action for damages in employees.[1] The rationale behind this is that it should not lie within an employer's power to terminate its obligations by the expedience of terminating its existence.

1. *Reigate* v. *Union Manufacturing*, [1918] 1 K.B. 592 (C.A.).

D. Dissolution of firms

278. As was seen above, where one of the parties to the contract of employment dies, the employment contract will be terminated. Where a firm is dissolved because one of the partners dies, the problem may be resolved differently. If the contract was of such a character as to make the personal attributes of the partners an essential element of the relationship then the result will be the same as if the contract had been concluded between two individuals viz., it will be considered terminated.[1] Where the personal attributes of the partners were of no concern, as will most often be the case, the contract will remain on foot.[2] Where a partnership's constitution has been changed by the retirement of one partner, the result will be the same, even though technically there has been a dissolution of the partnership. Where the retiring partner is replaced by another, the employee may treat this as a breach of contract because he cannot be forced to work with an employer he does not care for. But such a breach will be waived if the employee continues in service.[3] In any event, even if the employee should sue for damages for breach of contract in such circumstances, the amount awarded is likely to be nominal.[4]

1. *Tasker* v. *Shepherd*, (1861) 158 E.R. 237.
2. *Phillips* v. *Alhambra Palace*, [1901] 1 K.B. 59; *Harvey* v. *Tivoli, Manchester*, (1907) 23 T.L.R. 592 (D.C.).
3. *Hobson* v. *Cowley*, (1858) 27 L.J. Ex. 205.
4. *Brace* v. *Calder*, [1895] 2 Q.B. 253 (C.A.).

279. Where an employer's business is sold, common law would treat the contract as terminated. But, as was noted earlier, minimum standards legislation provides that where there is a sale (which usually includes a lease, a transfer or any other manner of disposition) of a business (which usually includes an activity, trade, undertaking or any part thereof), the employment shall not be deemed to be terminated and duties and obligations that the vendor owed to his employees shall now be borne by the purchaser.[1]

1. See paras. 162–163; *Re Bennie Electric*. An appeal under the Employment Standards Act – 3 Feb. 1972, Ont.

E. Termination by notice

1. Common law

280. A contract can be terminated because its object has been fulfilled. At common law, it could also be terminated at the will of either party, without the giving of prior notice, if the hiring was at will in the first place.

281. Sometimes the termination used to be made conditional on the doing of an act on the part of the employee which is prejudicial to the employer in the employer's opinion. Courts held that, in such cases, the employer merely had to show that he exercised this discretion given by the terms of the contract in a *bona fide* manner. The fact that the employer was wrong in his assessment was not significant.

282. Where the contract is for a definite duration, then it must run its course. But it is not always clear that it is for a definite duration. The abandonment of the presumption of yearly hiring has already been discussed above. It is still possible to have a yearly hiring and where there is one, the hiring continues for the full year, having become a contract of definite duration.

283. Where the contract is one of indefinite duration, as will be the usual case, it will be possible for either party to terminate it by giving appropriate notice. One of the most frequently raised issues, therefore, is the appropriateness of notice. In England there was a common law rule that menial servants were entitled to one month's notice.[1] This precept was manifestly the result of a social organization which was peculiar to England in those days. There being no corresponding social development in Canada, the English rule is not accepted here. Apart from this rule, the judiciary has adopted the approach that, in the absence of a specific term, the custom in the industry in the relevant geographic area will determine the amount of notice which ought to be given. If no established custom can be discerned, the courts must determine what reasonable notice in the circumstances would be. One very influential factor has been the periodicity of payment. It is common to hold that where an employee gets paid on weekly basis, he should be entitled to a week's notice. But this could not be, and is not, a hard and fast rule. The courts will take into account the difficulty the employee will have in being hired again. There seems to be an assumption that less skilled workers will find it easier to get new jobs than more skilled or specialized ones, leading to decisions which hold that reasonable notice in the latter kinds of cases should be longer than in the former groups. But, again, this can be treated as no more than a general trend. Cases are treated on a one-by-one basis within the general rules set out. Some examples follow.

1. *Pearce* v. *Lansdowne*, (1893) 69 L.T. 316.

284. An employee, working on a yearly contract, who was given one week's notice was held to have been given sufficient notice because he was paid on a weekly basis.[1] An executive who had worked as such for twenty-seven years was given three months' salary in lieu of notice, the employer saying that he was an employee hired by the month. It was held that, in view of the employee's position, a year's notice was the appropriate termination period.[2] An employee, who left a managerial position to supervise development of a new business, was given no notice at all when his new employers terminated his contract as the business venture was faltering. The court held that his managerial functions entitled him to six months' notice.[3] Finally, an employee hired as chief auditor for at least a year and who was paid on a monthly basis, had his contract of employment terminated after being given nine days' notice. He had agreed, prior to this event, to be paid on a weekly basis. It was held that he should have received three months' salary.[4] The old adage that much depends on the particular facts of the case has practical application in this area.

1. *Ek* v. *Eagle Shoe*, [1952] C.S. 85 (Que. S.C.).
2. *Duncan* v. *Cockshutt Farm Equipment*, (1956) 19 W.W.R. 554 (Man. Q.B.).
3. *Sky Rentals*, (1970) 70 C.L.L.C. para. 14,024 (Ont. S.C.).
4. *Fraser-Brace Terminal Contractors* v. *Mckeen*, [1955] 5 D.L.R. 267 (N.B.C.A.).

2. Statutes

285. Most legislatures have provided for minimum periods of notice which must be given to employees covered by the particular statutes.[1] They vary a good deal. Some minimum periods of notice are tied directly to the way wages are paid. Thus, if payment is made every week, a week's notice will be required. In the majority of jurisdictions, the minimum protection is only available to employees who have been employed for a specified length of time (usually three months). The amount of notice may vary with the length of time of service, increasing as length of employment increases (Alberta, Nova Scotia, Ontario) or be specified independently of length of service (Canada, Prince Edward Island, Saskatchewan). A particularly noteworthy provision is to be found in Nova Scotia. There an employee who has had more than ten years of employment with one employer cannot have her/his contract of employment terminated by notice. The employer must establish just cause to end the relationship.[2] The employer is given the right to pay an amount equal to the wages that would normally be earned by employees during the statutorily required notice period instead of giving notice. If the contractually agreed-upon or customary notice in the industry is longer than the statutory minimum, the employee is to get the benefit of the longer notice period. The employer is not required to give the statutory notice in a variety of circumstances which are the equivalents of frustration or conduct by the employee which amounts to a breach entitling the employer to repudiate the contract. Thus, impossibility of performance may avoid the need to give notice. Where there is an established practice which permits an employer to require an employee to retire at a particular age, the statutory provision will not apply. Nor will it where the employer has just cause to terminate the contract, or where the employer has offered reasonable alternative work to an employee, or different work as a result of an application of an agreed-upon seniority system and the employee refuses to accept such new work. The statutory notice period does not normally apply where an employee is put on temporary lay-off, as this is not a permanent termination of the contract provided this is not a breach of the contract or, if a breach, is waived. Where an employee has been asked to return after a temporary lay-off and refuses to do so after a specified time (usually seven days), the employer can terminate the contract without giving notice.

1. Canada, Part III, Division V.3; Alberta, s.38; The Employment Standards Act, R.S.M. 1970, c.E 110, s.35; The Labour Standards Act, S.N. 1977, c.52, Part VIII; Labour Standards

Code, S.N.S. 1972, c.10, ss.67A–73; The Employment Standards Act; S.O. 1974, c.112, Part XII; Prince Edward Island, s.79. Quebec Civil Code, Art. 1668; The Labour Standards Act, R.S.S. 1978, c.L–1, s.43.
2. At the federal level, employees employed for more than one year can only be dismissed for just cause, see section 5 below.

Group termination
286. In addition to these statutory protections, employees are also given some legislative aid in respect of mass lay-offs.[1] Most jurisdictions provide that where an employer intends to lay-off more than 50 employees in a four-week period (10 in Nova Scotia and Quebec), the employer is to notify the appropriate Ministry. This notice must also be given to the employees concerned, individually or by public notification. Thus the employees will be given at least four weeks' notice. As the number of intended lay-offs increases, so does the period of required notice. For instance, federally the provisions are: more than 50 less than 100, 8 weeks; more than 100 less than 300, 12 weeks; more than 300, 16 weeks. Pay instead of notice may be given. The employer is required to collaborate with the appropriate ministry in finding employment for the laid-off people. The intent behind notifying the ministry is to assist manpower organizational efforts.

1. Canada, Part III, Division V.2; The Employment Standards Act, R.S.M. 1970, c.E 110, s.35.1; The Labour Standards Act, S.N. 1977, c.52, s.53; Labour Standards Code, S.N.S. 1972, c.10, s.68(2), (3), (4); The Employment Standards Act, S.O. 1974, c.112, s.40 (and regulations under it); Manpower Vocational Training and Qualification Act, S.Q. 1969, c.51, s.45.

F. Termination for cause

287. In the discussion of termination by notice, it was indicated that there is no need for an employer to give notice of termination where the employer has cause to dismiss an employee. The examination of the legally implied obligations of an employee in paras. 255–260 made it clear that failure by an employee to obey may amount to a breach of contract entitling the employer to treat the contract as at end forthwith. The nature of the disobedience necessary was also discussed. Similarly it was noted that failure to exercise due skill and care would not amount to such a repudiation by the employee as would permit the employer to treat the contract as terminated, unless it was of a continuing, deliberate nature. It was indicated that much depended on the circumstances. In particular, if disobedience and/or lack of care is associated with insolence, the employer may have sufficient cause to end the contract of employment without giving notice. In a relatively recent English case, a gardener refused to obey an order to do a particular task on a Saturday morning and, when confronted by his employer, told him: 'I couldn't care less about your bloody greenhouse and your sodding garden' and walked off. This was held to amount to disobedience of a kind which entitled the employer to treat the contract as being ended.[1] It may well be that this kind of conduct might not, in modern

Canada, be so characterized, although, in the past, there are instances of similar displays of judicial respect for employers' dignity. The question is one of evaluation of operative industrial relationships. Sometimes, the employee's conduct on which termination without notice is justified is labelled wilful misconduct. Once again, the varied circumstances which can give rise to a finding of misconduct inhibit an attempt at description. Perhaps the best way of putting it is that where the conduct of the employee can be said to be a wilful repudiation of his obligations to abide by the essential elements of the contract, it can be treated as wilful misconduct. Thus, repeated insolence,[2] drunkenness[3] or morally improper behaviour[4] would amount to wilful misconduct. Similarly, criminal activity by an employee may be so characterized.[5] If the criminal offence occurs at the place of work it will usually amount to misconduct justifying termination without notice. Where the criminal activity occurs elsewhere and outside the normal hours of work, the crucial question will be how the conduct relates to the duties of the employee, or his ability to carry out such duties and to the business position of the employer.

1. *Pepper* v. *Webb*, [1969] 2 All E.R. 216 (C.A.).
2. *Markey* v. *Port Weller Dry Docks*, (1975) 4 O.R. (2d) 12 (C.C.).
3. *Clouston* v. *Corry*, [1906] A.C. 122 (P.C.).
4. *Chow* v. *Paragon Café*, [1942] 1 W.W.R. 519 (Sask. D.C.); *Denham* v. *Patrick*, (1910) 20 O.L.R. 347 (D.C.).
5. *Stewart* v. *King Motor Supplies*, [1941] 2 W.W.R. 634 (Sask.); *Pearce* v. *Foster*, (1886) 17 Q.B.D. 536 (C.A.).

288. The employer loses the right to treat the conduct of an employee as a repudiation of the contract of employment entitling him to terminate the contract of employment without notice if he accepts the employee's breach. The employer must, of course, be aware of the employee's breach to be defeated by his condonation of the conduct. He is also entitled to a reasonable time to react to a breach. Once again, much will turn on an assessment of the circumstances.[1]

1. *Warren* v. *Super Drug Markets*, (1965) 53 W.W.R. 25 (Sask. Q.B.); *Empey* v. *Coastal Towing*, [1977] 1 W.W.R. 673 (B.C.S.C.).

§5. Remedies for Breach of Contract

A. Employer remedies

1. Summary dismissal

289. As has just been seen, there are many situations in which an employer will be permitted to exercise a right of self-help in response to a breach of contract by an employee. He will be entitled to summarily dismiss the employee. This is by far and away the most potent weapon employers have in their arsenal and the remedy most frequently used by them. At common law the employer does not have the right to use any other form of discipline. For instance, an employer is not entitled to suspend an employee for a period without terminating the contract. If an employer seeks to penalize an employee in this way in response to a breach by that employee, the employer will himself be in breach of contract entitling the employee to remedial action.[1] Of course, an agreement to the contrary by the parties, or a custom to the contrary which is implied to be a term of the agreement, overcomes this rule. The rule sharply differentiates the common law of the contract of employment from the jurisprudence applicable to collective agreements. Many of the grounds giving an employer just cause to dismiss employees without notice may give good cause to an employer to discipline employees working under a collective agreement. But, after initial difficulties, it has become legislatively accepted that arbitrators interpreting the agreement have the remedial authority to substitute other forms of discipline for dismissal. Employers are also acknowledged to have a whole range of disciplinary powers available to them over and above the right to summarily dismiss employees for unacceptable conduct; see para. 742 *et seq.*

1. *Hanley* v. *Pease*, [1915] 1 K.B. 698.

290. In the federal jurisdiction, the standard collective bargaining regime's technique of reviewing the employer's right of summary dismissal has supplanted the common law doctrines. Any employee working under the umbrella of the Canada Labour Code and who has been employed for twelve months by one employer and who does not belong to a group of workers covered by a collective agreement, may complain within 30 days of his dismissal. An inspector will be asked to investigate and mediate the problem. Where this does not give the employee satisfaction, the employee may ask for an adjudicator for final determination. The adjudicator has the same powers to settle the dispute as does an arbitrator interpreting a just clause of a collective agreement.[1]

1. Canada, Part III.

2. Damages

291. Where the conduct of an employee does not amount to a breach which warrants the employer to terminate the contract without notice, the employer will be entitled to sue for damages incurred. For instance, there may be damage to property belonging to the employer. The employer also has the right of suing for damages where the employee leaves without giving appropriate notice. (Note here that the notion of agreed-upon, reasonable and statutorily provided minimum notice also applies to employees. As, in practice, the issue is usually whether the employer has given sufficient notice, little attention has been paid to this. The principles are the same as those which apply to employers.)

292. The measure of damages to which the employer is entitled is calculated in the same way that damages in contract law at large are assessed. There is to be liability for those losses which can be said to arise fairly and reasonably naturally from the breach or for losses which, although they do not arise naturally from the breach, may reasonably be supposed to have been in the contemplation of the parties at the time of contracting as being the likely result of breach. The latter part of this standard formulation means that, where the loss is of an extraordinary kind, to recover damages for it the possibility of its occurrence will have had to be spelled out explicitly when contracting.

293. Apart from damage done to inventory or property, it will be rare that the employer will be able to show more than nominal damages. Unless a worker is irreplaceable because of some special knowledge or skill, the requirement that a person suing for damages in contract has a responsibility to mitigate his losses, makes it unlikely that great loss will be incurred by an employer. The employer is not entitled to deduct the amount he claims in damages from any wages owing to the employee at the time of the breach. Nor can a term of the contract which is characterized as a penalty clause be enforced. It is conceivable that a contract has in it a provision that, in case of breach, a sum certain shall be payable to the aggrieved party. Where a court believes that this term is merely one intended to deter breach as opposed to being an agreed-upon estimate of the probable damage caused by a breach, the term will not be enforced. Thus, it is likely that a stated amount for any breach, no matter what its gravity, would be unenforceable.

3. Injunctions and specific performance

294. A contract of personal service cannot be specifically enforced. The very personal nature of the relationship dictates that the parties should not be forced to work with each other. As was noted above, an employer cannot discipline an employee for a breach by suspending him in order to obtain conformity. The employer cannot positively enforce a particular mode of performance. On the other hand, where an employer has treated the contract as terminated because of the alleged breach by an employee and the employee proves to a court's satisfaction that the employer was wrong in his assessment and, hence, act of dismissal, the court cannot force the employer to re-employ the employee. That would be tantamount to forcing the employer to work with an employee whom he may not wish to hire. Once again attention is drawn to the situation under a collective bargaining regime. There arbitrators interpreting awards and labour relations' tribunals have power to reinstate employees, that is, to specifically enforce contracts of employment.

295. There are situations which arise under the common law controlling individual contracts of employment which seem to lead to something like specific performance of contracts of employment. Where a contract explicitly provides that an employee undertakes to render his services exclusively for the employer, this clause will not be upheld by the grant of an injunction sought by the employer to prevent an employee from leaving his service. But where a similar result is sought by seeking an injunction to prevent breach of a contractual stipulation to the effect that the employee will not, during the term of the contract, render any of the services to be rendered for the employer for any

115

other person, the courts may grant the order restraining an employee from accepting other employment. The distinction made in the cases is between enforcing a positive covenant, that is, one requiring performance of the existing contract, and enforcing a negative covenant, that is, requiring the employee not to work in a particular way. The latter is acceptable because it may well leave the employee free not to perform the contract he wants to abandon. This assumes that the enforcement of the negative covenant will not, in fact, amount to the enforcement of the existing contract. To require the courts to make distinctions of this kind is to present them with unenviable tasks. To illustrate: The famous actress, Bette Davis, had entered into a contract which both required her to render her acting services exclusively to Warner Bros. and forbade her to accept acting work with any other person during the term of the contract. An injunction to force her to render services for the employer was refused; an injunction forbidding her to work as an actress with any other person for the remainder of the contract was granted. This was justified on the basis that the actress was a person of intelligence, capacity and means and that there was no evidence that, were she to refuse to fulfill her contract with Warner Bros., she would not be able to employ herself both usefully and remuneratively in other spheres of activity. That is, she was not effectively being forced to carry out the contract of employment.[1]

1. *Warner Brothers Pictures* v. *Nelson*, [1937] 1 K.B. 209; see also *Lumley* v. *Wagner*, (1852) 42 E.R. 687; *Bell and Atkins*, (1956) 56 C.L.L.C. para. 15,285.

B. Employee remedies

1. Damages

296. Where an employee has been dismissed summarily and he is able to prove that such dismissal was wrongful or where the claim is that the appropriate notice was not given, the employee is entitled to bring an action for damages. The measure of damages is the amount of wages the employee would have been entitled to receive had the correct period of notice been given. This amount is reduced if it can be shown that the employee had other suitable employment available before that period of notice would have elapsed. This is in accordance with the general law of contract rule that parties adversely affected by a breach of contract have a duty to mitigate their losses. The calculation of appropriate notice has already been discussed above. As to when the right to dismiss without notice arises, see para. 284. An employee entitled to damages for not having been given appropriate notice may seek to pursue his claim under the machinery of the minimum standards legislation, if the notice period for which recovery is sought coincides with the statutory minimum. Such procedures are quicker and less costly than the ones prevailing in the judicial system. All that is required in Ontario, for example, is a complaint by word of mouth or letter; an investigation will ensue and, if an employer appeals an adverse order which is subsequently made, a review will be ordered. In some provinces there are enactments which are descendants of very old English

Master and Servant Acts. These English statutes were aimed at restricting employees' freedom and they provided stiff criminal penalties for employees for leaving their masters' employ. One of the aspects of this stringent form of regulation was that it was also provided that masters would be committing a criminal offence if they failed to pay externally imposed remuneration. The modern Canadian equivalents provide a summary criminal procedure for the recovery of wages up to a limited amount. The claiming employee lays a complaint against his employer for non-payment of wages in the lowest court with criminal jurisdiction. The judge may discharge the employee from the service of the employer found to be in default and order the payment of wages for a certain period, or a lesser limited amount. In Alberta, reflecting the legislation's ancestry, the magistrate may impose a penalty on the defaulting employer.[1]

1. The Masters and Servants Act, R.S.A. 1970, c.228, s.5 (limit: lesser of 6 months or $500); Master and Servant Act, R.S.B.C., 1960, c.234, s.10 (limit: $50); The Master and Servant Act, R.S.O. 1970, c.263, s.4 (limit: $500 and costs).

297. Damages are not awarded for the manner in which a wrongful dismissal took place. It has already been noted that, contrary to the general rule, work is to be provided where working is more important than remuneration, as it is where an actor needs to perform to enhance his reputation. Thus, it is possible in such a case for an employee to recover loss of reputation damages. In addition, it is possible to recover damages where an employee has become depressed, anxious or ill as the result of a wrongful dismissal. In *Cox* v. *Philips Industries*[1] an employee was successful because the employer had, in breach of the agreement, not given the plaintiff an opportunity to do work of a prestigious kind. He had been relegated to being a mere cipher, embarrassing and discomfitting him. As this appears to be contrary to the traditional ruling that hurt and grief at dismissal are not compensable, it may well be that analytically this decision could be read down to a holding that to provide the employee with a certain amount of prestige and pleasure was within the parties' contractual expectations and that, therefore, damages were awarded for a breach of contractual term. Be that as it may, the development is an interesting one and may reflect a budding desire in the judiciary to recognize the increasing industrial demand for job satisfaction. Return to the parallel development noted in para. 237; see also para. 99.

1. [1976] 3 All E.R. 161. (Q.B.).

298. As was noted above, bankruptcy and the winding-up of a company may amount to a breach of contract. An employee may sue for damages in the usual way. Often there will be an arrears of payment of wages in the case of bankruptcy. The employee may then seek to recover as a creditor. This does not place the employee in a sound position. Under the Bankruptcy Act, the employees are not secured creditors and thus they take after secured creditors have exercised their rights. Amongst non-secured creditors, they rank fourth in order of priority of creditors. In addition, the statute does not protect employees in as many words, but rather clerks, servants, travelling salesmen, labourers or workmen, giving rise to interpretative difficulties.[1] Similarly, employees are creditors in respect of wages, salaries, commission or compensation, and questions such as whether severance pay due under a minimum standards statute falls under this rubric may arise. Such questions are complicated by the fact that the minimum standards legislation is provincial and the bankruptcy legislation is federal: issues as to whether the definition of wages in the former are applicable in the latter may arise.[2]

Protection is sometimes afforded to employees by making directors of corporations personally responsible for wages and vacation pay accrued. This has required legislative interference with the notion that the corporate entity is a person separate from its members.[3]

1. Bankruptcy Act, R.S.C. 1970, c.B–3, s.107.
2. *Re Lewis's Department Store*, (1973) 17 C.B.R. (N.S.) 113 (Ont.S.C.) (the provincial statute definition of wages including severance pay did not make severance pay wages for the purposes of the federal statute).
3. *E.g.*, The Business Corporations Act, R.S.O. 1970, c.53, s.139; Canada Business Corporations Act, S.C. 1974–75–76, c.33, s.114.

2. Quantum meruit

299. This means of recovery was discussed above. It will be available where there is no enforceable contract in existence, or where the employer's conduct is of such a kind that the employee is entitled to treat it as a repudiation and, therefore, to rescind the contract. The employee may then recover remuneration for the actual work done. He is not entitled to sue for damages on the basis of being entitled to notice and then for a *quantum meruit*. This remedy will seldom be of use to an employee, although it may be a way to recover remuneration for work done under a contract which is interpreted as not requiring pay unless a specified period of employment is completed. See para. 193.

Part II. Collective Labour Relations

Chapter I. Trade Unions and Their Organizations

§1. TRADE UNION MEMBERSHIP AND CHARACTERISTICS

300. The single most important feature of the modern Canadian trade union movement is that much of it is international in nature. International in this context means that the unions are American and Canadian in composition. In c.IV of the *Introduction* (*supra*), some of the major political, economic and social circumstances which give rise to developments of unionism in Canada were noted.

A. Size and number of trade unions

301. *Labour Organizations in Canada*, a publication of *Labour Canada*, reports that at the beginning of 1978, union membership stood at 3,277,968. This represented 31.3 per cent of the total work force and 39.0 per cent of the non-agricultural work force. As has been seen (Introduction, c.IV, *supra*), trade unionism is concentrated in a few major areas of the economy. Recently there has been a great increase in trade unionism in white collar sectors, particularly in the public services. At the time of writing the prospect of organizing banks has become a legal and practical reality. One of the remarkable aspects of the organized labour movement is the great number of unions which exist. There are 630 unions, only 18 having more than 50,000 members. The largest unions in the land at the beginning of 1978 were the Canadian Union of Public Employees (C.L.C.) with 231,000 members, the United Steelworkers of America (A.F.L.–C.I.O./C.L.C.) with 199,000 members, and the Public Service Alliance of Canada with 180,000 members. At that time, unions with headquarters in the United States accounted for 47.4 per cent of total union membership, as compared with 49.0 per cent in 1977. The slight decrease is, in large part, due to the development of national unionism in the white collar sectors mentioned above.

302. Finally note that, despite increasing consciousness, the amount of female participation in trade unionism is very low, hovering, at the end of 1977, somewhere between 7 per cent and 8 per cent of the total work force and 9 per cent to 10 per cent of the non-agricultural work force.

INTERNATIONAL AND NATIONAL UNIONS BY SIZE, 1978

Membership Range	International Unions		National Unions		Total	
	No. of Unions	Membership	No. of Unions	Membership	No. of Unions	Membership
Under 100	6	296	1	40	7	336
100–199	4	560	2	301	6	861
200–499	6	1,853	11	3,441	17	5,294
500–999	3	2,264	5	3,311	8	5,575
1,000–2,499	14	24,166	20	36,017	34	60,183
2,500–4,999	7	25,183	22	79,312	29	104,495
5,000–9,999	11	84,737	25	176,336	36	261,073
10,000–14,999	8	94,597	11	131,186	19	225,783
15,000–19,999	7	118,648	6	105,397	13	224,045
20,000–29,999	6	132,993	6	139,878	12	272,871
30,000–39,999	5	170,585	4	135,727	9	306,312
40,000–49,999	—	—	1	40,638	1	40,638
50,000–99,999	9	568,595	4	272,549	13	841,144
100,000 and over	2	329,000	3	513,493	5	842,493
Total	88	1,553,477	121	1,637,626	209	3,191,103

Source: Table 5, *Labour Organization in Canada 1978, Labour Canada.*

MEMBERSHIP OF REPORTING LABOUR ORGANIZATIONS AS A
PERCENTAGE OF NON-AGRICULTURAL WORKERS, 1962, 1970–1977

120

MEMBERSHIP OF REPORTING LABOUR ORGANIZATIONS AS A
PERCENTAGE OF TOTAL LABOUR FORCE, 1962, 1970–1977

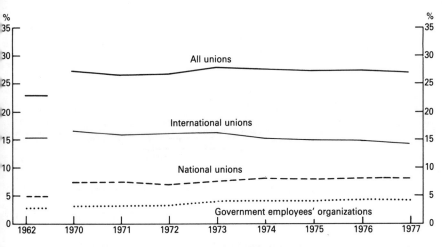

Source: Corporations and Labour Unions Reporting Act, 1977 (C.A.L.U.R.A.).

WOMEN MEMBERS OF REPORTING LABOUR ORGANIZATIONS AS A
PERCENTAGE OF NON-AGRICULTURAL PAID WORKERS, 1962, 1970–1977

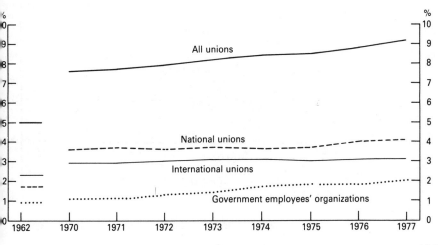

121

WOMEN MEMBERS OF REPORTING LABOUR ORGANIZATIONS AS A
PERCENTAGE OF TOTAL LABOUR FORCE, 1962, 1970–1977

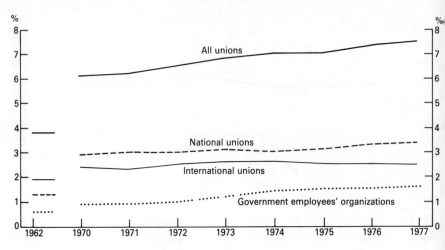

Source: Corporations and Labour Unions Reporting Act, 1977 (C.A.L.U.R.A.).

MEMBERSHIP OF THE SIX LARGEST INTERNATIONAL UNIONS
IN CANADA, 1962, 1970–1977

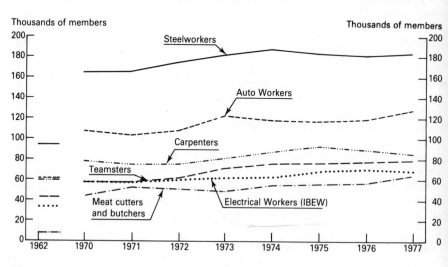

122

MEMBERSHIP OF THE SIX LARGEST NATIONAL UNIONS
IN CANADA, 1962, 1970–1977

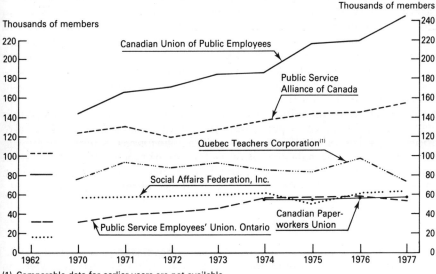

(1) Comparable data for earlier years are not available

Source: Corporations and Labour Unions Reporting Act, 1977 (C.A.L.U.R.A.).

B. Internationalism and nationalism

303. A fallacious impression would be given if it was thought that the formal structure of international trade unions meant that Canadian members of such unions are completely dominated by American governing bodies. This may be the case in some unions, but often, regardless of the formal structure, the Canadian branches of international unions have assumed a great deal of autonomy over their everyday affairs. Frequently such branches represent districts of the international unions. For example, the Eastern and Western Canadian branches of the United Steelworkers form Districts 5 and 6 of that union, with all the autonomy of all other Districts of that union in the United States. This permits control over bargaining, political and social activity and most internal trade union matters.

304. In addition, the 8th Canadian Labour Congress Constitutional Conference resolved that, in respect of Canadian autonomy in international unions, certain minimum standards ought to be followed. They included the election of Canadian officers by Canadian members. In some affiliates of the CLC, officers of the Canadian sections of the international unions are appointed by the International Executive. Although this CLC guideline is voluntary in nature, it has had an effect. For example: the Seafarers' International Union permits its

123

Canadian membership to elect Canadian officers; the Canadian membership of the United Steelworkers of America elects one national director and three district directors who sit on the international's executive, and the United Automobile Workers of America's Canadian membership elects one Canadian director who sits as an international vice-president. The C.L.C. Conference also resolved that policies of Canadian concern should be dealt with by Canadian elected officers and that Canadian officers should have authority to speak for their members in Canada. All of this has created a climate of consciousness in international affiliates of the C.L.C. of the need to accommodate Canadian national aspirations. Further, as has been noted, the increase in white collar unionism increases the influence of national affiliates in the C.L.C. This too is having some influence in persuading the international unions to give more formal, as well as informal, autonomy to Canadian unions. A recent manifestation is the proposed amalgamation of the Canadian branch of the Oil, Chemical and Atomic Workers International with the Canadian Chemical Workers' Union into one large Canadian union with the assistance of the International body.

§2. The Canadian Labour Congress

305. This is a union of unions. *Labour Organizations in Canada 1978* reported that, at the commencement of 1978, 2,203,812 workers were in unions directly affiliated or directly chartered by the C.L.C. This represented 67.2 per cent of the total membership. Of the remainder, 25.1 per cent belonged to unions not affiliated with any central labour congress, and the rest of the unions were affiliated with the Confederation of National trade Unions, Centrale des Syndicats Démocratiques, the Confederation of Canadian Unions and other such minor labour congresses.

Union Membership by Congress Affiliation, 1978

Congress Affiliation	Membership	
	Number	Per Cent
C.L.C.	2,203,812	67.2
A.F.L.–C.I.C./C.L.C.	1,281,495	39.1
C.L.C. only	922,317	28.1
C.N.T.U.	177,755	5.4
C.S.D.	38,083	1.2
C.C.U.	26,007	0.8
A.F.L.–C.I.O. only	10,573	0.3
Unaffiliated International Unions	96,278	3.0
Unaffiliated National Unions	665,088	20.3
Independent Local Organizations	60,372	1.8
Total	3,277,968	100.0

Source: Table 2, *Labour Organizations in Canada 1978, Labour Canada.*

306. The C.L.C. consists, thus, of international and national affiliates. It has 10 provincial affiliated bodies which look after provincial jurisdictional matters in respect of the provincial branches of the affiliates of the C.L.C. Amongst the major functions of the C.L.C. are the promotion of trade unionism and the protection of its members' rights. It has power to look for more members and has created organizing committees to this end. The C.L.C. has power to directly grant charters to unions, making them C.L.C. affiliates. But, in line with its aim to preserve existing unions, it is not to do so where the grant of a charter would mean the creation of a union whose jurisdiction would conflict with that of an affiliated national or international union. In a similar vein, the constitution of the C.L.C. forbids any of its members from seeking to organize workers where another has existing collective bargaining rights or rights to deal on behalf of certain workers (which is known as having a working relationship). Further, where some members agree to merge, thereby blurring jurisdictional lines, the C.L.C. has to approve of the agreement. An Impartial Umpire may be appointed to this end. In determining whether or not C.L.C. guidelines are being infringed, regard can only be had to what the concerned members' jurisdiction has been in the past, not to what it ought to be. The C.L.C. has moral authority, but very few sanctions to enforce these guidelines. It can, where a member has offended the C.L.C. rules (by raiding, espousing totalitarianism, acting discriminatorily, etc.) expel a member union if the majority of members so decide at the C.L.C. convention.

307. Conventions are held every second year. All members and local unions are entitled to send delegates and to present resolutions. These resolutions, if adopted, form the policy to be followed by the C.L.C. The C.L.C. frequently presents submissions to government in line with these policies, the provincial representative federations of the C.L.C. contacting the provincial legislatures, the C.L.C. lobbying the federal Parliament. Such submissions are not restricted to bread and butter labour issues. As well as being related to labour legislation, they may include briefs on the economic situation, wage and price guidelines, regional economic development, bilingualism, consumer affairs, immigration and the like. In addition, there has been a movement in the C.L.C. to assert itself as a major participant in executive decision-making at a national level. The notion is that major employer groupings, the C.L.C. and government should consult and negotiate on a formal, recurring basis in respect of matters affecting their and the nation's interests. This has been dubbed 'tripartism'. It has met with great opposition from some trade unionists. These people view the development with suspicion because they see it as a potential aggrandization of autonomy for the C.L.C. as a body separate from its member unions, and at these members' expense. Further, they are concerned that in the three-party bargaining structure proposed, government and employers would be natural allies, to the disadvantage of the labour movement. At the moment, the C.L.C. has stepped back from overt support for tripartism.

308. The C.L.C. provides research facilities and publicity for its members. It also has set up extensive educational programmes, including schools on bargaining, administration of agreements and on organizing. Through the International Confederation of Free Trade Unions, the C.L.C. maintains and supports ties with trade unions all over the world.

The international–national debate

309. Canadian trade union development was described in Chapter IV (*supra*, Introduction). It was noted that there always was both a symbiotic relationship between the American and Canadian trade union movement as well as a tension born out of nationalistic and political differences. This remains true to-day. On the whole, the reasons which led to the development of international unionism on the scale it did are still valid. In any event, the phenomenon is so well-entrenched that it is more difficult to change the situation than it once might have been. Dissidents find it hard to explain to workers what the situation would be if the dominance of international unions was diminished. Over recent years, it is fair to say, the best conditions have been obtained by workers in the major international unions. As times for workers generally get tougher, it may be that the old arguments about a different political role for trade unions will be raised again. In the federal election of 1979, the union movement in Canada openly set out to support the New Democratic Party. This development was not without opposition in the labour movement. This opposition argued that non-party politically based alliances had served the business unionism of international unions well. The debate is current and may well lead to conflict between the Canadian leadership of international unions and their parent groups in the United States.

310. Similarly, the sharpening of Quebec's separatists' desires underscores a potential problem relating to international unionism. Unions in Quebec in which franco-Canadians are not given a primary rôle may become less viable. It has already been noted that the Confederation of National Trade Unions is the modern descendant of what was a Quebec-based Catholic union movement. The Quebec Federation of Labour is the numerically dominant trade union representative group. It is associated with the Canadian Labour Congress and, therefore, international unionism. It often complains of the fact that, in the recent past, international unions have been insensitive to the French fact of Quebec by, for instance, publishing their newspapers in English.

311. One of the great attractions of international unionism in Canada is that, because of the huge size of this country, its small scattered population and quite disparate regional needs, it is difficult for a union to provide adequate collective bargaining resources. Being associated with an American-based union which, because of its sheer size, can provide co-ordination, expertise and funds, makes independent, small unions, which are sensitive to local needs, viable. This very benefit has in it the seeds for dissidence. Canadian branches of international unions sometimes feel that they are neglected and actually pay more in dues to the international parent than is returned by way of services in the form of advice, administration and strike funds. Sometimes figures in reports made under the *Corporations and Labour Unions Reports Act*[1] are cited in support of such claims. Unfortunately, the statistics kept under that Act are not informative enough to come to precise conclusions. What is of significance, though, is that there is such controversy from time to time. A somewhat contradictory argument is occasionally raised by people who oppose the presence of international unions. It is that the viability of so many small unions (because of their support by giant American unions) prevents the development of multi-craft, multi-industry Canadian unionism.

    1. R.S.C. 1970, c.C–31.

312. Overall, however, the dominance of international unionism is, at present, not seriously threatened and, in as much as international unions command a slightly declining proportion of the unionized work force, this seems to be due to the increase of unionism in the public sectors where American unions are clearly inapposite. So far, however, these emerging national unions have, in the main, affiliated themselves with the C.L.C., the body through which the internationals operate in Canada. They do not seem to feel uncomfortable at all about this co-existence.

§3. Legal Status of Trade Unions

A. At common law

313. Trade unions are groups of people who have come together to further their interests by acting in concert. They intend to combine in the giving and withholding of their members' labour to control the amount and kind of labour available. This will enable them to improve their bargaining position vis-à-vis potential employers. This notion of adversariness of interest to employers is endorsed by collective bargaining legislation such as that of Ontario which requires that a trade union has a constitution which specifies its objectives in this way.

314. At common law this made trade unions bodies which had purposes in restraint of trade. As such they were illegal bodies and thus were not recognized as legal entities for the purposes of suing and being sued. In addition, not being corporations or natural persons, they were, for the purposes of law, merely unincorporated or voluntary associations. That is, even if their purpose had not been in restraint of trade, they were merely to be treated as clubs were by the law. In nineteenth-century England this meant that trade unionists could be attacked as criminals, that they could not enforce agreements they obtained and that they could not protect their property. Despite these barriers, the development of trade unionism blossomed and legislation remedying the situation was passed.

315. In Canada, the common law position was the same. In 1872, an equivalent of the 1871 English *Trade Unions Act* was passed.[1] It defined a trade union as a body which, but for the statute, would have been treated as unlawful because its purposes were in restraint of trade. The effect of this has been, as will be shown below, that courts have treated trade unions as entities which can sue and be sued. But, as the Act only applies to registered trade unions and very few unions have ever been registered it is of minimal effect. In addition, there is a serious question as to whether the federal legislation is constitutionally valid. The argument is that in as much as it deals with civil rights and property questions, the jurisdiction to legislate is properly vested in provincial legislatures.[2]

1. *The Canadian Trade Unions Act* 1872 (Can)., c.30.
2. *Chase* v. *Star*, [1924] 4 D.L.R. 55; *Polakoff* v. *Winters Garment*; [1928] 2 D.L.R. 277; *Amalgamated Builders' Council* v. *Herman*, [1930] 2 D.L.R. 513.

316. The English and Canadian nineteenth-century statutes provided that agreements entered into by trade unions would not be enforceable merely because they were in restraint of trade, nor were the members of a trade union liable to criminal prosecution merely because the union had such purposes. By registration, trade unions could enable themselves to transfer property from trustee to trustee and empower trustees to bring or defend actions concerned with the property rights and claims of the union. The protection against criminal prosecution proved inadequate. The criminal law was amended to give immunity to a charge of criminal conspiracy if the relevant conduct engaged in took place during a trade dispute as defined. It also delimited the area of molestation and obstruction which would give rise to criminal responsibility by defining the circumstances in which watching and besetting (commonly referred to as picketing) was an excusable practice.[1]

1. *Criminal Code*, R.S.C., 1970 C–34, s.381.

317. The upshot of all this was that trade unions had some, but not all of the attributes with which a legal person such as a corporation or a natural person are endowed. Agreements between trade union members as to how they were to transact business or as to how they were to be employed, were unenforceable. Agreements about how trade union funds were to be used, how penalties were to be imposed, how subscriptions were to be raised and paid, were all unenforceable. This legislation advanced the cause of trade unions in as much as they could use concerted action, protect their property and escape some internal financial structures, although they were hampered in their fund-gathering activities and imposition of internal discipline. But the English judiciary, which seemed set on breaking down trade unionism, used this pro-trade union legislation to do so.

318. The courts had developed the torts of inducing a breach of contract and civil conspiracy. These torts did not present trade unions as such with much of a threat after the passing of the 1871–76 legislative measures. Trade unions had been partially legalized, but had not been made into legal entities which could sue and be sued apart from the statute. In 1901, the English House of Lords decided that a trade union could be sued in its registered name.[1] It is not clear from the judgments whether they were merely saying that to hold the union responsible in this way was merely a convenient way of allowing representative actions (which will be discussed below) or that they could be read as saying that, as a result of the legislation, trade unions had acquired sufficient of the attributes to become an entity which could sue and be sued as a corporation could. In any event, the threat to trade unions was so great that the English legislature passed a statute in 1906 to overcome the problems presented by the judicial reasoning.[2] In 1901 a precursor of the bill which finally overcame the effects of *Taff Vale* had been presented in England. A similar Act had been passed in British Columbia in 1902. The effect of this statute was to ban actions of a civil kind against trade unions. This Act was replaced in 1959.[3] Apart from that, Canadian jurisdictions have not passed protective legislation of the English kind. The decision in *Taff Vale* can, theoretically, only burden unions registered under the federal *Trade Unions Act* 1872, although occasionally courts have held unregistered trade unions capable of suing and being sued, perhaps on a seemingly mistaken notion of the applicability of English doctrine in Canada.[4] It is to be noted, however, that recent dicta in the Supreme Court of Canada suggested that the *Taff Vale* doctrine applies to unregistered unions.[5]

1. *Taff Vale Railway* v. *Amalgamated Society of Railway Servants*, [1901] A.C. 426. Similar later decisions are represented by *Amalgamated Society of Railway Servants* v. *Osborne*, [1910] A.C. 87 and *Bonsor* v. *Musicians' Union*, [1956] A.C. 104.
2. *Trade Disputes Act 1906*, 6 Edw. VII, c.47.
3. *Trade-unions Act of 1902*, (B.C.) replaced by *Trade-union's Act*, R.S.B.C. 1960, c.384.
4. *Metallic Roofing Co.* v. *Amalgamated Sheet Metal Workers' International Association* (1903), 5 O.L.R. 424 held: unregistered unions were not suable entities; to the contrary, *Centre Star Mining* v. *Rossland Miners* (1902), 9 B.C.R. 403.
5. *International Longshoremen's Association, Local 273* v. *Maritime Employers' Association* (1978), 89 D.L.R. (3d) 289, 296–302.

319. Apart from the effect of that federal statute, the question of legal personality of trade unions is determined by nineteenth- and early twentieth-century English common law as understood in Canada, except where it is varied by collective bargaining regime principles. We turn now to those principles.

B. Under collective bargaining

320. It is obviously impossible to treat trade unions as if they were unincorporated or voluntary associations which had no legal personality of their own for the purposes of the legislative collective bargaining schemes in Canada. The essence of those schemes is that trade unions are to be participants in their own rights. They are parties to enforceable collective agreements; they are responsible for the administration of the agreements; they may complain and be guilty of unfair labour practices as defined by the schemes; they are fixed with the responsibility of ensuring compliance by their members with statutes and agreements; they are, as trade unions, forbidden from engaging in discriminatory practices contrary to human rights legislation or anti-discriminatory provisions of the collective bargaining statutes. Manifestly, trade unions have been

129

given sufficient legal status under the regimes to accept and enjoy these responsibilities and privileges. But, because of the strange evolution of acceptance of trade unionism, there is no clear statement that trade unions are legal entities in the same way as corporations or natural persons. Conceptual difficulties remain as various jurisdictions have adopted differing resolutions of intractable problems.

321. Ontario and Saskatchewan, reacting to the common law situation and wishing to put trade unions in a position where they could use concerted conduct to bargain effectively, enacted legislation which defined trade unions as unincorporated associations. That is, they were groups which could neither sue or be sued as entities, unless the common law permitted it.[1] But, for the purposes of collective bargaining they are to be treated as entities, capable of enforcing collective agreements, enforcing arbitrators' awards, being subjected to prosecution, forcing the labour relations' board to carry out its functions, etc. Thus, although trade unions are not legal entities for all purposes, they are for many significant ones.

  1. The *Rights of Labour Act*, R.S.O. 1970, c. 416; *The Trade Union Act*, R.S.S. 1978, c.T–17.

322. Alberta, British Columbia, Manitoba and New Brunswick have directly achieved the above position by making unions legal entities capable of suing and being sued for the purposes of the reigning collective bargaining statues.[1] In the federal jurisdiction and in Nova Scotia, the collective bargaining legislation provides that trade unions may be prosecuted or prosecute in their own names.[2] The Newfoundland and Prince Edward Island statutes provide that unions should be treated as legal entities in a general sense.[3] In Quebec, a similar result is achieved by allowing any group of 15 persons to form a professional syndicate, which, in turn, can form a union. Professional syndicates may own property, sue and be sued, enter into collective agreements, etc. Further, under the *Code of Civil Procedure*, any group with a common purpose which has no legal personality and is not a partnership, may defend any action at law against it as an entity. It may also institute, as an entity, any legal proceeding provided that it deposits an appropriately authorized certificate stating it is a trade union within the meaning of the *Labour Code*.

  1. Alberta, 1973 S.A. 1973, c.33, s.58; British Columbia, S.B.C. 1973, s.147; Manitoba, S.M. c.L10, s.127; New Brunswick, R.S.N.B. 1973, c.104, s.114(2).
  2. Canada, R.S.C. 1970, c.L–1, s.193; Trade Union Act, S.N.S. 1972, c.19, s.76.
  3. Newfoundland, 1977, S.N. 1977, c.64, s.137; Prince Edward Island, R.S.P.E.I., 1974, c.L–1, s.43.

323. As can be seen, the statutory provision of legal personality is, with two exceptions, not of a kind which equates trade unions with natural persons or corporations. It does seem clear that for the purposes of collective bargaining legislation, the courts are to treat trade unions as fully capable legal entities. A recent Supreme Court of Canada decision has made this explicit in a case concerned with the federal statute.[1] In as much as trade unions are involved in causes of action arising outside the collective bargaining sphere, there is uncertainty.[2] A great deal seems to depend on the context in which the question is posed. When the principles relating to the governance of internal trade are examined below, we shall see that trade unions involved in collective bargaining are still treated as unincorporated associations.

1. *International Longshoremen's Association* v. *Maritime Employers'* (1978), 89 D.L.R. (3d) 289.
2. This could even be said about Newfoundland and Prince Edward Island where the statutes simply say trade unions are legal entities. A court could read that as implying that this could only apply to the incidents relating to the empowering statute. See generally Ch. 23, Carrothers – *Collective Bargaining Law in Canada* (Butt. 1965). Note the previous reference to the *ILA* v. *MEA* case in which it was suggested, *obiter dicta*, that trade unions were entities for all employment related purposes.

C. Representative actions

324. As it is possible that, apart from some specific circumstances, a trade union cannot sue or be sued as an entity in its own right, recourse may have to be had to the use of a representative action. The notion is that unincorporated associations could sue or be sued in their name if certain requirements were met. These were that, in respect of the right in controversy, the members of the association had a community of interest. Where this can be established, members who are properly constituted representatives of the unincorporated association – union in our case – may appear to bring or to defend an action. The Rules of Court of each jurisdiction provide for this means of conducting a judicial proceeding. What must be shown is that the members bringing the action comprise a class with identical interests,[1] or that, if a trade union is a defendant, different members of the union do not have separate individual defences. Again, if the trade union initiates proceedings in this form, a defendant will be enabled to defeat the form of the action if he can show that he would have different defences against different members of the trade union which is bringing the action as a representative. Perhaps the most important limitation when bringing a tortious suit against a trade union in this way is that, should a judgment against the trade union be obtained, a question will arise as to how the judgment is to be satisfied. It has been held that unless the plaintiff can show at the outset that the unincorporated association has set aside a special fund out of which such debts can be paid, a court will not allow a representative action to be brought against the association.[2] But note that, despite these difficulties, injunctions prohibiting picketing have been granted against trade unions on a representative basis.[3]

1. *Ross* v. *C.N.R.*, [1927] 3 W.W.R. 405; *Ackworth & McNair* v. *General Accident Assurance & Edwards* (1962), 31 D.L.R. (2d) 352, and see for application *Winnipeg Builders Exchange* v. *Operative Plasterers* 50 W.W.R. 72
2. *Body* v. *Murdoch*, [1954] O.W.N. 515; *Smith Transport* v. *Baird*, [1957] O.W.N. 405; *Anderson Block & Tile* v. *Mior*, [1961] O.W.N. 282.
3. *Cotter* v. *Osborne*, [1911] A.C. 137; *Canaday's Apparel* v. *Ross* (1957), 8 D.L.R. (2d) 273.

D. Legal status and democratic rule in trade unions

1. The need for democracy and the conceptual difficulty

325. Whatever the principles about the legal limitations on the right to sue and be sued by a trade union as a legal entity are, they arise out of common law decisions and statutory provisions which have never addressed themselves to the internal organization of trade unions. For this purpose, a trade union is still treated as if it were a gentlemen's club, that is, an unincorporated, voluntary association. Legally, the essence of such groups is that they are an aggregation of individuals who have agreed to effect certain purposes on the basis of agreed-upon rules. That is, there is a number of contracts whose terms are the rules or constitution of the association. As such, these rules could have any contents the members desire, provided they are not illegal.

326. But trade unions are not gentlemen's clubs. They have a vital effect on the lives of members and non-members. They affect employers and other sectors of society by the implementation of their rules in order to achieve their objectives. In such a context, it is significant what the contents of trade union rules are. In as much as the main business of trade unions is collective bargaining, it is premised on the notion that the suppression of individuals' desires is worthwhile because all individuals in the group will, eventually, be better served by such suppression. But, in line with societal values, there will be a perceived need to ensure that individuals' rights are not suppressed unduly, that majoritarian principles do not ride roughshod over minority interests. This imports precepts of democratic procedures and doctrines into collective bargaining. Yet, to require a trade union to behave as a democratic institution such as a legislature might derogate from its ability to carry out its tasks. Bargainers must appear to have full authority when sitting at the bargaining table; decisions must be capable of being made without having to go back to the membership for authorization; freedom must exist to bargain away some people's rights to obtain a better overall package, etc. That is, democratic principles will be reached out for, but they must necessarily be compromised. It would be difficult enough to do this even if the relationships within a trade union could be settled by external fiat of those who regulate collective bargaining. It is exceedingly difficult where, for these purposes, a trade union's internal affairs are treated as a matter of private contract-making, as if a trade union were a gentlemen's club with all the rights to restrict and control membership according to its whim. Accommodation of these very different concepts inevitably leads to complexity in the law.

2. The local–parent relationship

327. The pivotal organization for the purposes of collective bargaining is the local bargaining agent or trade union. When discussing the structure of trade unionism in Canada above, the emphasis was on national and international unions and their affiliations. These central bodies, however, are made up of many branches, the locals, who usually bargain directly with a particular employer. Where this is the situation, the local may have been created by the central union granting a charter to a local association which seeks to establish itself as a bargaining agent. This gives the local a ready-made constitution. This is important because it enables a labour-relations' board, familiar with the chartering union, to find that the applicant local is a trade union which satisfies the requirements for certification. In addition, the local obtains the valuable assistance and services of a large, well-organized entity. The C.L.C. can also issue charters. Sometimes a local group's members will agree that they will not become a union until they have obtained such a charter. Sometimes, however, a local seeks affiliation after formation as a trade union and/or certification as a bargaining agent. Other local groups never seek affiliation with anyone else. The concern here is with the situation in which a parent–local relationship has been created.

328. In such cases, the decision to organize in a particular way was made for collective bargaining purposes. Conceptually this ought to mean that difficulties should be resolved from within the framework of collective bargaining logic. For instance, if the local is merely a creature of the parent in order to bolster its jurisdiction and, hence, power in the industry, it might make sense to say that, should the parent withdraw its charter from the local, the local would cease to exist, or, if the parent sought to merge with another union, that it could dictate what should happen to the local and its assets. But, on the whole, the courts have resisted this approach. They prefer to treat the relationship of local and parent as a contractual one. If it is seen that, as a matter of contract, there was never any local organization, then they will treat the withdrawal of a charter by the parent as a termination of the local.[1] Where this is not seen to be the contractual relationship, questions of the survival of the local,[2] the splitting-up of assets upon attempted dissolution,[3] the right of a parent to create a competing local[4] and the right of the parent union which puts a local union under its trusteeship (for failure to comply with the parent's and/or collective bargaining rules) to bargain on behalf of the local membership are all decided by reference to contract principles. That is, the rules of the local, the parent and the terms of their agreed-upon relationship are treated as the terms of a contract which require interpretation. This may not adequately reflect the purposes and aims of the various groupings or the needs of the collective bargaining regime, given the fact that the parent-union/local union relationship is one concerned with economical and political power and the mechanism to create the relationship, contracting, is merely a legal convenience and is not likely to express the real goals and aspirations of the participants. Let us, by illustration, make these abstractions a little clearer.

1. *Jubilee Lodge No. 6* v. *Carmen's Council Section 'A'*, [1920] 56 D.L.R. 318; see also *Kuzych* v. *White*, (1947) 2 D.L.R. 496.
2. *Re International Nickel of Canada, Shedden* v. *Kopinak*, [1949] O.R. 765; see also *Re International Union of Operating Engineers*, 4 W.W.R. (N.S.)264.

3. *Lakeman and Barrett* v. *Bruce*, [1950] 3 D.L.R. 146; see also *McMillan* v. *Yandell*, (1972) O.R. 146.
4. *Local 1571 I.L.A.* v. *International Longshoremen's Association and Local 1764 I.L.A.*, [1951] 3 D.L.R. 50.

329. In one case, the majority of a local wished to become a local affiliated with a rival parent union. It was held that the original parent union could, by withdrawing its charter from the local, have all the assets of the local returned to it. That is, the local was blocked from freely exercising its majority's wishes because of the particular contractual relations which had been created.[1] Again, in *Re International Nickel of Canada., Shedden* v. *Kopinak,*[2] the contract of affiliation between local and parent stipulated that, as long as there were 10 members who wanted to remain in the local, the local as such could not transfer its affiliation to another parent union. In that case, a large majority wished the local to change its allegiance but were prevented from doing so by the enforcement of this contractual term. Thus, democratic principles central to collective bargaining notions may be frustrated by judicial reliance on contract principles pertinent to the rules of gentlemen's clubs.[3]

1. *Lakeman and Barret* v. *Bruce*, n. 3.
2. N. 2.
3. See generally, Ch. 29, Carrothers – *Collective Bargaining Law in Canada* – (Butt. 1965).

3. The right to belong to a trade union

330. Perhaps the single most important right trade unions have won is the right to have enforceable security clauses inserted into collective agreements. Closed shop, union shop and the Rand formula are discussed in paras. 497–501. What they import is that in many – most – circumstances, membership of a trade union which has won collective bargaining rights is a prerequisite (subject to the limited right of conscientious objection) to obtaining or retaining a job. In the absence of protection, individuals' rights may be put in jeopardy. Because trade unions are still treated as unincorporated associations when the question of whether or not they can sue or be sued or participate in collective bargaining is not in issue this area is governed by legal rules which seem to be out of step with the reality of modern labour relations.

331. As the members of an unincorporated association are bound to each other contractually on the basis of the rules of the association, it follows that they have rights against each other should there be a breach of the rules adversely affecting them. It also follows that persons who are not parties to the contractual arrangements have no rights under it. Thus, applicants for membership have no standing in law to become members of a trade union. In one well-known English case it was suggested that, where a person had to belong to an unincorporated association to earn a living, such a person could not arbitrarily be denied access to membership. The suggestion was that there was something called a right to work, akin to a property right, which would give such a person legal standing to be considered for membership.[1] This notion has been raised in

Canada but not yet accepted. In *Kuzych* v. *White*,[2] it was held by one judge that, if a trade union had the right to have a closed shop, it would amount to unacceptable totalitarianism not to recognize the right of people to work at their trade by giving them access to membership of the trade union. This case went to the Privy Council where this argument was not adumbrated. Another way that the argument supporting a right to work has been advanced is by reasoning that, as the collective bargaining legislation gives employees a right to join a union, whenever a closed shop arrangement is entered into, employees must have a right to belong to the trade union concerned otherwise their right to join a union would be rendered meaningless. This argument is bolstered by contrasting the right to join with the right to belong which are the forms respectively used in the Ontario and Alberta Legislatures. But this arrangement has been judicially rejected, it being argued that if the right to join was intended to mean the absolute right to be a member of a particular union (if occupationally qualified), the legislation would have explicitly stated this.[3]

1. Per Lord Denning, *Nagle* v. *Feilden*, [1966] 2 W.L.R. 1027, 1033.
2. Per O'Hollaran, J. A., [1940] 4 D.L.R. 187, 191.
3. *Gee* v. *Freeman* (1958), 16 D.L.R. (2d) 65; see also *Guelph* v. *White and Carron* [1946] 4 D.L.R. 114.

332. Some of the disastrous effects of using inapposite common law concepts have been ameliorated by the practices of the labour relations board. As noted, boards will not certify as bargaining agents unions which have rules which would prevent members of the apposite bargaining unit from belonging to the union. Because practices may modify the rules of admission to membership, boards have been given discretion to interpret these rules.[1] This protection is well short of a right to join a union. An additional protection is available to prospective employees in that unions and employers are not permitted to enter into agreements which discriminate against people on certain bases. Similarly, some collective bargaining statutes, such as in Ontario, will not grant bargaining rights to trade unions with rules which discriminate on such bases as sex, age, race, national origin, etc.

1. *Metropolitan Life Insurance Company* v. *International Union of Operating Engineers, Local 796* (1970), 11 D.L.R. (3d) 336 and legislative reaction to this decision.

4. The right to remain in a trade union

333. Trade union security provisions may require dismissal of employees who cease to belong to a trade union. Usually the employer will not have to dismiss a person expelled from a trade union if the reason for that expulsion is that that person became a member of another trade union, agitated against the union at a rival union's behest or otherwise dissented in a reasonable manner, etc.[1]

1. *E.g.*, s.38(2) *Labour Relations Act*, R.S.O. 1970, c.232, as am.

334. The question of whether or not an expelled member has a right of redress against a trade union has been approached by the courts on the basis of interpreting the contract between the members. Consequently, if the rules of the trade union, non-compliance with which led to the expulsion, were illegal in themselves or had illegal purposes, the courts have held the expulsion wrongful.[1] But where the circumstance was not so obviously contrary to enforceable public policy, the judiciary has taken its starting point as being that it ought not to question the contents of the rules. But, because the possible danger to individual rights is high, given the power of trade unions in the labour market, the courts have used age-old manipulative techniques to provide some remedial processes.

1. *SIU* v. *Stern* (1961), 29 D.L.R. (2d) 29; *Tippett* v. *International Typographers Union* (1976), 63 D.L.R. (3d) 522; *Pollock* v. *Alberta Union of Provincial Employees* 12 A.R. 398.

Judges as contract interpreters

335. Courts have been adamant that a domestic tribunal such as, say, a disciplinary body of a trade union, cannot arrogate to itself the right to interpret the contractual terms of the association. The courts are to be the final arbiters of how the contractual terms binding the members, i.e., the rules, should be interpreted. This, of course, allows them – should they so desire – to imply terms into the contract between the members. Such a tack is most likely to be taken when a court feels moved to protect an individual from the economic power a trade union wields. That is, where a court implicitly has some sympathy for the notion of a right to work. Thus, in one case it was held to be an implied term of the membership contract that, where a hiring hall was operating, the trade union could not discriminate between its members with respect to job opportunities in order to follow an unreasonable policy.[1] But courts are limited in their scope when implying terms. They cannot be too fanciful. In any event, this technique for implementation depends so much on unarticulated premises that its merits are dubious.

1. *Hornak* v. *Patterson* (1966), 58 D.L.R. (2d) 175; *C.P.R.* v. *Building Materials etc. Union*, (1972) 2 W.W.R. 535 and Lord Denning in *Lee* v. *Showmen's Guild*, [1952] 2 Q.B. 338, 341.

Requirement of good faith

336. The domestic tribunal, set up under the trade union's rules to deal with alleged breaches of the rules, must act without bias. While reasonableness of result is a good indication of a lack of malice, a court should not find a lack of good faith merely because it does not like the determination of the tribunal. Indeed, because it is a domestic tribunal, the mere fact that the members of the tribunal have a view of the policy which they wish to see pursued relating to the matter in dispute will not amount to lack of good faith. What a court will be looking for in the tribunal is an openness to listen to argument, no more.[1]

1. *Gee* v. *Freeman* (1959), 16 D.L.R. (2d) 65; *Bimson* v. *Johnston* (1957), 10 D.L.R. (2d) 11; *Evaskow* v. *International Brotherhood of Boilermakers* (1970), 9 D.L.R. (3d) 715.

Natural justice
337. The two previous devices could have been grouped under this rubric. They frequently are and were merely separated out for simplicity in presentation. Natural justice seems to imply that there should be a fair hearing. As the courts are to be the arbiters of what is fair, it is not surprising that the procedural safeguards they insist on (in addition to requiring good faith) closely resemble the practices surrounding the judicial processes. Thus, notice must be given to the member under attack.[1] He cannot be denied the opportunity to attend union meetings at which his fate is to be discussed and determined. Indeed, where a trade union claimed its rules permitted such exclusion, a court held that such terms of the membership contract were not acceptable.[2] The right to cross-examine and other such adversarial process trappings do not necessarily have to be available to the member under attack, but if too many of these tools are denied a court may well determine that there has been a lack of natural justice.[3]

1. *Re Busche and Nova Scotia Teachers* (1976), 62 D.L.R., (3d) 330.
2. *Hughes* v. *SIU* (1962), 31 D.L.R. (2d) 441.
3. *Gee* v. *Freeman, supra.*; *Tippett* v. *International Typographers, supra.*

338. One of the limitations on the right of an aggrieved member to seek redress in the courts is that the member may have to exhaust all remedial avenues available under the trade union's rules. This is certainly so where the union's rules provide so expressly, but a court might be willing to imply such a term where the rules of the union provide a system of appeals. The Privy Council has authoritatively decided that the complaining member should exhaust his remedies under the rules first.[1] Although this is, therefore, the basic principle it is more honoured in breach than by acceptance. The courts have undermined it in two ways. They have held that if the original disposition was totally unacceptable because the action taken by the trade union was outside the scope of its own rules, there is no need to exhaust the remedies under the rules. Thus, when a union purported to expel a member at a general meeting, without attempting to adhere to its own rules for laying charges and processing them, it was held that the expelled member could get a declaration of his rights and damages straight away from a court.[2] Another possible means of circumventing the rule is by holding that, if the union acted in breach of the rules of natural justice, there will be no need for an aggrieved member to exhaust his remedies. The reasoning is that, whatever the rules of the union are, they cannot deny natural justice. But the argument is contrary to the founding decision, *Kuzych* v. *White*, where there was a breach of natural justice, yet the plaintiff was held to the obligation of exhausting his remedies. To counter this, it has been noted that in *Kuzych* v. *White* the breach of natural justice could be repaired if the grieving member went through the appeal procedures and that, therefore, it was fair to require him to continue to pursue the internal processes. It will not always be fair. This has brought us to the third and most significant way of avoiding the requirement of exhaustion of domestic remedies. It may well be that the appeal procedures provided for in the union rules are inadequate. This is particularly likely in Canada in respect of international unions. These unions can in no way be said to be unfair in respect of the democratic nature of their rules. To the contrary: as their rules may be based on the American parents' which, in turn, have to comply with legislation requiring a good number of protective safeguards for individual members, they are, on the whole, likely to be as satisfactory as any national union's rules. But, it may be that the final appeals have to be heard in the United States. This could be treated by courts in Canada as unreasonable. Further, the ultimate appeal may be to a convention of the union which may only be held every two years. In one case in which this was so, a court held that the plaintiff could be asked to exhaust his remedies in the union because he could not show he would suffer any damages as a result of the delay.[3] In another case, where it was not clear when the next union convention – which was the final appeal – would take place, the court did not force a plaintiff to comply with an exhaustion clause in the trade union's rules.[4]

1. *Kuzych* v. *White*, [1951] 3 D.L.R. 650.
2. *McCrae* v. *Cargo and Gangway Watchmen of St. John, N.B.*, [1953] 1 D.L.R. 327.
3. *Local 471, I.L.A.* v. *International Longshoremen's Association*, [1951] 3 D.L.R. 50.
4. *Gee* v. *Freeman, supra*.

Status as a tool

339. From time to time, the absurdity of treating the relationship between members and their trade unions as being contractual in nature leads to an argument that, while it takes the legal concept of contract to set up the relationship, once it exists it creates rights and duties which are distinct from the contract. That is, the trade union member has a status which is to be recognized by law as giving him certain rights which the union cannot erode, regardless of the terms of the original contract. Such a legal concept would enable courts to reflect the economic and political reality of labour relations. The Supreme Court of Canada has addressed the argument. Only one of the justices accepted the reasoning; it was explicitly rejected by others.[1] This does not mean that this development has no future. It is still open to courts to say the question has not been finally decided and that possibility alone permits courts to make decisions on status-like notions while ostensibly using contract principles. If there are enough decisions of this kind, courts may eventually be able to say that the status of a member of a trade union has been legally recognized. This speculation is offered because it seems a desirable and likely development.

1. *Orchard* v. *Tunney*, (1957) 8 D.L.R. (2d) 273. Locke, J. supported the notion of status, but Rand, J., whose judgement was a leading one, rejected it.

5. Fair representation

340. As well as the power a trade union has over the employment opportunities of workers, it also has very important influence over the nature of working conditions workers obtain if employed. As the sole bargaining agent for a group of employees, it is in a position to differentiate between these employees when bargaining with an employer. Collective bargaining principles would be undermined by telling a trade union how to use its economic power. This inhibits the imposition of requirements on how to bargain. But, gradually, some rules are developing which oblige trade unions to take into account the needs of individual workers in the unit.

341. The first relevant development took place in the United States. Unsurprisingly, it was the judiciary which took up the cudgel for individuals. It is not wedded, conceptually, to the collective aspect of labour relations. It held that implicit in a statute giving exclusive bargaining rights, there is a duty to exercise that power fairly, without hostile discrimination against any of the employees represented.[1] Another 18 years elapsed before a labour relations' board accepted this notion.[2] This reluctance can be understood because of the labour relations' board inherent respect for freedom in collective bargaining. But now it is a well-established doctrine and can best be described by saying that the bargaining representative has a duty not to draw irrelevant and arbitrary distinctions amongst those it represents. Further, it has been recognized that this duty is applicable to the administration of the collective agreement as this, notionally, is part and parcel of a continuous bargaining process. In Canada, the courts have been much more reluctant to develop similar doctrines, but there has been some fruitful statutory evolution.

1. *Steele* v. *Louisville and N.R.R.*, 323 U.S. 192 (1944), *Wallace Corp.* v. *N.L.R.B.*, 323 U.S. 248 (1944), *Ford Motor* v. *Huffman*, 345 U.S. 330 (1953).
2. *Miranda Fuel Co. Inc.* 140 N.L.R.B. 181 (1962).

(a) Common law

Bargaining
342. There seem to be very few decisions which impose a duty on a union to fairly represent its members during the agreement-making process. In one case it was held that a union should keep its members informed about its proposed actions, such as telling them that picket lines were to be established, boycotts imposed or strikes called.[1] It could be that courts could spell out, as their American counterparts did in respect of similar statutes granting exclusive bargaining agency rights, impairing the duty to bargain in good faith, prohibiting discriminatory eligibility rules and terms in collective agreements, a duty to fairly represent members in the bargaining process. But note that the American statute had a specific provision allowing for the enforcement of rights under the labour legislation by way of civil remedy, a provision not found in Canadian statutes. Further, the manifest difficulty of assessing what the contents of such a duty ought to be is a powerful dissuader. It is not surprising that the judiciary has so far restricted itself to spelling out that, if there is such a duty, it merely requires a union to abide by procedural safeguards.

1. *Tippett* v. *International Typographers* (1976), 63 D.L.R. (3d) 522, 547.

Grievance process

343. There is only one important judicial pronouncement to the effect that a union has a duty to fairly represent a member of the bargaining unit in the grievance process. With few exceptions,[1] the union being the party to the collective agreement has the sole right to bring grievances about the interpretation of that agreement. Thus, an employee could be seriously disadvantaged if his bargaining agent chose not to process his claim. In *Fisher* v. *Pemberton*,[2] the plaintiff alleged that the union had not treated him fairly because he was a member of a rival union. The court upheld his claim that he had been discriminatorily treated. The American courts had, once they had devised a cause of action on the basis of the implications arising from the statutes, characterized it as a tort action. This entitled the successful plaintiff to damages regardless of his rights under the collective agreement. In *Fisher* v. *Pemberton*, the court seemed to take a different approach. Having found that the union had acted improperly, the court then considered whether the plaintiff would have succeeded in an arbitration should it have come to pass. It decided that he would not have and awarded him $1 damages.

1. *E.g.* Part IV *Public Service Staff Relations Act*, R.S.C., c.p–35.
2. (1970), 8 D.L.R. (3d) 521. For another judicial decision in which the duty of fair representation was raised, see *Longmore and Gebbie* v. *U.A.W., and Ford Motor*, 74 CLLC., par. 14, 222.

(b) Statute

344. There have been enactments in British Columbia, Quebec, and Ontario, as well as federally, which explicitly provide that the bargaining agent is not to act arbitrarily, discriminatorily or in bad faith in the representation of members of the bargaining unit.[1] For the sake of convenience, when specific legislative references are made, they are to the Ontario statute.

1. British Columbia S.B.C. 1973, c.122, s.7(1); Labour Relations Act, R.S.O. 1970, c.232, as am., ss.60 60(a); Labour Code, L.Q. 1977, c.41, s.38*b*; Canada, R.S.C. 1970, c.L–1, s.161.1.

345. The draftsmen relied on the American experience in defining the duty of fair representation. Despite some controversy, the dominant theme in the United States is that the weight of a grievance is to be measured in terms of the group interest as assessed honestly by the bargaining agent. Accordingly, the Ontario Labour Relations Board has stated that a complaint under s.60 must be evaluated in light of the industrial realities and practices. It will take into account the fact that trade union officials are not professional advocates and that they do not have much time for reflection when making daily decisions. In the same vein, trade union arguments that they had to weigh the effect of bringing a grievance on future settlements and bargaining are to be given serious weight. The Board has concerned itself with defining arbitrariness, discrimination and lack of good faith from within a very particularized framework.[1]

1. *E.g., Ford Motor* [1973] O.L.R.B. Rep. 519; *Essex International*, [1972] O.L.R.B. Rep. 104.

Discrimination and bad faith

346. The Board emphasizes that what is required is a subjective evidencing of hostility or malice. It sees this aspect of the statutory duty of fair representation aimed squarely at eliminating discrimination by the bargaining agent on the basis of race, creed, colour, sex, age, as well as to prevent internal trade union political differences leading to invidious conduct and to inhibit interpersonal breakdown in a trade union.[1] A complainant will have established his claim under the statute where it is shown that the benefits of representation are conferred on one member of that bargaining unit and not him and where the union offers no legitimate reasons for such discrimination. Legitimate reasons are ones which relate to the collective agreement or to the conduct or skills of the employees involved.[2] It will be bad faith where there has been no open and frank discussions of the merits of the grievance.[3]

1. *Walter Princesdomu* (1975) O.L.R.B. Rep. 444; *Vancouver General Hospital Employees, and a Group of Employees*, [1978] 2 Can. L.R.B.R. 508 (B.C.T.R.B.); *Frank J. Nowotniak and George E. Ostby and Grain Workers*, [1979] 2 Can. L.R.B.R. 467 (C.L.R.B.).
2. *Ford Motor* [1973] O.L.R.B. Rep. 519; *Napanee Industries* (1972) O.L.R.B. Rep. 353.
3. *Ford Motor, supra* n. 2.

Arbitrariness

347. This head of the duty of fair representation arises most frequently. It seems that where a union's treatment of a grievance has been perfunctory, a breach of the duty will have been established.[1] The test is an objective one. It requires the union to put its mind to the grievance. Mistakes, if honestly made, even if due to human shortcomings such as laxness, will not make the union's conduct arbitrary.[2] The union must give an opportunity to the employee to present his case[3] and where there are internal trade union rules prescribing how a grievance ought to be processed, they must be followed.

1. *Diamond 'Z' Association*, [1975] O.L.R.B. Rep. 791.
2. *Walter Princesdomu*, [1975] O.L.R.B. Rep. 444; *B.E. Kreber and Douglas Aircraft of Canada, U.A.W.*, [1979] 3 Can. L.R.B.R. 235 (O.L.R.B.).
3. *O'Donnell*, [1972] O.L.R.B. Rep. 423; *R.C.A.* [1974] O.L.R.B. Rep. 60; *Britnell*, [1974] O.L.R.B. Rep. 275.
4. *R.C.A.*, [1974] O.L.R.B. Rep. 60.

Procedure

348. The complaint of a breach of the duty of fair representation is made to the Ontario Labour Relations Board under s.79 of the Act. A field officer is sent out to investigate and help attain a settlement. If this fails, a report is made to the Board which, after screening by a panel of the Board, may lead to a hearing. At such a hearing the board must determine whether there has been a breach of the duty and, if so, what damage the complainant has suffered.

Remedies

349. Section 79 of the Ontario Labour Relations Act under which the complaint is made gives very wide powers to the Board, including recommending reinstatement and awarding compensatory damages. Where there is a breach of duty of fair representation, it will usually mean that the complainant should have had a right to have a claim arbitrated. At this point, the Board will usually defer to the grievance arbitration process under the collective agreement. This permits honouring the integrity of the collective agreement as well as alleviating the effect of the unfair labour practice constituted by the breach of the duty of fair representation.[1]

1. For a full discussion see *Imperial Tobacco Products (Ontario)*, [1974] O.L.R.B. Rep. 418.

350. But, sometimes deferral to the grievance process is unsuitable. This will be to where there clearly is a clash between the union's interest and that of the grievor and arbitration might not be an acceptable remedy for the grievor. This can be solved as it was in *Imperial Tobacco*.[1] There had been a complaint under s.60 which, if established, would also constitute a breach of the collective agreement. The Board accepted the union's proposal that an arbitrator acceptable to the three parties – the employer, the union and the grievor – should determine whether or not the collective agreement had been breached. If it had not, the Board would have no further interest in the matter. If the collective agreement had been breached, then the complainant had to prove that the breach was caused by a violation of the duty of fair representation. If this was done, the Board would fashion an appropriate remedy. Apart from such unique situations, the Board will provide a remedy where the grievance process could not. This will involve it in interpreting the collective agreement.

1. *Supra*, n. 1.

351. One of the difficulties is that, in searching for adequate remedies, it may be necessary to make an employer accept a resolution such as reinstatement, a new job assignment, a change in seniority orderings, and the like. The Board has accordingly made employers parties to such proceedings where necessary. Indeed, it may be that failure to notify the employer and to give him standing in the proceedings may amount to a denial of natural justice.

(c) Natural justice again

352. As has just been noted, there will be occasions when a union's interests will conflict with that of some of the employees it represents. It could come about that, when a trade union seeks redress for some of the employees in the unit, the result obtained will be adverse to other persons in the unit. The logic of collective bargaining dictates that, if the union is acting honestly to promote the good of the majority over the long haul, this is a cross that individuals must bear. But there have been some startling judicial developments which give remedies to employees aggrieved in this fashion over and above the jurisprudence relating to the duty of fair representation discussed thus far.

353. In one case, a grievance was brought to interpret the promotion clause of a collective agreement. The arbitrator ordered that a majority of the grievors be given positions filled at that time by other persons in the unit. Three of those incumbents were present at the hearing but played no part in it. Altogether six positions had been contested. The six incumbents claimed, in a judicial hearing, that the arbitrator's ruling should be set aside because they were not given an opportunity to participate in the hearing. The Ontario Court of Appeal agreed with this argument. Acknowledging that a union has to differentiate between employees, it was nonetheless felt that where the interests directly in issue were of a kind which related to substantial employment benefits, the employees whose interests would be so affected were entitled to the safeguards provided by the principle of natural justice. This was so, even though in many cases the union's opponent in the grievance, the employer, would put forward much of the argument that the non-represented employees might make. This, apparently, was not sufficient protection because the employer would only be putting forward those coincidental arguments and evidence which suited his personal interest.[1]

1. *Re Bradley and Ottawa Professional Fire-Fighters Association*, [1967] 2 O.R. 311.

354. This reasoning was re-affirmed by the Supreme Court of Canada. There the union had sought arbitration in respect of the interpretation of the collective agreement. There was no particular employee whose grievance was being processed. In fact, however, the arbitration process was being used by the union to force a recalcitrant bargaining unit employee to pay union dues or be dismissed. The arbitrator knew this full well and made this clear in his ruling. He not only upheld the union's interpretation of the agreement but concluded that the obstinate employee, Hoogendoorn, would have to be dismissed if he continued to refuse to pay union dues. The Supreme Court held that Hoogendoorn should have been allowed to participate in the proceedings.[1] In as much as this case could be treated as that of an individual whose substantial benefits were being directly affected by an arbitration, the decision would merely be an echo of *Bradley*. But this case was not one which concerned an individual's grievance, that is, one relating to the seniority of individuals, promotion, wage rates or opportunity to work overtime, but rather a policy grievance, that is, one in which the parties as part of the on-going collective bargaining process attempt to mould and shape the collective agreement.

1. *Re Hoogendoorn and Greening Metal Products and Screening Equipment* (1968), 65 D.L.R. (2d) 641.

355. The need to satisfy the doctrine of natural justice in such cases requires that the affected employees be given notice of the arising of the issue in such a manner and in sufficient time to allow adequate preparation for an appearance to be made. In addition, the employee ought to be permitted to be represented by counsel if this is his desire. Manifestly, this development threatens one of the very fundaments of collective bargaining. It undermines the trade union's right to behave authoritatively and diminishes the possibility of maintaining an informal, expedited means of settling problems which arise during the life of the collective agreement. This latter aspect is serious: there is no right to use the economic sanctions of lock-out or strike during this period. The parties, therefore, need to have access to a mechanism which expertly settles disputes on the basis of an understanding that these parties have an on-going relationship which is best maintained by respecting their autonomy and wisdom.

356. Unsurprisingly, arbitrators have been loath to give these judicial developments much scope. In some cases, arbitrators have insisted on full compliance with the requirements of natural justice. In others, substantial compliance has been had, for instance, by informing employees after the hearing had commenced that they had a right to participate and then rehearsing the evidence and argument thus far so that they could join in.[1] In yet other cases, failure to have compiled has been seen by the arbitrators as not being significant because the grievor's case had been dismissed. As the employee who should have been notified could only have been adversely affected if the grievor had won, failure to so notify was rendered unimportant.[2] In some instances, verbal notice rather than formal notice was seen as sufficient adherence to the doctrine by arbitrators[3] and, sometimes, a hearing is held, an award made but not made effective; notice is then given to employees who are likely to be affected. If the notified employees show no interest, the arbitrators then go on to give the award life.[4] But, most importantly, a study done by S. Tacon shows that in 50 per cent of policy grievances and 40 per cent of individual grievances, arbitrators have ignored the requirement altogether. Further, even where notice is given, more than 50 per cent of the people notified did not attend; only 27 per cent participated in the hearing and only 9 per cent were separately represented. S. Tacon predicts that, despite the judiciary's clear wish for the *Bradley–Hoogendoorn* doctrine to prevail, the realities of labour relations will relegate it to insignificance.[5]

1. *Re Orenda* (1972) 1 L.A.C. (2d) 73.
2. *Re Carling Breweries* (1968), 19 L.A.C. 110.
3. *Re Canadian Acme Screw & Gear* (1970), 22 L.A.C. 80.
4. *Re Edwards of Canada* (1974), 6 L.A.C. (2d) 137.
5. S. A. Tacon – *The Effect of Judicial Review on Grievance Arbitration* – (1976), 14 Osgoode Hall Law Journal 661, 680–702.

Chapter II. The Right to Organize

§1. THE NEED FOR STATUTORY PROTECTION

357. With the removal of criminal prohibitions against union organizations in the last quarter of the nineteenth century, workers were in principle free to join unions and to participate in their collective bargaining and related activities. However, this theoretical freedom was translated into practice only relatively infrequently, and with great difficulty.

358. Workers who sought to organize a union confronted, first of all, the possibility of economic reprisals by their employer. An employer could, with impunity, refuse to employ unionists, to negotiate with the union, or to abide by any undertakings given to the union. Whether he would, as a matter of prudence, actually adopt such a position depended upon the relative power of the parties. If the employer chose to dismiss unionists or to refuse to recognize a union, the union could respond by calling a strike or imposing other economic sanctions. However, the employer, in turn, could seek relief in the civil or criminal courts against such sanctions and, as the law stood down to the 1940's, be reasonably confident of success. Thus, the freedom to organize often amounted, in practical terms, to no more than the freedom to suffer serious, adverse legal and economic consequences.

359. Moreover, the absence of effective legal protection for trade union organization imposed at least two significant costs upon the community. First, the resulting weakness of trade unions may have exacerbated the deflationary effects of the great depression of the 1930's. This at least was a premise explicitly adopted in the protective legislation enacted in 1935 in the United States, the National Labor Relations Act (the 'Wagner' Act). Second, again reflecting the American experience, economic conflict over the issue of union recognition was costly and disruptive. Nonetheless, legal protection for the right of workers to organize came to Canada only at a relatively late date.

360. Following the enactment of the Wagner Act in the United States, many Canadian provinces enacted legislation which purported to protect workers' rights to organize and bargain collectively. However, for the most part, this legislation was declaratory and unaccompanied by effective mechanisms for enforcement. An amendment to the federal Criminal Code in 1939 did prohibit refusal of employment, dismissal or threats which were intended to inhibit union membership and organization.[1] However, certain textual difficulties, and the inefficacy of criminal prosecution in labour relations matters, largely vitiated this provision.

1. Now Criminal Code, R.S.C. 1970, c.C–34, S.382.

361. Only in the 1940's, in part to avoid disruptions which might damage the war effort, was Canadian legislation enacted on the model of the Wagner Act. The Ontario Collective Bargaining Act of 1943, the first effective provincial legislation in this regard, was superseded in 1944 by the enactment of P.C. 1003, the federal Wartime Labour Relations Regulations. These, in turn, provided the basis for post-war provincial and federal labour relations acts. Common to all were the essential and familiar features of the American Wagner Act: a mechanism for the designation, by majority choice, of one union as the exclusive bargaining agent of the employees; a legally-enforceable duty of the employer to recognize, and bargain in good faith with, that union; and the prohibition of employer 'unfair labour practices' which might interfere with selection of, or participation in, the union by employees.

362. The first two of these features – exclusivity of representation and the duty to bargain – will be considered elsewhere. Of immediate concern is the third, protection against unfair labour practices. Within the framework of a basic commitment to the promotion of collective bargaining, the suppression of unfair labour practices involves a balancing of the respective interests of the employee, the union, and the employer.

§2. Protection of the Rights of Individual Employees

363. At common law, subject to contractual constraints, an employer might refuse to hire, cease to employ, or otherwise deal with workers more-or-less as he saw fit. As a practical matter, written employment contracts, and contracts for a fixed term are very rare, so that most Canadian workers must look to legislation, if anywhere, for protection of their rights. As has been seen, various statutes do establish minimum conditions of work, safety and health standards, and protection against racial, religious, sexual or age discrimination. Workers within federal jurisdiction also enjoy statutory protection against unjust dismissal on any grounds.[1] But save to the extent that the employer's common law rights are thus specifically displaced by statute, they remain virtually absolute.

1. Canada Labour Code, s.61.5.

364. The labour relations acts provide a further, but limited, incursion into the employer's domain: he cannot exercise his rights vis-a-vis workers so as to interfere with their right to join a trade union or to participate in its lawful activities.[1] Thus, the mere showing that an employee has been arbitrarily dismissed or treated inequitably does not amount to proof that an 'unfair labour practice', in the technical sense has been committed.[2] Only when the employer's conduct is shown to proceed from an intention to interfere with union organization is it forbidden. However, the apparent narrowness of this protection, with its obvious difficulties of proof, is overcome by statutory or adjudicatively-developed presumptions.[3] Unless he can demonstrate the contrary, an employer will be presumed to have dismissed, or otherwise adversely treated, an employee for union activities. This presumption can be rebutted if the employer is able to tender credible evidence as to another motive, particularly if there is no record of other activities exhibiting an anti-union animus. On the other hand, the credibility of the employer's alternate explanation may be undermined if he can be shown to be engaging in a series of anti-union manoeuvres.[4]

1. Canada, s.184(3); British Columbia, s.3; Ontario, s.58; Quebec, s.13.
2. *CKOY*, (1976) 77 C.L.L.C. para. 16,067 (C.L.R.B.).
3. Canada, s.188(3); Ontario, s.79(4*a*); British Columbia, s.8(6); Quebec, s.16. And see *National Automatic Vending*, (1963) 63 C.L.L.C. para. 16,278 (O.L.R.B.).
4. *Fielding Lumber*, [1976] 1 C.L.R.B.R. 216 (O.L.R.B.).

365. Typical of circumstances which have been held to support a presumption of dismissal for union activity, or to undermine the credibility of an alternative explanation, are the following: the dismissal for 'poor work' of employees of whom no previous complaint has been made, or who have recently been promoted;[1] the selection for discharge on grounds of 'redundancy' only of employees active in the union; and the discharge of employees whose admitted misbehaviour was first condoned or forgiven by the employer, and then relied upon to justify discharge when their union membership was discovered.[2] Typically, it has been held that discharge for union membership or activity need be only one amongst several motives in the employer's mind, in order to stigmatize the discharge as an 'unfair labour practice'.[3] Discrimination against union members or activists is similarly forbidden, as is the imposition upon them of monetary or other penalties, or the attempt to secure a promise to abstain from union membership or activities as a condition of employment.[4]

1. *Forana*, [1974] 1 C.L.R.B.R. 13 (B.C.L.R.B.).
2. *National Automatic Vending, Fielding Lumber, supra.*
3. *R v. Bushnell Communications*, (1974) 4 O.R. (2d) 288 (C.A.).
4. Ontario, s.58(b),(c); Canada, s.184(3)(e); British Columbia, s.3(2)(c); Quebec, s.13.

366. The employer is also forbidden, typically, to use threats or promises to induce or coerce workers to abandon union membership or activities.[1] Such promises include both the direct offer of individual bribes and the suggestion that general wage increases would be forthcoming if workers did not organize, and withheld if they did.[2] Moreover, even apart from such overt threats and promises, statutes typically prevent an employer from unilaterally altering terms of employment during critical periods of a union's organizing campaign, to avoid a situation in which employees, either through gratitude or fear, decline to participate in the union.[3]

1. Ontario, ss.56, 58(c), 61; Canada, s.184(3)(a),(e); British Columbia, ss.3(2)(c), 5; Quebec, ss.12, 13.
2. *Martel Lumber*, [1972] O.L.R.B. 811.
3. Canada, s.124(4); Ontario, s.70(2); British Columbia, s.51(1).

367. Finally, some statutes protect employees from victimization by their employer prompted by the fact that they have given adverse testimony in labour relations proceedings.[1] Such statutes generally seek to maintain the integrity of legal mechanisms designed to protect the right to organize.

1. Ontario, s.71; Canada, s.184(3). Quebec, s.135, specifically protects the identity of complainants.

368. On the other hand, it must be reiterated that employees involved in union activities do not enjoy complete immunity. They may be disciplined or discharged for acting violently, for example, whether in connection with illegal work stoppages, or in support of a lawful strike.[1]

1. *Infra.*

§3. PROTECTION OF TRADE UNION RIGHTS

369. If a trade union is to represent workers effectively and authentically, it must be completely free of employer control, and deal with the employer at arm's length. The labour relations acts ensure this effective and authentic representation by forbidding, as unfair labour practices, the participation of management in the formation or administration of a union, its selection by employees, or its representation of them, as a bargaining agent.[1] Even the contribution of financial or other support by the employer to the union is forbidden, except in circumstances where the autonomy of the union is unlikely to be impaired.[2]

1. Ontario, s.56; Canada, s.184(1); British Columbia, s.3(1): Quebec, s.11.
2. *Super City*, (1964) 64 C.L.L.C. para. 16,005 (O.L.R.B.) (payment by employer of full-time union staff member unobjectionable because originally provided for in collective agreement and openly undertaken for over twenty years).

370. Thus, for example, an employer is forbidden to infiltrate and spy upon union activities,[1] to interrogate workers regarding their union membership,[2] to support one of two unions competing for members amongst his workers,[3] to provide a union with money (or some means of making money) to support its activities,[4] to pay for a union's legal representation,[5] or to enter into a collective agreement with a union which does not represent his employees.[6] On the other hand, after the employees have freely selected a union as their bargaining agent, the employer may permit it to use plant facilities for meetings, may grant time off to union officers for union business,[7] and may enter into a collective agreement providing that union membership shall be a condition of employment.[8]

1. Saskatchewan, s.11(h); *Grand Footwear*, (1960) 60 C.L.L.C. para. 16,176 (Q.R.L.B.).
2. *Jones & Laughlin Mining*, [1967–68] O.L.R.B. 202.
3. *Canadian Fabricated Products*, (1954) 54 C.L.L.C. para. 17,090 (O.L.R.B.).
4. *Toronto Electric Commissioners*, (1946) 46 C.L.L.C. para. 10,649 (O.L.R.B.).
5. *Norfish*, [1965–66] O.L.R.B. 414.
6. *Sunrise Paving and Construction*, [1972] O.L.R.B. 199.
7. *Kelvinator*, (1952) 52 C.L.L.C. para. 17,046 (O.L.R.B.).
8. See *infra*.

371. The exclusion of the employer from union affairs generally extends to the lowest level of management, foremen or supervisors.[1] However, recognizing that their managerial status may be merely temporary and that they may have residual ties to a union, membership by such persons in a union is not automatically suspect. Where their support of the union can be shown to be contrary to the wishes of their employer, foremen and supervisors have occasionally been permitted to participate in union activities,[2] although not legally protected in their right to do so.[3] However, where such individuals have been dismissed for union activities, it has been held that the employer may thereby have illegally undermined the union loyalties of non-supervisory employees.[4]

1. *Infra*.
2. *Air Liquide*, (1964) 64 C.L.L.C. 16,002 (O.L.R.B.).
3. *Jarvis* v. *Assoc. Medical Services*, (1964) 44 D.L.R. (2d) 407 (S.C.C.)
4. *A.A.S. Telecommunications*, [1977] 2 C.L.R.B.R. 73 (O.L.R.B.).

372. Unions which are the beneficiaries of illicit employer support are denied status as bargaining agents under the labour relations acts, their collective agreements are denied recognition[1] and, at least in Quebec, they are liable to be dissolved by administrative order.[2]

1. Canada, s.134; Quebec, s.24d; British Columbia, s.50(a); Ontario, s.40.
2. *Tremblay* v. *F.T.Q.* [1967] S.C.R. 697; Quebec, s.132.

§4. RECONCILING EMPLOYEE, EMPLOYER AND TRADE UNION RIGHTS

373. While labour relations acts expressly or impliedly protect trade union rights, as a necessary component of the statutorily-guaranteed collective bargaining system, it does not follow that such rights are always to be preferred when they clash with the opposing interests of individual employees and employers.

374. On the one hand, there is the need to protect individual workers against abuses of union power. Unions, therefore are forbidden to use intimidation or coercion to compel employees to join their ranks. Membership so procured, and union representational claims based on such membership, have no legal effect.[1]

1. *Milnet Mines*, (1953) 53 C.L.L.C. para, 17,063 (O.L.R.B.).

375. While the institutional interests of the union and the exigencies of the labour market are generally accepted as justifying arrangements which (with varying degrees of stringency) require trade union membership as a condition of employment, such arrangements typically operate within statutorily defined limits.[1] The countervailing right of employees to be free from unwanted union membership, and particularly to retain their jobs in the face of union hostility, is protected by a variety of devices. In some jurisdictions, the right of employees to object, on conscientious grounds, to union membership is protected.[2] In others, the union is forbidden to deny membership to employees arbitrarily, or to seek the discharge of members who have been expelled for improper reasons.[3] Unions which practice racial, religious, sexual, or other invidious forms of discrimination, may themselves be denied status under the governing legislation.[4]

1. Canada, s.161; Ontario, s.38; Quebec, s.50; British Columbia, ss.3(2)(e), 9, 10.
2. British Columbia, s.11; Ontario, s.39; Manitoba, ss.68(3), 68.1.
3. Canada, s.185(e); Ontario, s.38(2); British Columbia, s.9(2).
4. Ontario, s.12; British Columbia, s.50.

376. In other words, while it is inevitable that some individual interests will be sacrificed under a collective regime premised on majority rule, the countervailing claims of individual non-union employees are, in certain circumstances, protected.

377. On the other hand, the employer is also typically conceded to enjoy important interests, worthy of legal protection, with which trade union interests must be reconciled.

For example, an employer is entitled to maintain order and efficiency in his operations, even when the effect of so doing might be to interfere with union organizing campaigns or other union activities.[1] There is normally no privilege to solicit union membership or transact union business on company premises, during working hours.[2] Similarly, the normal right of an employer who is the owner or occupier of premises, to control access to those premises, is generally unimpaired, although it may make more difficult the union's ability to reach employees whom it wishes to organize.[3] Or again, the right of an employer to close a plant or discontinue or suspend operations is, in principle, secure despite the detrimental effect of such action upon the union and its supporters.[4]

1. *Rosco Metal Products*, (1964) 64 C.L.L.C. para. 16,303 (O.L.R.B.).
2. R. Milrod Metal Products (1964) 64 C.L.L.C. para. 16,007 (O.L.R.B.).
3. Canada, s.185(d); Ontario, s.62; Quebec, s.5; British Columbia, s.4(1). This had posed a particular difficulty for employees who lived on company premises in remote mining or lumber camps, see *R.* v. *Labelle*, (1964) 48 D.L.R. (2d) 37 (Ont.C.A.), and *infra*.
4. *Alitalia*, (1976) 76 C.L.L.C. para. 16,006 (C.L.R.B.); British Columbia, s.3(2)(h); Ontario, s.68.

378. So long as an employer can be shown to be pursuing his legitimate business interests, he is unconstrained by labour relations legislation. Thus his 'right' to so act must not be used for improper purposes, or as a mask for anti-union manoeuvres. The employer's motive is of crucial importance.

379. The maintenance of order and efficiency may justify the promulgation by an employer of a rule against all forms of employee solicitation or personal discussion during working hours. But such a rule must not be framed explicitly to prohibit discussion about unions nor, if framed generally, discriminatorily enforced only against employees involved in union activities.[1] The owner's proprietary or possessory rights over his premises are assured. But where employees not only work on the employer's premises but also reside there (as for example in mining and logging camps) the denial of access to union organizers so that they may meet the employees after work and in their living quarters, is excessive and gratuitous. Here, statutory intervention has created a special right of access for union organizers, so that they can bring the message of collective bargaining to employees in these remote and isolated locations.[2] An employer is clearly entitled to discontinue unprofitable operations, or to move his plant nearer markets or sources of supply. But when the interruption of employment cannot be justified by reference to any such business motive, it may well be construed as having only an anti-union purpose.[3]

1. *Associated Medical Services*, (1961) 61 C.L.L.C. para. 16,218 (O.L.R.B.).
2. Canada, s.199; B.C., s.4(2); Ontario, s.10; Quebec, ss. 8,9.
3. *Academy of Medicine*, [1977] O.L.R.B. 783.

380. In all such circumstances, when the motive of anti-unionism can be detected or inferred, otherwise apparently legitimate employer conduct may be found to be illegal.

381. The balance is nowhere more difficult to strike than in connection with appeals by an employer to his employees not to unionize. On the one hand, the employer is generally recognized to possess a right of free speech.[1] Through the exercise of this right, it is hoped, both the attractions and the drawbacks of unionization will be presented for consideration by the employees, so that they can make a rational and informed choice. On the other hand, the exercise of the employer's right of free speech may be so fraught with sinister significance for his employee audience that it will effectively destroy union support. Limits on the employer's right of free speech are thus inevitable. Of course, the employer may not use threats, coercion, intimidation, promises, or undue influence in addressing his employees on the subject of unionization.[2] But the difficult issue in any given case is whether apparently innocuous employer language may reasonably be construed as having such an effect upon employees.

1. British Columbia, s.3(2)(g); Ontario, s.56; and see *City and Country Radio*, [1975] 2 C.L.R.B.R. 1 (C.L.R.B.).
2. Canada, s.184(3)(e); British Columbia, s.3(2)(c); Ontario, ss.56,58; Quebec, s.12.

382. Labour relations boards seeking to gauge the true impact of employer appeals have generally accepted that the employer's economic power over his workers, prior to the advent of a union, makes them highly responsive to his wishes, especially where his message is delivered in a manner or under circumstances which serve to exacerbate this undesirable effect. Labour relations boards will look with suspicion at an appeal to employees who are a 'captive audience', compelled by an order of their employer to attend a meeting on company premises during working hours.[1] They will be similarly concerned with messages which predict, and especially with those which threaten, that employees will lose their jobs or employment benefits if they support the union.[2] Indeed, several jurisdictions have specifically outlawed employer speech which includes threats to move the employer's place of operations, or unilaterally to alter wages and working conditions.[3]

1. *Ex-Cell-O*, [1977] 2 C.L.R.B.R. 233 (O.L.R.B.).
2. *Bell and Howell*, [1968–69] O.L.R.B. 695; *Viceroy Construction*, [1978] 1 C.L.R.B.R. 22 (O.L.R.B.).
3. Newfoundland, s.26; Saskatchewan, s.11(1)(i).

383. Above all, labour relations boards will be especially vigilant in situations where employer appeals are made against a background of other, overt anti-union behaviour, or as a part of a sustained and egregious campaign of anti-union propaganda.[1]

1. *Dylex*, [1977] O.L.R.B. 357, *aff'd*. (1977) 18 O.R. (2d) 58 (D.C.).

§5. REMEDIES

A. Representation proceedings

384. The occasion for employer interference with the right to organize is usually the union's initial attempt to gain bargaining rights by securing employee membership and support. Once these rights have been secured, either by the granting of a labour relations board certification order or by execution of a collective agreement, the employer will usually acquiesce in the union's existence, and focus his opposition instead upon the union's substantive demands for wages and working conditions. Only if the union's status is subsequently called into question, or if it appears to have a tenuous command of employee loyalties, is the employer likely to be tempted to renew a campaign of serious interference with the union and its members. For this reason, some of the important remedies for employer unfair labour practices are connected with representation proceedings.

385. If the employer has violated the rights of the union and of its members, and thus created a coercive atmosphere in which the true wishes of the employees concerning union representation are unlikely to be ascertained, the union may be given bargaining rights, notwithstanding the absence of majority employee support.[1] In addition, the board may disregard evidence of opposition to, or resignations from, the union procured by or as a result of employer illegality,[2] and may disqualify one of two competing unions which is the willing beneficiary of improper tactics directed against its competitor.[3] All of these remedies are made available in the context of representation proceedings, and do not require the aggrieved union or individual to launch separate proceedings.

1. British Columbia, s.43(3); Ontario, s.7*a*; Nova Scotia s.24(9).
2. *Re Clark Leatherdale and Upholsterers' Int'l Union*, (1972) 26 D.L.R. (3d) 450 (Man. Q.B.).
3. S. W. Fleming, [1964–65] O.L.R.B. 144.

B. Administrative sanctions

386. Throughout the 1970's, Canadian labour relations boards generally acquired statutory powers to deal effectively with unfair labour practices.[1] While these vary somewhat from jurisdiction to jurisdiction, they do share certain typical characteristics.

1. D. D. Carter, *The Expansion of Labour Board Remedies: A New Approach to Industrial Conflict* (Kingston, 1976).

387. First, the labour relations board's initial response to a complaint is to attempt to resolve matters by informal processes. A board officer is sent out to investigate and to attempt to settle the complaint. Only if this attempt is unsuccessful is the matter set down for formal adjudication.

388. Second, while carriage of unfair labour practice proceedings rests with the complainant, the board does not make available to him the results of the initial investigation by the board's officer.[1] In view of the importance of motive in assessing employer conduct, and of the notorious difficulty of proving motive, it might be thought that the absence of this report would confront a complainant with an almost impossible task. However, the complainant is assisted, in almost all jurisdictions, by the creation of a legal presumption (either by statute or by labour board decision) that any discharge is for union activity, unless the employer can demonstrate the contrary.[2]

1. Ontario, s.100, and see *A. J. (Archie) Goodale*, [1977] 2 C.L.R.B.R. 309 (C.L.R.B.).
2. *Supra*.

389. Almost all boards have power at least to order reinstatement and compensation for employees who are victims of employer unfair labour practices. In addition, most boards have remedial powers framed in very general terms, which include the power to require the cessation of prohibited conduct, and the taking of affirmative action to remedy its effects.[1] In the exercise of this power, labour relations board have developed, for example, the 'make whole' remedy, by which the employer is required to compensate the union for the entire cost of an organizing campaign frustrated by his unfair labour practice, as well as the costs of litigation leading to the order.[2] At least one labour relations board has flirted with the notion of requiring an employer to re-open operations closed deliberately to forestall unionization, although it chose instead to award both 'make whole' damages to the union, and very substantial compensation to the employees who lost their jobs.[3] In another case employees were awarded compensation for the loss of possible salary increases, due to the employer's failure to bargain with the union.[4]

1. Canada, s.189; British Columbia, s.8(4); Ontario, s.79(4); Quebec, s.14.
2. *Kidd Bros. Produce* [1976] C.L.R.B. 304 (B.C.L.R.B.).
3. *Academy of Medicine*, [1977] O.L.R.B. 783.
4. *Radio Shack*, [1980] 1 C.L.R.B.R., 99 (O.L.R.B.).

390. Boards have recently been concerned, particularly, to undo the adverse effects of hostile employer action upon employee attitudes towards unionization. Thus, one board ordered the senior official of a large bank to write to all of its employees rescinding illegal management edicts, apologizing for interference with employee rights, and assuring employees of their right to organize.[1] In another case, a board required that such a statement should also be read to a meeting of employees assembled on company premises for the purpose, following which the union was to be afforded an opportunity to address the meeting.[2]

1. *Canadian Imperial Bank of Commerce*, (1980) 80 C.L.L.C. para. 16,002 (C.L.R.B.).
2. *Radio Shack*, [1980] 1 C.L.R.B.R. 99 (O.L.R.B.).

391. Of course, specific powers may be conferred which broaden the normal scope of the board's general remedial power. For example, one province authorizes the labour relations board to dissolve a dominated union, rather than merely deprive it of status under its Labour Code.[1] Another province authorizes the labour relations board to award punitive, rather than compensatory, damages to an employee whose rights are interfered with by an employer's unfair labour practice.[2]

1. Quebec, s.132.
2. Manitoba, s.22(6)(d).

392. In any case, remedial orders of the labour relations board are typically made registrable in the provincial supreme court, and are thereafter enforce-

153

able as court orders.[1] Continued disobedience of the order following registration may result in a contempt citation by the court, leading to fine or imprisonment for individual contemnors, sequestration of corporate contemnors, or to enforcement of money judgments by seizure of the assets of the offending party.

1. Canada, s.123; British Columbia, s.30; Ontario, s.79(5); Quebec, s.18a.

C. Criminal prosecution

393. Prosecution in the criminal courts remains a possible, if not favoured, response to employer interference with the right to organize.

As has been mentioned, such interference constitutes an offence under the federal Criminal Code.[1] However, this provision is seldom resorted to in practice.

1. *Supra.*

394. In almost all Canadian jurisdictions, a violation of the provisions of the labour relations act, or disobedience of the orders of any tribunal administering those provisions, is a quasi-criminal offence, typically punishable by a fine which may be imposed after prosecution in the lowest level of criminal courts in the province. The fine, again typically, cumulates daily while the offence continues, and is a greater amount in respect of trade union and corporate offences than it is in relation to offences by individuals.[1] However, recourse to prosecution, where available, is discouraged by both practical obstacles and specific statutory provisions.

1. Canada, s.191; British Columbia, s.138; Ontario s.85. Quebec, s.126, makes no such distinction.

395. As to the practical obstacles, carriage of a prosecution rests with the complainant. Unlike normal criminal prosecutions, the aggrieved party is thus charged with the obligation of gathering the evidence, and presenting it to a criminal court. Of course, the full costs of the prosecution and of any resulting appeals must be borne by the complainant. But if the prosecution is successful, any fine imposed goes not to the complainant but to the state. Moreover, conviction does not, of itself, result in an order to terminate the offending conduct; it simply exposes the offender to future prosecution. And finally, the criminal courts are presided over by judges who are largely unfamiliar with labour relations matters, who naturally require the same high standard of proof as they impose in other criminal proceedings, and who tend to interpret labour relations statutes without a developed understanding of underlying policies. For all of these reasons, therefore, there are important practical impediments to prosecution as a useful vehicle for enforcing the legislation and the policies it embodies.

396. More important even than the practical problems, are the typical statutory provisions which require that the labour relations board must consent

154

to all prosecutions.[1] While the board may use the application for consent as an occasion for clarifying the rights of the parties and, if possible securing mutually acceptable solutions, it is in fact loath to give its consent to prosecution. Prosecution is seen as accomplishing little of a positive nature, and on the contrary, as tending to embitter the relationship, and to inhibit the resumption of amicable dealing between the parties. Thus, consent to prosecute is given only in the most extreme circumstances.[2]

1. Canada, s.194; Ontario, s.90; neither British Columbia nor Quebec appear to interpose a requirement of consent to prosecute.
2. *A.A.S. Telecommunications*, [1976] O.L.R.B. 751; *Arthur G. McKee*, [1977] 1 C.L.R.B.R. 176 (O.L.R.B.).

D. Other remedies

397. Some collective agreements echo the statutory prohibition against employer conduct which interferes with the right of the union to represent the employees, or of the employees to be represented by the union. Where the employer in fact takes action during the currency of an agreement which can be so stigmatized, the union is free to seek redress through the grievance procedure and arbitration, as established by the agreement itself.[1] The arbitrator, typically, has sufficient remedial power at least to give compensation and order reinstatement of employees discharged for union activity, and perhaps has power as well to order the employer to abandon the offending practices.

1. Where arbitration is available, labour relations boards may require the parties to use it rather than seeking relief under statute, see *National Showcase*, (1960) 61 C.L.L.C. para. 16,185 (O.L.R.B.), and *contra Ludger Harvey* v. *Cossette*, (1968) 69 C.L.L.C. para. 14,212 (Que.C.A.).

398. It is notionally possible for employees to frame an action in tort against their employer for conduct which might amount to an unfair labour practice. However, this possibility is at most a theoretical one.[1] It certainly does not lie within the contemplation of unions confronting employer interference.

1. *Teamsters* v. *Midland Superior Express*, (1974) 43 D.L.R. (3d) 540 (Alta. C.A.).

E. Self-help

399. It has quite generally been held that a union, or employees, who are themselves the victims of employer unfair labour practices, are not free to visit reprisals upon the employer by means of strikes, picketing or boycotts.[1] If recourse is sought to these self-help remedies, the union and employees leave themselves vulnerable to prosecution, civil suit, or administrative proceedings at the instance of the employer. Only very rarely is a labour relations board given explicit power to deny an employer relief against illegal union or employee conduct on the ground that the employer's unfair labour practices have brought down the offending union or employee conduct upon himself,[2] although it is occasionally assumed to exist.[3] While the courts do possess an

analogous discretion to refuse injunctive relief to employers who have provoked their employees into illegal conduct by their own illegality, this discretion is seldom exercised.[4]

1. *Corcoran Foods*, [1964–65] O.L.R.B. 94.
2. British Columbia, s. 28(1)(c).
3. For example, the labour relations board has exercised its discretion in refusing an employer
consent to prosecute illegal strikers, because 'prosecution . . . should not be a manifestation of
retributive justice', *Savage Shoes*, (1953) 53 C.L.L.C. para. 17,060 (O.L.R.B.).
4. *Hiram Walker* v. *Distillery Workers*, (1974) 48 D.L.R. (3d) 618 (B.C.S.C.); *Crozier* v.
Western Publishers, (1974) 51 D.L.R. (3d) 96 (Sask.C.A.).

400. Thus, as a practical matter, it can be said that there is no legal privilege
to respond to employer unfair labour practices by means of economic reprisals.
To this general statement, there is, of course, always the overriding exception:
if the conduct is not illegal because, for example, it is a timely strike under the
Labour Relations Act, the fact that it is mounted in reprisal for the employer's
unfair labour practice does not alter its legality.

Chapter III. Legal Recognition of Collective Bargaining Rights

§1. THE SOURCE OF COLLECTIVE BARGAINING RIGHTS

401. Collective bargaining rights flow from the labour relations legislation
of the different Canadian jurisdictions. Such matters as the acquisition of
bargaining rights, the definition of the collective bargaining structure, the
transfer of bargaining rights, and the termination of bargaining rights are
covered in some detail by these statutes.

402. The responsibility to administer and interpret this legislation has been
given to the labour relations boards.[1] A variation of this general pattern,
however, is found in Quebec where the responsibility for administering collective bargaining laws is divided between investigative commissioners and a
labour court. The primary function of labour boards is still to grant or withdraw
collective bargaining rights, applying criteria either found in the legislation
itself or developed through the tribunal's own decision-making process.

1. *Supra*, Introduction C.III §1 *'Labour Law' Defined*, and C.V-§2 *The Role of Government
Institutions*.

§2. ACQUISITION OF COLLECTIVE BARGAINING RIGHTS

A. Eligible employees

403. The benefits and protections provided by collective bargaining statutes
extend only to those persons who can be considered to be 'employees',[1] and
who have not also been excluded, either expressly or implicitly, from the scope
of these statutes. In the context of collective bargaining legislation the term

employee' has a somewhat different meaning than when it is used in its more general legal sense. Even though certain persons may not be regarded as being employed at common law, they may still be considered as employees as that term is defined in collective bargaining statutes, and entitled to the benefits flowing from that legislation.[2] Conversely, there are some persons, clearly working under an employment relationship at common law, who are expressly or implicitly excluded from the coverage of collective bargaining legislation. The extent of these inclusions and exclusions varies slightly among the different Canadian jurisdictions, reflecting different policy judgments about the appropriate scope of collective bargaining legislation.

1. *Supra*, Introduction C.III §2 *'Labour Law Defined'*.
2. It has been held, however, that retired workers do not fall within the definition of employee. See *Cominco*, [1979] 2 C.L.R.B.R. 322 (B.C.L.R.B.).

1. Dependent contractors

404. Not all persons work under arrangements exhibiting all the characteristics of a straightforward employment relationship. Some contractual arrangements under which work is performed may display certain features indicating that the worker may be in the business of selling his services, and not just performing work for wages. Persons working under such hybrid arrangements have been referred to as 'dependent contractors'.[1] Many of these dependent contractors share the same labour market with employees, raising the question of whether there is a sufficient justification for excluding them from the scope of collective bargaining legislation. A justification put forward for the exclusion of dependent contractors from collective bargaining is that they are entrepreneurs and, as such, prohibited from acting in combination by the public policy found in federal competition legislation.[2] Weighing against this justification for the exclusion of dependent contractors from collective bargaining is the argument that groups in closely analogous economic positions, such as employees and dependent contractors, should receive the same legislative treatment. One particular problem for collective bargaining which stems from a failure to treat employees and dependent contractors alike is that collective bargaining rights may be eroded as employers seek to obtain services on a dependent contractor basis.

1. For a thorough discussion of the problems raised by this type of arrangement, see H. W. Arthurs, *The Dependent Contractor: A Study of the Legal Problems of Countervailing Power* (1965–6) 16 U. of T. L. J. 89.
2. It should be noted that the Combines Investigation Act, R.S.C. 1970, c.C–23, as am. by S.C. 1975, c.76, while now prohibiting restraints on competition in respect of services, still exempts from such prohibitions 'combinations or activities of workmen or employees for their own reasonable protection as such workmen or employees'.

405. There has been a tendency on the part of labour boards to give a wide interpretation to the term 'employee', bringing within the scope of collective bargaining legislation workers such as owner-drivers of transport trucks, who might otherwise be characterized as dependent contractors. The extent to which labour boards can extend the definition of employee, however, has been restricted by the existence of the common law test of employment status. This fourfold test, as it is commonly known, takes into account four factors: the ownership of the tools used to perform the work; the degree of control asserted over the person performing the work; the chance of profit arising from the activity; and the risk of loss that might also result. The appropriateness of this test for determining the extent of coverage provided by collective bargaining legislation has been questioned.[1]

1. Rather surprisingly, the source of this test is *Montreal* v. *Montreal Locomotive Works*, [1947] 1 D.L.R. 161 (J.C.P.C.), a case raising the issue of whether a manufacturer enjoyed immunity from municipal taxation.

406. Some Canadian jurisdictions by embracing a statutory definition of dependent contractor have permitted labour boards to take greater account of the economic substance of a relationship when determining the reach of collective bargaining legislation.[1] The widest of these definitions simply require that a person be in a position of economic dependence, and under an obligation to perform duties analogous to that of the employee. Labour boards have interpreted this definition as bringing within the scope of collective bargaining legislation persons who have made a considerable capital investment in the equipment used to perform their work,[2] and who employ others to assist them in the performance of their work.[3] Such diverse groups as owner-drivers of dump trucks, driver-salesmen employed by dairies, oil burner servicemen, free-lance journalists, and house parents working for welfare agencies have been considered to be dependent contractors.

1. Canada, s.107(1*a*), B.C., s.1(1), Ontario s.1(*ga*).
2. *Fownes Construction*, [1974] 1 C.L.R.B.R. 453 (B.C.L.R.B.); *Adbo Contracting*, [1977] 2 C.L.R.B.R. 1 (O.L.R.B.).
3. The extent to which the employment of others may point to a person being other than a dependent contractor is discussed in *Superior Sand, Gravel and Supplies*, [1978] 1 C.L.R.B.R. 421 (O.L.R.B.).

2. Managerial employees

407. Persons employed to exercise managerial functions are not included within the concept of employee as it is defined by collective bargaining legislation.[1] The rationale for the exclusion from collective bargaining of this group of persons who are regarded generally by the law as employees is that the scheme of collective bargaining requires an arm's length relationship between an employer represented by management and those employees represented by trade unions.[2] The exclusion of managerial employees from collective bargaining serves to keep management and labour insulated one from the other, protecting the union from management domination and, on the other side, ensuring that the management presence is not weakened. This rationale may also apply to exclude from the bargaining unit employees related to management,[3] or even employees closely identified with management.[4]

1. See Canada, s.107(1), British Columbia, s.1(1), Ontario, s.1(3)(b), Quebec, s.1(m).

2. *District of Burnaby*, [1974] 1 C.L.R.B.R. 1 (B.C.L.R.B.).
3. *Bruce-Clark*, [1979] 1 C.L.R.B.R. 149 (B.C.L.R.B.); *Feed-Rite*, [1979] 1 C.L.R.B.R. 296 (C.L.R.B.).
4. *Diversey*, [1979] 3 C.L.R.B.R. 77 (B.C.L.R.B.).

408. The identification of management employees is one of the more difficult tasks faced by labour boards. This difficulty is particularly pronounced in larger organizations where authority has become diffused through a number of bureaucratic layers. A distinction has to be drawn between those persons in an organization who exercise control and authority over employees, and those persons who participate in an organization's general decision-making process but have no direct control over other employees.[1] In most Canadian jurisdictions front-line supervisors who exercise a substantial degree of control and authority over other employees are considered to exercise managerial functions.[2] In the case of persons involved in the general decision-making process, however, labour boards have looked to the degree and extent of independent decision-making authority. In both situations labour boards often make reference to a person's ability to make effective recommendations, recognizing that managerial authority may be more diffuse in larger organizations. There appears to be no single test, or factor, that can be used to determine whether a person exercises managerial functions. The final determination is often the product of the particular facts of a case. Such factors as the nature of the organization, the manner in which it is organized, the person's position in that organizational structure, the extent of the person's authority over other employees, and the amount of non-managerial work performed by the person are all taken into account in determining whether a person exercises managerial functions.

1. *Carleton University*, [1975] O.L.R.B. 500; *McIntyre Porcupine Mines*, [1975] 2 C.L.R.B.R. 234 (O.L.R.B.); *Inglis*, [1976] O.L.R.B. 270.
2. For example, see *Chrysler*, [1976] 1 C.L.R.B.R. 447 (O.L.R.B.).

409. In some Canadian jurisdictions there appears to have been a greater tendency to extend collective bargaining to persons who formerly might have been regarded as managerial employees.[1]

1. *B.C. Telephone*, [1976] 1 C.L.R.B.R. 273 (C.L.R.B.); *Tahsis*, [1977] 2 C.L.R.B.R. 452 (B.C.L.R.B.); but see *B.C. Ferry*, [1979] 1 C.L.R.B.R. 116 (C.L.R.B.).

3. Confidential employees

410. Persons employed in a confidential capacity in matters relating to labour relations are expressly excluded from the scope of collective bargaining legislation. This exclusion reflects a clear recognition of the need for management to have some office and technical support when conducting collective bargaining exercise. Labour boards, however, have been careful about extending this exception too far, since its effect is to exclude from collective bargaining persons who would be in the same economic position as those employees who fall within the bargaining unit. Office and clerical employees in general are often privy to a certain amount of sensitive information that would not be available to their counterparts in the plant, and this fact of life also appears to be recognized by labour boards in refusing to give a wide interpretation to the confidential exclusion. In order for an employee to be considered as employed in a confidential capacity in matters relating to labour relations, it must be shown that the confidential matters relate to labour relations and not some other potentially sensitive area for the employer, that the employee has regular access to such confidential labour relations matters, and that these matters are integral to the collective bargaining process.[1]

1. *Falconbridge Nickel Mines*, [1966] O.L.R.B. 379; *Transair*, [1974] C.L.R.B.R. 281 (C.L.R.B.).

4. Public employees

411. Many public employees are either expressly or implicitly excluded from general collective bargaining legislation. The Crown by operation of the rules of interpretation is not bound by legislation unless there is an express provision to the contrary in the statute.[1] Legislative silence has by implication excluded public servants from the general scheme of collective bargaining in many jurisdictions. Express restrictions, however, have been necessary in order to exclude such groups of public employees as policemen, firemen, and teachers from collective bargaining legislation. As a general rule, municipal employees (other than firemen and policemen) are not excluded from general collective bargaining legislation, nor are the faculties and staffs of universities. Even where public employees are not excluded (either expressly or implicitly) from general collective bargaining legislation, restrictions may be placed on the exercise of general collective bargaining rights (such as recourse to strike action) by separate and more specific legislation. The general pattern, however, has been to establish special collective bargaining regimes for public employees, reflecting a reluctance to extend fully the private sector collective bargaining model to the public sector. While public employee collective bargaining statutes vary from jurisdiction to jurisdiction, the dominant pattern has been some restriction of the right to strike and significant limitation upon the range of bargainable issues.

1. In Quebec, Manitoba and Saskatchewan the Crown has been expressly included within the definition of employer and is bound by the statute (Quebec, s.1(1); Manitoba, s.3; Saskatchewan, s.2(g).

5. Professional employees

412. The exclusion of certain types of professional employees,[1] usually those belonging to the more traditional professions, such as law, medicine, dentistry and architecture, is still found in the collective bargaining legislation of some jurisdictions.[2] These exclusions appear to reflect a view that the economic interests of professional employees are best advanced through their own professional associations in the same manner as their self-employed colleagues. As the number of employed professionals has increased, there has been a much greater acceptance of collective bargaining by professionals and, concurrently, a reduction, or elimination, of the statutory exclusion for professional employees.[3] Nurses, engineers, para-medical professionals and, to a lesser extent, medical residents and lawyers, have used the collective bargaining structure rather than their own professional associations to assert their economic interests.

1. See generally, S. B. Goldenberg, *Professional Workers and Collective Bargaining* (Ottawa, 1970); G. W. Adams, *Collective Bargaining by Salaried Professionals*, (1977) 32 Rel. Ind. 184.
2. Ontario, s(3)(a).
3. Canada, s.107(1), s.125(3); Ontario, s.6(3).

6. Students

413. Whether collective bargaining legislation extends to cover those persons who receive their training on the job is problematical. Such persons may perform some of the work ordinarily performed by employees, but this work forms a part of their training programme and may be both supervised and paid by someone other than the employer. In order for these persons to be considered to be employees for the purpose of inclusion under general collective bargaining legislation their relationship with an employer must possess most of the characteristics of the normal employment relationship.[1] Labour boards have held that residents and interns,[2] prison imates participating in a rehabilitative programme,[3] persons employed under a publicly-subsidized works programme,[4] and student research assistants,[5] can be considered to be employees, and therefore, covered by collective bargaining legislation.

1. *Cranbrook District Hospital*, [1975] 1 C.L.R.B.R. 42 (B.C.L.R.B.).
2. *St. Paul's Hospital*, [1976] 2 C.L.R.B.R. 161 (B.C.L.R.B.).
3. *Guelph Beef Centre*, [1977] 1 C.L.R.B.R. 368 (O.L.R.B.).
4. *Kelowna Centennial Museum*, [1977] 2 C.L.R.B.R. 285 (B.C.L.R.B.).
5. *Carleton University*, [1978] 1 C.L.R.B.R. 452.

7. Other exclusions

414. Collective bargaining legislation in some jurisdictions also excludes from its coverage persons employed in particular occupations, such as agricultural workers and domestics.[1] The only supportable rationale for these exclusions is that a sufficient number of these workers would not be employed by a single employer to justify the formation of a collective bargaining relationship.[2] This rationale is now less convincing in the case of agricultural workers as the recent growth of 'agribusiness' has meant that the small farmer is no longer the typical agricultural employer.[3]

1. Ontario, for example, excludes persons employed in agriculture, hunting, trapping, domestics, and some persons employed in horticulture (s.2).

161

2. See Quebec, s.20 requiring bargaining units of agricultural workers to contain at least three persons ordinarily and continuously employed.
3. See K. Neilson & I. Christie, *The Agricultural Labour in Canada: A Legal Point of View*, (1975) 2 Dal. Law Journal 330; *South Peace Farms*, [1977] 1 C.L.R.B.R. 441 (B.C.L.R.B.).

B. Eligible trade unions

415. Collective bargaining by definition requires that the interests of employees be represented through the collectivity of a trade union. Not every organization of employees, however, has legal status as a trade union as certain qualifications have been imposed by the legislation in order to ensure that the organization is capable of representing the interests of its individual members in collective bargaining. Organizations that do not meet these qualifications are considered to lack status for collective bargaining purposes, and cannot acquire bargaining rights or enter into valid collective agreements.

1. Arm's length relationship

416. The scheme of collective bargaining legislation contemplates that there be an arm's length relationship between the trade union and employer. To achieve this end the legislation expressly defines a trade union as an organization of 'employees',[1] and prohibits employers from supporting or interfering with the formation, selection or administration of a trade union.[2] Perhaps even more importantly, if improper domination can be established, the impugned organization does not qualify for legal status as bargaining agent and any agreement made by such an organization would not be considered as a collective agreement.[3]

1. Canada, s.107(1); British Columbia, s.1(1); Quebec, s.1(a); Ontario, s.1(1)(h).
2. *Supra*, c.11–S3 *Protection of Trade Union Rights*.
3. Canada, s.134; British Columbia, s.50; Ontario, s.12, s.40.

417. The requirement of an arm's length relationship, however, has been interpreted by the labour boards in such a way as to take into account the fact that the character of organizations may change over time. While an organization actually comprising both employees and managers cannot be considered a trade union,[1] it is possible for an organization to purge itself of its managerial members by making such persons ineligible for membership.[2] In this way an organization can acquire trade union status even though it may have begun as a staff association that included in its membership persons exercising managerial functions.

1. *Hydro Electric Power Commission of Ontario*, [1971] O.L.R.B. 501.
2. *Children's Aid Society*, [1977] 1 C.L.R.B.R. 129 (O.L.R.B.).

418. Problems in applying the requirement of an arm's length relationship may also arise when a person exercising managerial functions, lends some support to union activities. Such support may not always be regarded as amounting to management domination if it can be established that the person was not perceived by the employees as acting on behalf of the employer.[1] This type of situation may occur where the manager lending support to the union acts under the erroneous belief that he is a member of the bargaining unit, or where he is clearly acting in opposition to management.

    1. *Air Liquide*, (1964) 64 C.L.L.C. para. 16,002 (O.L.R.B.); *General Aviation Services*, [1979] 2 C.L.R.B.R. 98 (C.L.R.B.).

419. Not all forms of employer–employee co-operation are treated as being incompatible with collective bargaining. An interesting question is whether employee participation on a board of directors may disqualify a trade union where the employee-director has been active in the union's organizing campaign. In certain circumstances such participation has been held not to taint the union as being management dominated.[1]

    1. *S. D. Adams Welded Products*, [1978] 2 C.L.R.B.R. 36 (O.L.R.B.).

420. Moreover, some forms of employer–union co-operation are not considered as impairing the arm's length relationship, especially where there has been a long standing collective bargaining relationship. It has been recognized that unions may negotiate such benefits as paid leave for employees conducting union business and use of the employer's premises for union business.[1]

    1. Canada, s.184(2).

2. Collective bargaining purpose

421. The definition of 'trade union' in Canadian collective bargaining legislation expressly contemplates that such organizations have as one of their purposes the regulation of relations between employers and employees. Employees who organize for other purposes such as the encouragement of social and recreational activities might not satisfy this requirement of a collective bargaining purpose.[1] This requirement, however, does not preclude the acquisition of bargaining rights by employee organizations not affiliated with national or international trade unions, provided that such organization have a collective bargaining purpose and do not suffer from the taint of employer domination.

    1. *Burlington-Nelson Hospital*, (1962) 63 C.L.L.C. para. 16,269 (O.L.R.B.).

422. In British Columbia the legislation takes a slightly more parochial approach imposing the additional requirement that collective bargaining be carried out within the province.[1] Such a requirement would appear to preclude a trade union from bargaining on a strictly national basis where it represents employees falling under that province's jurisdiction.[2] This restriction, however, may not prohibit all forms of national bargaining, provided that the requirements of the provincial legislation are met.

    1. S.1(1).
    2. *Otis Elevator* v. *Elevator Constructions*, (1973) 35 D.L.R. (3d) 566 (B.C.C.A.).

423. The general pattern in Canada of separating private sector and public sector collective bargaining may also be a factor to be taken into account when determining whether an organization has been established for collective bargaining purposes. It has been held that an organization formed for the purpose of representing government employees could not properly bargain for employees falling within the private sector.[1] This impediment appears to be easily surmountable, however, as such organizations are permitted to establish separate but related entities to carry on bargaining in the private sector.

    1. *Oshawa General Hospital*, [1970] O.L.R.B. 765.

424. The requirement of a collective bargaining purpose has been interpreted on occasion as disqualifying from trade union status organizations that have been regarded as having an overriding political purpose,[1] even though the legal justification for such a disqualification appears to be doubtful.[2] Nevertheless, it is clear that the requirement of a collective bargaining purpose has never been interpreted as precluding trade unions from engaging in the usual political activities connected with the advancement of their interests.[3]

    1. *Branch Lines*, (1950) 52 C.L.L.C. para. 16,622 (C.L.R.B.).
    2. *Smith and Rhuland* v. *The Queen*, [1953] 3 D.L.R. 690 (S.C.C.).
    3. *Supra*, Introduction c.IV *The Canadian Labour Movement*.

3. Formal structure

425. Canadian collective bargaining legislation appears to contemplate that trade unions operate within at least a rudimentary framework of constitutional organization. Some Canadian jurisdictions provide that a trade union may be required to file with the government its constitution and by-laws.[1] In Ontario a proper constitutional framework has long been regarded as a pre-condition to certification and that the Board has not only required that the formation of the trade union follow accepted procedures[2] but also that trade union officers be responsible and accountable to the membership.[3] These restrictions, however, have not been applied so as to prevent a local trade union that has been placed under the control of its parent union (usually referred to as trusteeship) from acquiring bargaining rights.[4] These decisions appear to reflect only a more narrow concern that a sufficient organizational structure be established, and not the wider concern that internal trade union procedures conform to generally accepted standards for democratic institutions.

    1. Canada, Corporations and Labour Unions Returns Act, R.S.C. 1970, c.C–31; British Columbia, Reg. 552/73, s.18 as am. 162/74; Ontario, s.75; Quebec, s.23.
    2. *Associated Hebrew Schools of Toronto*, [1978] O.L.R.B. 797.
    3. *J. Harris*, (1960) 60 C.L.L.C. para 16,177 (O.L.R.B.); *Canada Trustee Mortgage*, [1977] 1 C.L.R.B.R. 125 (O.L.R.B.).
    4. *S. McCord* v. *O.L.R.B.*, (1956) 4 D.L.R. (2d) 455 (Ont.H.C.).

4. Restrictions on membership

426. Even where an organization can establish that it functions within a basic

164

constitutional framework, problems may arise because that constitution restricts those eligible for membership in the organization. Once bargaining rights are conferred upon a trade union, it is required by law to bargain on behalf of all employees in its bargaining constituency. Where the trade union constitution disqualifies some of these employees from membership, there is the possibility that some members of the bargaining unit could find their jobs in jeopardy. If the union were to obtain a union security provision requiring that union membership be a condition for further employment, then those employees not belonging to the union would find themselves out of a job. As a result, labour boards have not granted bargaining rights where membership restrictions would have the effect of disqualifying some members of the bargaining unit.[1]

1. *Gaymer and Oultram* (1954) 54 C.L.L.C. para. 17,073 (O.L.R.B.); *Windsor Raceway Holdings*, [1979] 2 C.L.R.B.R. 89 (O.L.R.B.).

427. This type of constitutional restriction is more prevalent among craft unions operating primarily in the construction industry. Although the problems created by this type of restriction is reduced to some extent by the establishment of craft bargaining units (a bargaining constituency defined in terms of the skills employed by the members of the particular craft union), it still exists where craft unions attempt to organize along industrial lines.

428. Difficulties may occur even where a union has an established practice of not applying the membership restrictions of its constitution. While labour boards generally have overlooked such 'paper' restrictions where *de-facto* membership is granted, the courts have been less lenient.[1] As a result, legislation in some Canadian jurisdictions now expressly provides that eligibility requirements contained in union constitutions may be overlooked in determining whether a person is a member of a trade union.[2] Moreover, it is clear that, in the absence of any membership restrictions, trade unions are permitted to organize groups of employees not normally associated with the rest of the membership.[3]

1. *Metropolitan Life Insurance*, (1967) 67 C.L.L.C. para. 16,026 (O.L.R.B.).
2. Ontario, s.92(4); Quebec, s.24(j). In Canada and British Columbia the problem is overcome by only requiring a determination of the 'wishes' of the employees.
3. In *South Peace Farms*, [1977] 1 C.L.R.B.R. 441 the British Columbia board held that it was not inappropriate for an industrial union to seek to represent agricultural workers; but see *Caravelle Foods*, [1979] 2 C.L.R.B.R. 85 where the Alberta board held that it was inappropriate for a construction craft union to represent employees in the food processing industry.

429. The extent to which labour boards may regulate the structure of an organization by not granting it status as a trade union has been placed in some doubt by a recent court decision overruling a board decision holding that an organization could not be considered as a trade union because the constitution of that organization created a class of provisional members who were barred from holding any office in the organization.[1] The court in quashing this decision indicated that the Board had no legislative mandate to regulate intermembership rights in this manner. While this decision has not been construed by labour

boards as restricting their inquiry into the question of whether the organization
extends membership to all employees in the bargaining unit, it does appear to
have limited the ability of labour boards to regulate internal union affairs when
dealing with the issue of trade union status.

1. *Re CSAO National and Oakville Trafalgar Memorial Hospital*, (1972) 26 D.L.R. (3d) 63
(Ont.C.A.); see also *R* v. *N.B. Teachers*, (1971) 17 D.L.R. (3d) 72 (N.B.C.A.).

5. Discrimination

430. Canadian collective bargaining legislation provides that trade unions
are not to acquire bargaining rights if they discriminate on certain grounds
(usually those, covered by human rights legislation) and that any agreements
entered into by such unions are to be considered invalid.[1] The lack of labour
board jurisprudence dealing with these provisions would indicate that this type
of discrimination occurs infrequently. Instances of racial discrimination have
been considered on occasion,[2] as have situations raising the matters of creed
and nationality, ancestry or place of origin, and age. Creed has been equated
with religious belief and has not been extended to cover adherence to a
particular political ideology.[3] On the other hand, the prohibition against discrimination based on national ancestry or place of origin has been held to cover
citizenship requirements in union constitutions.[4] The provision relating to
discrimination based on age has been held by one labour board to be qualified
by the definition of such discrimination found in human rights legislation.[5]

1. British Columbia, s.50; Ontario, s.12, s.40; the federal legislation contains a different kind
of provision dealing generally with restrictions on membership (Canada, c.134(2)).
2. *T. Barbesin*, [1960] O.L.R.B. 80; *John Murdock*, (1955) 56 C.L.L.C. para. 15,286
(Q.S.C.).
3. *Steinbergs*, [1971] O.L.R.B. 329.
4. *Journal Publishing*, [1970] O.L.R.B. 925.
5. *Ontario Hydro*, [1978] 2 C.L.R.B.R. 109 (O.L.R.B.).

431. A more difficult question is whether organizations closely connected
with particular religious groups, such as the Christian Labour Association of
Canada, are permitted by law to acquire collective bargaining status. In one
case where the constitution of one such union expressly provided that one of its
aims was to apply Christian principles to collective bargaining, a labour board
refused status on the basis that this type of trade union would tend to impose a
particular religion on all members. This decision, however, was subsequently
overruled in the courts.[1] The result is that, even though trade unions that
organize along religious lines are not a common feature of Canadian collective
bargaining, such unions are not rendered illegitimate because of their religious
affiliation and can acquire trade union status provided that they meet the other
requirements of collective bargaining legislation.

1. *R* v. *Trenton Construction Workers*, (1963) 39 D.L.R. (2d) 593 (Ont.H.C.).

6. Presence within jurisdiction

432. One Canadian jurisdiction has also imposed the requirement that an organization have some independent presence within the jurisdiction in order to qualify for bargaining rights.[1] Presumably, the rationale for this restriction is that some presence within the jurisdiction is needed in order for the organization to answer both to the general laws of the jurisdiction and also to its own members.[2] While this restriction has not been construed as a complete ban on international and national unions operating within that provincial jurisdiction, it does require them to charter local unions operated by officials resident within the jurisdiction.[3]

   1. British Columbia, s.1(1).
   2. *Corcoat Engineering*, [1974] C.L.R.B.R. 530 (B.C.L.R.B.).
   3. *Bethlehem Copper*, [1978] 2 C.L.R.B.R. 410 (B.C.L.R.B.).

7. Councils of trade unions

433. It is also possible under Canadian collective bargaining legislation for a group of trade unions to join together as a council of trade unions and, as a council, acquire bargaining rights.[1] This form of multi-union bargaining often occurs in the situation where a number of trade unions organized along craft lines are faced with a single employer, or a group of employers bargaining as a single industry. In one jurisdiction, British Columbia, the minister of labour may refer the question of whether a council of trade unions is the appropriate bargaining structure to the labour board, and the board may in turn impose the council structure upon a group of trade unions.[2] By contrast, in Ontario a council of trade unions cannot obtain certification without first establishing that each of its constituent unions have vested the council with full authority as bargaining agent.

   1. Canada, s.130; British Columbia, s.1(1), s.57; Ontario, s.1.1(h), s.9.
   2. *British Columbia Railway*, [1977] 1 C.L.R.B.R. 289 (B.C.L.R.B.): *Construction Labour Relations Association*, [1978] 2 C.L.R.B.R. 203 (B.C.R.B.).

C. Method of acquisition

434. A distinguishing feature of Canadian collective bargaining legislation is that it provides an express method by which trade unions can acquire bargaining rights.[1] The legislation provides that a trade union may make application to the labour board and, if it can establish its representative character and meets all other requirements, it becomes entitled to receive a certificate.[2] The certificate gives the union the exclusive authority to represent employees in the bargaining unit and imposes upon the employer a corresponding obligation to bargain exclusively with that union. This procedure, referred to as certification, was established in order to meet the problems that occurred when unions attempted to obtain employer recognition by strike action.[3] Such recognition strikes, as they are called, have now been proscribed by collective bargaining legislation.

1. Canada, ss.124–136; British Columbia, ss.39–45; Ontario, ss.5–8, 108 (construction industry); Quebec, ss.20–31.
2. In Quebec the certification process is handled more informally by investigative commissioners rather than by a tribunal.
3. *Supra*, C.II–§.1 *'The Need for Statutory Protection'*.

435. While most unions acquire their bargaining rights through the process of certification, it is also possible to do so through the faster and more informal method of voluntary recognition by which an employer simply agrees to recognize a trade union as bargaining agent for its employees.[1] Voluntary recognition is more common in the construction industry where the short duration of many jobs often makes it the more attractive procedure. Bargaining rights acquired in this manner, however, are usually more open to challenge than those acquired through the certification process because of the possibility that employer recognition might constitute a 'sweetheart' arrangement precluding an employee voice in the selection of their bargaining agent.[2] As certification is the more common procedure for acquiring bargaining rights in Canada a number of the more important features of this process will be described.

1. Express reference to this procedure is found in Canada, s.107(1); Ontario, s.15(3).
2. Ontario, s.52.

1. Degree of formality

436. Since certification entitles a trade union to employer recognition, it should not be surprising that the certification process has been the focus of considerable labour–management disagreement. One of the more controversial issues is the degree of formality that the certification process should assume. Trade unions take the position that the process should be fast, informal, non-adversarial, and so should be conducted without hearing representations from employers or opposing employees. From the union perspective certification should be a simple matter of determining whether it has sufficient members to meet the criterion of representativeness. The employer position emphasizes due process in the sense of a full opportunity being afforded to any person possibly affected to make representation at judicial-style hearings, and the taking of a vote to determine employee support for the union. Certification procedures in the different Canadian jurisdictions appear to reflect a compromise between these two opposing points of view. The most informal procedures are found in Quebec where the process is in the hands of investigative commissioners, and the statute expressly provides that employers are not to be considered as an interested party where the representative character of the union is in issue.[1] By contrast, Ontario provides a full scale adjudicative hearing at which the employer has full standing on all issues raised by the certification application.[2] However, because of the need to process construction industry certifications more expeditiously, the Ontario board need not hold a hearing where an application arises out of that industry.[3]

1. Quebec, s.24e.
2. Statutory Powers Procedure Act, S.O. 1971, c.47.
3. S.91(13).

2. Proof of representativeness

(a) Membership evidence

437. The usual method by which trade unions establish representativeness in order to acquire bargaining rights is through evidence of membership. By establishing that more than a majority of employees[1] in the bargaining unit are union members, a trade union in all but one Canadian jurisdiction can acquire 'outright' certification without a vote of the employees having to be taken. The exception is Nova Scotia where an employee vote is required in all cases.[2] The form of trade union membership evidence has to meet certain standards established by law[3] and, since employers do not have access to this membership evidence, labour boards have tended to enforce these standards strictly.[4] Trade unions generally support this procedure for establishing representativeness since, from their point of view, it is faster and more efficacious than an employee vote.

1. In Ontario, however, more than 55 per cent is required for outright certification (s.7(2)).
2. Trade Union Act, S.N.S. 1972, c.19, s.24.
3. Generally it must be established that the employee has unequivocally applied for union membership and paid a certain sum of money to the union as either an initiation fee or as dues. The Canadian Labour Board now requires that at least $5 be paid, while $2 is required in Quebec, and only $1 in Ontario.
4. *Webster Air Equipment Co.*, (1958) 58 C.L.L.C. para. 18,110 (O.L.R.B.).

(b) Petitions

438. The straightforward process of determining membership support becomes more difficult in those cases where petitions, or statements of desire, are filed in opposition to the trade union. The problem occurs where employees who earlier had signed membership cards recant and indicate on the petition that they no longer support the union. Labour boards have treated these 'changes-of-heart' as casting sufficient doubt upon a trade union's membership evidence so as to justify the taking of an employee vote. Petitions are only given weight, however, if it can be established by the petitioner that the petition represents a voluntary expression of the desires of those employees who have signed it. Most petitions would appear to founder on this requirement since employer influence tends to be a common feature of petitions.[1]

1. The issue of the extent to which an employer may express his views to employees often arise where the board is assessing the voluntariness of a petition. *Supra*, c.II–4 *Reconciling Employee, Employer and Trade Union Rights*.

439. The reception of petitions is one of the more controversial aspects of the certification process. Not only do petitions tend to prolong the certification process, but they also appear to attract improper employer interference in trade union affairs.[1] To protect the integrity of the certification process the time within which a petition may be filed has been severely restricted in all Canadian jurisdictions.[2] In fact, in the federal jurisdiction membership evidence may even be determined as of a date occurring before the application has been filed in order to eliminate the effect of improper employer interference.[3]

1. *Canadian Imperial Bank of Commerce*, [1979] 1 C.L.R.B.R. 18 (C.L.R.B.).
2. In British Columbia membership support is determined as of the date of the application while in Ontario it is assessed as of a 'terminal date' set by the board and usually a week after the date of application.
3. S.126 (*c*).

(c) Votes

440. The employee vote is generally regarded as a secondary procedure for establishing representativeness. Although employers frequently advocate that votes should be held in all cases, this idea has received little support on the trade union side. Trade union reticence to adopt this position can be explained by the fact that studies have indicated that initial membership support is usually greater than employee support manifested later in a vote. As a result, trade unions enjoy a greater success rate where support is determined on membership evidence alone than where the vote is taken. The explanation for this phenomenon may relate to the fact that votes held in the context of the employment relationship are markedly different than the electoral process used to choose governments. The delays resulting from the holding of a vote and the dominant position of the employer are both factors that tend to erode voting support for a trade union.[1]

1. *Plateau Mills*, [1977] 1 C.L.R.B.R. 82 (B.C.L.R.B.).

441. In order for a certification vote to be held trade unions generally have to establish a certain minimum standard of employee support.[1] Some jurisdictions also provide for faster and more informal vote procedures in the form of prehearing vote.[2] Votes are conducted by labour board officials on the employer's premises, and scrutineers representing the union and the employer are appointed. Although a trade union must obtain a majority to gain bargaining rights, what constitutes a majority varies from jurisdiction to jurisdiction.[3] A vote may be set aside by the board if either side has engaged in improper electioneering practices.

1. Canada, 35%; British Columbia, 45% Ontario, 45% (but 35% for pre-hearing vote); Quebec, 35%.
2. British Columbia, s.44(1); Nova Scotia, s.24; Ontario, s.8.
3. Canada, a majority of those voting provided that at least 35% of employees have voted; British Columbia, a majority of those voting provided that at least 55% of employees have voted; Ontario, a majority of those voting; Quebec, a majority of all those in the bargaining unit.

(d) Proof of representativeness impaired by employer action

442. Some forms of employer interference in trade union organizing campaigns may actually render it impossible for the true wishes of employees to be ascertained either by means of membership evidence or a vote. Some jurisdictions provide that in these circumstances a trade union may still be certified as bargaining agent despite the lack of proven employee support.[1] These provisions would appear to serve as a disincentive to improper employer conduct by preventing employers from benefiting from their own wrongful conduct.

1. *Supra*, c.II–§5, *Remedies*.

3. Timeliness of application

443. In order to provide some stability for the established collective bargaining structure Canadian collective bargaining legislation places some limits on when applications to acquire (or terminate) bargaining rights may be made. The most important limitation is the one curtailing the making of certification applications when there is already a collective agreement covering the employees in question.[1] Generally, in this situation an application can only be made in the last two or three months of an agreement. The existence of this type of restriction, commonly referred to as the 'collective agreement bar' may give rise to the question of whether certain arrangements are in fact collective agreements. 'Sweetheart' agreements (non-arms-length arrangements between unions and employers) are expressly disqualified by law, and not considered to be collective agreements.[2] Moreover, it must be established that the trade union represented employees in the bargaining unit when the arrangement was entered into.[3] An agreement signed in the shadow of another union's organizing campaign, however, has been considered as a valid collective agreement.[4]

1. Canada, s.124(2)(c), Ontario, s.5; Quebec, s.21(d); in British Columbia, however, an application can be made in the seventh and eighth month of each year of the agreement (s.39).
2. Canada, s.134; British Columbia, s.50; Ontario, s.40.
3. *Niagara Crushed Stone* (1958) 58 C.L.L.C. para. 18,118 (O.L.R.B.).
4. Re *Brayshaws Steel* and *USWA*, (1971) 26 D.L.R. (3d) 153 (Ont.C.A.).

444. Even where there is no collective agreement present, existing bargaining rights may still bar the bringing of a certification application. Canadian collective bargaining legislation generally protects bargaining rights acquired through certification by not permitting any new certification application for a specified time.[1] As well certification applications are often curtailed during the period when parties are negotiating for a collective agreement.[2] In one jurisdiction, Ontario, bargaining rights acquired through voluntary recognition are also given some statutory protection.[3]

1. Canada, s.124(2)(b) – one year; British Columbia, s.39(2) – six months; Ontario, s.5(2) – one year; Quebec, s.21(b) – six months from the acquisition of right to strike.

2. Canada, s.124(3); Ontario, s.53.
3. S.5(3). But employees may apply to terminate bargaining rights acquired through voluntary recognition during the first year of the agreement, s.52.

4. Other bars to certification applications

445. The making of repeated certification applications is not permitted by Canadian collective bargaining legislation.[1] An interval between applications of from three to six months is usually required in order to protect the work place from the excessive disruption caused by repeated applications.

1. Canada, Regulations s.31; British Columbia, s.49; Ontario, s.92(2)(i); Quebec, s.31.

446. Strike action contemporaneous with a certification application may also bar the entertainment of that application. While there is no express legislative provision imposing such a bar, at least one labour board has imposed such a bar in order to enforce compliance with the prohibition against recognition strikes.[1]

1. *Radio Lunch*, (1950) 52 C.L.L.C. para. 17,012 (O.L.R.B.).

5. The fluctuating work force

447. The general requirement of determining employee support as of a specific point of time may cause problems where a work force is expanding. Balanced against the concern that certification not be delayed is a concern that prospective employees should have a say in the choice of the bargaining agent. Where employees currently employed do not constitute a substantial and representative segment of the work force to be employed, labour boards have followed the practice of delaying certification and ordering a later vote provided that there is a real likelihood that the increase in the work force will take place within a reasonable time.[1] Even though no specific legislative mandate exists for this practice, it has nevertheless been approved by the courts.[2] Once bargaining rights have been acquired, however, the addition of new employees is simply considered as an accretion to the existing bargaining unit.

1. *Frant and Waselovich*, (1957) 57 C.L.L.C. para. 18,057; but see *Uranerz Exploration and Mining*, [1978] 2 C.L.R.B.R. 193 (C.L.R.B.). S.108(2) of the Ontario legislation, however, expressly recognizes that this practice may not be appropriate for the construction industry.
2. *Noranda Mines* v. *R.*, (1969) 7 D.L.R. (3d) 1 (S.C.C.).

§3. THE SHAPE OF THE COLLECTIVE BARGAINING STRUCTURE

448. The task of shaping the collective bargaining structure in Canada has been largely left in the hands of the labour boards. Perhaps surprisingly, very little legislative guidance has been given to the boards as to how they should define the appropriate collective bargaining constituency (the bargaining unit) for the trade union, or go about identifying the employer on the other side of the bargaining table. It is in this area, more than any other, that the labour boards formulate policies that are legislative in nature, relying to a large part on their own labour relations expertise.

A. The collective bargaining constituency

449. Bargaining unit determination has been the primary influence shaping the collective bargaining structure in Canada. Labour boards have been given a general power to determine 'the unit of employees appropriate for collective bargaining' qualified only by legislative instructions relating to certain types of employees such as those who belong to established crafts or professions.[1] The general pattern has been the local bargaining unit confined to all employees of a particular employer in a particular municipality. In the federal jurisdiction, however, there can be found bargaining units national in scope covering all employees of such national undertakings as airlines and railways. The bargaining unit pattern for the construction industry is somewhat different, the geographic area being wider than a single municipality in order to take into account the ambulatory nature of construction activity. In the more organized sectors of the construction industry, moreover, there has been a move towards province-wide bargaining on a multi-employer level, and even a multi-union level. Multi-employer bargaining structures are more prevalent in British Columbia where this kind of bargaining structure is not confined to the construction industry.[2]

1. Canada, s.125; British Columbia, ss.40–42; Ontario, s.6; Quebec, s.20.
2. Section 40 of the British Columbia Labour Code provides a general procedure for multi-employer certification. See *Artisan Industries*, [1979] 3 C.L.R.B.R. 518 (B.C.L.R.B.). As well, s.132 of the Canada Labour Code provides for multi-employer bargaining for the long-shoring industry.

450. Labour boards must take into account a variety of often competing considerations when determining appropriate collective bargaining constituencies. Reference is often made by labour boards to the rather flexible notion of a 'community of interest' among employees when bargaining unit determinations are being made. Underlying this concept, however, is a basic tension between the desire of unions to organize employees in a manner most beneficial to their interests and the equally strong desire of employers to obtain a bargaining structure most conducive to their interests. Not to be overlooked, moreover, are the interests of employees, not all of whom may support the union. If certification is granted to a union, it then has the exclusive right to represent all employees in the bargaining unit regardless of the fact that a minority of those employees may not wish union representation. Finally, labour boards must also give some weight to what might be described as the public's interest in the creation of a rational and orderly bargaining structure. All of these considerations deserve to be examined in some detail.

1. Ability to organize

451. The shape and composition of the bargaining unit are factors clearly affecting a trade union's ability to organize employees. Generally trade unions find it easier to organize small, cohesive groups of employees working at a single location and, as a result, propose bargaining units reflecting this fact of life. Where trade unions have been successful in organizing a large group of employees, however, they may be more inclined to request a more comprehensive unit, knowing that existing employee support will be sufficient to sweep other employees into such a bargaining unit. Employers, as a general rule, tend to take the opposite approach, proposing more comprehensive bargaining units when a trade union's support is in doubt and more narrow units where it is clear that a trade union had adequate support for certification.

452. Labour boards in Canada have expressly recognized that the right of employees to organize must be taken into account when defining the appropriate bargaining unit. The most obvious situation where the right to organize had to be considered was in the case of bank employees. Banking in Canada has been dominated by a few large institutions with branches located throughout the country. The large number of employees involved and the geographic distances separating those employees meant that organization of these employees into one national bargaining unit was not a practical reality. Taking this factor into account, the Canada Labour Relations Board, reversing an earlier decision,[1] held that a single bank was a unit appropriate for collective bargaining a decision that opened the door for the organization of bank employees on a local basis.[2] Labour boards in other jurisdictions have also recognized that the ability of employees to organize is a factor influencing bargaining unit determination.[3]

1. *Bank of Nova Scotia*, (1959) 59 C.L.L.C. para. 18,152 (C.L.R.B.).
2. *Canadian Imperial Bank of Commerce*, [1977] 2 C.L.R.B.R. 99 (C.L.R.B.).
3. *Woodward Stores*, [1975] 1 C.L.R.B.R. 114 (B.C.L.R.B.); *Canada Trusco Mortgage*, [1977] 2 C.L.R.B.R. 93 (O.L.R.B.).

2. Viability of bargaining structure

453. An equally important consideration when determining the appropriate bargaining unit is the establishment of a viable collective bargaining structure for the long term. The primary concern is to avoid 'fragmentation' of the bargaining structure where a number of trade unions end up competing against each other for the same slice of the economic pie. The most obvious example of fragmentation is where employees of the same employer employed at the same location are represented by different unions, a situation likely to create inter-union rivalry in respect of both economic gains and work jurisdiction. Fragmentation sometimes work to the advantage of trade unions, but at times it imposes a handicap upon them. A small bargaining unit of highly skilled employees capable of shutting down an employer's operation possesses considerable bargaining power. On the other hand, if a small bargaining unit of employees is unable to shut down an employer's operation immediately through strike action, then it is unlikely to have the financial resources to carry on sustained strike activity.

454. The general bias of Canadian labour boards has been in the direction of defining more comprehensive units.[1] Once a bargaining unit is defined, moreover, labour boards have been reluctant to carve out smaller bargaining units from the existing structure.[2] The effect has been to somewhat even out trade union bargaining power and to reduce inter-union rivalries. Another effect has been to impose upon trade unions the difficult task of reconciling the divergent interests found within these more comprehensive bargaining units.

> 1. *Insurance Corporation of British Columbia*, [1974] 1 C.L.R.B.R. 403 (B.C.L.R.B.); *Stratford General Hospital*, [1977] 1 C.L.R.B.R. 70 (O.L.R.B.).
> 2. *Canadian Pacific*, [1976] 1 C.L.R.B.R. 361 (C.L.R.B.); but see *Canadian Broadcasting Corp.*, [1977] 2 C.L.R.B.R. 481 (C.L.R.B.).

3. Craft bargaining units

455. There has always been a certain tension within the Canadian trade union movement between those unions organizing employees along craft lines and those that organize employees on an industrial basis.[1] Craft unionism groups together workers who share common skills whereas industrial unionism groups together all employees employed in a particular operation regardless of their skills. Since the skills of their members are often in high demand, craft unions may wield considerable bargaining power. Craft unionism tends to be centred on the construction industry, but may also be found to some extent in the printing industry.

> 1. *Supra*, Introduction c.IV *The Canadian Labour Movement*.

456. Organization along craft lines gives rise to a number of problems. For one thing, the unskilled worker may be left outside the protective umbrella of collective bargaining. Just as troublesome is the fact that craft unionism fragments the bargaining structure giving rise to competition between trade unions. Since the craft or skill is the common denominator among its members, the craft union places great emphasis on its own work jurisdiction, and its members feel more closely bound to the craft than to any particular employment relationship. This attachment to a particular work jurisdiction often gives rise to 'jurisdictional disputes' where more than one union makes a claim to the same work. Usually such disputes cannot be resolved by a simple reference to bargaining unit descriptions since these tend to overlap.[1] As a result, some Canadian jurisdictions have established specific procedures for resolving such jurisdictional disputes.[2]

> 1. *Toronto Star Newspapers*, [1979] 2 C.L.R.B.R. 423 (O.L.R.B.).
> 2. Ontario, s.81.

457. In order to protect their work jurisdiction craft unions often rely upon 'sub-contracting' and 'non-affiliation' arrangements. The former type of arrangement, usually made with a general contractor, requires that any sub-contracting of work only be to employers with whom the union and other affiliated craft unions have bargaining rights. Enforcement of this kind of arrangement is often achieved by means of the non-affiliation arrangement that allows the members of the craft union to refuse to work alongside other employees not belonging to their union or another affiliated craft union. The Ontario Labour board has regarded the sub-contracting clause as a legitimate method of protecting a union's work jurisdiction,[1] and the British Columbia board has given its approval to the non-affiliation clause.[2]

1. *Metropolitan Toronto Apartment Builders*, [1979] 1 C.L.R.B.R. 197 (O.L.R.B.); *aff'd.* (1979) 79 C.L.L.C. para. 14,222 (Ont.Div.Ct.).
2. *R. M. Hardy*, [1977] 2 C.L.R.B.R. 357.

458. Despite the problems posed by craft bargaining units, it is generally recognized in Canadian jurisdictions that employees who have traditionally organized along craft lines are entitled to continue this pattern of organization.[1] Labour boards, though, have been reluctant to extend craft unionism beyond its traditional boundaries.[2] The recent growth in the organization of supervisory and professional employees, however, may be giving rise to a new type of craft unionism.[3]

1. British Columbia, s.41; Ontario, s.6(2); *Interior Contracting*, [1979] 1 C.L.R.B.R. 248 (C.L.R.B.).
2. *Firestone Tire & Rubber*, [1963] O.L.R.B. 491; *Collegiate Sports*, [1977] 1 C.L.R.B.R. 389 (B.C.L.R.B.); *Atomic Energy of Canada*, [1978] 1 C.L.R.B.R. 92 (C.L.R.B.).
3. *Infra*, paras. 463 and 464.

4. Agreed-upon bargaining units

459. In many situations unions and employers are able to reach agreement on the appropriate description of the bargaining unit. While such agreements usually serve to expedite certification hearings, they raise the problem of whether labour boards should accept such agreements where they appear to run contrary to prevailing policy. Most labour boards appear to accept such agreements unless they are obviously out of step with established policy.[1] This approach may be influenced by the fact that once bargaining occurs employers and trade unions often negotiate for a unit different than that set out in the certificate and, thereby, redefine their bargaining rights.[2] Such a practice appears to be acceptable provided that there is no encroachment upon other bargaining rights and no breach of the union's duty of fairly representing all the employees in the certified bargaining unit.[3]

1. *Fonthill Lumber*, (1964) 64 C.L.L.C. para. 16,305 (O.L.R.B.); but see *CJRP Radio* (1975) 77 C.L.L.C. para. 16,074 (C.L.R.B.).
2. *Beverage Disconsers* v. *Terra Nova Motor Inn*, (1974) 50 D.L.R. (3d) 253 (S.C.C.).
3. *Eastern Provincial Airways*, [1978] 2 C.L.R.B.R. 572 (C.L.R.B.).

5. Geographic proximity

460. The general pattern in Canada has been the local bargaining unit described in terms of all employees of an employer employed in a certain municipality, indicating that labour boards give considerable weight to the factor of geographic proximity. This factor, however, may not be determinative in all situations as the boards have at times confined the bargaining unit to a particular location in a municipality even though the employer's operation is conducted at more than one location in that municipality.[1] On other occasions, however, labour boards have described bargaining units embracing locations in the same municipality but several miles apart,[2] and even locations in different municipalities. Influencing these decisions have been such factors as the degree of interchange of employees between locations, the similarity of functions being performed at the different locations, and the difficulties of organizing employees at more than one location.

1. *Ponderosa Steak House*, [1975] 2 C.L.R.B.R. 10 (O.L.R.B.).
2. *Usarco*, [1967] O.L.R.B. 526.

6. Plant and office bargaining units

461. Some Canadian jurisdictions separate 'white-collar' and 'blue-collar' workers employed at the same location by placing them in separate bargaining units.[1] It is quite possible, however, that the separate office and plant bargaining units may be represented by the same bargaining agent. Technical personnel are usually included within the office unit. Generally, the larger plant bargaining units tend to fare better in collective bargaining than their office counterparts.

1. See W. G. Reed, *White-Collar Bargaining Units Under the Ontario Labour Relations Act* (Kingston, 1969).

7. Part-time employees and students

462. Some Canadian jurisdictions draw a distinction between full-time employees and part-time employees. In Ontario the general practice is to exclude part-time employees and students employed for the school vacation period from bargaining units of full-time employees. These excluded employees may form their own 'part-time' bargaining units. Ontario defines a part-time employee as a person employed for not more than 24 hours per week. Some jurisdictions, however, do not draw such a rigid distinction between full-time and part-time employees.[1]

1. See *Serre Rougemont*, (1977) 77 C.L.L.C. para 14,069 (Q.L.C.); *Toronto-Dominion Bank*, [1978] 1 C.L.R.B.R. 156 (C.L.R.B.); *Radio Station CHQM* (1975), 75 C.L.L.R. para. 16,166 (C.L.R.B.).

8. Professional employees

463. Legislation in some Canadian jurisdictions provides for separate bargaining units for professional employees.[1] Since professional employees have already organized themselves along professional lines for purposes other than collective bargaining, they generally seem to favour a collective bargaining structure that follows the same pattern. The problem is that bargaining units defined along purely professional lines create a fragmented bargaining structure that could result in the problems associated with a craft bargaining unit structure. As a result, labour boards have been generally reluctant to establish separate bargaining units for professional employees.[2] Nurses, however, have been able to establish a general pattern of organizing in separate bargaining units, and this pattern has been recognized by labour boards.

1. Canada, s.125(3); Ontario, s.6(3) (professional engineers only).
2. *Bell Canada*, [1976] 1 L.R.B.R. 345 (C.L.R.B.); *Stratford General Hospital*, [1977] 1 C.L.R.B.R. 70 (O.L.R.B.).

9. Supervisory employees

464. The trend in some Canadian jurisdictions in the direction of extending bargaining rights to supervisory employees raises the issue of the appropriate bargaining unit for such employees.[1] Labour boards appear to favour separate bargaining units as they serve to reduce the conflict of interest created by such employees supervising other organized employees.[2] Moreover, such units may flow naturally from the established collective bargaining structure as hourly-rated employees will usually have organized themselves already in their own bargaining units.

1. Section 124(4) of the Canada Labour Code and s.47 of the Labour Code of British Columbia expressly recognizes the possibility of supervisory bargaining units.
2. *B.C. Telephone*, [1977] 2 C.L.R.B.R. 385 (C.L.R.B.); *Tahsis*, [1977] 2 C.L.R.B.R. 452 (B.C.L.R.B.).

10. Dependent contractors

465. Dependent contractors, although having a close resemblance to other employees, can often be distinguished on the basis that they bring to their work a substantial investment in the tools of their trade.[1] The question is whether such differences justify a separate bargaining unit of dependent contractors. One jurisdiction, Ontario, expressly requires a separate unit unless a majority of dependent contractors prefer otherwise.[2] British Columbia, on the other hand, places dependent contractors within existing bargaining units of employees.[3]

1. *Supra* paras. 404 to 406.
2. S.6(4).
3. S.48.

11. Security guards

466. The potential conflict of interest resulting from the security guard's responsibility to monitor other employees has meant that this type of employee has usually been placed in a separate bargaining unit.[1] The legislation in some jurisdictions goes even further and requires that guards be represented by their own separate trade unions.[2] In order for an employee to be considered as a security guard it must be established that the person is more than a watchman and has responsibilities to monitor and admonish other employees.[3]

1. *St. Vincent's Hospital*, [1974] 1 C.L.R.B.R. 363 (B.C.L.R.B.); *Eastern Provincial Airways*, [1979] 1 C.L.R.B.R. 456 (C.L.R.B.).
2. Ontario, s.11; s.135 of the Canada Labour Code imposes a somewhat similar restriction but only in respect of 'private constables'.
3. *Grain*, (1963) 63 C.L.L.C. para. 16,291 (O.L.R.B.).

B. Defining the employer

467. Collective bargaining requires that there be on one side of the bargaining table a trade union representing employees and on the other side an employer. Employer is generally defined in collective bargaining legislation as simply a person who employs one or more employees.[1] In some jurisdictions, however, employer is defined in terms of a person employing more than one person.[2] While the task of defining the employer is usually not as difficult as determining the appropriate bargaining unit, problems sometimes arise when dealing with the employer side of the collective bargaining equation.

1. Canada, s.107; British Columbia, s.1(1); Quebec, s.(1).
2. Nova Scotia, c.19, s.1(1); Saskatchewan, s.2(g); The Ontario legislation contains no definition of employer but it provides that a bargaining unit must contain more than one employee (s.6(1)).

1. Identifying the employer

468. The functions normally performed by an employer are sometimes spread among more than one person. This spreading of employer functions tends to obscure the employment relationship giving labour boards some difficulty when determining the person with whom the employees should be bargaining. Often these situations occur where a business has contracted out some of its employment functions to an employment agency. Labour boards have taken the position that they will look beyond the outward trappings of such arrangements in order to identify the person exercising real control over the employees.[1] In doing so the boards must answer such questions as: who hires the employees; who controls the employees work; who effectively establishes wages and working conditions; who controls any negotiations relating to wages and working conditions?[2] The application of these tests make it difficult for employers to contract out of their collective bargaining obligations.

1. *Seafarers Int'l. Union* v. *Kent Line*, (1972) 27 D.L.R. (3d) 105 (Fed.C.A.); *Welland County Separate School Board*, (1972) 72 C.L.L.C. para. 16,063 (O.L.R.B.).
2. *MacCosham Van Lines*, [1979] 1 C.L.R.B.R. 498 (C.L.R.B.).

2. Related employers

469. Another situation where identification of the employer may be a problem is where associated activities are carried on through related businesses operating under common control.[1] A trade union may acquire bargaining rights in respect of a particular employer and then find that these are merely paper bargaining rights as the work being carried on by the employer has been transferred to another entity. This kind of problem often occurs in the construction industry where 'double-breasting' (the carrying on of the same business through more than one company) is a common phenomenon. In order to protect trade union bargaining rights from such changes of form, the legislation in many Canadian jurisdictions provides that labour boards may treat associated employers under common control and direction as a single employer for collective bargaining purposes.[2]

1. See *Industrial Mine Installations*, [1972] O.L.R.B. 1029 for a more detailed description of this problem.
2. Canada, s.133; British Columbia, s.37; Ontario, s.1(4).

470. In order for labour boards to exercise this discretion it must be established that the two employers are not only under common control or direction but also that the businesses carried on are associated or related. Common control is determined by an examination of such factors as: common ownership or financial control; common management; interrelationships of operation; representation to the public as a single related enterprise; and centralized control of labour relations.[1] Whether businesses are associated or related depends on such factors as the functional integration of the operations and the degree of employee interchange between operations.[2] To meet the evidential problems associated with establishing such factors, Ontario, has imposed upon employers the duty to adduce all facts within their knowledge relevant to these considerations.[3] A declaration that associated employers constitute a single employer may have retroactive effect and, as a result could give rise to substantial liability.[4]

1. *Walters Lithographing*, [1971] O.L.R.B. 406.
2. *Diversey*, [1978] 2 C.L.R.B.R. 535 (O.L.R.B.).
3. Ontario, s.1(5).
4. *Norfolk Hospital*, (1977) 77 C.L.L.C. para. 14,094 (Ont.Div.Ct.); *Caledonian Lands*, [1979] 3 C.L.R.B.R. 12 (B.C.L.R.B.).

471. Even where associated or related businesses are being carried on under common direction, labour boards in their discretion may refuse to treat these businesses as one employer. Such refusals have occurred where a labour board considered that a union was using the related employer provision as a substitute for obtaining bargaining rights under normal certification procedures,[1] where a trade union delayed unreasonably in seeking this remedy,[2] and where a trade union was attempting to strengthen its hand during bargaining.[3] From these decisions it is clear that labour boards have applied the related employer provisions only for the purpose of preventing the erosion of existing bargaining rights.

1. *Inducon Construction*, [1975] 2 C.L.R.B.R. 369 (O.L.R.B.).
2. *Farquhar Construction*, [1979] 1 C.L.R.B.R. 72 (O.L.R.B.).
3. *Calgary Television*, [1978] 1 C.L.R.B.R. 532 (C.L.R.B.).

3. Sale or transfer of business

472. Once collective bargaining rights have been acquired by a trade union, it is possible that the identity of the employer may change as the result of a sale or transfer of a business. Since collective bargaining rights are defined in terms of the employees of a particular employer, specific legislative provisions have been enacted in order to preserve collective bargaining rights where a business has been sold or transferred.[1] The effect of such provisions is to give collective bargaining rights some permanence. Where a collective agreement is in effect the buyer of the business inherits that agreement, and where a union is negotiating for a collective agreement, the buyer has the same obligation to negotiate with the union as had the predecessor employer. Although the scheme of the legislation is simple, its application gives rise to a number of problems.

1. Canada, s.144; British Columbia, s.53; Ontario, s.55; Quebec, s.36.

(a) The ingredients of a sale or transfer

473. Many transactions raise the question of whether a sale or transfer of the business actually occurred. Labour boards generally have given the successor rights provisions a liberal construction, looking to see if the evidence points to a continuation of the same business function as was carried on prior to the transaction.[1] In taking this approach the boards have tended to look beyond the form of the transaction in order to examine its real essence. The labour boards, however, have drawn a distinction between the continuation of the same business function and the commencement of a parallel business function – the latter not constituting a sale.[2] Emphasis appears to be placed on the extent to which the previous business has been continued. Such factors as the transfer of assets, the continuity of management, the continuity of the work performed by employees, and the continued employment of the same employees are all taken into account. No single factor is determinative as consideration has to be given to the business context in which the transaction occurs.

1. *Thorco Manufacturing*, (1965) 65 C.L.L.C. para 16,052 (O.L.R.B.); *Kelly Douglas*, [1974] 1 C.L.R.B.R. 77 (B.C.L.R.B.); *Radio CJYQ*, [1978] 1 C.L.R.B.R. 565 (C.L.R.B.).
2. *Thunder Bay Ambulance Services*, [1978] 2 C.L.R.B.R. 245 (O.L.R.B.) 565.

474. Labour boards have found a sale of a business to have occurred where a retail food store indirectly transferred its lease to a related company in the same business despite a considerable time elapsing before the business was re-opened.[1] The sale of a bankrupt business by a receiver has also been considered to be a sale even where the purchaser is in the process of winding the business down.[2] On the other hand, the replacement of one contractor by another providing the same services has not been treated as the sale of a business,[3] nor has a transfer of work accompanied by an incidental transfer of assets,[4] nor the purchase of assets to be put to a different business use.[5]

1. *Gordons Markets*, [1978] 2 C.L.R.B.R. 460 (O.L.R.B).
2. *Marvel Jewellery*, [1975] O.L.R.B. 733.
3. *K.J.R. Associates*, [1979] 2 C.L.R.B.R. 245 (C.L.R.B.).
4. *British American Bank Note*, [1979] 2 C.L.R.B.R. 122 (O.L.R.B.).
5. *Homco Industries*, [1979] 1 C.L.R.B.R. 453 (B.C.L.R.B.).

(b) Problems of proof

475. Usually the details of a particular transaction are facts peculiarly within the knowledge of the employers privy to that transaction. This fact may give rise to problems of proof when a trade union is attempting to establish that a sale or transfer of a business has occurred. Ontario now imposes upon employers a duty to adduce at the hearing all facts within their knowledge relevant to this issue.[1]

1. S.55(13).

(c) Intermingling of employees

476. The sale or transfer of a business may lead to the integration of what were previously separate businesses and the intermingling of employees working for those businesses. Such intermingling of employees gives rise to the question of whether collective bargaining rights attached to the predecessor employer should be continued. Two types of intermingling are possible – the intermingling of the unionized employees of the transferred business with the non-union employees of the successor employer and the intermingling of employees represented by different unions. Where intermingling occurs, labour boards usually order a vote in order to determine the wishes of employees as to the disposition of bargaining rights but may decline to do so where it is clear that a union represents a substantial majority of the employees in the bargaining unit.[1]

1. *Seaspan International*, [1979] 2 C.L.R.B.R. 213 (C.L.R.B.).

(d) Redefinition of bargaining rights

477. Even if intermingling of employees does not occur, there may still be the question of whether the bargaining rights inherited from the predecessor employer are appropriate as they relate to the successor employer. Labour boards have tended to preserve the bargaining structure established prior to the sale or transfer to the extent that it can be accommodated within the new employer's administrative structure.[1] This approach cuts both ways, however, as labour boards have not interpreted successor rights provisions as expanding the bargaining structure even though the scope clause of the inherited collective agreement may be sufficiently broad as to cover the unorganized employees of the successor employer.[2]

1. *City of Peterborough*, [1979] 2 C.L.R.B.R. 112 (O.L.R.B.); but see *Kelly Douglas*, [1974] 1 C.L.R.B.R. 77 (B.C.L.R.B.).
2. *Bryant Press*, [1972] O.L.R.B. 301.

(e) Change in character of business

478. One jurisdiction, Ontario, appears to qualify the general thrust of its successor rights legislation by giving its labour board a discretion to terminate bargaining rights passing upon a sale or transfer if the buyer has changed its character so that it is substantially different from the business of the predecessor employer.[1] The application of this exception to the general rule has not been without difficulty. While the Ontario board appeared to apply the exception rather broadly at the outset,[2] a more restrictive approach was taken in later cases. Recognizing that this exception ran against the grain of the general scheme of successor rights, the board has now taken the approach that for this exception to apply there must be a fundamental change in the business that would make continued representation by the trade union 'inadequate, inappropriate or unreasonable'.[3] Most of the cases where this exemption has been sought have arisen out of the hospitality industry where changes in business format are quite common.[4]

1. S.55(5).
2. In *Man of Aran*, [1973] O.L.R.B. 313, the board held that a conversion from a general tavern to an Irish pub was a change in character sufficient to justify termination of bargaining rights.
3. *Winco-Steak 'n Burger Restaurants*, [1975] 1 C.L.R.B.R. 296 (O.L.R.B.).
4. See, for example, *25168 Holdings*, [1978] 1 C.L.R.B.R. 28 (O.L.R.B.).

4. Multi-employer bargaining

479. Canadian collective bargaining legislation also recognizes that employers may wish to bargain collectively through associations rather than individually. Multi-employer bargaining, although usually associated with the construction industry, has now been embraced by other industries such as forest products and trucking. While it is common for multi-employer bargaining to occur on a voluntary basis, many Canadian jurisdictions now provide a formal legal structure – often referred to as accreditation – for multi-employer bargaining.[1] Accreditation allows an employer bargaining agency to acquire bargaining rights in respect of unionized employers, and to bargain on behalf of those employers with the union representing their employees. Like the trade union, the employer bargaining agency has exclusive bargaining rights and its individual members are not permitted to strike their own bargains with the union. While accreditation has served to stabilize construction industry collective bargaining by reducing the number of negotiations and strengthening the employer presence at the bargaining table, it has also caused problems by requiring employers regardless of their different interests to operate under a common bargaining structure. Small firms in particular may find it difficult to operate under terms and conditions that are acceptable to larger firms.

1. British Columbia, s.59; Canada, s.131(2); Ontario, ss.113–124, 125–136; Quebec, Construction Industry Labour Relations Act, S.Q. 1968, c.45.

§4. TRANSFER AND TERMINATION OF BARGAINING RIGHTS

A. Transfer of bargaining rights

480. The structure of trade unionism in Canada has never been static.[1] Mergers and breakaways occur with sufficient frequency to require that some legal provision be made for the transfer of bargaining rights between trade unions.[2] Affiliation with some other labour body, however, is not regarded as giving rise to a transfer of bargaining rights even where a change of name occurs.[3] Before giving their approval to such transfers of jurisdiction labour boards have required that the transfer be substantially completed, that the predecessor and successor union have approved the transfer,[4] that the transfer comply with any requirements in the unions' constitution,[5] and that it have the approval of the employees affected.[6]

1. *Supra*, Introduction c.IV *The Canadian Labour Movement*.
2. Canada, s.143; British Columbia, s.54; Ontario, s.54.
3. *Hydro-Electric Power Commission*, (1957) 57 C.L.L.C. para. 18,080 (O.L.R.B.).
4. *City of Brockville*, [1979] O.L.R.B. 76.
5. *Astgen v. Smith*, (1970) 7 D.L.R. (3d) 657 (Ont.C.A.); *Brewer's Warehousing*, [1975] 1 C.L.R.B.R. 34 (O.L.R.B.).
6. *Astgen v. Smith*, *supra*; *B.C. Ferry and Marine Workers*, [1978] 1 C.L.R.B.R. 17 (B.C.L.R.B.).

B. Termination of bargaining rights

481. The granting of collective bargaining rights does not always lead to the establishment of a continuing collective bargaining relationship. The failure of collective bargaining rights to take root usually reflects an erosion of employee support often attributable to the employer's continued resistance to collective bargaining. Occasionally, however, the failure of the collective bargaining relationship stems from the union's lack of interest in representing employees. Another possibility is that employee support may switch to another competing trade union so that employees may seek a change of bargaining agents. The procedures for terminating bargaining rights established by Canadian collective bargaining legislation take into account the full range of these possibilities.

1. Decertification

482. All Canadian jurisdictions provide for a review of the representativeness of a bargaining agent.[1] In order to provide some stability to the established collective bargaining structure, however, application for such reviews are subject to the same type of time restrictions as are applications for certification.[2] Labour boards carefully scrutinize such applications for improper employer influence, and will refuse to entertain such applications where there is the taint of employer involvement. The making of such an application following a bitter and protracted labour dispute, however, will not necessarily be considered as tainted.[3]

1. Canada, s.137; British Columbia, s.52; Ontario, s.49; Quebec, s.32.
2. *Supra*, S2 *Acquisition of Bargaining Rights*.
3. *Journal Publishing*, [1978] 1 C.L.R.B.R. 585 (O.L.R.B.).

483. If it can be established (usually by a vote) that a majority of the employees in the bargaining unit no longer support the bargaining agent, a declaration will issue from the Board to the effect that the trade no longer represents the employees in the bargaining unit. The effect of such a declaration is to terminate the bargaining rights and put an end to any collective agreement made in respect of that bargaining unit. Applications for decertification may conceal an attempt by another union to 'raid' the incumbent. Often the termination of bargaining rights is closely followed by an application for certification from another union. One labour board, however, has held that decertification is not appropriate where employees wish to continue to participate in collective bargaining.

1. *Hiram Walker*, [1974] 1 C.L.R.B.R. 517 (B.C.L.R.B.).

2. Displacement

484. Bargaining rights can also be terminated upon the making of a successful application for certification by another union. The procedures applicable to decertification, as a general rule, also apply to this more open form of raiding. The application must be timely, uninfluenced by the employer, and representativeness is usually determined by means of a vote. If the displacement application is successful, bargaining rights are taken from the incumbent and given to the challenger. Any collective agreement that might apply to the affected employees is terminated, and the new union must begin negotiating its own agreement.[1]

1. Canada, s.142; Ontario, s.48.

3. Union inactivity

(a) Statutory provisions

485. Canadian collective bargaining legislation also provides for the termination of bargaining rights where the trade union has been inactive. British Columbia and Quebec provide that a certificate may be cancelled where the trade union ceases to exist.[1] Ontario goes even further, providing that bargaining rights may be terminated for failing to give notice to bargain or failing to commence bargaining.[2] The Ontario board has been reluctant to terminate bargaining rights on these grounds, declining to do so except where no reasonable explanation for the trade union's inactivity is provided.[3] The Canada Labour Code considers trade union inactivity from a quite different perspective, providing that a decertification order may not be made where a collective agreement does not cover the employees in the bargaining unit unless the Board is satisfied that the incumbent bargaining agent has failed to make reasonable efforts to enter into such a collective agreement.[4]

1. British Columbia, s.52; Quebec, s.32.
2. Ontario, s.51.
3. *Dominion Stores*, (1956) 56 C.L.L.C. para. 18,047 (O.L.R.B.).
4. S.138(2); see *Radio CJYQ 930*, [1979] 1 C.L.R.B.R. 180 (C.L.R.B.).

(b) Abandonment[1]

486. The statutory provisions do not deal with all situations where a trade union has been inactive. It is possible that a trade union may make a collective agreement providing for automatic renewal but not actively administer that agreement. This agreement would normally stand as a bar to certification application from another trade union. The Ontario board, however, has taken the position that trade union inactivity can constitute abandonment of bargaining rights so that any subsisting agreement or certificate would not constitute a bar to a certification application.[2]

1. See generally, J. Dorsey, *Abandonment of Trade Union Rights and the Labour Code of British Columbia*, (1977) 11 U.B.C.L.Rev 40.
2. *Advanced Wire Die*, (1971) 71 C.L.L.C. para. 16,033 (O.L.R.B.).

487. Another possibility is that a trade union may wish to return to a bargaining relationship after a considerable period of inactivity. Such a possibility is more likely now that accreditation procedures are becoming more common. Under these accreditation schemes a trade union may attempt to gain access to a multi-employer collective agreement by reclaiming a collective bargaining relationship that it once had with an employer. The doctrine of abandonment has also been applied in these circumstances with the result that trade unions have not been able to reclaim inactive bargaining rights.[1] Underlying this approach appears to be the concern that the trade union, because

186

of its inactivity, may no longer represent the employees in the bargaining unit.

> 1. *J.S. Mechanical*, [1979] C.L.R.B.R. 87 (O.L.R.B.); see also *Whitehorse Hotels*, [1977] 1 C.L.R.B.R. 477 (C.L.R.B.).

488. The question of whether bargaining rights have been abandoned is essentially a question of fact. The length and degree of the union's inactivity, the reasons for such inactivity, the union's relationship with the employees, and the absence of employees from the bargaining unit are all considered. The statutory basis for the doctrine of abandonment is somewhat unclear. Labour boards have been given a wide power to reconsider previous decisions,[1] and this power may be sufficiently wide to justify revocation of bargaining rights previously granted. Bargaining rights alleged to flow from an agreement may also be put in question where the trade union no longer actively represents the employees covered by such an agreement.[2]

> 1. *Genaire* v. *Int'l. Machinists*, (1958) 14 D.L.R. (2d) 201 *aff'd.* (1959), 18 D.L.R. (2d) 588 (Ont.C.A.).
> 2. In Ontario the definition of collective agreement refers to a trade union 'representing' employees.

4. Fraud

489. Two jurisdictions, Canada and Ontario, expressly provide that if a certificate has been obtained through the use of fraudulent evidence, an application to revoke it may be made at any time.[1]

> 1. Canada, s.140; Ontario, s.50.

Chapter IV. The Collective Bargaining Process

490. The acquisition of bargaining rights by a trade union can be regarded as a prelude to the main objective of collective bargaining – the negotiation of a collective agreement with the employer. It is at this point that the union and the employer must attempt to work out between them the terms of their collective bargaining relationship. This relationship not only sets the conditions of employment for the employees in the bargaining unit but it also establishes the arrangements that are to exist between the union and the employer. Underlying these negotiations is the possibility that either party may resort to the use of the economic sanctions (the strike or lock-out) in support of its bargaining position.

491. Not only do the negotiations determine the terms of any agreement that might be reached by the union and the employer, but they also determine whether any agreement will be reached at all. At stake may be the survival of the union as bargaining agent, the jobs of the employees in the bargaining unit, and even the viability of the employer's operation. The manner in which negotiations are conducted is likely to set the tone for the future relationship of the parties. Long and bitter strikes are often the product of missed opportunities at the bargaining table. At this stage of the collective bargaining relationship common sense and a feel for the proper compromise play a more important role than rules and procedures.[1]

1. See generally J. P. Sanderson, *The Art of Collective Bargaining* (Toronto, 1979).

§1. THE UNION'S EXCLUSIVE AUTHORITY TO BARGAIN

492. A fundamental principle of Canadian collective bargaining law is that once a trade union has acquired bargaining rights for a particular bargaining unit, it enjoys exclusive rights to bargain collectively on behalf of the employees in that bargaining constituency. By establishing that it has the support of a majority of the employees in a bargaining unit a trade union gains the exclusive right to bargain for all employees included in that bargaining unit. The trade union's exclusive right to bargain imposes a corresponding obligation on the employer to recognize the trade union as bargaining agent for all employees in the bargaining unit, regardless of whether all of these employees are members of that trade union. A co-relative obligation imposed on the union, however, is the duty to provide fair representation to all members of the bargaining unit.[1]

1. See *Supra* para. 340 to 356.

493. These twin principles of 'majoritarianism' and 'exclusivity' are common threads running through all Canadian collective bargaining legislation. The only jurisdiction to deviate at all from these principles has been Quebec where special legislation establishing a multi-employer, multi-union collective bargaining structure of provincial scope for the construction industry has permitted competing federations of trade unions to share a common bargaining table.[1] Frequent amendments to that legislation attest to the fact that the Quebec experiment has not been free of difficulties.

1. Construction Industry Labour Relations Act, S.Q. 1968, c.45.

A. Exclusion of individual bargains

494. A corollary of the principle of 'exclusivity' is the illegitimacy of individual arrangements between employer and employee. It has been made clear by the courts that the presence of a collective bargaining relationship excludes 'private' negotiations except where permitted by the agreement itself.[1] One result is that the collective agreements in Canada generally establish the actual terms of employment for those in the bargaining unit rather than merely setting minimum terms.

1. *Syndicat Catholique* v. *Paquet*, (1959) 18 D.L.R. (2d) 346 (S.C.C.).

495. Another result has been the wholesale displacement of the law relating to the individual contract of employment by the newer legal regime of collective bargaining.[1] Even the act of hiring employees may be regulated by the collective arrangements between employer and bargaining agent rather than by earlier common law employment principles. An example of the extent of this displacement can be found in a recent decision of the Supreme Court of Canada holding that the law of the individual contract cannot be applied to relieve an employer from its obligation to make severance payments, even where employees have engaged in an illegal strike.[2] The strike, and the obligation to pay severance pay, were considered by the court as being matters to be dealt with according to general collective bargaining law and not by reference to the common law.

1. See *infra*, c.VI–82 *Unique Legal Effect*.
2. *McGavin Toastmaster* v. *Ainscough*, (1975) 54 D.L.R. (3d) 1 (S.C.C.).

B. Prohibition against bargaining collectively with others

496. Canadian collective bargaining legislation protects the union's exclusive authority to bargain by prohibiting employers from bargaining collectively with any person other than the bargaining agent, and also by prohibiting other trade unions from bargaining with the employer in respect of the employees in the bargaining unit represented by the bargaining agent. These prohibitions flow from the general statutory duty to bargain in good faith or, in some jurisdictions, from even more explicit legislative provisions.[1] This kind of prohibition raises the interesting question of the extent to which an employer may communicate directly with its employees during collective negotiations. The answer would appear to be that not all direct communications between employer and employees are prohibited, but only those that constitute an attempt to bargain directly with the employees in the bargaining unit.[2] Employers may attempt to set the record straight by explaining their bargaining position, but they may not disparage the bargaining agent or attempt to undermine its bargaining rights in other ways.

1. Canada, s.185 (*b*); Ontario, s.59.
2. *A. N. Shaw Restoration*, [1978] 2 C.L.R.B.R. 214 (O.L.R.B.); compare *The Ottawa Citizen*, [1979] 2 C.L.R.B.R. 251 (O.L.R.B.).

C. The right to bargain for union security provisions

497. One of the more important incidents of the union's exclusive authority to bargain is the recognition that the union as bargaining agent may bargain for its own financial security. Such arrangements include the 'closed shop' where a person must be a member of the union before being hired,[1] the 'union shop' where a person must join the union upon becoming employed, and the 'dues shop' or 'Rand formula' where a person, although not required to join the union, must pay union dues upon becoming employed.

1. The closed shop is usually found in the construction and longshoring industries where trade unions operate hiring halls.

498. Canadian collective bargaining legislation expressly recognizes the legitimacy of union security arrangements.[1] In addition some Canadian jurisdictions go even further by requiring that the 'Rand formula' be included in collective agreements,[2] or by at least requiring the employer to collect dues on behalf of the union where authorized by the employee.[3] This approach contrasts sharply with that taken in some United States jurisdictions where 'right to work' laws have the effect of restricting union security arrangements.

1. For example Canada, s.161; Ontario, s.38.
2. British Columbia, Quebec, Saskatchewan, Manitoba, Ontario.
3. Canada.

499. Canadian courts have recognized that the trade union's right to bargain for its own financial security flows from its exclusive authority to bargain. In the leading case on this point it was held that an employer could not refuse to remit union dues to a union after it had agreed to the inclusion of a compulsory check-off provision in the collective agreement.[1] Union security, therefore, is regarded as being a proper matter for collective bargaining and, once bargained for and included in the collective agreement, such arrangements bind both the employer and the employees in the bargaining unit.

1. *Syndicat Catholique* v. *Paquet*, (1959) 18 D.L.R. (2d) 346 (S.C.C.).

500. Some jurisdictions, however, do allow employees in the bargaining unit to seek some exemption from union security provisions where they object to supporting a trade union because of their religious convictions or beliefs.[1] Sometimes such employees, while objecting to their own bargaining agent, have indicated their support for another trade union. Even in this situation, however, labour boards have generally granted relief against the union security provision. The test applied is whether the employee has a sincere religious objection to the particular bargaining agent, and not whether the objection relates to all trade unions.

1. British Columbia, s.11; Ontario, s.39.

501. Despite the legitimacy of union security provisions, the issue of union security often presents an obstacle to the reaching of a collective agreement, especially where the parties are negotiating their first agreement. Trade unions generally regard the 'Rand Formula' (dues shop) as the minimum for which any respectable union should settle. Employers, on the other hand, are often not anxious to recognize trade unions to the extent of agreeing to a collective agreement provision that would make the bargaining agent more financially viable.

§2. THE STATUTORY FREEZE

502. A feature of Canadian collective bargaining legislation is the prohibition against either the trade union or employer unilaterally altering the arrangements existing between them once bargaining begins.[1] While such prohibitions appear to be straightforward on their face, their application has given rise to some difficulty. The question is whether this type of provision requires that there be no change in the actual state of employment existing at the point when the freeze is imposed, or whether it requires the employer to maintain the established pattern of the employment relationship. This question is particularly important where there has been a past pattern of periodic salary adjustments before the collective bargaining relationship has been established.

1. Canada, s.148; British Columbia, s.61; Quebec, s.47; Ontario, s.70. Some jurisdictions also impose the same kind of statutory freeze from the filing of the certification application until the certificate is issued.

503. One line of reasoning treats the union's exclusive right to bargain as dictating a freeze of the actual 'state of employment' and precluding any further salary reviews by the employer.[1] Another approach treats the statutory freeze as requiring an employer to conduct 'business as before'.[2] This approach requires the employer to run the business according to the pattern established before the freeze was imposed – a pattern that may require continued salary adjustments. The two approaches reflect more than a semantic quibble. The choice of approach is likely to affect the starting point for collective negotiations as the employer's last wage increase usually establishes the floor for negotiations.

1. *Royal Bank*, [1978] 2 C.L.R.B.R. 159 (C.L.R.B.).
2. *Spar Aerospace Products*, [1979] 1 C.L.R.B.R. 61 (O.L.R.B.); see now *Canadian Imperial Bank of Commerce*, (1980) 80 C.L.L.C. para. 16,002 (C.L.R.B.).

504. The statutory freeze not only refers to the terms and conditions of employment but also to other rights, privileges, and duties. This language has been held to be sufficiently wide to catch all incidents of a collective bargaining relationship, including a union security arrangement.[1] The term 'privilege' has been interpreted as covering such matters as free parking, a waiver of rights under an expired collective agreement,[2] and an expectation that a past pattern of wage review would be continued. A reversion to the pattern of employment conditions prevailing prior to the imposition of the freeze has been considered to fall outside the statutory freeze.[3]

1. *Kodak*, [1977] 1 C.L.R.B.R. 280 (O.L.R.B.).
2. *A.N. Shaw Restoration*, [1978] 2 C.L.R.B.R. 257 (O.L.R.B.).
3. *Parr's Print and Litho.*, [1973] O.L.R.B. 597.

§3. Dispute Settlement Procedures

505. A distinctive feature of the Canadian collective bargaining system is its array of dispute-resolution procedures. While some of these procedures have served a useful purpose by reducing industrial conflict, their presence may also have served to protract labour disputes by postponing the time at which the two parties have been able to resort to economic sanctions.

506. Canadian collective bargaining legislation usually requires the parties to exhaust certain dispute resolution procedures before striking or locking-out. Because these procedures have been made a pre-condition to the use of economic sanctions, they have often been regarded as being merely indirect restrictions upon the right to strike and lock-out. The restrictive side of these procedures, to some extent, has impaired their usefulness in resolving industrial conflict.

A. Conciliation

507. Compulsory conciliation has been a longstanding feature of the Canadian collective bargaining structure.[1] Well before the establishment of a legal structure to provide for the acquisition of collective bargaining rights, Canadian legislators had enacted provisions calling for non-coercive, third party intervention in labour disputes.[2] While these conciliation procedures did not prevent the employer and trade union from resorting ultimately to economic sanctions, they did have the effect, for better or for worse, of postponing strike and lock-out action.

1. For example, Canada, s.180; Ontario, s.63(2); British Columbia and Quebec do not make conciliation a pre-condition to the use of the strike or lock-out.
2. *Supra*, Introduction c.IV *The Canadian Labour Movement*.

1. The conciliation board

508. Conciliation may assume more than one form. In its inception the process was essentially an exercise in fact-finding, contemplating the intervention of a third party to investigate a dispute, make specific recommendations for its settlement, and to report these recommendations to the public. Such an approach assumed that public opinion focussed upon the dispute by means of a public report would influence parties to reach agreement. This fact-finding role was given to tri-partite conciliation boards composed of representatives of the two parties and an independent chairman.

509. The fact-finding technique employed by conciliation boards enjoyed only partial success. The influence of public opinion upon labour disputes has been at the very least unpredictable, and it has not always led to compromise and agreement by the parties. Publicity sometimes may serve to harden bargaining positions rather than soften them. Fact-finding, moreover, is a time-consuming exercise and it may have the effect of postponing the use of economic sanctions for long periods of uncertain duration. Because of the disadvantages of fact-finding, boards of conciliation at times abandoned their fact-finding role in order to play a more mediative function. Over time, as the mediative form of conciliation became recognized as being more effective than fact-finding, this latter procedure began to fall into disuse. In Ontario, for example, conciliation boards are now used only very infrequently. In the federal jurisdiction, use of conciliation boards continues to a somewhat greater extent, perhaps because labour disputes arising in that jurisdiction tend to receive more public attention.

2. The conciliation officer

510. Fact-finding by tri-partite conciliation boards has been largely displaced by mediation conducted by the single conciliation officer. This person is usually a full-time government employee whose function is to act as a channel of communication between the parties. The process contemplates that the parties may be brought to an agreement through the efforts of the conciliation officer (or mediator) rather than by the influence of public opinion. Instead of employing such tools as a public inquiry and a public report, the conciliation officer relies upon private discussions (usually with each party separately). An important factor is the parties' trust in the conciliation officer's ability to keep confidences. The conciliation officer does not prepare public reports, and only makes specific recommendations where it would benefit the parties themselves. Patience, perseverance, diplomacy, and discreetness are the characteristic qualities of the conciliation officer.

511. The need for confidentiality in the conciliation process has been expressly recognized by the creation of a special statutory privilege.[1] This privilege attaches to the conciliation officer, providing him with an immunity from giving evidence relating to information acquired in the course of conciliation or, in some jurisdictions, it may also attach to any information furnished to the conciliation officer during negotiations. Problems in applying this kind of privilege often arise when labour boards are dealing with complaints that one or other of the parties have failed to bargain in good faith. The nature of the complaint requires that bargaining conduct be examined, yet much of this conduct may be shielded by the statutory privilege attached to the conciliation process. Labour boards have taken the position that this privilege protects 'private communications' (those made to the conciliator when the other party is not present) but not to 'public statements' (those made to the conciliator in the presence of the other party).[2] Labour boards have also treated the privilege as not belonging to the parties but attaching to the conciliation process itself. A party, therefore, cannot waive the privilege and disclose communications made between it and the conciliator.[3]

1. Canada, s.208; British Columbia, s.127; Ontario, s.100.
2. *CCH Canadian*, [1974] 1 C.L.R.B.R. 388 (O.L.R.B.).
3. *Ibid*.

512. Recourse to the services of a conciliation officer is a pre-condition of the right to strike and lock-out in most Canadian jurisdictions. The compulsory aspect of this process has meant that at times it has been treated as a formality to be satisfied in order to gain the right to strike or lock-out. Other jurisdictions (for example, British Columbia and Qubec), perhaps recognizing the problem of making conciliation mandatory, do not stipulate that conciliation is to be a pre-condition of the use of economic sanctions.

513. In all Canadian jurisdictions, however, there does appear to be a recognition that the mediation function itself performs a particularly useful role in resolving labour disputes. Variations of the basic mediative approach can be found in many Canadian collective bargaining statutes. In addition to compulsory conciliation the legislation may provide for more specialized forms of mediation through the use of industrial inquiry commissioners[1] or mid-contract mediation.[2]

1. Ontario, s.34, 34 *b*; British Columbia, s.122.
2. Ontario, s.34 *a*; British Columbia, ss.113–121.

B. Strike votes

514. A number of Canadian jurisdictions make a favourable strike vote a pre-condition to the exercise of the right to strike.[1] The advocates of this type of procedure argue that it acts as a brake upon an over zealous trade union leadership. Union leaders, however, may not always be in front of the rank and file, and there is some danger that the requirement of a strike vote may lend an unnecessary rigidity to the negotiating process. At the very least such requirements tend to protract negotiations by postponing the use of economic sanctions until a favourable vote has been taken.[2]

1. Alberta, British Columbia, New Brunswick, Nova Scotia, P.E.I.
2. See *infra*, C.V–§4 *Unlawful Industrial Action*.

515. The procedure for the conduct of such votes varies from jurisdiction to jurisdiction. Only two jurisdictions require that a strike vote be supervised by a government official.[1] The timing of the vote is regulated in all but one jurisdiction,[2] the usual requirement being that it follow conciliation. Usually all employees in the unit affected are considered as eligible voters but one jurisdiction also allows other members of the trade union to vote.[3] In some jurisdictions the required majority is defined by reference to those who voted[4] while in others it is defined by reference to all employees in the bargaining unit.

1. Alberta, British Columbia.
2. The exception is Nova Scotia where there is no requirement as to when the vote must be held.
3. New Brunswick. However, the union must obtain both a majority of its members and a majority of the employees in the bargaining unit.
4. Alberta, British Columbia.

C. Arbitration

516. The general approach of Canadian collective bargaining legislation is to permit labour disputes arising in the private sector to be resolved through ultimate recourse to economic sanctions – the strike and the lock-out. Third-party intervention has been restricted to fact-finding and mediative functions, and no Canadian jurisdiction provides any general procedure for the ultimate resolution of bargaining impasses in the private sector by means of third-party intervention. Compulsory arbitration of such impasses, while receiving support in some quarters, does not appear to be widely favoured by either employers or trade unions.

517. The lack of enthusiasm for compulsory arbitration is understandable given the problems associated with this procedure.[1] Interest arbitration, as it is commonly called, requires an arbitration tribunal (usually tri-partite in composition) to hear representations from the employer and the union, and then to make the ultimate agreement for them. The procedure gives the appearance of being adjudicative, but the issues being dealt with are usually economic in nature, requiring a particular decision about the allocation of economic resources. The guidelines provided for the resolution of such disputes, not surprisingly, tend to be general in nature, and are often contradictory.[2] As a result, arbitration awards more often appear to be a compromise between the opposing positions of the parties than to be the result of the application of established principles. The presence of arbitration may also discourage the parties from making concessions prior to arbitration – placing the entire burden of establishing the appropriate compromise upon the arbitrator.[3] The adjudicative format that the process assumes, moreover, makes it slow and expensive – features that do not sit well with either trade unions or employers.

1. See generally, D. J. M. Brown, *Interest Arbitration*, Task Force Study No. 18 (Ottawa, 1968).
2. For an attempt to formulate more 'rational and objective' criteria, see *Welland County General Hospital*, (1965) 16 L.A.C. 1.
3. In order to avoid the problem some commentators have advocated 'final-offer selection', restricting the arbitrator to choosing between the final position of the two parties. This 'all-or-nothing' approach has been adopted to some extent in the educational sector. Problems with this technique may arise, however, where the dispute is complicated by a multiplicity of unresolved issues.

518. At a more philosophical level, there is the objection that the setting of wages through compulsory arbitration is incompatible with the operation of a free enterprise economy. It has been argued that, if wage levels are to be determined in this manner, then other prices should also be controlled. Unions tend to regard arbitration as an unwarranted intrusion in the free operation of the economy when they receive an unfavourable award, and employers make the same objection when they regard the award as being overly-generous. Given the problems associated with interest arbitration and the general lack of enthusiasm for it, this impasse resolution procedure is not a common feature of private sector collective bargaining. Nevertheless, interest arbitration is not entirely absent from the private sector collective bargaining system.

1. Voluntary arbitration

519. Many Canadian jurisdictions expressly provide that, for the purpose of resolving a particular dispute, the parties themselves may agree to be bound by the recommendations of a third party.[1] The existence of such provisions support the view that voluntary interest arbitration is not incompatible with collective bargaining legislation. An interesting question, however, is the extent to which the parties by agreement may bind themselves to a general procedure of interest arbitration for future disputes. Even though such a procedure leaves open the possibility that future arbitrators might continue this procedure indefinitely, it has been held by one labour board that such provisions are not inconsistent with the scheme of collective bargaining legislation.[2]

1. Canada, s.171; British Columbia, s.122; Ontario, s.34c; Quebec, ss.62–81.
2. *Haldimand-Norfolk Regional Health Unit*, [1978] 1 C.L.R.B.R. 475 (O.L.R.B.); but see *Wentworth Arms Hotel*, (1979) 79 C.L.L.C. para. 14,189 (S.C.C.).

2. First-agreement arbitration

520. Legislative provisions for the arbitration of unresolved first contract disputes are now found in three Canadian jurisdictions – British Columbia, Quebec, and the federal jurisdiction.[1] These provisions allow the minister of labour to refer bargaining impasses reached during the first set of negotiations to a third party[2] for final and binding resolution. The collective agreement imposed on the parties is for a limited duration,[3] and any future negotiations are left to be resolved through normal collective bargaining procedures that include the use of economic sanctions.

1. Canada, s.171.1; British Columbia, s.70, 71; Quebec, ss.81a–81i.
2. In British Columbia and the federal jurisdiction it is the labour board; in Quebec it is a board of arbitration.
3. One year in British Columbia and Canada; up to two years in Quebec.

521. The basic purpose of first agreement arbitration is to deal with those situations where an employer continues to refuse to deal with a trade union even after it has acquired bargaining rights.[1] The procedure of imposing a first contract prevents employers from benefiting from such conduct. In British Columbia, the jurisdiction with the longest experience in administering this type of provision, the available evidence would indicate that very few of these 'trial marriages' have matured into a permanent relationship. The proponents of first-agreement arbitration argue, however, that the major benefit of such a remedy is the deterrent effect that it has upon other employers who might be tempted to adopt the same kind of anti-union approach.

1. *London Drugs*, [1974] 1 C.L.R.B.R. 140 (B.C.L.R.B.); *Radiodiffusion Mutuelle*, [1979] 1 C.L.R.B.R. 332 (C.L.R.B.).

522. The legislation providing for first-agreement arbitration gives very little guidance as to what should be taken into account when the content of the collective agreement is being determined. The two most prominent factors appear to be bargaining conduct of the parties themselves, and the prevailing conditions of employment for other organized employees doing the same kind of work. The British Columbia board has indicated that it does not consider itself constrained to adopt a 'modest award', recognizing that collective bargaining must be sufficiently attractive to maintain employee support for the union.[1] Where an employer fails to honour an imposed first-agreement, the union may be able to obtain damages for its organizing and legal expenses, sometimes referred to as a 'make-whole' remedy.

1. *Century Plaza Hotel*, [1979] 3 C.L.R.B.R. 49 (B.C.L.R.B.).

3. Ad hoc intervention

523. Despite the absence of any general provision for compulsory arbitration of interest disputes, there has still been in Canada a limited amount of *ad hoc* legislative intervention where unresolved disputes have been considered as being contrary to the public interest. Such intervention usually takes the form of a back-to-work order and provision for the dispute to be resolved by binding arbitration. The service interrupted by the dispute must be regarded as being sufficiently essential to justify such an extraordinary response.

524. The question of what constitutes an essential service is not easy to answer.[1] It is generally accepted that at least some of the services provided by governments are essential and, as a result, most Canadian jurisdictions impose at least some restrictions on the use of the strike by government employees.[2] As well, other types of public employees are often regarded as providing services that are essential. Policemen, firemen, school teachers, hospital workers, and municipal transit workers may find restrictions upon their use of strike action, either in general legislation or as the result of an *ad hoc* intervention by the legislators. Such disparate groups as railway workers, elevator contractors and loggers have on occasion also discovered that their services are essential. It would appear that the definition of essentiality depends to a great extent upon public tolerance of the inevitable disruptions caused by collective bargaining disputes. As a general observation, Canadians appear to have been more tolerant of a disruption of services in the private sector and less tolerant where there have been disruptions of service in the public or quasi-public sectors.

1. See generally, H. W. Arthurs, *Public Interest Disputes in Canada: A Legislative Perspective*, (1967) 17 Buff. L.Rev. 39.
2. Most jurisdictions have separate legislation establishing a collective bargaining structure for public employees. For example, Public Service Staff Relations Act, R.S.C. 1970, c.P–35.

§4. Conduct of Negotiations

A. Commencement of bargaining

525. Under Canadian collective bargaining legislation the use of economic sanctions has been restricted in order to provide for periods of labour peace. As a general rule strikes and lock-outs are not permitted during the duration of the collective agreement nor are they permitted to be used as a weapon to obtain recognition.[1] Furthermore, the legislation also contemplates a period of negotiation during which the parties are not free to resort to economic sanctions. Resort to certain dispute resolution procedures during this period may also be required in order for the right to strike or lock-out to accrue.[2] Given these legislative restrictions, the commencement of bargaining is generally regarded as marking the beginning of the countdown to the time when economic sanctions may be applied.

1. See *infra*, c.V–§4. *Unlawful Industrial Action*
2. *Supra*, §3, *Dispute Settlement Procedures*

1. Notice to bargain

526. Collective bargaining legislation usually provides that bargaining is to commence by the giving of written notice to bargain by one party to the other. Usually it is the union that takes the initiative by serving notice to bargain. The notice is generally regarded as timely if it is given after bargaining rights have been acquired, or during the last months of an expiring collective agreement. Questions sometimes arise as to whether a party is entitled to give notice to bargain. Some of these challenges may raise the issue of the extent of the union's bargaining rights, but others may simply go to the timing of the notice to bargain.

527. Particular problems relating to the timing of the notice may arise where the parties are bargaining to renew a collective agreement. Collective bargaining legislation usually provides that notice to bargain may be given within the last months (usually three) of the expiring collective agreement. Where notice is given after this period expires, there is some question as to whether this notice is sufficient to set in motion the negotiation process contemplated by the legislation. Labour boards have held that the time for the giving of notice found in the statute is merely directory, and notice given after that time is sufficient to set the negotiation process in motion.[1]

1. *Peel Memorial Hospital*, [1977] 2 C.L.R.B.R. 211 (O.L.R.B.).

528. A different result would appear to follow, however, where the collective agreement by its own terms provides that it is to continue in effect for a further year. If notice is not given within the time specified in the agreement, the legal result would appear to be that the collective agreement is extended for a further year, having the effect of postponing the time at which notice to bargain may be given under the statute.[1]

1. *London Generator Service*, [1978] O.L.R.B. 932; *Hield Brothers*, (1957) 57 C.L.L.C. para. 18,071.

529. Problems may also occur where the expiring collective agreement provides that it is to remain in effect until replaced by a new agreement. Even though such an agreement may also provide for the giving of notice to bargain,

there remains the question of whether the parties can ever be free to invoke economic sanctions because of the continuing effect of the collective agreement. The Supreme Court of Canada has recently held that this type of continuation provision should not be read as perpetually excluding the parties from striking or locking-out.[1] The Court viewed the overriding collective agreement provision as being the one providing for notice to bargain. The giving of notice to bargain, therefore, serves to terminate the agreement at the end of its specified term allowing the parties to follow the normal set of procedures for renewal of the collective agreement. One Canadian jurisdiction now expressly allows a party to terminate the continuing operation of such agreements on the giving of thirty days notice to the other party.[2]

1. *Wentworth Arms Hotel*, (1979) 79 C.L.L.C. para. 14,189.
2. Ontario, s.44.(2).

2. Wage re-openers

530. Some collective agreements (usually negotiated during periods of high inflation) may provide for the re-negotiation of the wage scale during the term of the collective agreement. Whether this kind of provision is sufficient to set in motion the full range of negotiation procedures is problematical. Collective bargaining legislation as a rule provides that collective agreements are to be for a term of at least one year. In Ontario, the legislation also provides that if an agreement is for an unspecified term it shall be considered as being for a term of one year. The Ontario board has indicated that where the parties explicitly provide for the early termination of a collective agreement to re-negotiate wages the effect is to create a term of unspecified duration that would be reduced by operation of the statute to one year.[1] A clause merely providing for the re-negotiation of wages during the term of the collective agreement, however, has not been interpreted as being sufficiently express to terminate the agreement prior to specified expiry dates. One jurisdiction, British Columbia, provides for the early termination of collective agreements on the consent of the Minister.[2]

1. *Kroehler Mfg.*, [1977] 1 C.L.R,B.R. 107 (O.L.R.B.).
2. British Columbia, s.66(2)(3).

3. Bargaining over technological change

531. The introduction of new technology to the work place may have a very disruptive labour relations effect. Not only is it likely to require a reorganization of work assignments and the learning of new work methods, but it is just as likely to involve a reduction in the work force. Particular problems occur when such changes are made during the term of the collective agreement. Even though the introduction of new technology may have a substantial effect on the arrangements established by the collective agreements, legislation in most Canadian jurisdictions does not permit full negotiations over technological change with resort to strike and lock-out action until after the agreement has expired and the required dispute resolution procedures have been completed.[1]

Some jurisdictions, however, have recognized this problem and have established specific procedures to deal with the introduction of technological change during the collective agreement.[2] Under these procedures it is possible for the bargaining agent to obtain an order preserving the *status quo* and, in certain circumstances, to open the collective agreement for re-negotiation. Somewhat surprisingly, these procedures do not appear to have had much use, perhaps because of their complexity or perhaps because of the recent trend to shorter collective agreements.

1. See *infra*, c.V–§4 *Unlawful Industrial Action.*
2. Canada, ss.149–152; British Columbia, ss.74–78.

4. Bargaining over wage rollbacks

532. The recent Canadian experience with economic controls created a number of problems because of the basic incompatability between collective bargaining and a programme of wage restraint. One of the more interesting problems concerned the effect that a wage rollback had upon a negotiated collective agreement. Did the intervention of the federal Anti-Inflation Board serve to end the collective agreement, permitting the parties to return to the negotiation process, or did it simply amend the collective agreement according to the terms of the rollback? Canadian Labour Boards generally took the position that the rollback served to put an end to the collective agreement unless the parties made specific provision to the contrary.[1] The result was that the parties were able to negotiate the implementation of the rollback and, if agreement was not reached, could have ultimate recourse to economic sanctions provided that such negotiations were conducted within the parameters established by the Anti-Inflation Board. The expiry of the economic controls legislation, however, has meant that these issues have receded into the background of labour relations.

1. *Cyprus Anvil Mining*, [1976] 2 C.L.R.B.R. 360 (C.L.R.B.); *Croven*, [1977] 1 C.L.R.B.R. 394 (O.L.R.B.); *Trustees of School District No. 39*, [1977] 2 C.L.R.B.R. 201 (B.C.L.R.B.).

B. The duty to bargain in good faith

533. Once notice to bargain has been given the parties are under an express statutory obligation to bargain in good faith and to make every reasonable effort to negotiate a collective agreement.[1] Somewhat surprisingly, there has been until recently very few decisions defining the concept of 'good faith' bargaining in the context of Canadian labour relations. The reason for this lack of jurisprudence can be found in the fact that labour boards have only recently enjoyed a direct jurisdiction over bargaining complaints.[2] Prior to this extension of the boards' jurisdiction, such complaints had to be brought to the boards in the form of an application for consent to prosecute. If consent were granted, then the matter could proceed in the criminal courts by way of private prosecution. Because of the possibility of subsequent criminal proceedings being pursued, labour boards were reluctant to comment upon the evidence when granting consent to prosecution even though very few of these complaints were taken to the criminal courts after consent to prosecute was given. The result was a singular lack of both board and court decisions defining the duty to bargain in good faith. This gap, however, is now being rapidly filled by the growing jurisprudence of the labour boards.

1. Canada, s.148; British Columbia, s.63; Ontario, s.14; Quebec, s.41.
2. The Canada Labour Code, s.187(5), provides that no bargaining complaint may be made to the board except with the consent of the Minister. In British Columbia and Ontario, however, the complaint may be made to the board directly.

534. The obligation to bargain in good faith poses certain definitional problems. Collective bargaining requires that bargaining impasses be resolved ultimately by pitting the economic strength of the employer against the collective economic strength of the employees. Given the fact that economic strength is the ultimate arbiter of the dispute, it is often asked whether there is room for any concept of 'good faith' in collective bargaining.

535. A closer examination of the nature of collective bargaining provides the answer to this question. Collective bargaining is not merely an economic exercise, being just as much an exercise in human relations. This latter aspect of collective bargaining cannot be carried on successfully if the parties are left free to resort to tactics inherently destructive of the bargaining relationship. The presence of a duty to bargain in good faith serves to control such tactics while still leaving the parties free to resort to legitimate economic sanctions.

536. It should not be surprising, then, that labour boards in administering the duty to bargain in good faith have placed far greater emphasis on the manner in which negotiations have been conducted than upon the content of negotiations.[1] Generally speaking, the boards have not sought to determine whether a particular bargaining proposal should be carried to an impasse – a reticence that appears to reflect a concern that they should not be interfering unduly with the economic forces at play during negotiations. As a result, a great deal of the jurisprudence defining the duty to bargain in good faith deals with the manner in which negotiations are to be conducted.

1. *Noranda Metal Industries*, [1975] 1 C.L.R.B.R. 145 (B.C.L.R.B.); *Journal Publishing*, [1977] 2 C.L.R.B.R. 183 (O.L.R.B.); *CKLW Radio Broadcasting*, (1977) 77 C.L.L.C. para. 16,110 (C.L.R.B.).

1. Duty to meet

537. A primary function of the duty to bargain in good faith is to reinforce the bargaining rights acquired by the trade union. These bargaining rights give the trade union exclusive authority to bargain on behalf of the employees in the bargaining unit. The corresponding obligation upon the employer is to bargain in good faith and make every reasonable effort to reach a collective agreement. It should be self-evident, then, that implicit in the duty to bargain in good faith is an obligation to meet with the other party.

538. The boundaries of this obligation to meet are not capable of precise definition. Where the parties have fully discussed the issues at numerous meetings, a refusal to meet any further until there has been some alteration in position is likely to be legitimate. If such a refusal occurs at the commencement of negotiations, however, it is likely to be regarded as refusal to recognize the other party.[1] Moreover, it is clear that the presence of extenuating circumstances may justify such a refusal to bargain. Where a municipal council took the position that negotiations with the union would be conducted at meetings with the public and press in attendance, a trade union's refusal to meet under these circumstances has been considered to be legitimate.[2] On the other hand, it has been held that an employer was not justified in unilaterally breaking off negotiations simply because of an outstanding dispute under the expiring collective agreement.[3]

1. *DeVilbiss*, [1976] 2 C.L.R.B.R. 101 (O.L.R.B.)
2. *Borough of North York*, [1968] O.L.R.B. 66.
3. *Journal Publishing*, [1977] 2 C.L.R.B.R. 183 (O.L.R.B.).

539. A related question is whether the employer may refuse to meet with the union because it objects to the composition of the union's bargaining committee. Labour boards have held that, since employees are entitled to negotiate through their own freely-chosen representatives, an employer's objection to the composition of the union bargaining committee (even where it contains an employee of a business competitor) cannot justify a refusal to meet with the union.[1]

1. *Marshall-Wells*, (1955) 55 C.L.L.C. para. 18,002 (S.L.R.B.); *Journal Publishing*, [1977] 2 C.L.R.B.R. 183 (O.L.R.B.).

2. Circumvention of bargaining agent

540. Legal recognition of the trade union as bargaining agent gives it the exclusive right to bargain on behalf of the employees in the bargaining unit. Employers are not permitted to circumvent the bargaining agent by bargaining directly with the employees or with some other union.[1] Moreover, attempts by employers to unilaterally alter wage and working conditions, even after the statutory freeze has expired, have in some circumstances been considered as violations of the duty to bargain in good faith.[2]

1. Supra, §1, *The Unions Exclusive Authority to Bargain*; see also *Davidson Rubber*, (1969) 69 C.L.L.C. para. 14,190 (Ont.Prov.Ct.).
2. *DeVilbiss*, [1976] 2 C.L.R.B.R. 101 (O.L.R.B.).

3. Requirement of full discussion

541. The duty to bargain in good faith not only requires the parties to acknowledge the collective bargaining relationship between them but also to engage in a full and informed discussion during the course of that bargaining relationship. The requirement of full discussion means that more mature bargaining relationships may come under the scrutiny of labour boards. While lack of recognition is not usually a problem associated with such relationships, difficulties may arise because of a breakdown in communications. Labour boards have made it clear that mutual communication is an essential element of the duty to bargain in good faith.

542. The requirement of mutual communication appears to reflect a concern that negotiations not break down because of a lack of understanding of the positions taken at the bargaining table. An adamant refusal to discuss alternative interpretations of wage control guidelines has been considered as a failure to bargain in good faith,[1] as has a refusal to explain the rationale underlying a wage offer.[2] An insistence by one party upon discussing an issue to the exclusion of all others has also been regarded as falling short of the required standard.[3]

1. *Canadian Industries*, [1976] 2 C.L.R.B.R. 8 (O.L.R.B.).
2. *St. Joseph's Hospital*, [1976] O.L.R.B. 255; *Board of Health of Haliburton, Kawartha, Pine Ridge District Health Unit*, [1977] 1 C.L.R.B.R. 221 (O.L.R.B.).
3. *Journal Publishing*, [1977] 2 C.L.R.B.R. 183 (O.L.R.B.).

543. Labour boards, however, have recognized that this requirement of mutual communication must take into account the realities of collective bargaining, and some allowance appears to be made for the normal wear and tear of collective bargaining. A mere lack of tact is not by itself sufficient to constitute a failure to bargain in good faith.[1] It has also been recognized that the parties may reach a point in the bargaining process where further discussions are no longer fruitful. Once such a point is reached, a breaking off of negotiations[2] or the adoption of a 'take it or leave it' position is not likely to be regarded as a failure to bargain in good faith.[3] As well, a refusal to discuss an issue on the periphery of the negotiations may not be considered as bad faith bargaining.[4]

1. *Board of Health of Haliburton, Kawartha, Pine Ridge District Health Unit*, [1977] 1 C.L.R.B.R. 221 (O.L.R.B.).
2. *CKLW Radio Broadcasting*, (1977) 77 C.L.L.C. para. 16,110 (C.L.R.B.).
3. *The Ottawa Citizen*, [1979] 2 C.L.R.B.R. 251 (O.L.R.B.).
4. *Pulp and Paper Industrial Relations Bureau*, [1978] 1 C.L.R.B.R. 60 (B.C.L.R.B.).

4. Duty to supply information

544. An interesting question arising from the requirement of full discussion concerns the extent to which an employer is obligated to supply wage data and more general financial data about its operation to the bargaining agent. While it has been recognized that there is some duty upon the employer to supply information, the full extent of that duty has not been clearly defined.[1] In one case a refusal by an employer to supply existing wage and classification data was taken into account in determining that a failure to bargain in good faith had occurred.[2]

1. *Noranda Metal Industries*, [1975] 1 C.L.R.B.R. 145 (B.C.L.R.B.); but see *Marshall-Wells* v. *Retail Wholesale*, (1956) 2 D.L.R. (2d) 569 (S.C.C.).
2. *DeVilbiss*, [1976] 2 C.L.R.B.R. 101 (O.L.R.B.).

5. Untimely use of economic sanctions

545. Canadian collective bargaining legislation generally provides that the parties may resort to economic sanctions only after they have had recourse to certain dispute-settlement procedures. The result is that there is a period of negotiation when economic sanctions are proscribed. At times, however, one of the parties may yield to the temptation of 'jumping the gun'. Untimely strikes or lock-outs are clearly illegal and a remedy can be sought through the special procedures established to deal with such untimely economic action. Picketing at this time, however, may not be illegal *per se*, but its use during this 'quiet' period may be considered as a failure to bargain in good faith.[1]

1. *Nipissing Hotel* v. *Hotel & Restaurant Employees*, (1962) 36 D.L.R. (2d) 81 (Ont.H.C.).

6. Duty to complete the negotiations

546. Negotiating problems sometimes arise at the very end of the negotiating process. While labour boards appear to have given the parties more leeway at this stage of the negotiations, they have intervened where one of the parties attempts to renege on committments previously made. A tabling of additional demands by a party after a dispute has been defined has been considered to be a failure to bargain in good faith.[1] Moreover labour boards have gone so far as to order an employer to execute a formal agreement where a mutual understanding had been reached on all issues.[2]

1. *Graphic Centre*, [1976] 2 C.L.R.B.R. 118 (O.L.R.B.); *Morris Rod Weeder* [1978] 2 C.L.R.B.R. 232 (S.L.R.B.).
2. *Municipality of Casimir, Jennings and Appleby*, [1978] 2 C.L.R.B.R. 284 (O.L.R.B.); *British Columbia Institute of Technology*, [1976] 2 C.L.R.B.R. 129 (B.C.L.R.B.) Section 65(2) of the British Columbia Code requires both parties to execute the agreement where an agreement has been reached in bargaining.

7. Supervision of the content of bargaining

547. The development of the duty to bargain in good faith has focused primarily on the manner in which negotiations are to be conducted. Despite this emphasis, labour boards on occasion have concerned themselves with the content of negotiations. Unlike the well-developed jurisprudence in the United States, however, the Canada case law does not usually draw a distinction between mandatory and voluntary demands.[1] Nevertheless, Canadian labour boards have considered the making of demands that are tainted by illegality as a failure to bargain in good faith and,[2] going even further, have treated demands that are inconsistent with the scheme of the collective bargaining statute as bad faith bargaining.[3]

1. In *Otis Elevator*, (1973) 73 C.L.L.C. para. 14,166 (B.C.C.A.) a distinction was made between mandatory and non-mandatory bargaining proposals.
2. *Trustees of School District No. 39*, [1977] 2 C.L.R.B.R. 201 (B.C.L.R.B.).
3. *Carpenters Employer Bargaining Agency*, [1978] 2 C.L.R.B.R. 501 (O.L.R.B.).

548. A demand may be rendered illegal by legislation other than the collective bargaining statute. For example, the insistence that the collective agreement contain a restriction upon the hiring of members of a particular ethnic group contrary to human rights legislation has been considered to be bad faith bargaining.[1] Labour boards have also indicated that insistence upon a demand in contravention of wage control legislation would amount to a failure to bargain in good faith.[2]

1. *T. Barbesin*, [1960] O.L.R.B. 80
2. *Trustees of School District No. 39*, [1977] 2 C.L.R.B.R. 201 (B.C.L.R.B.)

549. The illegality of the demand, however, is more likely to result from a conflict with the collective bargaining legislation itself. A failure to bargain in good faith can occur where a party seeks to bargain for a national agreement yet the applicable provincial labour legislation requires bargaining to be provincial in scope.[1] An attempt to extend bargaining rights during negotiations has been held to be inconsistent with the scheme of collective bargaining legislation.[2] Employer demands to restrict the scope of a bargaining unit have been considered as illegal, as have demands relating to the assignment of work between competing trade unions.[3] As well, bargaining demands that interfere with the conduct of the internal affairs of a trade union may also be considered to be illegal such as an employer demand that a union not discipline employees who crossed picket lines during a strike.[4] And, finally, insistence that a collective agreement be of shorter duration than required by law has been considered as a failure to bargain in good faith.[5]

1. *Otis Elevator*, (1973) 73 C.L.L.C. para. 14,166 (B.C.C.A.).
2. *Carpenters Employer Bargaining Agency*, [1978] 2 C.L.R.B.R. 501 (O.L.R.B.).
3. *British Columbia Telephone*, [1977] 2 C.L.R.B.R. 404 (C.L.R.B.); *Toronto Star Newspapers*, [1979] O.L.R.B. 451; [1979] O.L.R.B. 811.
4. *Morris Rod Weeder*, [1978] 2 C.L.R.B.R. 49 (S.L.R.B.); but see *A.N. Shaw Restoration*, [1977] 1 C.L.R.B.R. 103 (O.L.R.B.).
5. *Canada Bread*, (1945) 46 C.L.L.C. para. 16,430 (O.L.R.B.).

550. Despite these decisions curtailing the scope of bargaining, labour boards in general have allowed a great deal of latitude for the parties to determine the content of their negotiations. For example, issues such as the improvement of the pension benefits of retired employees have been considered as being bargainable.[1] Bargaining demands by themselves only give rise to a failure to bargain in good faith when they conflict with the scheme of the collective bargaining legislation or with some other statute.

1. *Pulp and Paper Industrial Relations Bureau*, [1978] 1 C.L.R.B.R. 60 (B.C.L.R.B.).

8. Compulsory provisions

551. The latitude given the parties to bargain the content of their collective agreement, however, has been restricted to some extent by legislation requiring that certain types of provisions be included in the collective agreement. Canadian collective bargaining legislation generally requires that there be included in a collective agreement a provision establishing a procedure for final and binding arbitration of any disputes arising from the agreement that cannot be resolved by the parties themselves.[1] In some jurisdictions the collective agreement must also contain a related provision barring strikes and lock-outs during its term.[2] Another general requirement is that collective agreements operate for a minimum term of one year.[3] Many jurisdictions also make compulsory a provision recognizing the union as exclusive bargaining agent and may, in addition, require some minimum form of union security.[4] These mandatory provisions have the effect of reducing the scope of bargaining to the extent that they establish a minimum below which the parties cannot bargain.

1. Canada, s.155; British Columbia, s.93; Ontario, ss.36, 37.
2. Ontario, s.36.
3. Canada, s.160; British Columbia, s.66; Ontario, s.44, Quebec, ss.53, 54.
4. Supra, S1 *The Union's Exclusive Authority to Bargain*.

9. Duration of the duty to bargain in good faith

552. Some negotiations may drag on over an extended period of time without being resolved. An interesting question is whether the duty to bargain in good faith may be weakened, or even disappear, over the passage of time. It has been recognized that the duty applies even where the law permits the parties to resort to the strike or lock-out.[1] Although it would appear that the duty to bargain in good faith cannot be extinguished by the passage of time, it is also apparent that the duty may have a different effect in the situation where extensive negotiations have already taken place.[2] Moreover, if negotiations are too protracted, the bargaining agent may find itself facing a timely application for de-certification. Where bargaining rights are divested by de-certification, then the duty to bargain in good faith is extinguished as a matter of course.

1. *New Method Laundry & Dry cleaners*, (1957) 57 C.L.L.C. para. 18,059 (O.L.R.B.).
2. *CKLW Radio Broadcasting*, (1977) 77 C.L.L.C. para. 16,110 (C.L.R.B.).

10. Remedies

553. The usual remedy for a failure to bargain in good faith is a declaration that a violation of the duty has occurred and a general bargaining order directing that future negotiations be in compliance with the duty to bargain in good faith. Such remedies as the imposition of terms that might have been reached had there been no failure to bargain in good faith,[1] and the postponement of a pending de-certification application[2] have been expressly rejected by labour boards on the basis that they would interfere unduly with the existing balance of bargaining power. One labour board has been prepared to order an employer to reimburse the union for its extra negotiating costs flowing from the employer's breach of the duty to bargain in good faith, and even to order the employer to reimburse the employees from the loss of opportunity to negotiate a collective agreement.[3] Another labour board has treated good faith bargaining as a pre-condition to the use of economic sanctions, although this view does not appear to have gained wide acceptance elsewhere.[4] Where bargaining demands have been considered to be illegal or inconsistent with the general scheme of collective bargaining, labour boards in effect have taken them off the bargaining table by declaring that such demands cannot be taken to an impasse.[5]

1. *Journal Publishing*, [1977] 2 C.L.R.B.R. 183 (O.L.R.B.).
2. *Journal Publishing*, [1978] 1 C.L.R.B.R. 84 (O.L.R.B.).
3. *Radio Shack*, (1980) 80 C.L.L.C. para. 16,003 (O.L.R.B.).
4. *Trustees of School District No. 39*, [1977] 2 C.L.R.B.R. 201 (B.C.L.R.B.); but see *Journal Publishing* footnote 1, *supra*.
5. *Carpenters Employer Bargaining Agency*, [1978] 1 C.L.R.B.R. 50 (O.L.R.B.).

Chapter V. Industrial Conflict

§1. THE ROLE OF CONFLICT IN THE CANADIAN SYSTEM OF INDUSTRIAL RELATIONS

554. It is accepted that the practice of collective bargaining necessarily involves the risk that parties will not successfully conclude negotiations, and will not arrive at mutually acceptable terms of agreement. When this risk eventuates, there must be recourse to some method of resolving the impasse. Except in a few essential industries,[1] or if the parties should so agree[2] (as they virtually never do), the Canadian system does not envisage recourse to arbitration in such circumstances. However, the parties are offered – indeed are required to have recourse to – the services of a mediator or conciliator who will assist them in their negotiations. But the mediator or conciliator cannot compel them to agree; he can only assist them to do so. If agreement is not forthcoming, the parties are free to mount economic pressures in order to force the opposite party to make concessions. The most common form of pressure is a strike, typically supported by picketing and other forms of appeals for sympathetic action against the employer. However, on occasion, an employer will conduct a lockout, which is the notional equivalent of a strike, denying his employees the opportunity to work until they are prepared to accept his terms.

1. *Infra*.
2. Ontario, s.34c.

555. The earliest serious efforts at government intervention in labour-management relations centred on this policy of conciliation. From 1907, with the enactment of the Industrial Disputes Investigation Act,[1] Canadian legislative policy has consistently sought to minimize the incidence of strikes through compulsory, elaborate and time-consuming peacemaking procedures. However, during the 1950's and 1960's, there was a growing consensus that these procedures were dysfunctional, that instead of reducing the number of strikes and minimizing their duration, the procedures were in fact protracting, intensifying, and perhaps actually causing, strikes. Various legislative reforms ensued which were designed to make conciliation or mediation less time-consuming and predictable, more flexible and responsive to the exigencies of particular situations.[2]

1. S.C. 1907, c. 20.
2. See *e.g.* H. D. Woods, *Canadian Collective Bargaining and Dispute Settlement Policy*, (1955) 21 Can. J. Ec. & Poli. Sci. 447; W. B. Cunningham, *Conciliation: The End of Compulsory Boards*, (1970) 25 Ind. Rel. 62.

556. What has not changed has been the determination that economic conflict in labour disputes should be used only to resolve differences over the terms of a new collective agreement. As will be seen,[1] strikes in all other situations are presumptively, if not conclusively, contrary to public policy and illegal.

1. Infra.

557. However, although the legitimate occasion for strikes has been very narrowly defined, their frequency has not thereby been inhibited. On the contrary, Canada has had, rather consistently over the past two decades, a rather unenviable record of strikes, as compared with other western industrialized countries.[1] As the following statistics[2] demonstrate, Canada has generally lost more man days through strikes, relative to man days worked, than other countries.

1. For an analysis of Canada's strike record see Malles, *Canadian Industrial Conflict in International Perspective* (Ottawa, 1977).
2. Table 6; Source: P. Malles, *Canadian Industrial Conflict in International Perspective* (Ottawa, 1977).

558. Apart from these overall, discouraging comparative statistics, certain features of the Canadian strike record should be identified. Obviously, in Canada as in other countries, the strike record is, in part, the product of social, economic, political and demographic factors. Some special features of the Canadian situation are these: considerable fluctuations in the growth of the economy, especially during the late 1960's and early 1970's, when expansion encouraged workers aggressively to seek a share of the growing wealth, and a

TABLE 6
Industrial conflict in selected countries
annual averages 1965–1969 and 1970–1974

| | (1) Number of Conflicts | | (2) Workers Involved | | | | (3) Working Days Lost per Worker Involved | | (4) Days Lost per 1,000 Workers | |
| | | | Numbers | | % of Paid Labour Force | | | | | |
	1965–1969	1970–1974	1965–1969	1970–1974	1965–1969	1970–1974	1965–1969	1970–1974	1965–1969	1970–1974
Canada	563	735	273,142	429,700	4.4	4.2	17.8	15.0	775	863
United States	5,422	5,458	2,302,200	2,665,600	3.5	3.6	15.8	15.5	558	562
Japan	1,473	3,164	1,224,542	2,203,422	4.0	6.3	2.7	2.7	109	172
Australia	1,537	2,553	671,738	1,323,100	17.1	28.9	1.6	2.5	269	718
Belgium	67	187	30,411	75,860	1.1	2.5	8.6	11.8	92	292
Denmark	29	96	19,927	109,803	1.1	5.8	3.6	7.5	41	434
France[1]	1,508	3,690	2,211,323	3,435,975	14.8	13.4	1.0	1.5	167	209
Germany	n.a.	n.a.	75,321	235,768	0.4	1.1	2.0	5.3	7	57
Italy[2]	3,080	4,694	3,762,272	5,195,113	31.0	40.2	4.1	3.7	1,274	1,517
Netherlands	25	33	10,593	33,707	0.3	0.7	2.1	6.4	6	48
Sweden	18	74	7,835	23,671	0.2	0.5	12.0	9.1	29	62
United Kingdom	2,380	2,885	1,175,320	1,573,340	5.1	7.0	3.3	8.9	171	627

1. For the year 1968 in which the May/June upheavals occurred no figures are available. The annual averages for the period 1965–1969 are therefore based on the period 1965 to 1967 plus 1969. Also excluded from the French figures are so-called political strikes.
2. Excluding political strikes.
3. The figures in column 4 differ somewhat from those in the EEC based Table 1, most likely due to rounding and updating of national data. However in almost all instances the differences are of no real significance.
Source: Year Book of International Labour Statistics, 1976, International Labour Office, Geneva, and OECD Labour Force Statistics, 1975, Paris.

subsequent period of inflation, during the middle 1970's, when government-imposed wage restraints postponed wage claims, and prompted first a 'National Day of Protest' – a one-day general strike – and then a series of 'catch up' strikes after the end of the period of controls; the proximity of the United States and the intimate connection between the economies of the two countries, which has provided Canadian workers with a perhaps unrealistically high level of aspiration and collective bargaining claims; the relatively recent advent of public sector unionism which has graduated into a posture of militancy at the very moment when government spending restraints have made collective bargaining more difficult; the vivid impact, in a relatively small national labour market, of lengthy strikes by a few, large groups of workers; and the exacerbating effects of social and economic unrest in Quebec, translated especially into militancy amongst public sector unions.

559. However, there are also suggestions that certain structural features of the Canadian industrial relations system contribute to the country's poor strike record: the highly decentralized nature of collective bargaining in most industries promotes inter-union competition for wage increases and other benefits; the relative rigidity of complex collective agreements for fixed and lengthy terms often of two or three years, means that the parties play for high stakes at their periodic negotiations; and the protracted nature of negotiations, in part due to compulsory conciliation procedures, leads to the build-up of resentments and the hardening of positions.

560. For all of these reasons, and no doubt others, there has been considerable concern in Canada in recent years about the cost to the economy both of strikes and of what are sometimes viewed as excessively high wage settlements, secured through the assertion of economic power.

§2. FORMS OF CONFLICT

A. The strike

561. The strike is the most obvious and widely-practised form of economic sanction employed in industrial relations. Most labour relations statutes contain a definition of 'strike', which has three components: (1) a refusal to work or cessation of work, (2) by employees, (3) in combination or in concert or in accordance with a common understanding.[1] In addition, the Labour Code of British Columbia, and several other provincial statutes, introduces a further component: (4) the purpose of compelling an employer to agree to terms and conditions of employment.[2] Each of these components presents certain problems.

1. Canada, s.107(1); Ontario, s.1(1)(m); Quebec, s.1(h).
2. British Columbia, s.1(1); Alberta, s.49(1); Manitoba, s.1(v); Nova Scotia, s.1(1)(v).

562. The 'cessation of' or 'refusal to' work implies that an obligation to work exists. However, it has been held that a strike may include a refusal to work overtime,[1] or to operate new machines,[2] or a slowdown or work to rule,[3] or an attempt by the union to adhere to unilaterally made restrictive work rules.[4]

1. *Mobile Paint*, [1975] 1 C.L.R.B.R. 248 (O.L.R.B.); *Weyerhaueser* [1976] 2 C.L.R.B.R. 41 (B.C.L.R.B.); *MacMillan Bloedel (Alberni)* v. *I.W.A.* (1971) 13 D.L.R. (3d) 741 (B.C.C.A.).
2. *R* v. *B.C.L.R.B.*, *Ex p. Pulp & Paper Workers* (1964) 45 D.L.R. (2d) 437 (B.C.S.C.).
3. *Pacific Press* v. *Vancouver Typographical* (1970) 15 D.L.R. (3d) 212 (B.C.C.A.); *Transport Labour Relations* v. *Truck Drivers*, (1974) 54 D.L.R. (3d) (B.C.S.C.); *Winnipeg Teachers' Assoc.*, v. *Winnipeg School Division No. 1*, (1975) 59 D.L.R. (3d) 228 (S.C.C.).
4. *Alps Construction*, [1964–65] O.L.R.B. 131.

563. Significantly, it has been held that a 'strike' may occur notwithstanding a provision in the collective agreement purporting to relieve employees of the obligation to work in specific circumstances, for example, where to do so would require them to cross the lawful picket line of another union. Such a clause is invalid because it would defeat the statutory policy of not permitting employees to strike during the term of their collective agreement.[1]

1. *Re Otis Elevator and Elevator Constructors*, (1973) 36 D.L.R. (3d) 402 (N.S.C.A.); *Associated Freezers of Canada* [1972] O.L.R.B. 445.

564. Only 'employees' may strike. Hence, in principle, a refusal to accept employment should not amount to a strike. However, a recent Supreme Court of Canada decision[1] held that the refusal of workers to cross picket lines to accept assignments to unload ships was a strike, although there was no subsisting employment relationship as between individual workers and the specific stevedoring firms to which they were sent by the union hiring hall from time to time. On the other hand, while the quitting of employment for cause is not *per se* a strike,[2] resignations must be *bona fide* and not a mere subterfuge.[3]

1. *I.L.A.* v. *Maritime Employers' Assoc.*, (1978) 89 D.L.R. (3d) 289 (S.C.C.).
2. Ontario s.68.
3. *Aubin Plumbing & Heating*, [1967–68] O.L.R.B. 898.

565. Concerted activity is of the essence of a strike. Thus, the refusal by individual employees to cross the picket line of another union to go to work will not be treated as a strike if it can be ascribed to individual motivations, *e.g.*, the fear of violent reprisals,[1] or a *bona fide* belief that individual employees enjoyed a contractual right to respect the picket line.[2] On the other hand, the mere fact that a large group of employees refuses to work at the same time creates a very strong presumption that they are acting 'in accordance with a common understanding', and hence striking.[3]

1. *MacMillan Bloedel (Alberni)* v. *Swanson*, (1972) 26 D.L.R. (3d) 641 (B.C.S.C.).
2. *Nelson Crushed Stone*, (1977) 78 C.L.L.C. para. 16,117 (O.L.R.B.).
3. *Winnipeg Builders' Exchange* v. *I.B.E.W.*, (1966) 57 D.L.R. (2d) 141 (Man. C.A.), *aff'd.* (1968) 65 D.L.R. (2d) 242 (S.C.C.).

566. The special element of 'purpose' found in the British Columbia Labour Code, and elsewhere, is of potentially great importance. This point is illustrated by a series of cases relating to the National Day of Protest, in effect a one day general strike, called by the Canadian Labour Congress to protest the federal government's anti-inflation legislation. A number of unions were charged, in various provinces, with violation of no-strike provisions in collective agreements or statutes. Their defence was, that such provisions were not intended to restrict activity which was essentially directed towards political, rather than industrial relations, objectives. This argument failed in virtually all forums in which it was advanced,[1] except British Columbia, whose labour relations board relied upon the special statutory requirement of 'purpose' to confine the inhibiting effect of no-strike clauses to situations where the strike was intended to exact concessions from the employer.[2] However, this argument did not prevail in other jurisdictions whose statutes had similar, purposive provisions.[3]

1. See *e.g. Domglas*, [1976] 2 C.L.R.B.R. 394 (O.L.R.B.) *aff'd.* (1978) 19 O.R. (2d) 353 (D.C.); *Re U.S.W.A. and Inco.*, (1978) 87 D.L.R. (3d) 274 (Ont.H.C.); *Kendall*, (1978) 17 L.A.C. 408 and cases cited; but see *contra Dominion Bridge*, (1977) 15 L.A.C. (2d) 295.
2. *B.C. Hydro & Power Authority*, [1976] 2 C.L.R.B.R. 410 (B.C.L.R.B.).
3. *Re Robb Engineering and U.S.W.A.*, (1978) 86 D.L.R. (3d) 307 (N.S.C.A.); *Re Inco and U.S.W.A.*, (1978) 86 D.L.R. (3d) 407 (Man.C.A.).

B. The lock-out

567. The 'lock-out' is also defined by almost all labour relations statutes.[1] Common elements in these statutory definitions are that the lock-out must involve: (1) a closing of a place of employment, the suspension of work, or a refusal to continue to employ, and (2) the purpose of compelling employees to agree to terms and conditions of employment. Thus defined, the lock-out is clearly a legitimate employer tactic, if exercised in accordance with the procedural requirements which also govern strikes, and if used in aid of the employer's collective bargaining objectives. However, the Ontario statute[2] contains a further element: (3) in the alternative, to compel or induce employees to abandon their rights under the Labour Relations Act. A 'lock-out' of this type is an unfair practice, and illegal.[3]

1. Canada, s.107(1); British Columbia, s.1(1); Quebec, s.1(i); the Saskatchewan Trade Union Act contains no definition.
2. S.1(1)(i); to the same effect: New Brunswick, s.1(1); Prince Edward Island s.7(1)(k).
3. *C.P.R.* v. *Zambri (Royal York Hotel case)*, (1962) 34 D.L.R. (2d) 654 (S.C.C.).

568. Lock-outs are relatively rare, although not unknown in industries where employer associations are comparatively strong and capable of preemptive, coordinated action to prevent a union from striking each employer in turn.

C. Picketing

569. Although picketing is a familiar feature of strikes and lock-outs, and indeed may be encountered even where there has been no work stoppage at all, the term is not one which is, typically, defined with precision. Only the Labour Code of British Columbia purports to contain an authoritative definition.[1]
1. S.1(1).

570. Generally, picketing is understood to involve these elements: (1) the presence of one or more persons, (2) communication by spoken or written messages, or through behaviour, and (3) an intention by presence or communication to secure a sympathetic response from third persons, *e.g.* customers who will cease to deal with a struck employer, prospective employees who will decline to accept employment in a struck enterprise, or suppliers who will interrupt shipments of materials required to sustain production in a struck plant.

571. As will be seen,[1] it is the interaction of these elements which creates analytical difficulties. The presence of individual picketers in conflict situations which are often volatile and emotional, may produce, reasonably or otherwise, the fear of illicit reprisal or violence in the minds of customers, prospective employees or suppliers, who refuse to respond sympathetically to the picketers. However, it is not possible to reassure those who are afraid, without at the same time interfering with the freedom of communication of the picketers, a freedom which is exercised in all social, economic and political controversies. This is a fact of special significance because the picket line is more than an appeal to third persons. It is, as well, a means of communication and association amongst those picketing. It may provide an occasion for meaningful activity to ease the monotony and idleness of the strike; it may help to stimulate a sense of solidarity and effective action which bolsters morale; and it may serve to discourage those who are considering abandoning the cause.

1. *Infra.*

572. At the same time, there is a sense that communication in the context of an industrial dispute has a greater impact than in other contexts. On the one hand, the solidarity of the labour movement gives any appeal for support special cogency and the consequences of support greater impact. On the other hand, to the extent that occasional incidents of picket line violence do occur, the mere presence of a picket line may induce behaviour on the part of someone contemplating crossing it which is not entirely reasonable. Because of these factors, there is particular concern that picket lines should be mounted only for limited purposes, and not in situations where the impact they might have would be disproportionate to the good they might accomplish. Finally, picketing may involve the invasion of rights of personal security, property and reputation, about which the law traditionally has been especially solicitous. Both courts and legislatures have had considerable difficulty in striking the proper balance between the vindication of these traditional interests, and the newer interests of labour unions implicit in the use of picketing as a legitimate weapon of industrial conflict.

D. Boycott

573. A 'boycott' is an invitation to the public to express sympathetic support of the cause of a trade union by avoiding or ending economic involvement with an employer with whom it is in dispute. The term is also broad enough to embrace appeals to workers not to accept employment with that employer, or to handle goods produced by or destined for him, in the course of their employment by some third person. This latter aspect of boycotts will be treated separately.[1]

1. *Infra*, 'The Scope of Ancillary Activities: Secondary Picketing'.

574. A boycott may be solicited by picketing at the employer's place of business or at a place where his products are sold, or by approaches to his customers or suppliers through letters or individual interviews, or simply by appeals to the community at large, or some sympathetic portion of it, by means of leaflets or newspaper advertisements.

575. Except to the extent that such appeals constitute an invitation to violate the law, *e.g.* an invitation to strike illegally, it might be thought that they should be protected by law as the exercise of the right of free speech. But the trend of the law is otherwise.[1]

1. *Hersees of Woodstock* v. *Goldstein*, (1963) 38 D.L.R. (2d) 449 (Ont.C.A.), discussed, *infra*.

§3. LAWFUL ECONOMIC SANCTIONS

A. The right to strike

576. The right to strike in Canada rests neither upon constitutional guarantees nor, surprisingly, upon explicit statutory language. Rather its juridical basis has been variously ascribed to the absence of common law decisions denying its existence ('what is not forbidden is permitted'), or to common law *dicta* which affirmed the right, or to inferences derived from modern labour relations statutes which, by regulating its exercise, assume that strikes properly conducted are lawful.[1] Whatever its basis, a 'right to strike' is now generally thought to exist. However, specific legislation relating to certain essential industries and, in a few provinces, to public employment, may abrogate this right, and compel recourse to such definitive procedures as final and binding arbitration of interest disputes.[2]

1. These positions are taken in various judgments in *C.P.R.* v. *Zambri (Royal York Hotel case)*, (1962) 34 D.L.R. (2d) 654 (S.C.C.).
2. *Infra*.

577. In a preliminary way, it is reasonably accurate to state that the only lawful strikes are those which are designed to gain economic objectives, and which are timely in the sense that they follow exhaustion of the compulsory conciliation procedures laid down in the legislation. Even a strike for collective bargaining objectives is unlawful if it is untimely.[1] As well, strikes for recognition,[2] sympathy strikes designed to bring pressure to bear on a secondary employer,[3] strikes designed to force the employer to accept the union's interpretation of an agreement,[4] strikes of political protest,[5] are all unlawful.

214

Not only are such strikes unlawful, but activities conducted in association with them, or in substitution for them, are equally unlawful.

1. Canada, s.180; British Columbia, ss.79, 80; Ontario, s.63; Quebec, s.46.
2. *Gagnon* v. *Foundation Maritime*, (1961) 28 D.L.R. (2d) 174 (S.C.C.).
3. *The Citizen*, [1976] 2 C.L.R.B.R. 474 (O.L.R.B.); *Mark Fishing* v. *United Fishermen*, (1972) 24 D.L.R. (3d) 585 (B.C.C.A.), *aff'd*. (1973) 38 D.L.R. (3d) 316n (S.C.C.).
4. *Teamsters* v. *Therien*, (1960) 22 D.L.R. (2d) 1 (S.C.C.).
5. *Supra*.

B. The effect of a lawful strike on employment status and benefits

1. Employment status

578. An employee who participates in a lawful, timely strike does not thereby either resign his employment or render himself liable to discharge. In the historic *Royal York Hotel* decision,[1] the Supreme Court of Canada pointed out that employees who participate in such strikes are exercising a statutorily protected right to participate in the lawful activities of a trade union, violation of which is an unfair labour practice. Moreover, the Court pointed out, the Labour Relations Act in question specifically (but typically) precluded any inference that strikers ceased to be employees 'by reason only of . . . ceasing to work . . . as the result of a lock-out or strike.'[2]

This holding, in turn, raises a number of issues, the resolution of which indicates the extent to which the right to strike may or may not be rendered meaningless by employer counter-measures.

1. *C.P.R.* v. *Zambri, supra*.
2. See Ontario Ontario, s.1(2); to the same effect: British Columbia, s.1(2); Canada Labour Code, s.107(2); Quebec, s.98.

2. The right to hire replacements

579. While the point has not been squarely decided in Canada, it has been assumed that the employer has the right to hire replacements for his striking employees. Certainly, a contrary holding by a court would provoke much astonishment. Resort by the employer to the labour market to keep his plant running is part of the test of economic realities which the strike is intended to be. When there is unemployment, presumably replacements will easily be found at the wages offered by the employer; when there is a labour shortage, he will have to offer higher wages, whether to arrive at settlement with the union or to attract new workers. Despite labour claims that this right of the employer gives him an unwarranted advantage in the bargaining contest, to outlaw the hiring of replacements (except perhaps for a ban on professional strike-breakers, such as that enacted by British Columbia in 1973)[1] would drastically alter the present balance of power. Against this background, recent Quebec legislation which prohibits the use of either non-striking employees or replacements to maintain operations during a strike, must be seen as a dramatic departure from the norm.[2] A much more limited restraint upon this traditionally-accepted employer right is legislation in several provinces which gives to non-striking employees the right to refuse to perform work normally done by strikers.[3]

1. S.3(2)(d).
2. Quebec, Ss.97a–97c. (as am. S.Q. 1977, c.41); an employer is entitled to take 'necessary measures to avoid the destruction or serious deterioration' of his property.
3. Manitoba, s.12; Alberta, s.153(3)(g); Nova Scotia, s.51(3)(c).

3. The striker's right to his job

580. Almost inevitably strikes are settled on terms which include the return to work of all strikers.

581. However, not all strikes are won. Sometimes the employer is strong enough to deny any concessions to the union, and *ex hypothese*, to withstand a union claim that all strikers be returned to work. Then a new set of equities comes into play. Senior employees within sight of pension rights may never serve out their few remaining years; employees in their middle years may find themselves on an inhospitable labour market; employees of only a few years' service may depend on their job to feed young families. For all of these groups, the consequences of losing their jobs are so severe that they may be prepared to desert the strike and return to work. While there is no authoritative decision on point, it is reasonably clear that the employer cannot deny a striking employee the opportunity to return to work to fill a vacant job, or at least must treat his application to do so without discrimination based on strike participation or union membership. However, this general principle might be qualified in two respects.

582. First, it is clear that the strikers' right to his job will yield to certain economic exigencies. If the employer decides to shut down or suspend an operation for reasons other than anti-unionism, and in response to legitimate business considerations, he is entitled to do so even though the result will be to terminate the employment of strikers.[1]

1. *Webster & Horsfall*, (1969) 69 C.L.L.C. para. 16,050 (O.L.R.B.).

583. Second, recent legislation guarantees strikers an absolute right to reinstatement in their former jobs, provided that work is still being performed, either for an indefinite period[1] or, in the case of Ontario, for a period of six months.[2]

1. Manitoba, s.11; Quebec, s.98a.
2. Ontario, s.64. The limitation of the right to reinstatement to a period of six months raises the possibility that the court might decide that the employer is free to refuse reinstatement thereafter. However, no such finding has yet been made, and such an interpretation would appear to conflict with underlying policies of the statute.

584. Assuming reinstatement of the striker, there remains the difficult question of what happens to the host of employment benefits which were rooted in the expired collective agreement? If a new agreement is signed, these benefits will usually be renewed by it. If no new agreement is signed, the continued existence of the benefits theoretically is the subject of bargaining between the employer and the individual worker, but practically is unilaterally determined by the former.

4. Employment benefits during strikes

585. Prima facie, an employee who goes on strike thereby forfeits the right not only to his regular pay, but also to all other benefits which are associated with his employment. So long as a collective agreement is in operation, it will usually provide the employee with a number of such benefits (often building upon a legislatively-required minimum): annual vacations, paid holidays, severance pay, pensions, life, accident, health and dental insurance, and preferment in the event of lay-offs or promotions, based on seniority. When a collective agreement expires, if the employee remains at work, it can fairly be inferred that he does so on the same terms as formerly prevailed under the collective agreement, except to the extent that specific changes are announced by the employer and acquiesced in by the employee. In effect, the employee is then working under an individual contract of employment the terms of which are assumed to be those of the former collective agreement. But when a strike begins, and work stops, an employer is clearly entitled to cease paying wages to his striking employees. By the same token, he may refuse to continue to provide them with employment-based benefits which are, in effect, wages paid in monies' worth.

586. Thus, with the outbreak of a strike, the employer is free to terminate insurance coverage, pension contributions and benefits, paid vacations and holidays etc. In practice, a union and an employer will often make arrangements whereby contributions may be made by or on behalf of employees to avoid the forfeiture of such benefits. Often, too, after a strike, a collective agreement is signed which relates back to the date of expiry of the previous collective agreement, and retroactively restores the *status quo ante*. Pursuant to the terms of such an agreement, the employer may make up any deficiency in payment of premiums or pension contributions, and rectify any violation of seniority.

587. But, in the heat of battle, an employer may refuse to agree to any such arrangements, and thereby generate considerable pressure on his striking employees, for example, by threatening them with loss of pension benefits when they are very close to retirement age. While this situation was the subject of sympathetic comment in the *Royal York Hotel* decision in the lower courts,[1] and has been to a limited extent addressed by specific legislation,[2] the position remains essentially as stated. The Supreme Court of Canada has been unable to find any foundation upon which to construct the protection of benefits which had been provided by the expired collective agreements.[3] And various arbitration decisions have held that (subject always to the specific terms of a subsequent collective agreement) strikers forfeit sick pay and severance pay and pay for holidays and annual vacations which occur during the strike.[4]

1. *R.* v. *C.P.R.*, (1962) 31 D.L.R. (2d) 209 at 220 per McRuer, C. J. H. C. (Ont.H.C.), *aff'd. sub nom. C.P.R.* v. *Zambri, supra.*
2. Canada, s.184(3)(d); Alberta, s.153(3)(c); Manitoba, s.14(a); Newfoundland, s.24(2); Nova Scotia, s.51(3)(d); Saskatchewan, s.11(1)(l).
3. *C.P.R.* v. *Zambri, supra,* at 666, (per Judson, J.).
4. See generally, G. England, *The Legal Response to Striking at the Individual Level in the Common Law Jurisdictions of Canada,* (1976) 3 Dalhousie L.J. 440.

588. Obviously, if benefits are to be protected during a strike, legislative intervention is required. This has already happened in regard to pension benefits and in Saskatchewan, possibly, in regard to all benefits.[1] But such protection is not widespread.

1. Saskatchewan, s.11(1)(1), prevents employer interference with 'pension rights or benefits *or any benefits whatever'.*

589. Finally, assuming that a striker is disentitled to various employment-related benefits during a strike, to what extent is this loss offset by eligibility to receive benefits under various state-sponsored schemes? Under unemployment insurance legislation,[1] strikers are disqualified from receiving benefits for the duration of the labour dispute. Likewise, they may be ineligible even for social assistance benefits, because they are not considered to be 'persons in need' within the contemplation of welfare legislation.[2]

1. Unemployment Insurance Act, S.C. 1971, c.48, s.44; see M. A. Hickling, *Labour Disputes and Unemployment Insurance in Canada and the United Kingdom* (Toronto, C.C.H., 1975).
2. The provinces administer welfare programmes funded (in part) by federal grants, and subject to general federal standards and policies. See Canada Assistance Plan, R.S.C. 1970, c. C–1, s.2. However, the provinces have considerable latitude in defining eligibility for benefit, and some have done so in such a way as to exclude strikers, see *Alden* v. *Gaglardi,* (1973) 30 D.L.R. (3d) 760 (S.C.C.).

590. Deprived of income by both his employer and the state, the striking employee is left largely to his own resources. These are, at least minimally, supplemented by payments from the strike funds established by most unions. Such payments are, however, typically meagre, and their duration limited by the union's ability to renew its resources through contributions from non-striking members in other enterprises, and from other unions. Beyond this, unions are occasionally able to borrow funds by pledging their capital assets, but are obviously reluctant to do so.

591. In sum, a striking employee is almost certain to confront severe economic loss, both of his regular wages, and of 'fringe benefits'.

5. *Employee obligations during a strike*

592. Obviously, an employee is not bound to report for work during a strike.

He is not, however, relieved of all obligations towards his employer. While a worker does not terminate his employment relationship, 'by reason only of participating in a lawful strike' he is not thereby completely insulated from discharge.

593. Specifically, an employer has a privilege to dismiss employees for cause, without committing an unfair labour practice, for such serious misconduct as sabotage against plant property or violence on the picket line.[1]

1. See *e.g. Re Canadian Gypsum and Nova Scotia Quarryworkers*, (1960) 20 D.L.R. (2d) 319 (N.S.S.C.); *Inmont*, (1970) 21 L.A.C. 411.

594. While there is little debate over the employer's right to discharge employees for such serious acts of misconduct, the application of the principle poses certain problems. Foremost amongst these is the difficulty of assessing employee conduct in the volatile atmosphere of a strike. Provocative employer action, for example, may actually be designed to elicit misconduct on the picket line for the very purpose of affording the employer a convenient excuse for the discharge of strikers. Moreover, the usual forum for adjudication of discharge grievances is arbitration. But, by definition, arbitration which is established by a collective agreement is not available during the course of a strike. Thus, if the discharge of employees for alleged misconduct during the strike is to be arbitrated, the parties must almost inevitably make some provision for such arbitration when they execute a new collective agreement following the termination of the strike.

6. The duration of the employment relationship

595. To hold that neither a strike nor the illegal discharge of the strikers severs the employment relationship throws up the obvious questions, how long does the relationship last and what will sever it? The questions are important for psychological and legal reasons. As to the former, when there are no more striking 'employees', the strike is over. Thus announcement that no more strikers are employed may destroy union morale, just as continued assertion that the strikers are 'employees' bolsters it. As to the latter, employment status may determine entitlement to various welfare benefits, and may affect the continued existence of the union's bargaining rights.

596. Obviously, if a striker dies, or becomes unemployable, or clearly renounces his employment status, he ceases to be a striking 'employee'.[1] But usually matters are not so clear. For the duration of the conflict, strikers may take full-time or part-time jobs in order to supplement their meagre strike pay. Can it be said that by so doing they are acting inconsistently with continued employment by the struck employer, and thus that they have renounced their jobs as well? While in principle this might be a sound position, in practice it is not. The relative ease with which workers move from job to job throughout the economy suggests the striker is unlikely to regard his new job as 'permanent'.

Especially if the former job is one in which the striker is experienced and has seniority, and in which there is a prospect of renewed pension and other benefits, he is likely to regard his new job as only 'temporary'.

1. *R.* v. *C.P.R.*, *supra*, at 220 per McRuer, C. J. H. C.; but this position was challenged in the Supreme Court of Canada, (1963) 34 D.L.R. (2d) 654 at 657, per Locke, J., dissenting; see also England, *supra*, at 449.

597. While some indication of continued interest by the striker in his former employment can be demonstrated through such activities as picketing, their absence is not necessarily conclusive; all aspects of the employee's behaviour must be examined in order to determine whether employment status survives a protracted strike in any individual instance.[1]

1. G. England, *supra*, at 449.

C. Ancillary tactics in support of lawful strikes

1. The legal rules governing picketing

598. The law governing picketing, in all Canadian jurisdictions, is essentially the ordinary law of tort or delict, administered by the regular courts. Exceptions to this generalization can be easily identified and will be dealt with in detail elsewhere: the federal Criminal Code controls coercive and excessive forms of 'watching and besetting';[1] British Columbia integrates the law of picketing with its general code of labour relations, administered by the Labour Relations Board;[2] and several provinces have modified common law principles by either protecting conduct which might otherwise constitute a civil wrong,[3] or forbidding conduct which would not.[4]

1. Criminal Code, s.381.
2. British Columbia, ss. 28035, ss.84–91.
3. *E.g.* The Petty Trespass Act, R.S.M. 1970, c.P50, s.5, as am. S.M. 1976, c.71, s.2; The Queen's Bench Act, R.S.M. 1970, c.C–280, as am. S.M. 1970, c.79, s.60.2; Rights of Labour Act, R.S.O. 1970, c.416; British Columbia, s.87.
4. *Infra*.

599. In Quebec, the general provisions of the Civil Code concerning intentional wrongs are applied to conduct in labour disputes. In common law jurisdictions, several torts, largely developed in nineteenth-century England to regulate trade union activity, are relied upon: conspiracy, inducing breach of contract, and wrongful interference with economic relations. These torts can be briefly defined, although extensive doctrinal analysis is, in this context, neither possible nor useful.[1]

1. See H. W. Arthurs, *Tort Liability for Strikes in Canada: Some Problems of Judicial Workmanship*, (1960) 38 Can. B.Rev. 346; A. W. R. Carrothers, *Collective Bargaining Law in Canada* (Toronto, 1965) esp. Part III *The Limits of Lawful Picketing and Boycotting*; I. M. Christie, *The Liability of Strikers in the Law of Tort: A Comparative Study of the Law in England and Canada* (Kingston, 1967); S. Tacon, *Tort Liability During the Various Phases of the Collective Bargaining Relationship* (Toronto, 1980).

600. a. Conspiracy, as a civil wrong, involves the agreement of two or more persons to accomplish a wrongful purpose, or a proper purpose through the use of wrongful means. 'Wrongful' in this sense is not confined to means or ends explicitly proscribed by the positive law; it includes all conduct which a judge might stigmatize as 'wrongful'. However, as the case law has developed, if a union has as its predominant purpose the pursuit of its own economic self-interest, that purpose will not be found to be unlawful.[1] And, as for 'means', these are increasingly tactics which are proscribed by the labour relations act,[2] as well as by the various doctrines described below.

1. *Crofter Hand Woven Harris Tweed* v. *Veitch*, [1942] A.C. 435 (H.L.).
2. *Gagnon* v. *Foundation Maritime*, (1961) 28 D.L.R. (2d) 174 (S.C.C.); *Jacobsen Bros.* v. *Anderson*, (1962) 35 D.L.R. (2d) 746 (N.S.S.C.).

601. b. It is wrongful for a third person to *interfere in existing contractual relationships* either by persuading one of the parties to a contract to break it, or by preventing him from performing. In principle, any such interference by means of picketing or otherwise should involve a union in liability; there is a very limited privilege to induce breaches of contract and it has never been extended to cases where a union is vindicating its own economic interests. But in practice, the tort is not applied in ordinary situations where picketing takes place at the premises of a lawfully struck employer.[1] However, along with other torts, it is one of the bases upon which courts rely in prohibiting labour union activity which is thought to violate the labour relations act.[2] The tort does not apply in relationships where there is no existing contract, nor to interference by means of appeals to one of the parties to exercise a right not to enter into, or to withdraw from, a contract with another, rather than to break it.[3]

1. This result has been accomplished by specific legislation in Newfoundland, s.99.
2. *Smith Bros.* v. *Jones*, [1955] 4 D.L.R. 255 (Ont.H.C.).
3. *Newell* v. *Barker & Bruce*, [1950] 2 D.L.R. 289 (S.C.C.).

602. c. Wrongful interference with economic relationships does not depend upon the existence of a contract, but protects such economic interests as a course of dealing, past or prospective. In determining what interference is 'wrongful', the courts have expressed a willingness to be guided by either common law or statute law. In effect, the courts rely upon violations of the labour relations act as important indicators of unlawfulness.[1]

1. *Teamsters* v. *Therien*, (1960) 22 D.L.R. (2d) 1 (S.C.C.).

603. Increasingly, it becomes clear that apart from any other sources of law upon which they might rely, the courts in purporting to apply common law doctrine are in fact enforcing what they conceive to be the policies and express requirements of the labour relations act. Indeed, there is a growing tendency to do so directly and without obfuscating references to common law doctrine.[1]

1. See *e.g. I.B.E.W.* v. *Winnipeg Builders' Exchange*, (1967) 65 D.L.R. (2d) 242 (S.C.C.); *I.L.A.* v. *Maritime Employers' Assoc.*, (1979) 89 D.L.R. (3d) 289 (S.C.C.).

604. This trend, while perhaps defensible on jurisprudential grounds, has attracted negative comment on the grounds that courts are extrapolating provisions of labour relations statutes beyond the contemplation and intention of the legislature that enacted them, that judges are insufficiently familiar with industrial relations policies and practices to apply such statutes in a sophisticated and constructive way, and that the intervention of the courts in policing the rules of industrial conflict impedes the development of an integrated scheme of enforcement under the aegis of the labour relations board.

605. In the discussion that follows, no attempt will be made to explain the doctrinal bases of the courts' decisions. For the most part, the doctrines outlined above have little application in the context of 'lawful' strikes; they are more typically used to render unlawful conduct which supports, or is in substitution for, illegal strike action.[1]

   1. *Infra*, §4 *'Unlawful Industrial Action'*.

2. Timeliness

606. As has been indicated, the essential test of the legality of a strike is whether or not it is timely, *i.e.* whether it follows exhaustion of the negotiation and conciliation procedures prescribed by statute. Although not all labour relations statutes specifically address the use of 'ancillary' tactics such as picketing,[1] it can generally be said that where a strike would be unlawful, so will ancillary activity be forbidden.[2] Conversely, where a strike is lawful, picketing is presumptively lawful.[3]

   1. British Columbia, ss.85, 88, re-enacting that province's Trade-unions Act, S.B.C. 1959, c.90, permits picketing during a lawful strike, but not otherwise. To the same effect: Alberta, s.134; New Brunswick, s.104; Newfoundland, s.124.
   2. Ontario and Quebec legislation, for example, contains no direct reference to picketing, but judicial decisions in those provinces have generally reached this conclusion. See *infra*.
   3. *Williams* v. *Aristocratic Restaurants*, [1951] 3 D.L.R. 769 (S.C.C.).

3. Behaviour on the picket line

607. This presumption in favour of picketing in support of a lawful strike will yield to a showing that behaviour on the picket line is improper. An earlier view that peaceful picketing is 'a negation in terms'[1] in now obsolete, and peaceful picketing is *prima facie* lawful.[2] But the courts will not permit picketing which is perceived to interfere with the personal security, property rights or reputation of either the employer who is its primary target, or other persons to whom appeals for support are directed.

   1. *Hollywood Theatres* v. *Tenney*, [1940] 1 D.L.R. 452 at 459 per O'Halloran, J. A. (B.C.C.A.).
   2. *Williams* v. *Aristocratic Restaurants*, *supra*.

(a) Personal security

608. Anyone has the right to pass through a picket line without being subjected to violence or threats of violence. Violent picketing may well constitute the crime of assault, or of watching and besetting, although the latter offence specifically excludes mere 'attending for the purpose only of obtaining or communicating information'.[1] In addition, such picketing may give rise to an action for an injunction, which will restrain not only violence *per se*, but, if it is egregious, will completely, or virtually, forbid all picketing.[2] The courts are relatively quick to detect such threats even where picketers, for example, merely point, grimace or stare,[3] or congregate in large numbers in a confined area.[4] Thus, the courts routinely limit the numbers of picketers who may be present at any one time at each entrance to a plant, and police are generally able to assure access to struck premises by means of informal agreement with the picketers, rather than by bringing charges.

1. Criminal Code, s.381(2).
2. *Hallnor Mines* v. *Behie*, [1954] 1 D.L.R. 135 (Ont.H.C.); *Bulk-Lift Systems* v. *Drivers*, (1976) 64 D.L.R. (3d) 208 (Ont.H.C.).
3. *Hammer* v. *Kemmis*, (1956) 3 D.L.R. (2d) 565 (B.C.S.C.).
4. *Hanes* v. *McConnell*, [1969] 2 O.R. 782 (H.C.).

609. On the other hand, there have been situations where serious violence has broken out, either as a result of union frustration, or as a result of deliberate employer provocation. In these situations, recourse may be had to both the criminal law and the court's injunctive powers.

(b) Property rights

610. Normally, picketing takes place on a sidewalk or roadway in front of struck premises. However, the Criminal Code prevents the blocking or obstructing of a highway,[1] so that picket line activity is not permitted to interfere with the flow of supplies into the plant, or of goods departing. Interference with ingress or egress may also be treated as a civil wrong, subject to injunction.

1. Criminal Code, s.381(1)(g).

611. Where a struck enterprise is located on land owned by a third person, and shared with other tenants, *e.g.* a shopping centre, picketers are confronted with an awkward situation. If they picket on the sidewalk or road surrounding the entire premises, there is a risk that neutral employers who share those premises but have nothing to do with the dispute may be injured, and have good grounds for complaint. On the other hand, although picketing may be confined to the immediate vicinity of the struck enterprise, if it occurs on privately owned land, *e.g.* on the sidewalk of a shopping centre, the owner of the land will be able to vindicate his property rights by a trespass action.[1]

1. *Harrison* v. *Carswell*, (1976) 62 D.L.R. (3d) 68 (S.C.C.).

612. This dilemma, which virtually immunizes employers in such circumstances from picketing, has been resolved in some provinces by legislation which in effect confers upon the picketers a licence to go on to privately owned land, such as shopping centres, to which the public is ordinarily admitted.[1]

1. British Columbia, s.87; Petty Trespass Act, R.S.M. 1970, c. P50, s.5, as am. S.M. 1976, c.71, s.2.

(c) Reputation

613. Early cases had held that such pejorative terms as 'unfair' or 'scab' amounted to defamation of the persons at whom they were directed. However, these terms have now become sufficiently commonplace that they are accepted as part of the permissible – if unpleasant – vocabulary of the picket line.

614. But in one special sense, the courts remain concerned to control messages conveyed by picket signs. Under the general rubric of defamation, the courts have enjoined false and misleading statements by unions against management. For example, the courts have prevented a union from displaying a sign which might have conveyed the impression that a dispute was at the picketed location, rather than another, although the true location was stated accurately, albeit in smaller-sized, less easily noticed, letters on the picket sign.[1]

1. *F. W. Woolworth* v. *Retail Clerks*, (1961) 30 D.L.R. (2d) 377 (B.C.S.C.).

(d) Picketing as the exercise of fundamental civil liberties

615. A *leitmotif* of the law of picketing has been the attempt to claim protection for peaceful public appeals as the exercise of freedom of speech, and for the physical presence of picketers as the exercise of freedom of assembly and association. By and large, this attempt has been unsuccessful.

616. A threshold problem is the Canadian constitutional position. Civil liberties have no independent constitutional value. They may be regulated by whichever level of government, provincial or national, has jurisdiction over the subject area with which the 'civil liberty' is associated. For example, a recent Supreme Court of Canada decision has held that parades and demonstrations may be banned by a municipality (acting under provincial legislation) because the highways and parks upon which such manifestations occur fall under provincial legislative jurisdiction.[1] Similarly, it has been held that a province could competently enact a statute which forbade all picketing not associated with a lawful strike (and presumably such picketing as well, if it desired) even though the picketers whose presence was prohibited in the particular case were not shown to be acting on behalf of a union.[2] The position must be, therefore, that either the provinces or the federal government may expand or contract freedom of speech and assembly in the context of a labour dispute to any extent, so long as the dispute itself occurs in an enterprise which is one that that level of government is constitutionally competent to regulate.

1. *A. G. Canada* v. *Dupond*, (1978) 84 D.L.R. (3d) 420 (S.C.C.).
2. *Koss* v. *Konn*, (1961) 30 D.L.R. (2d) 242 (B.C.C.A.).

617. However, even in the absence of constitutional protection, the basic libertarian aspects of picketing are not entirely ignored. For example, the federal Criminal Code expressly protects informational picketing,[1] a Manitoba statute protects 'communication . . . on a public thoroughfare' as 'the exercise of . . . freedom of speech' which is not subject to restraint by injunction,[2] while legislation in British Columbia specifically excepts general public appeals from prohibitions against illegal picketing 'at or near' the employer's place of business.[3]

1. Criminal Code, s.381(2).
2. Queen's Bench Act, R.S.M. 1970, c. C280, as am. S.M. 1970, c.79, s.60.2.
3. British Columbia, ss.1(1), 84. New Brunswick, s.104(3) and Newfoundland, s.124(3) protect such appeals provided they are not conducted by means of picketing, no matter where located.

618. Of somewhat greater potential importance than these relatively rare legislative attempts to protect picketing as free speech, is the willingness of judges implicitly to recognize that a residuum of picketing should be preserved. Some judges have been prepared, indeed, to be explicit on this point,[1] but others have merely relied upon the general legal presumption that what is not forbidden by law is permitted.[2]

1. *General Dry Batteries* v. *Brigenshaw*, [1951] 4 D.L.R. 414, *per* McRuer, C.J.H.C. (Ont. H.C.); *Williams* v. *Aristocratic Restaurants, supra* at 790, *per* Rand, J; *Channel Seven Television* v. *Broadcast Employees & Technicians*, (1971) 21 D.L.R. (3d) 424 at 441, *per* Hall, J. A. (Man.C.A.).
2. *Canada Dairies* v. *Seggie*, [1940] 4 D.L.R. 725 (Ont.H.C.).

619. But by and large, even while conceding that there is a free speech aspect of picketing, courts have held that it is outweighed by other, competing interests such as the preservation of commercial activity,[1] of traditional property rights,[2] and of industrial peace.[3] The most that can be said is that the courts generally do not interfere with peaceful informational picketing at an employer's place of business, by small numbers of picketers, in support of a lawful strike.

1. *Hersees of Woodstock* v. *Goldstein*, (1963) 38 D.L.R. (2d) 449 (Ont.C.A.).
2. *Harrison* v. *Carswell, supra*.
3. *Winnipeg Builders' Exchange* v. *I.B.E.W., supra*.

4. The scope of ancillary activities: secondary pressure

(a) Definition

620. If it is reasonably clear that a union may peacefully picket the premises of an employer against whom it is lawfully on strike, it is by no means clear what other economic sanctions it may bring to bear against him. Specifically, union attempts to secure sympathetic action by other means may well be categorized as 'secondary', and illegal.

621. 'Secondary' pressure is not a term of art. However, it is generally taken to include any situation where the union brings pressure to bear against the primary employer by actual or threatened sanctions mounted against third persons. For example, a union may picket a retail store selling goods produced by the struck primary firm, or may picket the supplier of materials or services to the struck primary firm to persuade the retailer's or supplier's employees not to perform their duties for their own employer, until his relations with the struck firm are abandoned. Also treated as 'secondary' pressures are more generalized appeals to the public not to purchase goods from a struck firm, or to the labour movement, not to handle goods moving to or from the struck firm.

(b) The legality of secondary picketing and boycotts[1]

622. The legal reaction to the problem of secondary pressure has varied somewhat from one Canadian jurisdiction to another. The particular rationale (if any) accepted by a court or legislature for regulation of such pressure will obviously determine the form and extent of the prohibition it adopts against it.

1. See generally A. W. R. Carrothers, *Secondary Picketing*, (1962) 40 Can. B. Rev. 57; J. C. Paterson, *Union Secondary Conduct: A Comparative Study of the American and Ontario Positions*, (1973) 8 U.B.C. L. Rev. 77; D. Beatty, *Secondary Boycotts: A Functional Analysis*, (1974) 52 Can. B. Rev. 388.

623. Secondary pressures may be viewed with concern for at least three distinct reasons, each of which has been relied upon to justify complete or partial judicial or legislative restrictions upon their use. First, the potential harm to the primary employer of a secondary boycott may be much greater than that of a strike and picketing at his premises. It may be argued that the use of secondary pressures thus disturbs the balance of power and should for that reason alone be forbidden. In the absence of any authoritative standards for measuring the appropriate balance of power, this is an unacceptable rationale. Second, secondary boycotts have ramifying consequences for the interests of other businesses and of consumers, who may be injured by the dispute although not parties to it. Such consequences are to some extent inevitable even as a result of primary strikes and picketing but, it is argued, they should be confined so far as possible. Third, where secondary pressure takes the form of appeals to other workers to cease work, such action not only invites widespread industrial disruption, but usually involves as well violations of various no-strike provisions in statutes or collective agreements.

624. The response of common law courts has essentially been divided into two phases. A series of decisions concerning secondary picketing prior to 1963 had exhibited, for reasons which were peculiar to each case, a 'fundamental judicial indisposition' to such picketing.[1] In 1963, however, the Ontario Court of Appeal in the well-known *Hersees* decision held that secondary picketing was 'illegal *per se*', because it sought to 'benefit . . . a particular class only' while the right of a neutral retailer handling struck products was 'a right far more fundamental and of far greater importance as one in which its exercise affects and is for the benefit of the community at large'.[2] This conclusion, however opaque, has generally prevailed in subsequent decisions,[3] although it has not yet been specifically accepted by the Supreme Court of Canada.

1. Carrothers, *supra* at 74.
2. *Supra* at 454.
3. But see *contra Channel Seven Television* v. *Employees & Technicians, supra.*

625. Legislatures, however, have reacted in a more limited and specific way to secondary picketing. Ontario, for example, only prohibits conduct which might, as a reasonable and probable consequence, cause an unlawful, sympathetic strike.[1] Alberta has specifically outlawed boycotts in the transportation of goods.[2] British Columbia, New Brunswick, and Newfoundland, while generally forbidding picketing except where conducted at an employer's place of business operations, specifically preserve the right to make public appeals by means other than picketing.[3]

1. S.67.
2. S.156.
3. *Supra.*

626. The difficulty is that, save for the Labour Code of British Columbia which specifically ousts the courts,[1] legislation – whether specific or merely silent – is largely ignored by judges as they reach their conclusion concerning the legality of secondary picketing on common law grounds. Thus, for example, in the *Hersees* case, the Court of Appeal pronounced a complete ban on secondary picketing, although the legislature had only a few years earlier specifically declined to follow the recommendation of a legislative committee to the same effect, and had instead adopted the much narrower prohibition referred to above.[2]

1. Ss.31 and 32. The courts retain only a vestigial jurisdiction under s.32(4) to award damages if the Labour Relations Board, having regard to the purposes and objects of the statute, consents to the commencement of proceedings for this purpose.
2. H. W. Arthurs, *Comment*, (1963) 41 Can. B. Rev. 573.

(c) Problems of characterization: primary versus secondary

627. Jurisdictions which legislatively confine picketing to the employer's place of business operations, as well as those which judicially prohibit all secondary picketing, are confronted with a difficult task of determining whether, in a given case, picketing does fall within permissible limits.[1] For example, in some industries such as taxi cabs, the primary employer's place of business is ambulatory, and unless pickets are permitted to follow the employer from place to place, wherever he makes contact with customers, the right to picket would be entirely negated. Again, in other industries such as construction, the employer's place of business is typically shared with a number of other firms, each of which employs workers who belong to different unions. There is a risk that if the primary employer's striking employees are permitted to picket the common workplace, the picket line will cause a work stoppage by the unionized employees of all other firms. Yet it would be unfair, for that reason, to deny them a right to picket which they would otherwise enjoy. A compromise position, adopted in some cases, is to permit picketing but to confine its undesired effects by requiring the picketers to clearly identify their primary target, and to avoid interfering with employees of other firms. A more difficult question relates to the right of a union to picket businesses which have a close connection with that of the primary employer. Unions are entitled to picket all locations at which the primary business is conducted, although they may represent workers at only some of the locations, because the employer draws strength from his entire enterprise. The position in relation to corporate affiliates of the struck firm is somewhat more ambiguous. But the real difficulty is to identify those firms which are active allies of the primary employer in the industrial conflict. It has been recognized both by courts and at least one legislature[2] that a firm which knowingly intermeddles in a dispute to assist the struck employer is no longer a neutral deserving of protection, and is itself liable to be picketed. This 'ally' doctrine extends at least to firms whose assistance is active, as for example the performance of work on behalf of the struck firm, rather than passive, as for example a public warehouse continuing to provide storage facilities used by the primary employer prior to the strike.

1. The cases discussed in this paragraph are conveniently collected and analyzed in D. Beatty, *supra* and S. Tacon, *supra*.
2. British Columbia, s.85(3),(4).

§4. UNLAWFUL INDUSTRIAL ACTION

A. Generally

628. In Canada, a strike which is 'timely' is almost always lawful, and one which is 'untimely' is almost always not. Timeliness is the touchstone of the lawfulness of a strike. Moreover, as will be seen, by a process of judicial extension to the development of common law tort doctrines, the courts have held that unlawful picketing and other conduct which induces, supports, or is in substitution for, an untimely strike is similarly unlawful.

629. Whether framed in terms of compulsory recourse to conciliation procedures,[1] or of specific time delays during which conciliation may run its course,[2] or of compliance with strike notice and strike vote requirements,[3] Canadian labour legislation generally provides that all lawful strikes must be postponed until various peacekeeping measures have been exhausted. But to introduce this requirement of timeliness is also to define the purposes of the strike itself, since such measures are provided only in specific circumstances.

1. Ontario, s.63(2); Canada, s.180.
2. Quebec, s.46.
3. British Columbia, ss.80, 81.

630. First, conciliation is available only to certain unions – those which have already secured the right to represent employees and therefore to call upon the employer to enter upon negotiations. Second, conciliation is available only for certain kinds of disputes – those which involve conflicts of interests arising upon the expiry of the collective agreement (whose term is of fixed duration), and not those which involve conflicts of rights arising out of the administration of the agreement. Third, conciliation is available (at least arguably; the point has not been decided) only to resolve certain kinds of interest disputes – those whose subject matter falls within the statutorily-defined scope of collective bargaining. And, finally, while strike notice and strike vote requirements help to safeguard important employer and employee interests, it is questionable whether non-compliance with them should result in open-ended liability for resulting damage to both those interests and all others. Each of these points must now be considered in detail.

B. Strikes for union bargaining rights

631. Canadian law contains elaborate administrative procedures, known as certification,[1] by which a union's claim to act as the bargaining agent of employees may be tested and validated, if an employer declines to accept that claim at face value. In principle, it is not surprising that the courts should take the view that any economic pressure designed to secure union bargaining rights amounts to an attempt to 'short circuit' the statutory certification mechanism.[2] Indeed, the desire to avoid industrial action to secure recognition was a prime objective of the original American and Canadian labour relations statutes. However, it must be noted that in some jurisdictions legislation does not explicitly restrict activity other than strikes, so that in this latter conclusion the courts may arguably be said to be extending the reach of the statutory prohibition. Moreover, the premise of these cases is that the availability of certification makes impermissible any recourse to economic sanctions. While it might be argued that, if in given circumstances there are practical obstacles to certification, the use of economic sanctions should be permitted, this position has not been accepted.[3]

1. *Supra.*
2. *Smith Bros. Construction* v. *Jones*, [1955] 4 D.L.R. 255 (Ont.H.C.); *Gagnon* v. *Foundation Maritime*, (1961) 28 D.L.R. (2d) 174 (S.C.C.).
3. This was, for some years, a particular problem in the construction industry. The time required to gain certification often exceeded the duration of the job, after which the workforce would be disbanded. As a result, unions often felt obliged to use strikes and picketing to gain recognition. Reform and acceleration of certification in the construction industry significantly alleviated the problem.

632. The general question of civil, criminal and administrative sanctions for illegal conduct will be canvassed below. A special issue arises, however, in the context of economic pressure to secure bargaining rights. On occasion, a union which resorts to such pressure may simultaneously seek to win bargaining rights through certification. The Ontario Labour Relations Board has used its control over certification procedures as a lever to bring illegal strikes to an end, by adjourning the application for certification until the strike has terminated.[1]

1. *Robert McAlpine*, [1961–62] O.L.R.B. 178; The Board's early policy was to dismiss outright any application for certification by a striking union, *Radio Lunch*, (1950) 52 C.L.L.C. para. 17,012 (O.L.R.B.).

C. Industrial action during a collective agreement

633. Legislation in all Canadian jurisdictions, provides procedures by which disputes concerning the interpretation, administration or violation of a collective agreement may be adjudicated. By much the same reasoning as in cases concerned with bargaining rights, the courts have relied upon such provisions to prohibit industrial action to enforce the collective agreement.[1]

1. *Teamsters* v. *Therien*, (1960) 22 D.L.R. (2d) 1 (S.C.C.).

634. However, at least some controversies which arise during the term of the collective agreement do not fall neatly into the categories of disputes which are intended to be adjudicated. An example of such controversies is those which arise out of a radical technological change, requiring fundamental revision of the collective agreement rather than the application of its provisions. In effect, wages and working conditions premised upon a now-obsolete assumption concerning the nature of the work performed can hardly be referred to the terms of the former agreement. The parties are left with the problem of resolving an interest dispute – whether such a change shall be instituted and, if so, with what consequences – through an adjudicative procedure designed for rights disputes. The intractability of this situation has led, from time to time, to the use of strikes, both legal and illegal, by frustrated unions. These, in turn, have led to public inquiries,[1] and to legislative attempts to deal specifically with the consequences of mid-agreement industrial change, by permitting the use of strikes in certain circumstances.[2] Except as provided by such legislation, however, mid-agreement strikes are forbidden, even though the parties confront problems which cannot be resolved through adjudication. In such circumstances, the employer's initiative is allowed to prevail unless and until it is revised at subsequent negotiations, following the expiry of the agreement.

1. *Report of the Industrial Inquiry Commission on Canadian National Railways 'Run-Throughs'*, (Ottawa, 1965).
2. British Columbia, ss.76, 77 (as am, S.B.C. 1975, c.33); Manitoba, ss.72–75; Canada ss.149–153; Saskatchewan, s.43.

635. Safety problems present another example of controversies which cannot easily be resolved within the adjudicative mechanism of the collective agreement. Here, the concerns of workers may be too urgent and the mechanisms of decision too slow-moving to justify a total prohibition of work-stoppages. Recent legislation has conferred upon workers a privilege to stop work during the currency of a collective agreement where there is a *bona fide*, reasonable belief that they are in imminent danger.[1]

> 1. Canada, s.82.1; Occupational Health and Safety Act, S.O. 1978, c.83, ss.23–24; British Columbia, s.83(3).

636. Save where expressly permitted, then, strikes and ancillary activity during the term of a collective agreement may give rise to civil, criminal, or administrative proceedings. In addition, however, there are three distinctive consequences of such strikes which must be addressed as a result of the fact that collective agreements (whether by legislative compulsion or by free choice) generally contain a 'no strike' clause.[1]

> 1. Ontario, ss.36, 37; Canada, s.155; British Columbia, s.93(2). (Quebec, s.95 forbids strikes during a collective agreement, unless the parties have included in it a clause permitting renegotiation of its terms.)

637. First, the question immediately arises as to whether breach of a no strike clause by the union or its members constitutes such a fundamental breach of the collective agreement as to relieve the employer of his obligation further to be bound by it. The Supreme Court of Canada has answered this question in the negative.[1] A strike in violation of a collective agreement does not bring it to an end.

> 1. *McGavin Toastmaster* v. *Ainscough*, (1975) 54 D.L.R. (3d) 1 (S.C.C.).

638. Second, given that the agreement remains in force for its full term, what recourse does the employer have against the union for such violations? That the union should be made to answer before an arbitrator or other adjudicative forum for breach of its promise not to strike is apparent, since all other breaches of the agreement are similarly subject to adjudication. But it has also been held that a union is answerable for failing to take reasonable measures to bring to an end a spontaneous work stoppage which it did not officially promote or condone.[1] In either case, a union is liable for any financial loss suffered by the employer by reason of the illegal strike.[2]

> 1. *Polymer*, (1958) 10 L.A.C. 31, *aff'd. Imbleau* v. *Laskin*, (1962) 33 D.L.R. (2d) 124 (S.C.C.).
> 2. *Re New Brunswick Power Commission and I.B.E.W.*, (1976) 73 D.L.R. (3d) 94 (N.B.C.A.).

639. Third, although an employee does not cease to be employed by reason only of striking (either legally or illegally)[1] he does expose himself to employer sanctions, including discharge.[2] However, that discharge may itself be questioned as a violation of the usual requirement in a collective agreement that employees should only be disciplined or discharged for 'just cause'. Arbitrators have held that discharge is too harsh a penalty for employees whose strike was, in effect, provoked by the employer.[3] On the other hand, a line of arbitration decisions which had held union stewards and officers to a particularly high standard of conduct, and held them strictly liable for organizing work stoppages, has been overturned on review by the courts.[4]

1. *McGavin Toastmaster* v. *Ainscough, supra*; *Praesto Aluminum Products*, (1959) 59 C.L.L.C. para, 18,137 (O.L.R.B.).
2. *Dresser Electric*, [1966–67] O.L.R.B. 906; *Berlet Electronics*, (1968) 19 L.A.C. 152; *Re Canadian Gypsum and Nova Scotia Quarryworkers*, (1959) 20 D.L.R. (2d) 319 (N.S.S.C.).
3. *Aerocide Dispensers*, (1965) 16 L.A.C. 57.
4. *Re McConnell and Douglas Aircraft*, (1976) 14 O.R. (2d) 1 (H.C.).

D. Industrial action for improper purposes

640. As has been suggested, strikes may lawfully occur only following collective bargaining and conciliation. However, there is some authority for the proposition that even when these requirements of timeliness are met, strikes for certain purposes extrinsic to, or inconsistent with, the labour relations act, are unlawful.

641. Politically-motivated strikes have almost inevitably been held unlawful (although admittedly in cases where they were also untimely),[1] as has picketing to secure changes in government policy,[2] or to support the struggle of foreign workers involved in a labour dispute.[3] Sympathetic strikes to aid other workers within the same industry are also unlawful.[4] There is some suggestion, as well, that industrial action, concededly for collective bargaining purposes, may become unlawful if the particular concessions sought are contrary to the policy of the labour relations act,[5] although this suggestion has not received authoritative approval.

1. *R.* v. *Russell*, (1920) 51 D.L.R. 1 (Man.C.A.); and see cases re National Day of Protest, *supra*.
2. *Ellis* v. *Willis*, (1972) 30 D.L.R. (3d) 397 (Ont.H.C.).
3. *Pietro Culotta Grapes* v. *Moses*, [1968] 1 O.R. 89 (H.C.); *Darrigo's Grape Juice* v. *Masterson*, (1971) 21 D.L.R. (3d) 660 (Ont.H.C.); *Slade & Steward* v. *Retail Wholesale*, (1969) 5 D.L.R. (3d) 736 (B.C.S.C.).
4. *Antonsen* v. *United Fishermen*, (1963) 64 C.L.L.C. para. 15,497. (B.C.S.C.).
5. *Otis Elevator* v. *Elevator Constructors*, (1973) 35 D.L.R. (3d) 566 (B.C.C.A.); *Carpenters Employer Bargaining Agency*, [1978] 2 C.L.R.B.R. 501 (O.L.R.B.).

642. Finally, there has been some attempt specifically to outlaw so-called 'jurisdictional' or 'demarcation' strikes and picketing. Such tactics are employed when a union demands that work be assigned to its members rather than to workers associated with some other union, trade, craft or class. Typically, such disputes arise in the construction industry which is organized on a craft union basis, with each union representing workers of only a single craft, and each employer typically employing workers associated with that craft and union. In effect, disputes over jurisdiction or demarcation amount to a contest for available work or employment opportunities, between groups of workers, claiming supposed rights based upon traditional skills, industrial custom, or 'job property'.

643. Being essentially multilateral, involving two unions and two or more employers, such disputes do not yield easily to adjudication in traditional forums. Several solutions have evolved. On the one hand, a variety of permanent and *ad hoc* tribunals have been established on a purely consensual basis by various employer and union initiatives.[1] On the other hand, in several provinces the labour relations board is specifically empowered to terminate jurisdictional strikes and picketing, and to settle the underlying controversy which gives rise to such industrial action.[2]

1. J. H. G. Crispo and H. W. Arthurs, *Jurisdictional Disputes in Canada: A Study in Frustration*, in E. E. Palmer (ed.), III *Current Law and Social Problems* (Toronto, 1963).
2. Ontario, s.81; Alberta, s.160; Nova Scotia, s.50; Prince Edward Island, s.37; New Brunswick, ss.82–89. These statutes, in varying degrees, contemplate resort by the parties to procedures of their own creation.

E. Compliance with notice and strike vote procedure

644. Various Canadian jurisdictions provide that notice of a strike must be given to an employer,[1] or that a secret ballot vote of employees must be held,[2] prior to the commencement of a strike. These provisions are, respectively, designed to protect the interests of the employer against precipitate strike action, and of individual workers against strikes which are not democratically mandated. However, they also serve the latent function of delaying strikes because of the formalities involved and the time consumed.[3]

1. Alberta, s.125(1)(c); New Brunswick, s.97; British Columbia, s.81(3)(b); British Columbia also provides for greater notice where the strike involves perishable goods, s.82A.
2. British Columbia, s.81(1); Alberta, s.125(1)(b); New Brunswick, s.94(1).
3. The experience with strike votes has been that they almost always are in the affirmative, and that their effect may be to heighten the possibility of strikes by making rank-and-file support more visible. F. R. Anton, *Government Supervised Strike Votes* (Toronto, 1961).

645. Non-compliance with these provisions is obviously at least a minor violation of the statute, in principle giving rise to a quasi-criminal sanction.[1] However, some Canadian courts have also treated non-compliance as rendering illegal not only the strike – a sufficiently significant conclusion – but all activities associated with the strike, including otherwise innocuous picketing.[2] And they have done so even when the statutory provisions themselves were obscure and the breaches of a highly technical nature.

1. *Industrial Wire and Cable*, [1960–61] O.L.R.B. 451; *Keddy v. R*, (1961) 130 C.C.C. 226 (N.S.S.C.).
2. *Contractors Equipment & Supply v. Teamsters* (1965), 54 D.L.R. (2d) 726 (Man.C.A.); *Jacobson Bros. v. Anderson*, (1962) 35 D.L.R. (2d) 746 (N.S.S.C.); *Culinary Workers v. Terra Nova Motor Inn*, (1974) 50 D.L.R. (3d) 253 (S.C.C.).

646. Of special interest is the extent to which other forms of industrial action may be permitted at a time when strikes are not, specifically when such action is intended to spur current negotiations. In an early case, the Supreme Court of Canada had noted that, although strikes were forbidden prior to compliance with the strike vote procedures, no such restraints were imposed upon 'ancillary means of advancing the interests of either party.'[1] In that case, picketing was permitted even though the required strike vote was not held, and no strike had been called. However, a later decision held that picketing of their employer's premises by off-duty employees, in an effort to stimulate bargaining concessions, was illegal because they were not yet entitled to strike.[2]

1. *Williams* v. *Aristocratic Restaurants, supra* at 791, per Rand J.
2. *Nipissing Hotel* v. *Hotel and Restaurant Employees*, (1962) 36 D.L.R. (2d) 81; (1963) 38 D.L.R. (2d) 675 (Ont.H.C.). The precise grounds of decision are unclear. Landreville, J., dealing with the matter on a preliminary motion, held that any pressure asserted during negotiation violated the obligation of the parties to negotiate in good faith. Spence, J., not primarily addressing himself to that point, held at trial, that a common law duty of fidelity precludes employee conduct which may injure the employer.

F. Boycotts

647. Reference has already been made to the use of consumer and other boycotts in the context of secondary picketing following a lawful strike.[1] They may also be treated as conduct utilized in substitution for other industrial action in circumstances when such action would be unlawful. Where the boycott is conducted by means of an unlawful work stoppage, it is actionable.[2] Moreover, the courts have been prepared to extend a statutory prohibition on untimely picketing to all forms of appeal, including newspaper advertisements, handbills and letters.[3] Nor will a union be allowed to institute a boycott by means of provisions in its collective agreement precluding the employer from dealing with the party at whom the boycott is aimed, whether an employer or a rival trade union.[4]

1. *Supra*.
2. *Mark Fishing* v. *United Fishermen*, (1972) 24 D.L.R. (3d) 585 (B.C.C.A.), *aff'd.* (1974) 38 D.L.R. (3d) 316n (S.C.C.).
3. *Sonoco* v. *I.B.P.W.* (1970) 13 D.L.R. (3d) 617 (B.C.C.A.); *Coles Bakery* v. *Bakery Workers*, (1962) 36 D.L.R. (2d) 772 (B.C.S.C.). (The specific holding in these cases was overruled by the enactment of British Columbia, s.84.).
4. *Int'l Iron Workers* v. *Canadian Ironworkers* (1971) 21 D.L.R. (3d) 469 (S.C.C.); *C.P.R.* v. *Teamsters*, (1975) 60 D.L.R. (3d) 249 (B.C.C.A.).

§5. REMEDIES FOR UNLAWFUL INDUSTRIAL ACTION

A. Employer self-help

648. An employer confronted with an illegal strike by his employees, or by unlawful conduct on the picket line during the course of a lawful strike, may impose appropriate discipline, including outright dismissal.[1] However, the mere occurrence of unlawful industrial action does not of itself bring to an end any existing collective agreement.[2] Thus, the employer's self-help measures are liable to be tested in arbitration by employees who claim that they have been disciplined or discharged without just cause.[3] If no collective agreement is in force, the employer's action may still be tested under the unfair labour practice provisions of the labour relations act, if it is discriminatory or designed to interfere with the rights of employees,[4] rather than to vindicate the employer's legitimate business interests.[5]

1. *Supra*.
2. *McGavin Toastmaster* v. *Ainscough*, (1975) 54 D.L.R. (3d) 1 (S.C.C.).
3. See generally, D. J. M. Brown and D. M. Beatty, *Canadian Labour Arbitration* (Toronto, 1977) at 509.
4. *Praesto Aluminum Products*, (1959) 59 C.L.L.C. para. 18,137 (O.L.R.B.); *Robinson, Little*, [1975] 2 C.L.R.B.R. 81 (B.C.L.R.B.); *Central Broadcasting*, [1975] 2 C.L.R.B.R. 65 (C.L.R.B.); *Hydro Electric Power Commission of Ontario*, [1969] O.L.R.B. Rep. 249, *aff'd*. (1970) 70 C.L.L.C. para. 14,031 (Ont.C.A.).
5. *Skinner School Bus Lines*, [1968–69] O.L.R.B. 1309; *Seven-Up Bottling*, (1962) 62 C.L.L.C. para. 16,227 (O.L.R.B.).

B. Administrative remedies[1]

1. Declaration

649. Several labour relations boards have power to declare that a strike or lock-out is unlawful. Originally a remedy with no compulsive effect, the declaration was nonetheless a useful device for educating the parties as to their rights in situations in which there was some doubt about the legality of a strike. Moreover, a mere declaration, unaccompanied by other sanctions, sometimes brought a strike to an end because it amounted to a useful prediction as to how a court would react to the legality of such conduct in a subsequent proceeding. During the 1970's, however, the declaration became increasingly the prelude to authoritative labour relations board orders requiring cessation of illegal activity,[2] or triggering other important remedies.[3]

1. See generally: P. C. Weiler, *The Administrative Tribunal: A View from the Inside*, (1976) 26 U.T.L.J. 193; D. D. Carter, *The Expansion of Labour Board Remedies: A New Approach to Industrial Conflict*, (Kingston, 1976).
2. Canada, s.182 (as am. S.C. 1977–78, c.27); Ontario, ss.82, 83.
3. Ontario, s.84, provides that following the making of a declaration, a claim for damages may be pursued through a special arbitration mechanism.

2. Investigation and settlement

650. Typically, labour relations boards which enjoy power to issue authoritative orders against illegal industrial action do so only after making preliminary efforts to solve the underlying industrial relations problems. Upon the filing of a complaint seeking the intervention of the board, it typically despatches an official who meets informally with the parties and seeks to bring unlawful conduct to an end without recourse to further, formal proceedings. This effort may involve not merely pointed reminders to the employees of the consequences of continued illegality, but as well resolution of the differences which initially provoked it.

3. Cease and desist orders

651. Generally, labour relations boards have power to·order an offending party to cease and desist from his illegal conduct.[1] This power is amplified, in some statutes, by explicit language permitting the board to rectify underlying problems,[2] to withhold or attach conditions to such remedies in order to achieve equitable results,[3] to provide relief on an emergency basis,[4] and to modify any order in the light of subsequent developments.[5]

1. Canada, s.189; British Columbia, s.28; Ontario, ss.82, 83 123.
2. Ontario, ss.79, 81; British Columbia, ss. 97, 113 ff.
3. British Columbia, ss.28(1)(c), 28(1)(a), 29, 91.
4. British Columbia, s.35(1); Nova Scotia, s.49; Ontario, s.81(3)(8).
5. British Columbia, s.29; Nova Scotia, s.49(11); Canada, s.183.1(2).

C. Criminal and quasi-criminal sanctions

1. Criminal Code

652. The federal Criminal Code contains several offences pertinent to industrial conflict, commission of any one of which may result in prosecution, leading to fines or imprisonment. These offences include 'watching and besetting', i.e. coercive and obstructive picketing,[1] assault,[2] unlawful assembly,[3] criminal conspiracy,[4] and criminal breach of contract involving public utility workers.[5] In addition, two provisions of the Code of general application provide penalties for disobeying the order of a court,[6] and for violating a law for which no penalty is elsewhere expressly provided.[7]

However, as a practical matter, only assault charges are laid with any frequency, and then only following violent episodes on a picket line.

1. Criminal Code, s.381.
2. S.245.
3. S.64.
4. Ss.423, 424.
5. S.380.
6. S.116.
7. S.115.

2. Labour relations acts

653. Violation of the provisions of a labour relations act, or in some cases of orders made under the act, is an offence punishable by summary procedure in the lower criminal courts.[1] However, in this situation, initiation of prosecutions may require the prior consent of the labour relations board.[2] The decision by a labour relations board to allow prosecution is discretionary, and consent will not lightly be given. For example, the Ontario board has said that it will not allow prosecution to be used as 'a vehicle of retributive justice',[3] when strikers have been fired,[4] or selected randomly for prosecution,[5] or where the strike resulted from a genuine mistake as to the legal position of the union,[6] or has already been ended with no pattern of prior illegality or likely prospect of resumption.[7] Moreover, as with all labour relations board proceedings, an application for consent to prosecute is usually the occasion for formal and informal settlement efforts.

1. Ontario, s.85; Canada, ss. 190, 191; British Columbia, s.138; Quebec, s.124. In Quebec, prosecution takes place before the Labour Court, s.103.
2. Ontario, s.90; Canada, s.194.
3. *Savage Shoes*, (1953) 53 C.L.L.C. para. 17,060 (O.L.R.B.).
4. *Canal Cartage*, [1961–62] O.L.R.B. 251; *Joyce and Smith Plating*, (1956) 56 C.L.L.C. para. 18,049 (O.L.R.B.); *Toronto Western Hospital*, [1972] O.L.R.B. 1018.
5. *Canadian Elevator Manufacturers*, [1975] O.L.R.B. 722; *Arthur G. McKee*, [1976] O.L.R.B. 637.
6. *Savage Shoes*, (1953) 53 C.L.L.C. para. 17,060 (O.L.R.B.).
7. *Foundation Co.*, [1971] O.L.R.B. 29.

654. As a practical matter, apart from the reluctance of the labour relations board to encourage prosecution, it is not a remedy much favoured by the parties as a means of enforcing their rights under labour legislation.[1] Criminal proceedings are slow and technical; proof to the standard of 'beyond a reasonable doubt' required in criminal cases is difficult; judges are generally unfamiliar with industrial relations or labour law; the effect of even a successful prosecution is likely to be a rather small fine – not an order prohibiting continuation or repetition of the offence; and the burden of the whole prosecutorial function is borne by the complainant rather than the state, which normally conducts prosecutions.[2]

1. A. M. Minsky, *A Study of Consent to Prosecute Applications Disposed of by the Ontario Labour Relations Board From April 1, 1965 to March 31, 1968*, [1969–70] Pt. 1. O.L.R.B. (Supplement).
2. Quebec, s.131, prosecution may be undertaken by the Procureur-général or the labour commissioner-general, as well as by aggrieved parties, as in the other provinces.

D. Civil remedies

1. General

655. In affording relief to persons injured by unlawful industrial action, the courts ostensibly apply the ordinary law of civil wrongs – tort or delict, and occasionally contract – although they increasingly place reliance upon labour relations legislation as the ultimate basis of liability.[1] The usual remedies in civil litigation are money damages and injunctions (prohibitory or mandatory orders). While occasionally civil remedies are sought by unions or employees against employers, typically it is employers who institute such proceedings. The following analysis assumes, therefore, that the union is the defendant.

1. *Supra*.

2. Problems of suing unions

(a) Union responsibility

656. When a wrong is committed during a labour dispute, liability may of course fall on the individual worker who has committed the act complained of – assault, defamation, inducing breach of contract, etc. But that individual's identity may be difficult to establish, his degree of participation obscure and, in any event, his assets so limited that a damage award against him would be worthless. Hence, the employer may prefer to proceed against the union.

657. The question thus arises as to when the union itself can be made responsible. Clearly, a union will be held liable for conduct which it officially authorizes, encourages or directs, or in which its responsible officials participate.[1] However, insofar as wrongful conduct is that of mere rank-and-file members or of stewards or other junior union officials, the union's responsibility is more difficult to establish. Essentially, the union itself will be held liable for unauthorized and illegal industrial action only if it fails to take reasonable measures to dissociate itself from such action, and to bring any unlawfulness to an end.[2] However, in practice this question is not always addressed. The union will often feel obliged to stand behind its members and officers if they are sued in their personal capacities, although no question arises of the union's direct or vicarious liability.

1. *U.S.W.A.* v. *Gaspe Copper Mines*, (1970) 10 D.L.R. (3d) 443 (S.C.C.), but *cf. Western Construction & Lumber* v. *Jorgensen*, (1973) 40 D.L.R. (3d) 613 (S.C.C.).
2. *Re New Brunswick Electric Power Commission and I.B.E.W.*, (1976) 73 D.L.R. (3d) 94 (N.B.C.A.); *Oliver Sawmills* v. *I.W.A.*, (1969) 6 D.L.R. (3d) 48 (B.C.C.A.).

(b) The juridical status of unions

658. Most labour relations statutes implicitly or explicitly make unions legal entities for purposes of proceedings under those statutes. But, at common law, a union was simply an unincorporated collection of individuals with no legal personality; it could neither sue nor defend in its own name in ordinary civil proceedings.[1]

1. D. J. Sherbaniuk, *Actions by and against Trade Unions in Contract and Tort*, (1957–58) 12 U.T.L.J. 151.

659. The inconsistency between these two views of the union's status had to be resolved, especially in cases where the substantive basis of liability was framed as a common law action, although in fact heavy reliance was placed on the union's alleged contravention of the letter or spirit of a labour relations statute. In the pivotal case of *Therien*,[1] the Supreme Court of Canada held that a union had wrongly interfered with the economic interests of the plaintiff by threatening to picket a construction project on which he was engaged, in order to enforce its view that the collective agreement precluded his presence; 'wrongfulness' resided in the union's failure to seek arbitration of the relevant provisions of the collective agreement, contrary to its terms, and the provisions of the Labour Relations Act. The Court went on to hold that the union was itself answerable in damages, on the grounds that the Labour Relations Act had conferred rights and obligations upon unions, thus impliedly endowing them with juridical status sufficient to make them subject to civil suits, although such an intention was not expressly manifested by the words of the statute. Although criticized in the literature, this decision now prevails in all Canadian jurisdictions,[2] except Ontario and Saskatchewan, where legislation[3] expressly preserves the union's former common law immunity from suit.[4]

1. *Teamsters* v. *Therien*, (1960) 22 D.L.R. (2d) 1 (S.C.C.).
2. Most recently, in the federal sphere: *I.L.A.* v. *Maritime Employers' Assoc.*, (1978) 89 D.L.R. (3d) 289 (S.C.C.).
3. Rights of Labour Act, R.S.O. 1970, c.416, s.3(2); Saskatchewan, s.29.
4. *Nipissing Hotel* v. *Hotel & Restaurant Employees*, (1963) 38 D.L.R. (2d) 675 (Ont.H.C.).

660. Even before the *Therien* decision, however, unions did not, and now do not, enjoy complete immunity from suit. First, as mentioned, they often choose to stand behind individual members who are sued and to pay for their legal representation and any damage awards that might be made against them. Second, court rules in many jurisdictions provide that a member of an unincorporated group may be appointed by the court to act as its representative for purposes of litigation.[1] By this device of a 'representative action' a union might in effect be sued, although this possibility was diminished by a judicial gloss restricting representation orders to cases where the group has a common interest in a fund specifically designated as being available for the payment of damages;[2] few unions obligingly maintain such funds. Third, in injuction proceedings, an employer is entitled to seek relief against named individual defendants, but as well against 'their servants and agents, and anyone acting with knowledge' of the court's order, in effect all other members of the union.[3] And finally, some statutes specifically make unions suable entities.[4]

1. Supreme Court of Ontario, Rules of Practice, R.R.O. 1970, Reg. 545, Rule 75.
2. *Body* v. *Murdoch*, [1954] O.W.N. 658 (H.C.).
3. *Infra*.
4. Alberta, s.58(1)(b); Manitoba, s.127(3); Prince Edward Island, s.43(1); New Brunswick, s.114(2); Newfoundland, s.137(1). An old, unrepealed, federal statute, Trade Unions Act, S.C. 1872, c.30, afforded trade unions the opportunity to register if they wished to hold property; if they chose to register, they would also be liable to suit; virtually none are now registered.

3. Common law actions to enforce collective agreements[1]

661. Collective agreements could not be sued upon at common law.[2] This position was called into question in a lower court judgment on the grounds that the Labour Relations Act was tantamount to legislative recognition of the collective agreement, and the reversal of the common law position,[3] an inference clearly precluded in Ontario and Saskatchewan.[4] While the issue has not been definitively decided, it was somewhat outflanked by the Supreme Court of Canada's espousal of the proposition that it should not enter upon the interpretation of collective agreements where arbitration is established as the exclusive forum for their enforcement.[5] It might be assumed, therefore, that the employer could not bring an action in the regular courts to enforce the no-strike provisions of a collective agreement. However, without clearly addressing its own self-imposed rule against interpreting a collective agreement, the Supreme Court has at least twice given relief against industrial action which violated the no-strike provisions of a collective agreement.[6] As has been mentioned, arbitration is also available for damage claims arising from such violations.

1. *Supra*.
2. In *Young* v. *Canadian Northern Railway*, [1931] A.C. 83 (P.C.), the Privy Council – then Canada's final appellate court – held that if the employer violated the collective agreement '. . . the effective sequel would be, not an action by any employee, not even an action by [the union] against the employer for specific performance or damages, but the calling of a strike until the grievance was remedied.' (at 89).
3. *Nelsons Laundries Ltd.* v. *Manning*, (1965) 51 D.L.R. (2d) 537 (B.C.S.C.). This result was specifically accomplished by statute in Manitoba, s.127(2).
4. Ontario Rights of Labour Act, s.3(3); Saskatchewan, s.30.
5. *Hamilton Street Railway* v. *Northcott*, (1966) 58 D.L.R. (2d) 708 (S.C.C.); *General Motors* v. *Brunet*, (1976) 77 C.L.L.C. para. 14,067 (S.C.C.).
6. *I.B.E.W.* v. *Winnipeg Builders' Exchange*, (1967) 65 D.L.R. (2d) 242 (S.C.C.); *I.L.A.* v. *Maritime Employers' Assoc.*, (1978) 89 D.L.R. (3d) 289 (S.C.C.).

4. Damages

(a) Compensatory Damages

662. Damages are primarily intended to restore the injured party to the *status quo ante*. However, the courts have not been willing to scrutinize with excessive care the causal relationship between the wrong done by the defendant and the loss suffered by the plaintiff. For example, in one case, the court held that a technical breach of strike vote procedures not only made the strike itself unlawful, but fixed liability upon the union for all business loss subsequently suffered by the employer due to either the strike or to activities supporting it.[1]

1. *Jacobson Bros.*, v. *Anderson*, (1962) 35 D.L.R. (2d) 746 (N.S.S.C.).

(b) Punitive or exemplary damages

663. Where there is a deliberate or calculated infliction of harm,[1] rather than a mere failure to bring an illegal strike to an end,[2] in addition to any compensatory damages, a court may also award a sizeable, discretionary sum to punish the defendant for high handed conduct, and to discourage repetition of the act in the future.

1. *Johnston Terminals & Storage* v. *Miscellaneous Workers*, (1975) 61 D.L.R. (3d) 741 (B.C.S.C.); *Canadian Ironworkers* v. *Int'l. Ironworkers*, (1973) 31 D.L.R. (3d) 750 (B.C.S.C.), *aff'd*. (1974) 45 D.L.R. (3d) 768*n* (B.C.C.A.).
2. *Weins Contracting* v. *MacMillan Bloedel (Alberni)*, (1973) 40 D.L.R. (3d) 593 (B.C.S.C.).

(c) Mitigation or diminution of damages

664. As a matter of general principle, any plaintiff is under a duty to act in his own self-interest in order to minimize his loss. He cannot simply stand by following the defendant's wrong, and allow financial consequences to multiply. This general principle presumably applies to tort actions arising out of industrial action as well. Moreover, it has been argued that the courts ought to reduce damages to which a plaintiff employer would otherwise be entitled if he has acted improperly in such a way as to provoke the illegal industrial action of which he complains. The Supreme Court of Canada has rejected this argument on the particular facts of a case in which it was raised, but not as a matter of principle.[1]

1. *U.S.W.A.* v. *Gaspe Copper Mines*, (1970) 10 D.L.R. (3d) 443 (S.C.C.); *cf. Brown's Bread* v. *Bakery Workers*, [1971] 5 W.W.R. 577 (Man.Q.B.).

(d) Extended liability

665. Normally, a wrongdoer is civilly liable only to someone whom he deliberately or foreseeably injures by his wrong. A strike, or other industrial action, however, may trigger a chain of consequences by which a struck employer is, for example, unable to supply promised goods to his customers, and they to theirs. A union will, presumably, not be liable for such extended consequences, so long as its strike is a lawful one.[1] However, when the strike is unlawful, it is at least possible that a union may be fixed with liability.[2]

1. This principle seems generally to be accepted at common law, and is made explicit in Newfoundland, s.99.
2. Manitoba, s.127(1) imposes liability upon anyone violating the act 'for general or special damages, or both, to *anyone* who is injured or suffers damage' by the violation. See also, *Canadian Ironworkers* v. *Int'l. Iron Workers*, (1970) 13 D.L.R. (3d) 559 (B.C.C.A.).

5. Injunctions

(a) General[1]

666. The injunction has been by far the most frequently sought remedy in conflict situations. It has the attraction of being available speedily with relatively little formality of proof or pleading, and of stopping illegality and the resulting loss or damage, rather than attempting to compensate for it.

1. A classic American work on this subject, F. Frankfurter and N. Greene, *The Labour Injunction* (New York, 1930) contains much historical and scholarly criticism which would apply to recent Canadian injunction law. Two important Canadian studies are A. W. R. Carrothers, *The Labour Injunction in British Columbia* (Toronto, 1956) and A. W. R. Carrothers and E. E. Palmer, *Report of a Study on the Labour Injunction in Ontario*, esp. Part I, H. Krever, *The Labour Injunction in Ontario: Procedures and Practice*, (Toronto, 1966).

667. On the other hand, the injunction has also given rise to great political and social controversy. First, the very virtues of speed and informality have been seen to involve an undue sacrifice of procedural fairness. Second, the courts' intervention is limited to the suppression of illegality (itself defined according to rather vague common law standards) and is not directed to the underlying causes of conflict. Third, there has been the appearance of anti-unionism in the reaction of some judges to strikes and picketing. As a result, reforms during the 1970's in various Canadian jurisdictions have either entirely displaced the injunction or radically altered the procedure by which it is obtained.

(b) Procedural problems

668. Injunctions may be granted either temporarily (interlocutory injunctions) or permanently. Permanent injunctions are granted only after a full-scale trial, but because of delays in mounting such trials, they are almost never sought. Temporary injunctions are granted, typically, upon motion, supported only by affidavit evidence, on brief notice or no notice, and on the explicit understanding that they will last only for a fixed period of days, or until the trial of the action. While summary procedures are the key to the usefulness of temporary injunctions, they do undoubtedly pose problems.

669. Where an injunction against picketing is given without notice (*ex parte*) even for a few days, the effect may be to disrupt and demoralize the union's activities. If it should turn out that the injunction was wrongly obtained, and even though it is ultimately dissolved, the employer will still have won a tactical advantage. Even when an injunction is given on notice, typically only of two days' duration, a union's chance to prepare reply evidence is very limited. Moreover, the use of affidavit evidence offers the employer an opportunity for artful equivocation or distortion of the facts in order to elicit the judge's sympathy. It is very difficult, as a practical matter, to either cross-examine or rebut witnesses (deponents) whose affidavits are the only evidence before the court. Because motions are hurriedly scheduled, usually in courts crowded with other business, and heard in an atmosphere of urgency, the opportunity for extended argument and calm deliberation is not easily achieved. And because, in principle, the injunction is only temporary and in prospect of a future full-scale trial (which, however, seldom occurs) rights of appeal against the granting of a temporary injunction are severely limited. Finally, although the plaintiff must promise to indemnify the defendant if it should turn out that the injunction has been wrongly obtained, in practice the defendant almost never has a chance to enforce this promise, since the matter becomes moot after the injunction has run for even a limited period.

670. Added to all of these problems are the facts that courts of general jurisdiction contain relatively few judges who have specialist knowledge of industrial relations or labour law; that such courts lack power to make an independent investigation of the facts or to probe, let alone resolve, the underlying controversies; and that ordinary doctrines of tort, delict or contract administered by them are somewhat obscure and not necessarily consistent with contemporary industrial relations policies and realities.

671. As will be seen, many of these problems have been addressed by reforming legislation.

(c) The scope of injunctions: conduct and persons

672. A temporary injunction is, in theory, intended to hold matters *in status quo* pending trial. It is thus essentially negative in character, and orders that wrongful conduct should cease. Because such an order interferes with the defendant's freedom of action, certain doctrines had emerged in non-labour situations which were designed to avoid overreaching. A plaintiff, for example, was required to show that he had a strong, *prima facie* case which would likely prevail at trial; that the balance of convenience lay in favour of restricting the defendant rather than allowing him to continue his conduct; and that any harm done by the defendant would not be compensable by the payment of money damages. In the light of such doctrines, it is rather surprising, for example, that an injunction has been given anticipatorily to restrain possible future unlawful behaviour, the occurrence of which is neither imminent nor certain.[1] Indeed, none of these limiting doctrines is rigorously adhered to in the context of labour injunction litigation, although all of them are occasionally reaffirmed by *dicta* in the higher courts.

1. *Foundation Co.* v. *McGloin*, (1963) 42 D.L.R. (2d) 209 (Ont.H.C.).

673. Because injunctive relief was, historically, administered by the courts of equity, in principle a plaintiff seeking such relief must come to the court 'with clean hands', *i.e.* he must not himself be guilty of conduct which is unconscionable or improper. On occasion, the argument has been made that an employer, seeking an injunction, ought not to receive it, although otherwise entitled, because he has behaved unacceptably in the conduct of his relationship with his employees or their union. This argument has seldom persuaded courts to exercise their discretion to withhold the relief sought.[1]

1. *A. G. Canada* v. *Whitelock*, (1973) 37 D.L.R. (3d) 757 (B.C.S.C.).

674. Moreover, because the injunction is sought at the instance of a private party, the plaintiff must normally sue to vindicate some interest of his own. An injunction will not, in principle, lie at the suit of a private party to enforce the criminal law or other statutes protecting the public interest.[1] This doctrine has also been abandoned in practice in the context of labour injunction litigation, and the courts will in fact enjoin conduct upon an allegation of injury by the plaintiff, merely because it amounts to a violation of the labour relations act[2] or the Criminal Code, and without regard to whether the plaintiff actually pleads a cause of action based on the violation of some right personal to himself.

1. *Robinson* v. *Adams*, [1925] 1 D.L.R. 359 (Ont.C.A.).
2. *I.L.A.* v. *Maritime Employers'*, *supra*.

675. Injunctions are, in principle, designed to restrict unlawful conduct. In the context of picketing, especially, the labour injunction has become a rather refined instrument. For example, the courts will often stipulate by injunction that a union is limited in its picketing to a fixed number of persons patrolling a designated area, that particular offending words on a picket sign be removed, that picket line conduct be modified in stipulated ways, or that union officers issue statements to their members to ensure compliance with the court's orders. In effect, the courts have become intimately involved in the case-by-case development of a detailed code of picketing, a task for which, critics argue, they are ill-equipped.

676. The issuance of injunctions requiring strikers to return to work has been an especially radical development in the scope of the injunction, given that its traditional role was to preserve existing situations by stopping unlawful conduct. And such injunctions are even more surprising in view of the historic reluctance of the law to require performance of employment contracts, except by providing damages upon breach. But the Supreme Court of Canada has clearly set aside any such traditional inhibitions, and has authorized the issuance of such orders.[1]

1. *I.B.E.W.* v. *Winnipeg Builders' Exchange*, *supra*.

677. Finally, an injunction is in principle directed against a named wrong-doer. That defendant thus has the opportunity to challenge factual allegations against him and to persuade the court that his conduct does not constitute an actionable wrong. But labour injunctions are typically directed to a named defendant, 'his servants or agents, and anyone having knowledge of the order'. There can be little objection to an order which binds persons acting on behalf of the named defendant. However, the restriction upon the rights of 'persons having knowledge' is more questionable, and not merely because such an order was unknown in traditional injunction practice. A general order of this sort binds people who have no advance knowledge of the proceeding, and thus no chance to influence the scope of the order as it might affect them. Not being parties to the action, they lack standing to either seek modification of the original order or to appeal it. And, of course, their interests or circumstances may differ from those of the named defendants.

(d) Enforcement

678. Disobedience of an injunction is contempt of court, so-called 'civil' contempt. But any conduct, including disobedience, by any person, whether a party to the proceeding or not, amounts to the much more serious offence of 'criminal' contempt, if it interferes with the administration of justice. In either case, a court whose order has been disobeyed has the power summarily to try the contemnor and impose sanctions in its discretion. These sanctions may include imprisonment until the contempt is purged by compliance, or penalties such as fixed terms of imprisonment and heavy fines imposed upon both unions and individuals.

679. At various periods in recent Canadian labour history, the use of the contempt power to enforce labour injunctions has aroused great political controversy[1] and, ultimately, led to various projects of law reform.

1. Amongst the more controversial examples of the use of the contempt power are its invocation against an alleged political demonstration against injunctions, *Re Tilco Plastics* v. *Skurjat*, [1966] 2 O.R. 547 (H.C.), the jailing of forty-four senior leaders of *le front commun* of public service unions in Quebec, *A. G. Quebec* v. *Charbonneau*, (1974) 40 D.L.R. (3d) 65 (Que.C.A.), and the jailing of many postal leaders following their failure to obey legislation, and a supporting court order, requiring them to end a strike.

(e) Law Reform

680. Given the intensity of resentment against labour injunctions and the apparent validity of some of the criticisms made against them, it is not surprising that several Canadian jurisdictions have adopted reforming statutes.

681. The most far-reaching of these is the Labour Code of British Columbia[1] which specifically deprives the civil courts of the power to issue injunctions against strikes or picketing, except in cases involving immediate and serious danger to individuals, or physical damage to property.[2] In place of the courts' injunction jurisdiction, the labour relations board is given full remedial powers in relation to industrial action,[3] including power to decide whether the case is an appropriate one for subsequent litigation before the courts.[4] The effect of these provisions is to unite within the grasp of a single, knowledgeable tribunal all aspects of industrial relationships, including that of conflict, and to enable that tribunal to deploy the full range of appropriate responses, described above.[5]

1. H. W. Arthurs, *'The Dullest Bill': Reflections on the Labour Code of British Columbia*, (1974) 9 U.B.C.L. Rev. 280.
2. S.32(2).
3. Ss.28–32.
4. S.32(4).
5. *Supra.*

682. Ontario has adopted a more tentative approach. Injunction procedures have been substantially reformed, particularly in relation to problèms of proof, notice, and other aspects of fairness.[1] Indeed, there is some suggestion that so long as the controversy involves a 'labour dispute', as that term is statutorily defined,[2] no injunction may issue except after unsuccessful recourse to police action.[3] By implication, such a holding would confine the issuance of labour injunctions to cases involving violence and obstruction and other matters of a criminal nature, leaving the remaining aspects of illegality to be dealt with by the labour relations board. The labour relations board, in turn, has acquired extensive new remedial powers in relation to industrial action which is forbidden by the Labour Relations Act.[4] However, the Labour Relations Act does not purport to be an integrated and complete code, as does the Labour Code of British Columbia, and there is conduct to which it is apparently not addressed. It would seem unlikely, therefore, that the courts will ultimately be prepared (in the absence of express legislation such as the Labour Code of British Columbia) to concede to the labour relations board plenary and exclusive jurisdiction over industrial action.[5] The present position may be characterized as one of relative equilibrium: the courts are less active and less subject to criticism than formerly; the labour relations board is acquiring experience with its new remedial powers.

1. Judicature Act, R.S.O. 1970, c.228, s.20. See also Newfoundland, s.130; Alberta, s.131.
2. Judicature Act, s.20(1). *Darrigo's Grape Juice* v. *Masterson*, [1971] 3 O.R. 772 (H.C.), held that secondary picketing was not a 'labour dispute'.
3. *Nedco* v. *Nichols*, [1973] 3 O.R. 944 (H.C.); *Charterways Transportation* v. *Alexander*, (1975) 9 O.R. (2d) 198 (H.C.); *Sasso Disposal* v. *Webster*, (1975) 10 O.R. (2d) 304 (H.C.). This interpretation is not likely to prevail in the higher courts.
4. *Supra*.
5. But see *Re C.J.M.S. Radio Montreal* v. *C.L.R.B.*, (1978) 91 D.L.R. (3d) 388 (Fed.T.C.); *McKinlay Transport* v. *Goodman*, (1978) 90 D.L.R. (3d) 689 (Fed. T.C.); *Chevron* v. *Teamsters*, (1978) 91 D.L.R. (3d) 649 (B.C.S.C.).

E. Arbitration

683. Collective agreements, usually by compulsion of statute, contain a promise that there will be no strike or lock-out for the duration of the agreement. They also contain, again usually by compulsion of statute, a provision for arbitration of all alleged violations of the no-strike clause. It follows that, if a strike occurs in violation of a no-strike clause, the aggrieved employer may have recourse against the union in arbitration.

684. The arbitrator has effective remedial powers. Most importantly, he may award money damages for an unlawful strike.[1] These damages may include all business loss incurred by the employer as a result of the interruption of work,[2] although the sum may be reduced if the employer has, in some way, contributed to his own loss by provocative or inept response to the union's concerns.[3] It is also possible that the arbitrator may have authority to enjoin future violations of the agreement.[4]

1. *Re Polymer and Oil Workers Union*, (1962) 33 D.L.R. (2d) 124 (S.C.C.).
2. Maritime Employers' Assoc., (1975) 10 L.A.C. (2d) 225; *Windsor Star*, (1974) 4 L.A.C. (2d) 207.
3. *Lake Ontario Steel*, (1968) 19 L.A.C. 260.
4. *Re Samuel Cooper and Ladies' Garment Workers*, (1973) 35 D.L.R. (3d) 501 (Ont.H.C.).

685. Of course, recourse to arbitration generally assumes the existence of a collective agreement, and is available only when the employer alleges violation of the no-strike clause, one of the terms of the agreement. If there is no agreement in force, or if the industrial action took some form other than a strike, arbitration is not normally available. However, the relative attractions of arbitration as a forum for determining the consequences of illegal strikes has led Ontario to provide access to arbitration to deal with damage claims arising out of illegal strikes, even when there is no collective agreement in effect.[1]

1. S.84.

Chapter VI. Collective Agreements

686. The making of a collective agreement represents the culmination of the collective bargaining process. At this stage the union and the employer have not only defined their future relationship but they have also established the terms and conditions of employment for all of the employees in the bargaining unit. The legal incidents flowing from the collective agreement and its administration now form a very large part of Canadian labour law.[1]

1. See generally L.R.L.C. (eds.), *Labour Relations Law: Cases, Materials and Commentary* (3rd ed., Kingston, 1980) c.7.

§1. THE COLLECTIVE AGREEMENT

A. Legal requirements

687. In order for arrangements between an employer and trade union to be considered as collective agreements they must be sufficiently formalized. Canadian collective bargaining law generally requires that such arrangements be in writing,[1] and that the assent of the trade union and employer be evidenced by the signatures of persons having the authority to act on their behalf.[2] An unconditional memorandum of settlement reached upon the completion of negotiations would appear to be considered as a binding collective agreement provided that it sets out the agreement of the parties with sufficient particularity, even though the parties might intend to replace it with a more formal document at some later date.[3] Where the agreement is made subject to ratification, however, it would not be treated as binding until the fact of ratification has been established.[4]

1. Canada, s.107(1); British Columbia, s.1(1); Ontario, s.1(1)(e); Quebec, s.1(e).
2. *Graphic Centre*, [1976] 2 C.L.R.B.R. 118 (O.L.R.B.).

3. *John Inglis*, [1974] 1 C.L.R.B.R. 481 (B.C.L.R.B.); *Ferranti-Packard*, [1977] 1 C.L.R.B.R. 503 (O.L.R.B.).
4. *Ibid*.

688. Some Canadian jurisdictions have legislative provisions allowing only one collective agreement to be made for a bargaining unit during any particular period of time.[1] This requirement, however, does not prohibit the parties from entering into supplementary agreements relating to such matters as pension and insurance plans provided that such arrangements do not contradict the terms of the collective agreement. Such supplementary arrangements are not considered as being part of the collective agreement unless it can be established that they have been incorporated by reference into the agreement.

1. Ontario, s.41; Quebec, s.55.

B. Unique legal effect

689. A collective agreement can be regarded as a unique legal relationship – it not only defines the rights and obligations of the two principal parties, the trade union and the employer, but it also sets the terms and conditions of employment for all of the employees in the bargaining unit regardless of whether they happen to be members of the trade union.[1] This first aspect of the collective agreement has been referred to as the 'contractual effect', while the latter aspect has been described as the 'normative effect'.

1. See generally B. L. Adell, *The Legal Status of Collective Agreements, in England, the United States and Canada* (Kingston, 1970).

1. Contractual effect

690. Collective agreements define the relationship between the trade union and the employer in a variety of ways. For one thing, a description of the bargaining unit is a feature of all collective agreements. It is generally accepted that, once a collective agreement is reached, the union's bargaining rights flow from the collective agreement, and not from the earlier certificate.[1] It is quite possible that the parties through bargaining may redefine the bargaining constituency by agreeing upon a different description of the bargaining unit. Such a practice appears to be acceptable provided that it does not involve a breach of the duty of fair representation on the part of the union in relinquishing its bargaining rights, or a breach of duty to bargain in good faith on the part of either the union or employer by insisting on re-defining the bargaining unit during negotiations.

1. *Culinary Workers* v. *Terra Nova Motor Inn* (1975), 50 D.L.R. (3d) 253 (S.C.C.).

691. Even more importantly, the collective agreement is likely to contain some sort of language requiring as a condition of further employment that the employees falling within the bargaining unit either join the union or support it financially. Such arrangements, known as union security provisions, are a common feature of Canadian collective agreements.[1] As well as bargaining for its own financial security, a trade union may bargain for and obtain other provisions of direct benefit to themselves, such as provisions permitting union officials to take time off work to conduct union business or provisions providing greater job security to union officials in the event of a reduction of the work force.

    1. *Supra*, c.IV, §1, *The Union's Exclusive Authority to Bargain*.

692. An almost universal feature of Canadian collective agreements is a provision establishing informal settlement mechanisms for disputes arising from the agreement with binding arbitration as the final step. Most Canadian jurisdictions prohibit resort to the strike and lock-out during the term of the collective agreement[1] and, as well, require that the parties include in their collective agreement a provision explicitly promising not to resort to economic sanctions during the term of the agreement. The *quid pro quo* for this restriction is generally considered to be the legislative stipulation that grievance arbitration be the means of finally resolving collective agreement disputes. The parties may design their own arbitration procedure through bargaining provided that this procedure meets the requirement for arbitration found in the legislation.[2]

    1. The Saskatchewan legislation, however, does not contain this prohibition.
    2. Canada, s.155; British Columbia, s.93; Ontario, s.37; Quebec, s.88.

693. Despite the general prohibition against striking or locking out during the term of the agreement, the parties may still include in their collective agreement other provisions affecting the use of economic sanctions. They may, for example, agree that the members of the bargaining unit are not to be disciplined for refusing to cross picket lines,[1] or they may agree following a strike or lock-out that neither party is to take disciplinary action in respect of incidents arising from the dispute.

    1. See *Nelson Crushed Stone*, [1978] 1 C.L.R.B.R. 115 (O.L.R.B.).

694. The fact that the collective agreement serves to define the relationship between the trade union and the employer raises a question as to the extent to which the traditional prerogative of the employer to manage has been curtailed by the establishment of a collective bargaining relationship. Most collective agreements contain a broadly worded provision recognizing the general right of the employer to manage the enterprise and, where such provisions have been absent, arbitrators usually have read into the collective agreement a general right to manage. On the other hand, collective agreements also contain specific provisions dealing with such matters as discharge and discipline,[1] seniority, job classification, wages, and hours of work that clearly limit the general power of the employer to manage. The potential conflict between these two types of provisions has given rise to some debate as to how this contractual language should be read.

    1. In one jurisdiction such a provision is mandatory (British Columbia, s.93).

695. One approach would treat the collective agreement as only restricting the traditional prerogative of the employer to manage to the extent that it does so through specific contract language. This approach, often called the 'reserved rights' approach is premised on the assumption that management when entering the collective bargaining relationship does not surrender its traditional right to manage. The other approach, however, would treat the collective agreement as creating a new legal regime that puts the trade union and employer on an equal footing.[1] Under this approach fundamental changes affecting the bargaining unit could not be made unilaterally by the employer but would have to be the subject of mutual agreement. Neither approach has received general acceptance by Canadian labour arbitrators who appear to prefer less philosophical, and more pragmatic, approaches toward the resolution of collective agreement disputes.[2]

1. *Peterboro Lock Mfg.*, (1953) 4 L.A.C. 1499.
2. *Russelsteel*, (1966) 17 L.A.C. 253.

2. Normative effect

696. It has now been authoritatively recognized that the collective agreement dictates the terms and conditions of employment for all of the employees in the bargaining unit. The trade union, as bargaining agent, has the exclusive authority to bargain for such employees, leaving no room for private negotiations between the employer and individual employee.[1] The terms negotiated between the union and employer, moreover, are by operation of law binding upon all the employees in the bargaining unit.[2] It is the collective agreement that establishes the norms of the employment relationship for the individual employees in the bargaining unit, operating in much the same manner as legislation.

1. *Supra*, C.IV, §1, *The Union's Exclusive Authority to Bargain*.
2. Canada, s.154; British Columbia, s.64; Ontario, s.42; Quebec, s.55.

3. Exclusion of Common Law Principles

697. There exists in Canada a body of common law principles dealing with the individual employment relationships.[1] Where a collective bargaining relationship exists, however, the legal arrangements between the employer and the employee have been dictated by negotiations between the union and the employer rather than by any direct bargaining between employer and employee. Recognizing this 'reality', the Supreme Court of Canada has clearly indicated that the common law of employment, as a general rule, is no longer relevant to the determination of the rights and obligations of employees covered by collective agreements.[2] The practical result of this ruling is to leave the legal position of such employees to be defined by reference to the law of the collective agreement rather than by reliance upon imported common law principles.

1. *Supra*, Part I, c.1.
2. *McGavin Toastmaster* v. *Ainscough*, (1975) 54 D.L.R. (3d) 1 (S.C.C.).

4. *Limited standing in the courts to enforce the collective agreement*

698. The trade union's exclusive authority to represent the employees in the bargaining unit encompasses not only the negotiation of the collective agreement but also its administration. As a general rule, an individual employee cannot turn to the courts in order to enforce the terms of the collective agreement. Any matter that requires the interpretation or application of the collective agreement must be resolved through the grievance and arbitration procedures provided in the collective agreement.[1] Except where specific provision is made for the involvement of individual employees, it is the union as bargaining agent that has the exclusive right to take any matter through the grievance and arbitration procedures. Despite this wide restriction on the standing of the individual employee to assert a claim arising from the collective agreement, it still appears to be possible for an employee to bring a simple claim for unpaid wages in the courts provided that it does not raise an issue requiring the interpretation of the collective agreement.[2] Moreover, in at least some jurisdictions, it may be possible for the employer to enforce the terms of the collective agreement through an action in the courts.[3]

1. *General Motors*, (1976) 77 C.L.L.C. para. 14,067; the *Rights of Labour Act*, R.S.O. 1970, c.416, s.3(3), expressly provides that 'a collective bargaining agreement shall not be the subject of any action in any court unless it may be the subject of such action irrespective of any of the provisions of this Act or The Labour Relations Act'; see also *Bergeron* v. *Kingsway Transports Ltd*, (1979) 23 O.R. (2d) 332 (H.C.).
2. *Re Grottoli* v. *Lock*, (1963) 39 D.L.R. (2d) 128 (Ont.H.C.); *Hamilton Street Railway* v. *Northcott*, (1966) 58 D.L.R. (2d) 708 (S.C.C.).
3. *Nelsons Laundries* v. *Manning*, (1965) 51 D.L.R. (2d) 537 (B.C.S.C.).

5. *Potential legal vacuum upon expiry of the collective agreement*

699. Collective agreements, unlike many individual contracts of employment, are not of indefinite duration and must be renewed at periodic intervals. Negotiations for renewal may be protracted and often extend past the expiry of both the collective agreement and the period of the statutory freeze. Where employees continue to work beyond both the expiry of the collective agreement and the freeze period a question may arise as to whether their terms and conditions of employment are still governed by the expired collective agreement.

700. It appears to be recognized that the provisions of the collective agreement relating to the terms and conditions of employment of the employees in the bargaining unit survive both the expiry of the collective agreement and the period of the statutory freeze.[1] At that point the right to alter unilaterally these terms of employment is not entirely unqualified, since in some circumstances a unilateral alteration might be interpreted as a breach of the obligation to bargain in good faith. Moreover, at this stage, there is a question of how the surviving terms and conditions of employment might be enforced. It is open to argument as to whether these terms survive in the form of individual contracts between employer and employee that would be enforceable in the ordinary courts, or whether they still must be enforced through grievance and arbitration procedures administered by the trade union. One court has held that the grievance and arbitration procedures become part of the individual contracts of employment between the employer and the employees upon the expiry of the collective agreement.[2] Some doubt has been expressed, however, as to whether this type of provision, which is integral to the relationship between union and employer, is consistent with the terms usually found in individual contracts of employment.

1. *Telegram Publishing*, (1976) 76 C.L.L.C. para. 14,047 (Ont.C.A.).
2. *Re Prince Rupert Fishermen's Co-op. Assoc. and United Fishermen*, (1969) 66 W.W.R. 43 (B.C.S.C.).

701. The legal vacuum created by the expiry of the collective agreement usually poses a problem only where there has been a failure to renew the collective agreement. In those cases where the collective agreement is renewed the parties are likely to make the new agreement retroactive to the expiry date of the previous agreement. These retroactive provisions, however, have sometimes been interpreted by arbitrators as not touching all terms of the collective agreement. Where full retroactivity would lead to impractical and unintended results, then certain terms of the agreement may not be given retroactive effect.[1] Arbitral authority appears to be divided on the more specific question of whether persons who leave their employment prior to the signing of the collective agreement may still benefit from a retroactive wage increase.[2]

1. *Penticton and District Retirement Service* (1978), 16 L.A.C. (2d) 97 (B.C.L.R.B.).
2. See *Ont. Fed. of Labour*, (1978) 16 L.A.C. (2d) 265.

6. Status of the collective agreement in the courts

702. The primary method of enforcing collective agreements is the grievance arbitration procedure established in the agreement itself. The existence of this special procedure for enforcement is at least partially a result of an earlier reluctance on the part of the courts to recognize trade unions as legal entities as well as a judicial unwillingness to treat collective agreements as legally enforceable arrangements.[1] Moreover, the union's role of exclusive bargaining agent virtually eliminates any possibility of individual employees being able to use the courts in order to enforce the terms of employment established by the collective agreement. The result is that the courts in Canada have not played a direct role in the enforcement of collective agreements.

1. See *supra*, para. 658 to 661.

(a) Standing of trade unions in the courts

703. Even after the repeal of the laws of criminal conspiracy relating to trade unions, the common law of restraint of trade was still recognized by the courts as applying to trade unions. The survival of this common law doctrine until the advent of present-day collective bargaining legislation meant that trade unions found to be operating in restraint of trade were denied standing in the courts to enforce their collective agreements.[1] While present-day collective bargaining legislation has had the effect of legitimating trade unions,[2] other means of enforcing the collective agreement had already been established by the time that this incident of collective bargaining legislation was recognized by the courts.

1. *Polakoff* v. *Winters Garment*, [1928] 2 D.L.R. 277 (Ont.S.C.).
2. *I.B. F.W.* v. *Town Summerside*, (1960) 23 D.L.R. (2d) 593 (S.C.C.).

704. Even after the demise of the restraint of trade bar there remained a further obstacle to judicial recognition of the trade union as a legal entity. Initially, the trade union was regarded by the courts as just another unincorporated association and, as such, was not treated as a legal person in its own right. The result was that the trade union could only sue or be sued in the courts through the rather cumbersome procedure of the representative action.[1] This disability was not regarded as being entirely disadvantageous by trade unionists who harboured some distrust of the courts, and who feared the potential consequences of a damage action in the courts. In fact, some jurisdictions expressly preserved this disability even after the enactment of Wagner-style collective bargaining legislation.[2] However, most jurisdictions came to treat trade unions as having status to sue and be sued in the courts. By this time, though, grievance arbitration had become firmly entrenched as the method by which collective agreements were enforced by and against trade unions.

1. *Supra*, c.V.S.5, *Remedies for Unlawful Industrial Action*; see also *Seafarers Int'l.* v. *Lawrence*, (1979) 24 O.R. (2d) 257 (C.A.).
2. Ontario and Saskatchewan.

(b) Unenforceability of the collective agreement at common law

705. A further impediment to the enforcement of the collective agreement in the courts was an earlier judicial unwillingness to recognize collective agreements as giving rise to legally enforceable obligations. The courts took the view that the parties to the collective agreement had not intended to create legally enforceable obligations, and that any disputes arising from the agreement could only be resolved through negotiation and, if necessary, the use of economic sanctions.[1] The enactment of present-day collective bargaining legislation rendered this approach obsolete. One of the primary thrusts of this legislation is to limit economic conflict to the period when the collective agreement is being negotiated. Since the use of the strike or lock-out to resolve problems arising during the term of a collective agreement is expressly prohibited, the collective agreement cannot be the subject of continuous negotiation and must be treated as being enforceable during its term.[2] The procedure for enforcing the collective agreement is grievance arbitration – a procedure that is mandatory in almost all Canadian jurisdictions.

1. *Young* v. *C.N.R.,* [1931] 1 D.L.R. 645 (P.C.).
2. Some Canadian jurisdictions expressly provide that the collective agreement is binding upon both the bargaining agent and the employer – Canada, s.154; British Columbia, s.64; Ontario, s.42.

§2. ADMINISTRATION AND ENFORCEMENT OF THE COLLECTIVE AGREEMENT

706. The collective agreement establishes a continuing relationship between the employer, the union, and the employees represented by the union. In a sense these parties are partners in the operation of the enterprise. The administration of the collective agreement is very much a continuing process requiring the parties to work out within the framework of the agreement the numerous problems, some small and others large, arising from the day-to-day running of the enterprise. Most of these problems are resolved on a very informal basis by the parties themselves, sometimes without reference to the collective agreement. Where informal adjustment is unsuccessful more formal procedures for the administration and enforcement of the collective agreement can usually be found in the agreement itself.

A. Grievance procedures

707. Most collective agreements contain some sort of grievance procedure designed to resolve collective agreement disputes by means of discussion and agreement between the parties. The complexity of such procedures usually depends on the nature and size of the enterprise. In the small enterprise only a single meeting between the union representative and the owner may be called for. A more structured, multi-stage, procedure is likely to be found in the larger enterprise, each additional stage requiring the participation of management and union officials with greater authority than those participating in the preceding stage. These more complex grievance procedures have been designed to allow minor grievances to be settled at the earlier stages (or steps) of the grievance procedure, and to have more important grievances settled at a more senior level.

708. Carriage of a grievance through the grievance procedure is usually the function of the union, and not of the individual employee. Collective bargaining legislation in some jurisdictions, however, does permit employees to process their own grievances.[1] In the absence of such legislative provisions, or an express provision in the collective agreement allowing employees to have access to the grievance procedure, it is only the union and the employer who may set the grievance procedure in motion.

1. Canada, s.132; similar provisions exist in Manitoba, New Brunswick, Newfoundland, Nova Scotia and Prince Edward Island. It is clear, however, that this type of provision does not permit an employee to carry a grievance through to arbitration.

709. Many collective agreements establish time limits for the filing of the grievance and the taking of the various steps in the grievance procedure. As well, it may be stipulated in the collective agreement that the grievance be in written form and signed by the grievor. A distinction may also be drawn in the collective agreement between individual and policy grievances. All of these requirements can be waived by the parties in the interests of settling a grievance, and they only become an issue where one of the parties wishes to resist the grievance on procedural grounds. When this latter situation occurs, the grievance will usually end up at arbitration and the arbitrator will be faced with the question of whether a procedural defect renders a grievance no longer arbitrable.[1]

1. *Infra*, B.2. *Arbitrability of Grievances*.

B. Grievance arbitration

710. Those grievances that cannot be settled by the parties themselves are generally resolved through grievance arbitration. Grievance arbitration is mandatory in all jurisdictions but Saskatchewan, and even in that jurisdiction arbitration procedures are usually found in collective agreements. While only a small proportion of grievances go to arbitration, the process itself has a substantial impact upon the administration of the collective agreement. Over the years arbitral decision-making has given rise to a comprehensive body of principles relating to the rights and duties created by a collective agreement.[1] This law of the collective agreement undoubtedly influences decisions made at the earlier stages of the grievance procedure as to whether to proceed to arbitration. Moreover, the effectiveness of the grievance arbitration process itself, both in terms of cost and speed, has some bearing on whether a matter will be taken to arbitration or withdrawn at an earlier stage.

1. See generally, D. J. M. Brown and D. M. Beatty, *Canadian Labour Arbitration* (Agincourt, 1977); E. E. Palmer, *Collective Agreement Arbitration in Canada* (Toronto, 1978).

1. Nature of the process

711. Grievance arbitration is a hybrid process – containing both public and private elements. Although the process is mandatory in all but one jurisdiction, the parties still have a wide latitude to define the process in their own terms. The legislative requirement establishes only a minimum procedure, leaving the parties free to improve upon this basic model by devising procedures suited to their own particular needs. There exists in Canada a number of variations from the standard model of arbitration as evidenced by the rail, longshoring, trucking, mining and garment industries, which have each devised their own special procedures for the final resolution of grievances.[1]

1. See Labour Canada Study, *Industry and Expedited Arbitration. Alternatives to Traditional Methods* (Ottawa, 1977).

712. Grievance arbitration, moreover, is procedure separate and distinct from commercial arbitration. Recognizing this fact, all but two provinces[1] exclude grievance arbitration from the scope of the statutory structure established for the arbitration of commercial disputes.

1. Newfoundland and Nova Scotia.

(a) Constitution of the arbitration tribunal

713. The parties themselves are generally responsible for the establishment of the arbitration tribunal, an exercise usually performed on an *ad hoc* basis. Where a grievance is to be taken to a board of arbitration, the general practice is for each of the parties to nominate a representative member to sit on the board with the chairman being chosen by mutual agreement. Some arbitration procedures, however, contemplate the use of a sole arbitrator in which case the arbitrator is again selected by mutual agreement. In many cases the arbitration tribunal is constituted only after the grievance is referred to arbitration, although some collective agreements provide for less *ad hoc* procedures by establishing a panel of arbitrators to be used in rotation or, more exceptionally, a permanent umpire. The arbitration tribunal is only appointed by the government where the parties have failed to constitute the tribunal themselves.[1]

1. This situation has been somewhat altered by recent legislation in Ontario. Amendments to the Ontario legislation now permit either party to apply immediately to the Minister for the appointment of an arbitrator even though the collective agreement may establish a different procedure for the selection of the arbitrator. Section 103 of the Nova Scotia legislation goes even further for construction industry arbitrations, providing a mandatory statutory procedure for the expeditious appointment of a single arbitrator.

(b) Costs of proceedings

714. As a general rule the parties by agreement bear the costs of the arbitration tribunal equally. Where a board of arbitration is used, each party pays the fees and expenses of its own nominee to the board and the fees and expenses of the chairman are divided equally between them.[1] In the case of a sole arbitrator, the fees and expenses of the arbitrator would again be divided equally. Each party bears its own costs of presenting the grievance to the arbitration tribunal as it is the prevailing practice of arbitrators not to award costs against the losing party.

1. One jurisdiction, Nova Scotia, provides that the costs of the arbitration tribunal are to be divided in three ways among the union, the employer, and the government: s.41(2).

(c) Openness to public

715. There is some question as to whether arbitration tribunals are sufficiently private in nature so as to justify the exclusion of the general public from their hearings. Legislation in both Ontario and the federal jurisdiction appears to treat grievance arbitration tribunals as being different from statutory tribunals.[1] On the other hand, an arbitral ruling to the effect that the essentially private nature of the arbitration process precluded the opening of an arbitration hearing to the public has not met with judicial approval.[2] The result is that an arbitration tribunal now appears to have a discretion as to whether to exclude members of the public, including the press, from its proceedings.[3]

1. *The Statutory Powers Procedure Act*, S.O. 1971 (Vol. 2), c.47; Canada, s.156(3).
2. *Toronto Star*, (1975) 9 L.A.C. (2d) 193; overruled by (1977) 14 O.R. (2d) 278 (H.C.).
3. *Toronto Star*, (1977) 14 L.A.C. (2d) 155.

(d) The problem of bias

716. The *ad hoc* and representative nature of arbitration tribunals raises a question of whether the nominees to a board of arbitration may be so closely connected with their nominating party so as to be disqualified on the ground of bias. The appointment as nominee of an official of a trade union party to an arbitration or, on the other side, of an employee of an employer party is not an uncommon practice. In most of these situations no objection is taken to the constitution of the arbitration board and the problem of bias is effectively avoided. Where objection to the constitution of a board is made at the outset of the hearing, however, consideration has to be given to the relationship between a party and its nominee. The courts have indicated that they are not willing to approve of a nominee with too close a relationship with one of the interested parties, such as an official of the union which is itself a party to the arbitration.[1]

1. *Canadian Shipbuilding and Engineering*, (1973) 73 C.L.L.C. para. 14,185 (Ont.H.C.); but see *Re Gainers and Packinghouse Workers*, (1964) 47 W.W.R. 544 (Alta.S.C.).

(e) Conduct of hearings

717. Once constituted the arbitration tribunal usually convenes a hearing of the grievance at a time and place agreed upon by the parties. Hearings are almost always held in a location close to the place of work, often a conference room in a nearby hotel. The format of the arbitration hearing is usually more informal than that adopted by the courts. Often the parties are able to agree upon a statement of facts avoiding recourse to more formal evidential procedures. In many cases, the parties (more often the trade unions) do not use lawyers to present their case but, instead, make use of the services of their own officials. Despite this informality, it would appear that the courts still require arbitration tribunals to adopt an adjudicative format and to adhere to basic principles of judicial procedure. All parties having any interest in the outcome of the proceedings are required to be notified.[1] Parties are entitled to be represented by counsel,[2] and entitled to cross-examine the evidence of the other party at the hearing.[3] These procedural requirements imposed by the courts have introduced a substantial legal element into the process – a factor that may explain why many Canadian arbitrators have legal backgrounds.

1. *Re Hoogendoorn and Greening Motel Products & Screening Equipment*, (1968) 65 D.L.R. (2d) 641(S.C.C.).
2. *Men's Clothing Manufacturers Assoc. of Ont.*, (1979) 79 C.L.L.C. para. 14,224 (Ont.H.C.).
3. *Re Girvin and Consumers' Gas*, (1974) 40 D.L.R. (3d) 504 (Ont.H.C.).

(f) Sources of arbitral standards

718. Grievance arbitration is essentially an adjudicative process requiring the arbitration tribunal to make findings of fact and then to apply appropriate standards to these facts.[1] The primary source of the standards applied by the arbitrator is the collective agreement itself. Initially the arbitrator looks to the language of the collective agreement in order to determine whether the parties have formulated a rule that can resolve the immediate dispute. This exercise is not as easy as it would appear at first glance. Some collective agreements may contain language of so general a nature as to make it virtually impossible for the arbitrator to find a specific rule to deal with the particular problems. Even where contract language is more specific, collective agreement provisions may conflict with each other, making it equally difficult for the arbitrator to resolve the dispute by reference to the language of the collective agreement alone.

1. See generally, P. C. Weiler, *The Role of the Labour Arbitrator: Alternative Versions*, (1969) 19 U.T.L.J. 16.

719. The nature of the negotiation process is such that it is impossible for the parties to provide for every eventuality in their collective agreement. The crisis atmosphere of negotiations means that agreements are often drafted in haste, and that language may be deliberately left unclear in order to mask those issues on which complete agreement has not been reached. Even where the greatest care is taken in drafting the collective agreements, the limits of human foresight make it likely that contract language cannot provide the arbitrator with the answers in all cases.

720. In those situations where the language of the collective agreement does not clearly reveal a standard for the resolution of the case, the arbitrator may look outside the collective agreement. It has been recognized that where a collective agreement is ambiguous, arbitrators are permitted to rely upon extrinsic (or parole) evidence as an aid to interpreting the language of the contract.[1] Such extrinsic evidence usually takes the form of testimony as to the practice of the parties in previous cases of a like nature, or testimony as to the history of the negotiations that led up to the making of the collective agreement. Whether a collective agreement is sufficiently ambiguous to justify the use of such evidence will depend upon the relative plausibility of the conflicting interpretations of the collective agreement.[2] An ambiguity, however, may also be latent where the application to the facts of what appears to be unequivocal language is uncertain or difficult.[3]

1. *John Bertram*, (1967) 18 L.A.C. 362.
2. *U.B.C.*, [1977] 1 C.L.R.B.R. 13 (B.C.L.R.B.).
3. *Leitch Gold Mines* v. *Texas Gulf Sulpher*, (1969) 3 D.L.R. (3d) 161 (Ont.H.C.); but see *R.* v. *Barber, Ex p. Warehousemen's* (1968) 68 D.L.R. (2d) 682 (Ont.C.A.).

721. In cases where the language of the collective agreement does not supply a ready answer arbitrators may also rely upon the arbitral jurisprudence. Although arbitrators are not strictly bound to follow prior arbitration decisions, the very well-developed body of arbitral case law in Canada does have a substantial influence on the process. Arbitrators tend to assume that the parties have entered into their collective agreement with knowledge of the basic themes running through this jurisprudence.[1] Moreover, where there has been a previous decision relating to a similar provision in the collective agreement, arbitrators have taken the approach that they will follow the previous award unless convinced that the earlier interpretation is clearly wrong.[2] The extensive use of arbitral jurisprudence by Canadian arbitrators has meant that the parties now rely heavily upon previous decisions when presenting their cases at arbitration.

1. *Russelsteel*, (1966) 17 L.A.C. 253.
2. See J. F. W. Weatherill, *The Binding Force of Arbitration Awards*, (1958) 8 L.A.C. 323.

722. Even though the collective agreement is regarded as the primary source of the arbitrator's jurisdiction, it may still be necessary for the arbitrator to take into account relevant statutory provisions. The roots of the grievance arbitration process can be found in general collective bargaining legislation, and arbitrators may refer to this legislation in order to avoid giving the collective agreement an interpretation that would be inconsistent with this legislative scheme. An interesting question is whether the parties may restrict access to the arbitration process by placing language to that effect in their collective agreement. Although an arbitral consensus has not been reached on this issue, the more widely accepted view favours the primacy of those legislative provisions that make mandatory the arbitration of all disputes arising from the collective agreement.[1]

1. *Cassier Asbestos*, [1974] 1 C.L.R.B.R. 428 and [1975] 1 C.L.R.B.R. 212 (B.C.L.R.B.); *Transair*, [1978] 2 C.L.R.B.R. 354 (C.L.R.B.); *International Waxes*, (1978) 17 L.A.C. (2d) 62; *Toronto Star*, (1979) 20 L.A.C. (2d) 392.

723. Statutory provisions other than those found in collective bargaining legislation may also be relevant to the disposition of a matter at arbitration.[1] Where the provisions of a collective agreement clearly conflict with a statute, the arbitrator is obligated to take the statute into account even if it means having to treat the language of the collective agreement as a nullity.[2] In some situations, however, it may not be necessary for the arbitrator to render the language of the collective agreement inoperative. If the launguage of the agreement is open to alternative interpretations, the arbitrator can adopt the interpretation that is consistent with the statute by assuming that the parties did not intend to agree on language that would be in conflict with the general law.

1. See generally, P. C. Weiler, *The Arbitrator, the Collective Agreement and the Law*, (1972) 10 Osgoode Hall L.J. 141.
2. *McLeod* v. *Egan*, (1974) 46 D.L.R. (3d) 150 (S.C.C.).

724. To some extent arbitrators also rely upon general notions of equity and fairness when deciding grievances. Although the primary assumption is that the arbitrator must be faithful to the language of the collective agreement, there is still some latitude allowed for the introduction of certain equitable doctrines. At times arbitrators have invoked the doctrine of equitable estoppel to prevent one party from claiming its strict rights under a collective agreement where it has led the other party to believe that such rights would not be enforced and that other party has relied on the representation to its detriment.[1] Another equitable doctrine sometimes invoked by arbitrators is that of laches or undue delay. If a party delays unduly in processing a grievance and this delay results in some detriment to the other party, the arbitrator may refuse to hear the grievance even though it might be timely under the grievance procedure in the collective agreement.[2] The equitable doctrines applied by arbitrators tend to parallel those developed by the courts, although there has been some recent support for the adoption of a general doctrine of fairness by arbitrators.[3]

1. *Canadian General Electric*, (1971) 22 L.A.C. 149.
2. *Governing Council of U. of T.* (1976) 10 L.A.C. (2d) 417.
3. British Columbia, s.92, instructs arbitrators to 'have regard to the real substance of matters in dispute' and provides that arbitrators are 'not bound by a strict legal interpretation of the issues in dispute'; see also *Re Municipality of Metropolitan Toronto*, (1978) 79 D.L.R. (3d) 249 (Ont.H.C.) where the majority of the court indicated that there was an implied duty upon the employer to administer the collective agreement fairly.

(g) Remedial authority

725. The hybrid nature of the arbitration process has given rise to considerable debate about the proper limits of the arbitrator's remedial authority.[1] Those who characterize the arbitration process as being merely a creation of the collective agreement argue that the arbitrators remedial power cannot extend beyond those powers expressly conferred by the terms of the collective agreement. On the other hand, those who regard the arbitration process as being primarily the product of collective bargaining legislation take the position that a full range of remedial powers can be implied from the statutory language requiring final and binding settlement of grievances by means of arbitration.

1. See generally, P. C. Weiler, *The Remedial Authority of the Labour Arbitrator: Revised Judicial Version*, (1974) 52 Can. B. Rev. 29.

726. In the early stages of grievance arbitration in Canada there was some doubt as to whether, absent specific language in the collective agreement, an arbitration tribunal could do more than make a declaration as to the respective rights of the parties under the collective agreement. Judicial approval, however, was later given to an arbitral damage award[1] indicating that the courts were prepared to treat the legislative framework as providing the arbitrator with at least some authority to fashion an appropriate remedy. It is now clear that arbitrators have a wide authority to award damages for a breach of the collective agreement,[2] provided that the damages are essentially compensatory in nature.

1. *Polymer*, (1959) 10 L.A.C. 51; (1961) 26 D.L.R. (2d) 609 (Ont.H.C.); 28 D.L.R. (2d) 81 (Ont.C.A.); (1962) 33 D.L.R. (2d) 124 (S.C.C.).
2. In *Re Blouin Drywall Contractors and Carpenters and Joiners*, (1976) 57 D.L.R. (3d) 199 (Ont.C.A.) the court upheld the authority of the arbitrator to award damages to the union for breach of a hiring hall provision in the collective agreement.

727. In other situations, however, the courts have been less willing to recognize the remedial authority of the arbitrator. In the case of an improper discharge the usual remedy is a direction to the employer to reinstate the employee without loss of seniority and to compensate the employee for wages and fringe benefits lost during the period of discharge. While the power of the arbitrator to order full reinstatement has never been seriously challenged, the order of an arbitrator substituting a lesser penalty for discharge has been overturned by the courts on the basis that in making this remedial order the arbitrator exceeded the jurisdictional limits established by the collective agreement.[1] The effect of this judicial decision was to curtail the power of arbitrators to fashion a remedy falling somewhere between the two extremes of full reinstatement or dismissal of the grievance. Recognizing the problems created by this restriction, collective bargaining legislation in most Canadian jurisdictions has been amended to provide the arbitrator with a wide remedial authority in cases of discharge.[2]

1. *Port Arthur Shipbuilding* v. *Arthurs*, (1968) 70 D.L.R. (2d) 693; but see now *New Brunswick Electric Power Commission*, (1979) 79 C.L.L.C. para. 14,200 (S.C.C.).
2. Canada, s.157(d); British Columbia, s.98(d); Ontario, s.37(8); Quebec, s.88 *m*; a perceptive review of the evolution of the arbitrator's jurisdiction in this area is found in *Wm. Scott*, [1977] 1 C.L.R.B.R. 1 (B.C.L.R.B.).

728. The power of the arbitrator to relieve against provisions in the collective agreement restricting the time for the processing of grievances experienced a somewhat similar evolution. Attempts by arbitrators to provide relief against the harsh consequences of a missed time limit did not meet with judicial approval.[1] Some Canadian jurisdictions, recognizing the undesirability of grievances being forfeited on technical grounds, have amended their legislation to give arbitrators the explicit power to relieve against the forfeiture of a grievance because of a failure to meet contractual time limits.[2]

1. See, for example, *Truck Drivers* v. *Hoar Transport*, (1969) 4 D.L.R. (3d) 449 (S.C.C.).
2. British Columbia, s.98(e); Ontario, s.37(5a).

729. Whether an arbitrator has the power to rectify a collective agreement when there has been a mistake made in reducing the actual agreement reached by the parties into final written form is problematical. Although the courts themselves exercise such a power, they have been reluctant to recognize the arbitrator's authority to perform the very same remedial role.[1] Arbitrators themselves appear to be divided on the question of whether they have the authority to order rectification.[2] This reluctance to order rectification may be explained in part by the difficulty of determining what constitutes the actual agreement of the parties when it has not been reduced into final written form.

261

1. *Re Metropolitan Toronto Board of Commissioners of Police and Metropolitan Toronto Police Assoc.*, (1972) 26 D.L.R. (3d) 672 (Ont. C.A.).
2. See *B.C. Transformer*, (1976) 11 L.A.C. (2d) 233; *Okanagan Federated Shippers Assoc.*, [1977] 1 C.L.R.B.R. 21 (B.C.L.R.B.); compare *Prince Albert Pulp*, (1975) 7 L.A.C. (2d) 345.

730. The power of arbitrators to make affirmative orders to remedy breaches of the collective agreement appears to be more clearly established. These compliance orders, as they have been called, have been used not only to remedy past breaches of a collective agreement but also to restrain future anticipated breaches.[1] This type of relief, however, may be difficult to enforce and, as a result, arbitrators may not consider it to be appropriate in all circumstances.

1. *Polax Tailoring*, (1972) 24 L.A.C. 201; *Re Samuel Cooper and Ladies Garment Workers*, (1973) 35 D.L.R. (3d) 501 (Ont.H.C.).

731. Despite their approval of the general arbitral power to make compliance orders, the courts have not been inclined to recognize the power of the arbitrator to make a specific order awarding a job to a grievor where it has been found that an employer has improperly exercised its power to promote. In these circumstances the courts have held that, absent any specific remedial power in the collective agreement, the proper course for the arbitrator to take is to remit the matter back to the employer for reconsideration.[1]

1. *Re Falconbridge Nickel Mines and U.S.W.A.*, (1973) 30 D.L.R. (3d) 412 (Ont.C.A.).

732. Finally, it is interesting to note that arbitrators have not followed the practice of the courts of awarding the costs of the proceedings against the losing party, even in the situation where it is clear that one of the parties has been responsible for prolonging the proceedings. This arbitral reluctance to assume a jurisdiction to award costs by deviating from the general understanding that each party assumes an equal share of the costs of the process may be partly attributed to the consensual element of grievance arbitration. Arbitrators, being chosen and paid by the parties, do not enjoy the same position of authority as a judge or a member of a public tribunal, a factor that may explain their reluctance to single out one of the parties to bear all of the costs of the proceedings.

2. Arbitrability of grievances

733. At the outset of arbitration proceedings certain questions may arise as to whether the grievance should even have been brought to arbitration. It may be argued that a collective agreement was not in effect when the grievance arose, that the grievor was not covered by the collective agreement (perhaps because of probationary status), that the issue raised fell outside the ambit of the collective agreement, that the grievance was improperly submitted to arbitration, or that the grievance must be forfeited because of a failure to comply with the time limits contained in the collective agreement. All of these issues are generally regarded as going to the arbitrability of the grievance, and collective bargaining legislation in all jurisdictions provides arbitrators with a full jurisdiction to resolve this type of issue. While arguments contesting the arbitrability of a grievance usually raise issues that are preliminary in nature, in some cases the issues raised by a preliminary objection may be closely connected with the merits of the grievance. Some disagreement exists among arbitrators as to whether issues relating to the arbitrability of the grievance should be disposed of before proceeding to hear the merits.[1] As a general practice, any serious objection to the arbitrability of the grievance is usually dealt with before the arbitrator proceeds to the merits.

1. *Hiram Walker*, (1973) 3 L.A.C. (2d) 203; compare *Alcan*, (1974) 5 L.A.C. (2d) 300.

(a) Submission to arbitration

734. Union grievances submitted to arbitration generally fall into two categories – those that relate to a particular problem of an individual employee (the individual grievance) and those of a more general nature with implications extending beyond the particular situation of a single employee (the policy grievance). Arbitrators at first tended to draw a rigid distinction between these two types of grievances by not permitting matters that were in essence individual grievances to be brought to arbitration as policy grievances. Latterly, however, arbitrators have modified this approach by drawing this distinction only where the language of the collective agreement explicitly limits the use of policy grievances.[1] Despite this change of approach, arbitrators still recognize that a policy grievance cannot be used as a device to circumvent the time limits established for the processing of individual grievances.[2]

1. *Weston Bakeries*, (1970) 21 L.A.C. 308; *Toronto Star Newspapers*, (1979) 20 L.A.C. (2d) 392.
2. *Hydro Electric Commission of Borough of North York*, (1974) 6 L.A.C. (2d) 113.

(b) Carriage of the grievance

735. The general rule is that, regardless of whether a grievance may be an individual grievance, it is the union that has the right to take the grievance to arbitration. Individual employees are not permitted to take their grievance to arbitration on their own even where they are prepared to assume the costs of the process.[1] It is only possible for employees to have access to arbitration in their own right where the language of the arbitration provision in the collective agreement expressly so provides. Language to this effect is not commonly found in Canadian collective agreements, and the usual situation is that the trade union has the exclusive right to bring employee grievances to arbitration.

1. *Danby*, (1979) 79 C.L.L.C. para. 14,208 (Que.S.C.).

736. Two consequences of some importance flow from trade union control over the carriage of the grievance. First, it is clear that the trade union is permitted to settle or withdraw the grievance at any time without the consent of the individual grievor.[1] A second consequence is that the union may take a grievance to arbitration even where the individual is no longer interested in pursuing it any further.[2]

1. *Governing Council of U. of T.*, (1974) 5 L.A.C. (2d) 304.
2. *Int'l. Nickel*, (1975) 9 L.A.C. (2d) 83.

(c) Timeliness

737. Grievance procedures contained in most collective agreements stipulate certain time limits for the taking of each step in the procedure, including the submission of the grievance to arbitration and the constitution of the arbitration tribunal. A failure to comply with these time limits may often give rise to an objection that the grievance is no longer arbitrable. In dealing with this kind of objection arbitrators have drawn a distinction between time limits that are 'mandatory' in that they dictate the forfeiture of the grievance for noncompliance, and those time limits that are merely 'directory' and which do not by themselves invalidate the grievance.[1] The nature of a time limit is determined by an examination of the language used by the parties when drafting the grievance procedure and by consideration of the purposes intended to be served by the use of this language. The use of the word 'shall' does not necessarily make a time limit mandatory. However, where the grievance procedure provides a remedy for non-compliance, the time limit is generally considered to be mandatory. It does not follow, though, that the lack of a penalty provision makes a time limit directory. In all cases the language used must be interpreted in the context of the overall grievance procedure.

1. For a review of these decisions, see *Municipality of Metro. Toronto*, (1973) 3 L.A.C. (2d) 126.

738. Arbitrators have recognized that relief against the strict operation of mandatory time limits may be justified in some cases. While arbitrators do not have any general power to relieve against time limits in the absence of an explicit statutory mandate,[1] they have nonetheless been able to provide some relief in certain types of situations. One situation is where the time limit (or other procedural irregularity) has been clearly waived by the party otherwise entitled to insist upon its observance.[2] Another situation is where the grievance can be characterized as a continuing grievance in the sense that the conduct giving rise to the grievance is of a recurring nature. Here arbitrators have treated time limits as operating only to limit grievances relating to earlier breaches of the collective agreement, and not as restricting a grievance relating to a fresh recurrence.[3]

1. *Supra*, (a) *Nature of the Process* (7. *Remedial Authority*).
2. *Regency Towers Hotel*, (1974) 4 L.A.C. (2d) 440.
3. *Parking Authority of Toronto*, (1974) 5 L.A.C. (2d) 150.

739. In some jurisdictions legislation explicitly gives arbitrators a power to relieve against time limits.[1] This power is a discretionary one and when exercis-

ing it arbitrators consider such matters as the reason for the delay in processing the grievance, the length of the delay, the nature of the grievance, and the extent of prejudice to the other party if relief against the time limit were to be granted.[2] The existence of an explicit statutory power to relieve against time limits in these jurisdictions makes the distinction between mandatory and directory time limits much less significant.

1. British Columbia, s.98(e); Ontario, s.37(5a).
2. *Pamour Porcupine Mines*, (1977) 77 C.L.L.C. para. 14,078 (Ont.H.C.); *Becker Milk*, (1979) 19 L.A.C. (2d) 217.

740. Late grievances, on the other hand, may be inarbitrable even where they are not invalidated by time limits in the collective agreements. Arbitrators on occasion have applied the equitable doctrine of laches, refusing to hear the grievance on the ground that unreasonable delay in bringing the grievance has caused prejudice to the other party.[1]

1. *Supra*, (§2 B.1.f. *Source of Arbitral Standards*).

(d) Settlement, withdrawal and abandonment

741. The settlement, withdrawal, or abandonment of a grievance generally has the effect of rendering the grievance no longer arbitrable. Moreover, the disposition of a grievance in this manner usually precludes a party from bringing to arbitration another grievance raising the same matter as the earlier grievance. Arbitrators have recognized that the integrity of the earlier settlement process must be maintained, and have been reluctant to re-open issues where they appear to have been settled by the parties at an earlier stage in the process.

3. Discharge and discipline

742. The largest category of grievances carried to arbitration arises from those situations where employees have been disciplined or discharged by their employer. Discipline covers such matters as suspension without pay, formal warnings and, in some cases, demotion. Discharge, the most severe form of disciplinary sanction, is often considered as being distinct from other disciplinary sanctions.

743. Discipline and discharge cases raise questions concerning the extent to which the traditional prerogative of employers to manage has been restricted by collective agreement provisions requiring that the disciplinary sanctions only be imposed for just cause. Viewed from the employee perspective discharge and discipline can be regarded as sanctions that have been imposed for wrongful conduct, and the argument is that such cases must be resolved by reference to principles analogous to those found in the criminal law. Employers, on the other hand, tend to resist this analogy to the criminal law, arguing that the power to discharge and discipline is simply one facet of their general responsibility to manage the enterprise as efficiently as possible. A decision to discharge or discipline, according to this view, amounts merely to the enforcement of the contractual bargain with the employees – a function that is not analagous to the imposition of sanctions under the criminal law. The true nature of discharge and discipline probably lies somewhere between these two extreme positions. In some situations employers appear to be attempting to regulate the conduct of their employees by reference to what is often an unwritten code of employment conduct. Theft, dishonesty, participation in illegal strikes, fighting on the job, and insubordination are usually regarded as the more serious offences, and often result in discharge. On the other hand, employees may be discharged or otherwise disciplined simply because their work performance is inadequate. Inadequate work performance may occur for such diverse reasons as incompetence, excessive absenteeism, ill health, or the inability to get along with fellow employees.

744. Most collective agreements provide that the employer can only discharge or discipline an employee for just cause. In the absence of such a restriction, arbitrators have been reluctant to review management decisions to discharge or discipline, especially where there exists in the collective agreement a clause giving management a general right to discharge or discipline. One Canadian jurisdiction, however, makes it mandatory for the parties to include in their collective agreement a clause requiring that discharge or discipline be for just and reasonable cause.[1]

    1. British Columbia, s.93.

(a) Resignation

745. The term 'discharge' is not considered as including all terminations of employment. Where the employment relationship is terminated by the voluntary actions of the employee, such a termination is regarded as a resignation (or a quit) and is not arbitrable as a discharge. Arbitrators, however, have been cautious when characterizing employee conduct as a quit, requiring that there not only be evidence of an employee's intention to quit but also proof of conduct indicating that this intention has been carried out.[1] Both of these elements must be established clearly before arbitrators have concluded that the employee has voluntarily terminated the employment relationship.[2]

    1. *Anchor Cap and Closure*, (1949) 1 L.A.C. 222.
    2. For a review of the arbitral jurisprudence, see *University of Guelph*, (1973) 2 L.A.C. (2d) 351.

(b) Retirement

746. The retirement of an employee, regardless of whether it is involuntary, has not been considered to be the same kind of termination as a discharge.[1] The characterization of retirement as being different from discharge means that a compulsory retirement cannot be dealt with by an arbitrator in the same manner as other terminations of employment. While arbitral review of involuntary retirement is not entirely absent, the usual standard of 'just cause' is not applicable. The arbitral case law indicates, however, that an involuntary retirement cannot be made in an arbitrary, discriminatory, or unreasonable manner.[2] In applying this standard arbitrators have taken into account such considerations as the prevailing retirement age, equality of treatment in the application of a retirement policy, the amount of notice of a retirement policy given to the employee, non-discrimination clauses in the collective agreement,[3] and applicable human rights legislation.[4] In some situations arbitrators have found the involuntary retirement of an employee to be improper but, in general, it would appear that they have been reluctant to interfere with the application of compulsory retirement policies.

1. *Bell Canada*, (1973) 37 D.L.R. (3d) 561 (S.C.C.).
2. The case law is discussed in some detail in *Electrical Power Systems Construction Assoc.*, (1978) 18 L.A.C. (2d) 205 (O.L.R.B.).
3. *Oshawa Times*, (1977) 14 L.A.C. (2d) 375.
4. *Prince Rupert Fishermen's Co-op. Assoc.*, (1979) 19 L.A.C. (2d) 308; but see *Crestbrook Forest Industries*, (1980) 22 L.A.C. (2d) 25.

(c) Probationary employees

747. One of the more difficult problems facing arbitrators concerns the position of the probationary employee whose employment has been terminated prior to the expiry of the probationary period. Many collective agreements expressly provide that the discharge of a probationary employee is not to be judged by reference to as high a standard as that of the employee who has acquired seniority, and some agreements even go so far as to expressly preclude the matter from being arbitrated. This latter type of provision has usually been considered as being incompatible with the legislative provision making mandatory arbitration of all outstanding grievances, but this view has not received universal acceptance.[1] Even where the collective agreement does not explicitly deal with the situation of the probationary employee who has been terminated, arbitrators have generally taken the approach that in this type of situation the management decision to terminate the employment relationship will be subject to a less onerous standard of arbitral review.[2] The result is that the probationary employee, although generally entitled to all other benefits of the collective agreement, has far less job security under the collective agreement than the employee with seniority.

1. *Supra*, (B.1.f. *Sources of Arbitral Standards*).
2. *Porcupine Area Ambulance Service*, (1975) 7 L.A.C. (2d) 182.

(d) Loss of seniority

748. Some collective agreements may also provide for the loss of seniority where certain conditions occur, such as the absence of the employee without leave for a specified number of days. There is no arbitral consensus as to the consequences that flow from this type of situation. Some arbitrators have treated a loss of seniority in these circumstances as justifying the employee's discharge, while others have regarded it as having less severe consequences.[1] The question is whether the loss of seniority has the effect of returning the employee to probationary status, or whether the employee is simply to be considered as a permanent employee but with no seniority.

1. For a discussion of these two approaches see *Gates Rubber*, (1979). 20 L.A.C. (2d) 229.

(e) Demotions

749. There is some question as to whether demotions should be treated as a form of discipline. Arbitrators have drawn a distinction between those demotions which are in essence disciplinary measures, and those that are non-disciplinary in nature. A disciplinary demotion occurs where an employee, because of some form of misconduct, has been transferred to a lower-rated job. A non-disciplinary demotion occurs where the transfer to the lower-rated job does not relate to employee misconduct, such as where the employee is incapable of performing the job or where a lack of work requires a reassignment of the work force.[1] Arbitrators have applied a different standard to non-disciplinary demotions, usually restricting their inquiry to the question of whether the employer has acted in a manner that was arbitrary, discriminatory, or in bad faith.[2] In cases of disciplinary demotion, arbitrators initially tended to regard demotion as being an inappropriate form of penalty although, more recently, they have come to recognize that a demotion may be appropriate where the employee misconduct relates to that person's suitability to perform the job.[3]

1. *Cominco*, (1975) 9 L.A.C. (2d) 233. (B.C.L.R.B.).
2. *Canadian Canners*, (1975) 9 L.A.C. (2d) 396.
3. *Stelco*, (1975) 7 L.A.C. (2d) 132.

(f) Onus and standard of proof

750. It is now generally accepted that the employer bears the ultimate onus of establishing that discharge or discipline is for just cause.[1] This approach recognizes that it is the employer that has access to the reasons for the discharge or discipline and is in the better position to be able to introduce proof of these reasons. Because the employer bears the ultimate onus of proof in these cases, it is the usual practice for the arbitrator to have the employer adduce evidence before calling upon the union to present its case.

1. *Intl. Nickel*, (1969) 20 L.A.C. 51.

751. The standard of proof required of the employer in cases of discharge and discipline is that which applies in other civil matters – that the case be established on the balance of probabilities. While the application of the standard does not usually give rise to difficulty, problems can occur where the misconduct giving rise to the disciplinary sanction also constitutes a criminal offence. Arbitrators appear to be divided as to whether the civil standard of proof is still applicable, or whether a more stringent standard (approaching that of the criminal standard of proof beyond a reasonable doubt) should be applied.

(g) Alteration of grounds

752. On occasion employers advance at the hearing a justification that had not been relied upon when the disciplinary sanction was first imposed. As a general rule, arbitrators have been reluctant to receive this subsequent justification even though it might serve to justify the employer's conduct.[1] However, where it can be established that the employer was unaware of these alternative grounds at the time disciplinary action was taken, there appears to be greater arbitral willingness to allow the employer to raise such grounds at a later stage in the proceedings. In those situations where alternative grounds are received at the hearing, the usual practice is to adjourn the hearing to allow the union the opportunity to prepare a response.

1. *Aerocide Dispensers*, (1965) 15 L.A.C. 416.

(h) Culminating incident

753. Employers may sometimes attempt to justify disciplinary action by reference to the employee's previous unfavourable employment record. Such a justification can only be used where the event precipitating the imposition of the sanction by itself warrants the imposition of some kind of discipline.[1] Once this culminating incident, as it is called, has been established arbitrators have been prepared to consider previous incidents of misconduct as being relevant to the issue of just cause, provided that these incidents have been the subject of disciplinary action which has been brought to the employee's attention and placed on the employment record.

1. *Canadian Lukens*, (1976) 12 L.A.C. (2d) 439.

(i) Insubordination

754. Insubordination is one of the primary grounds for the imposition of disciplinary sanctions by employers. Employers place a high priority upon being able to run their enterprises in an orderly and disciplined manner and, not unnaturally, view employee challenges to their managerial authority in a serious light. From the employee and union perspective, however, some of these challenges to managerial authority raise important questions concerning the extent of an employee's civil rights in the work place.

755. Arbitrators when reviewing cases of insubordination have generally placed greater emphasis upon the employer's right to direct its work forces and to take immediate disciplinary action where such directions are not followed. The general rule is that the employee is expected to comply with the order of the employer, even where that order appears to be in violation of the collective agreement. This approach does not leave the union and employer without redress where the employer's conduct constitutes a violation of the collective agreement, since this is a matter that can be resolved subsequently through the grievance and arbitration procedure. This 'comply-now, grieve-later' rule is one that has received wide acceptance by Canadian arbitrators.[1]

1. This approach appears to have its origin in an American arbitral award, *Ford Motor*, 3 L.A. 779.

756. Like any rule, the 'comply-now, grieve-later' rule has certain recognized exceptions. Arbitrators take into account the fact that in some situations the grievance and arbitration procedure is not likely to provide the employee with adequate redress. Conduct that would ordinarily be considered as insubordinate has been excused when influenced by a legitimate concern for personal health and safety,[1] where compliance would require the employee to perform an illegal act,[2] where a union official is pursuing the legitimate interests of the union and its members,[3] and in some circumstances where there is an objection to a rule relating to the personal appearance of employees.[4]

1. *Stelco*, (1974) 4 L.A.C. (2d) 315.
2. *Int'l. Nickel*, (1974) 6 L.A.C. (2d) 172.
3. *Stancor Central*, (1970) 22 L.A.C. 184.
4. *Borough of Etobicoke*, (1974) 6 L.A.C. (2d) 251.

(j) Misconduct outside the work place

757. At times misconduct of an employee occurring away from the work place may be brought to the attention of the employer, usually where such misconduct has resulted in the machinery of criminal justice being put into motion. Where an employee has been charged with a criminal offence for conduct occurring away from work, arbitrators have considered that the suspension of the employee from work to be justified only where the employer can establish that the continued employment of that employee would prejudice the employer's interests in some material way.[1] This approach takes into account such employer concerns as the security of its own property and its reputation in the eyes of the public.

1. *Dorr-Oliver-Long*, (1973) 3 L.A.C. (2d) 193.

758. Much the same approach is taken by arbitrators where off-duty misconduct results in a criminal conviction. Again the question is whether the conviction is sufficiently prejudicial to the interests of the employer so as to justify the employer taking disciplinary action (in most cases discharge).[1] If the conviction carries with it a penalty of imprisonment, however, the employer

may be justified in terminating the employment relationship simply because
the employee is no longer available for work.[2]

1. *Borough of Scarborough*, (1973) 3 L.A.C. (2d) 213.
2. *Canadian Westinghouse*, (1956) 7 L.A.C. 94; but see *Alcan*, (1974) 6 L.A.C. (2d) 386.

(k) The appropriate penalty

759. Even where it can be established by the employer that just cause exists
for the imposition of some form of discipline, there still remains a question of
whether the disciplinary sanction chose by the employer is appropriate in the
circumstance of the particular grievance.[1] Arbitrators have taken a wide
variety of factors into account when reviewing the appropriateness of the
penalty, including the previous record and service of the grievor, the nature and
seriousness of the offence,[2] and equality of treatment among employees.[3]
Moreover, arbitrators now take into account the desirability of corrective
discipline,[4] and have even considered the rehabilitative potential of the
employee.[5]

1. See *supra*, §2 B.1.g. *Remedial Authority* for a discussion of the extent of the arbitrator's
remedial authority to substitute a lesser penalty.
2. *Steel Equipment*, (1964) 14 L.A.C. 356.
3. *Julius Resnick*, (1973) 3 L.A.C. (2d) 247.
4. *Ontario Produce*, (1976) 12 L.A.C. (2d) 235.
5. *Toronto East General Hospital*, (1975), 9 L.A.C. (2d) 311; but see *Northern & Central Gas*,
(1978) 16 L.A.C. (2d) 395.

4. Seniority

760. Just as important as the discharge and discipline cases are those grievances claiming that the employer has not acted with proper regard to the
seniority of the employee. Employee seniority rights substantially qualify the
general right of the employer to manage the enterprise. Length of service is not
only a factor that may affect entitlement to benefits such as vacations and
pensions but, even more importantly, it is usually a factor affecting employee
claims to job opportunities and job security. Most collective agreements provide that the employer cannot promote, demote, transfer, lay-off or recall
without giving at least some consideration to the relative seniority of the
employees. Generally, seniority is defined in terms of length of service with the
employer, regardless of whether some of that service relates to employment
outside the bargaining unit.[1]

1. *Gabriel*, (1967) 18 L.A.C. 373; *ICN Strong Cobb Arner*, (1974) 5 L.A.C. (2d) 105.

(a) Types of seniority provisions

761. Although there exists a great variation in the wording of seniority
clauses from agreement to agreement, such provisions are usually character-

ized by reference to two basic models – the competitive clause and the non-competitive clause.[1] The former type of clause, which is more common, requires the employer to consider seniority as the deciding factor only where the skill and ability of the competing employees is relatively equal. The latter type of clause, however, places much greater emphasis on seniority, making it the deciding factor so long as the more senior employee can perform the job competently. Both types of clauses may give rise to a grievance alleging that the employer has either established the qualifications for the job in an improper manner, or has improperly assessed the abilities of the more senior employee.

1. *Westeel Products*, (1960) 11 L.A.C. 199.

(b) Scope of arbitral review

762. Grievances relating to the establishment and assessment of job qualifications raise the vexing question as to the extent to which the arbitrator may properly review this type of managerial judgment. Although it is clearly recognized that it is not appropriate for arbitrators to usurp the functions of management, it is equally apparent that arbitrators must give meaning to seniority provisions contained in collective agreements. There has been no lack of arbitral effort spared in attempting to reconcile these competing concerns as evidenced by the numerous decisions that have attempted to formulate an appropriate approach.[1]

1. For a review of some of this jurisprudence, see *Hydro-Electric Power Commission of Ontario*, (1976) 11 L.A.C. (2d) 36.

763. Arbitrators in general have not applied the same scrutiny to a management decision respecting employee qualifications as they have to disciplinary decisions. Unless it can be established by a grievor that an employer has acted in bad faith, arbitrators have not been prepared to interfere with the setting of the qualifications for jobs.[1] Moreover, employer assessments of employee abilities have been usually respected by arbitrators, arbitral intervention occurring only where it has been established that management has acted in bad faith, has discriminated, or has been otherwise unreasonable.[2]

1. *Reynolds Aluminum*, (1974) 5 L.A.C. (2d) 251.
2. *Hydro Electric Power Commission of Ontario*, (1976) 11 L.A.C. (2d) 36.

764. A recent court decision in Ontario, however, suggests that arbitrators may have been taking a too narrow view of their authority to review managerial decisions relating to qualifications.[1] The court quashed a decision of an arbitration board which had simply asked itself whether the employer had acted 'honestly, reasonably, without discrimination and without bad faith'. According to the court, the arbitration board by taking this approach had failed to apply the language of the seniority clause in the collective agreement. Whether this judicial decision has made arbitrators less diffident when reviewing this type of management decision is not yet clear, although subsequent arbitration awards would indicate that there has not been much change of arbitral approach.[2]

1. *Great Atlantic and Pacific*, (1976) 76 C.L.L.C. para. 14,056 (Ont.H.C.).
2. *Dominion Stores*, (1977) 15 L.A.C. (2d) 403.

(c) Job posting

765. A usual incident of seniority provisions is a requirement in the collective agreement that job vacancies be publicly posted. In this way employees can be made aware of the job opportunities to which their seniority gives them some claim. Job posting requirements have been interpreted by arbitrators as binding employers only where the employer has actually determined that there is sufficient work available to justify the creation of the job.[1] Moreover, it is usually only the jobs described in the collective agreement that are considered to be subject to the posting requirement so that transfers within job classifications have been regarded as falling outside this requirement.[2]

1. *Tidewater Oil*, (1963) 14 L.A.C. 233.
2. *Kysor of Ridgetown*, (1967) 18 L.A.C. 63.

5. *Assignment of work*

766. The general right of the employer to assign work as it sees fit may be qualified by restrictions other than a requirement to consider the relative seniority of employees. Certain other qualifications, either explicit or implicit, upon the right of management to assign work may be found in the collective agreement.

(a) Bargaining unit work

767. Arbitrators have recognized that there is a core of work that is customarily performed by members of the bargaining unit. While the bargaining agent does not have any absolute right to claim this work for its employee constituents, it would appear that an employer is not allowed to make any substantial assignment of this core of bargaining unit work to either its supervisory employees, or to its non-supervisory employees not included in the bargaining unit. Arbitrators have recognized that this type of work assignment would substantially erode the seniority, classification, and wage structure created by the collective agreement.[1]

1. For a review of these decisions, see *Westroc Industries*, (1974) 5 L.A.C. (2d) 61.

768. A less restrictive approach, however, has been taken by arbitrators toward the contracting out of work by an employer. The general arbitral approach is that, in the absence of any explicit limitation in the collective agreement, an employer may enter upon a legitimate contracting out of work.[1]

Not all arrangements giving the appearance of a contracting-out have been regarded by arbitrators as being legitimate. Where an employer still retains substantial control over the employees of the person to whom the work has been allegedly contracted out, the arrangement made by the employer is likely to be regarded by an arbitrator as something less than a *bona fide* contracting-out of work.[2]

1. *Russelsteel*, (1966) 17 L.A.C. 253.
2. *Wean-McKay*, (1971) 23 L.A.C. 27.

(b) Classification structure

769. Many collective agreements contain a fairly elaborate system of job classification, setting out both descriptions of the job and the wage to be paid for the work falling within that job description. Such job classification systems serve the purpose of creating an equitable wage structure where remuneration bears some relation to the effort and skill required by the job. Although arbitrators have regarded job classification structures as creating a restriction upon the employer's discretion to determine the wage to be paid an employee, they have not treated such structures as restricting management's right to assign work.[1] As a general rule, management can create new job classifications and add to the job content of existing classifications.

1. *Algoma Steel*, (1968) 19 L.A.C. 236.

(c) Overtime

770. In the absence of an express provision in the collective agreement making overtime voluntary, arbitrators have taken the view that management has the right to require an employee to work overtime.[1] The employer's right to assign overtime on a compulsory basis, however, may be qualified by operation of minimum standards legislation. It is now clear that arbitrators must have regard to such legislation when determining the extent of an employer's right to assign overtime under the collective agreement.[2]

1. *Bridge & Tank*, (1976) 11 L.A.C. (2d) 301.
2. *McLeod* v. *Egan*, (1974) 46 D.L.R. (3d) 150 (S.C.C.).

771. Overtime is not always regarded by employees as a burden since many collective agreements provide premium pay for overtime work. As a result, collective agreements often contain provisions requiring the employer to distribute overtime so as to give all employees an equal chance to benefit from the extra work. Where such provisions have been breached, the employee may be awarded compensation for the lost overtime opportunity or, where appropriate, may receive a remedy 'in kind' providing the employee with an overtime opportunity to make up for the opportunity previously lost.[1]

1. *Canadian Johns Manville*, (1971) 22 L.A.C. 396.

6. Monetary grievances

772. An essential part of any collective agreement are those provisions establishing the compensation package for the employees in the bargaining unit. Collective bargaining in Canada is very much an economic exercise, and Canadian trade unions place great emphasis upon representing the economic interests of their members. As a result, many collective agreements not only provide for an elaborate wage structure, but they also provide a comprehensive system of fringe benefits, including such items as paid holidays, paid vacations, sick pay, medical and hospital insurance, disability insurance, pensions, and supplementary unemployment benefits. As the rate of inflation has accelerated in recent years, an increasing number of collective agreements have provided for the periodic adjustment of wages to take account of increases in the cost of living. A large number of grievances brought to arbitration involve the interpretation of these various kinds of monetary provisions.

7. Union rights and liabilities under the collective agreement

773. The trade union, as one of the two principal parties to the collective bargaining relationship may bargain on its own behalf as well as for the members of the bargaining unit. Certain clauses of the collective agreement may create special rights for the union, and for its officials. By the same token, however, arbitrators have recognized that the special position of the union and union officials may carry with it greater obligations than those imposed upon the members of the bargaining unit.

(a) Enforcement of union security provisions

774. Union security provisions are a common feature of Canadian collective agreements.[1] Most of these provisions make the payment of regular union dues a condition of employment, and some go further by making continued employment conditional upon union membership. Such provisions are enforced through the grievance and arbitration process in the same manner as any other clause of the collective agreement.

1. *Supra*, c.IV–§1, *The Union's Exclusive Authority to Bargain*.

775. The enforcement of a union security provision through arbitration, brings into conflict the interests of the trade union and those of the individual employee. While trade unions usually place great emphasis upon the protection of employment, in this situation they find themselves in the unusual position of insisting upon the termination of the employment relationship. Union security provisions have been recognized as being quite legal, and arbitrators have enforced them by ordering employers to terminate the employment relationship of employees who have not complied with the require-

ment of such provisions. However, these employees, since they would be directly affected by the disposition of the union's grievance at arbitration, are entitled to notice of the arbitration hearing, and also entitled to participate fully in the hearings.[1] The enforcement of a union security provision at arbitration may also entail an examination of the internal affairs of the trade union in order to determine the circumstances under which union membership has been divested or withheld.[2]

1. *Re Hoogendoorn and Greening Metal Products & Screening Equipment*, (1968) 65 D.L.R. (2d) 641 (S.C.C.).
2. *Orenda Engines*, (1958) 8 L.A.C. 116.

776. Union security provisions not only impose an obligation upon employees to contribute financially to the trade union, but they also impose an obligation upon the employer to collect such funds on behalf of the bargaining agent. Employers have not been permitted to impound these funds in order to satisfy some other financial obligation that might be owed to the employer by the trade union.[1] Where a union security provision requires, not only the collection of union dues, but also the hiring of union members, employer liability for breach of such a provision is likely to be even more extensive. A breach of a 'hiring hall provision gives the union the right to claim damages, not just for lost dues, but also for lost contributions to its welfare and vacation funds, and for the wages that its members would have earned had the clause been honoured.[2]

1. *Brooks Manufacturing*, (1969) 20 L.A.C. 298.
2. *Re Blouin Drywall Contractors and Carpenters & Joiners*, (1976) 57 D.L.P. (3d) 199 (Ont. C.A.).

(b) Special position of union officials

777. The collective agreement may also confer certain privileges upon union officials. Time-off for union business may be provided for in the collective agreement, permitting union officials to carry out their functions on the employer's time. Many collective agreements provide that the union official is to be indemnified for any loss of earnings resulting from performing union business during working hours. The right of a trade union official to take time-off for union business, however, is not an absolute right, and arbitrators have held that an employer may discipline a union official for abusing this right.[1] Union officials may also acquire super seniority under the collective agreement, giving them greater job security in the event of lay-off than that enjoyed by the other members of the bargaining unit and, sometimes, a better claim to overtime work. Arbitrators have also recognized that union officials should not be denied opportunity for promotion simply because they may have to spend some time performing their union responsibilities. However, employers are permitted to consider whether an official's union responsibilities would interfere substantially with performance of the job.[2]

1. *Massey-Ferguson Industries*, (1970) 21 L.A.C. 244.
2. *Northern Electric*, (1976) 11 L.A.C. (2d) 208; *Toronto Star*, (1977) 15 L.A.C. (2d) 326.

778. Union officials may also be allowed more latitude than other employees in their relationship with management. Emotions may run high in meetings between union and management giving rise to conduct that would normally be considered as insubordinate. Arbitrators, however, have not treated such conduct as justifying discipline where it is clear that the conduct occurred in circumstances where the union official was acting in a representative capacity.[1]

1. *St. Lawrence Seaway Authority*, (1979) 20 L.A.C. (2d) 24.

(c) Union obligations

779. Collective agreements usually contain a provision stipulating that there are to be no strikes or lock-outs during the term of the agreement. Most grievances brought to arbitration by employers relate to the breach of this particular obligation.[1] Arbitrators have generally characterized conduct as strike action in the same way as have the labour boards when dealing with the legislative strike prohibition. Where a strike occurs, an onus is placed upon the trade union to establish that it did not authorize or condone such activity.[2] Although arbitrators have interpreted the 'no-strike' obligation as requiring the union and its officials to make their best effort to end the strike, they have not imposed absolute liability upon the trade union, recognizing that a trade union and its officials may not always be able to control spontaneous or 'wildcat' strikes. If a trade union is found to be responsible for strike action occurring during the term of the collective agreement, the arbitrator has the power to award damages for losses flowing from breach of the no-strike provision in the collective agreement.[3]

1. *Supra*, C.V–§5 *Remedies for Unlawful Industrial Action*.
2. *Canadian General Electric*, (1951) 2 L.A.C. 608.
3. *Re Polymer and Oil Workers*, (1962) 33 D.L.R. (2d) 144 (S.C.C.).

(d) Obligations of union officials

780. There has been considerable debate over the extent to which union officials have a greater responsibility to an employer than other members of the bargaining unit. This issue usually arises in the context of an illegal strike, the question being whether the participation of union officials in a walk-out should draw more severe discipline than that meted out to other striking employees. Recent judicial authority would indicate that, although more severe discipline may be warranted where a union official bears more responsibility for a breach of the collective agreement, greater discipline cannot be justified simply by virtue of the fact of holding union office.[1] Where a trade union official assumes only a passive role in the particular incident drawing disciplinary sanctions, then the responsibility of that official is no greater than that of the ordinary employee.

1. *Douglas Aircraft*, (1979) 79 C.L.L.C. para 14,221 (S.C.C.).

781. The disciplining of union officials also raises the question of the appropriate sanction to be imposed in such circumstances. In one case where a union official had been discharged for irresponsible behaviour, the arbitrator ordered that the official be reinstated on the condition that the person not hold union office.[1] The imposition of this condition, however, was considered by the courts as being inconsistent with those provisions of collective bargaining legislation protecting employee freedom of association, and the arbitrators award was quashed.[2]

1. *Inglis*, (1976) 12 L.A.C. (2d) 435.
2. (1977) 77 C.L.L.C. para. 14,089 (Ont.H.C.).

§3. THE LIMITED ROLE OF THE COURTS

782. The existence of a well-developed system of grievance arbitration, and the legal barriers to the direct enforcement of collective agreements in the courts,[1] has meant that the judiciary has not played a major role in the enforcement of Canadian collective agreements. Nevertheless, the courts have influenced the development of Canadian arbitral jurisprudence through the exercise of their prerogative to review the decisions of lower tribunals and, as well, the enforcement process of the courts has had to be brought into play occasionally in order to ensure compliance with arbitral awards.

1. *Supra*, §1.B. Unique Legal Effect.

A. Judicial Review

783. Canadian courts have made it clear that their authority to review the decisions of lower tribunals extends to grievance arbitration tribunals.[1] While at one time the courts appeared to attach some significance to the difference between statutory grievance arbitration and consensual grievance arbitration when determining the scope of the judicial review,[2] more recent cases would indicate that this distinction has become less important.[3]

1. *Port Arthur Shipbuilding* v. *Arthurs*, (1968) 70 D.L.R. (2d) 693 (S.C.C.).
2. *Howe Sound* v. *Mine Workers*, (1962) 33 D.L.R. (2d) 1 (S.C.C.).
3. *Bell Canada* v. *Office & Professional Employees*, (1973) 37 D.L.R. (3d) 561 (S.C.C.);
Metro Toronto Police Assoc. v. *Metro Toronto Board of Commissioners of Police* (1974) 45 D.L.R. (3d) 548 (S.C.C.); *Volvo Canada*, (1979) 79 C.L.L.C. para. 14,210 (S.C.C.).

784. The scope of judicial review, however, does depend to some extent upon whether the applicable collective bargaining legislation has expressly restricted judicial review of grievance arbitration by means of a privative clause.[1] Where no private clause exists in the legislation, the courts have been prepared to review arbitration decisions on both matters of procedure and substance. The scope of this judicial review covers such matters as breach of the rules of natural justice (including the question of bias), excess of jurisdiction, and error of law on the face of the award. A privative clause has been considered by the courts as precluding review for error of law on the face of the award but not review on the other grounds.[2] Even where no privative clause is in force, however, the courts have demonstrated some deference to arbitral decision-making. On matters of collective agreement interpretation, the courts have indicted that they are not prepared to overrule an arbitrator where they simply disagree with the interpretation to the agreement given by the arbitrator, and that an arbitral award will be quashed only where an arbitrator has given the language an interpretation that it cannot reasonably bear.[3] The courts have been less deferential, however, where the arbitrator has had to construe a general statute.[4]

1. Canada, s.156; British Columbia, s.109. In British Columbia, moreover, s.108 of the Code expressly gives a power of review to the labour board.
2. *Re Canadian National Railway and U.T.W.*, (1970) 63 D.L.R. (3d) 385 (Ont.C.A.).
3. *Machinists & Aerospace Workers and Hudson Bay Mining and Smelting*, (1968) 66 D.L.R. (2d) 1 (S.C.C.).
4. *Mcleod* v. *Egan*, (1974) 46 D.L.R. (3d) 150 (S.C.C.).

B. Enforcement of arbitration awards

785. Arbitrators do not themselves have the coercive powers to enforce their awards, and collective bargaining legislation in Canada usually provides that arbitration awards are to be filed with the courts and enforced in the same manner as a judicial decision. The result is that the contempt power of the court is ultimately available to enforce compliance with the arbitrator's award. Generally speaking, non-compliance with arbitration awards does not appear to be a serious problem in Canada.

§4. THE EXPANDING ROLE OF LABOUR BOARDS

786. Until quite recently labour boards played a minor role in the grievance arbitration process. The adjudication of disputes arising under collective agreements was generally regarded as being the function of *ad hoc* arbitrators or boards of arbitration with the labour boards playing only a supporting role. Only such ancillary functions as ensuring whether a grievance arbitration provision met the statutory standard, and advising on whether there was authority in a Minister to constitute an arbitration tribunal, were given to labour boards by the legislation.[1] Even in situations where a violation of the collective agreement might also be construed as a violation of the collective bargaining statute itself, labour boards were still generally content to have the matter dealt with through the arbitration process.[2] More recently, however, there appears to have been a marked shift in some jurisdictions toward having labour boards play a more prominent role in the grievance arbitration process.

1. For example, s.37(3) and s.96 of the Ontario legislation.
2. This general policy of deferral to arbitration can be found in *United Gas*, (1965) 65 C.L.L.C. para. 16,056 (O.L.R.B.).

A. Direct jurisdiction

787. In two Canadian jurisdictions, British Columbia and Ontario,[1] labour boards have been given a direct jurisdiction over grievance arbitration. The jurisdiction of the British Columbia board is comprehensive in scope applying to grievances arising from any collective agreement so long as the parties in their collective agreement have not explicitly excluded the operation of this procedure. In Ontario, the jurisdiction of the board to arbitrate grievances applies only to the construction industry where conventional grievance arbitration had proved to be less than satisfactory. In contrast to British Columbia, however, the parties to a construction industry collective agreement in Ontario cannot opt out of the statutory arbitration procedure.

1. British Columbia, s.96; Ontario, s.112a.

788. The two boards have taken somewhat different approaches in exercising their arbitral jurisdiction. The British Columbia board has regarded its role as providing a procedure through which grievances can be resolved informally, primarily through the settlement efforts of its industrial relations officers. If settlement of a grievance is not possible, the board will take one of three approaches: informal investigative disposition of the case; formal adjudication of the matter with full hearing; or referral of grievance back to the parties for arbitration under the collective agreement.[1] Apparently that Board's usual practice is to refer a grievance back to the parties where it cannot be compromised or resolved by means of an informal investigative disposition.

1. Statement of Policy, 2 C.L.L.R. para. 30,601; see also, P. C. Weiler, *The Role of the Labour Board as an Alternative to Arbitration in Proceedings of the 30th Annual Meeting of the National Academy of Arbitrators* (Washington, 1977).

789. In its early stages, the procedure of the Ontario board resembles that followed in British Columbia as settlement efforts are initially made by the board's labour relations officers. If a grievance is not settled, however, a different approach is taken by the Ontario board. Unlike its British Columbia counterpart, the Ontario board does not resolve the matter by investigative disposition nor does it refer the grievance back to the parties. Instead, the unsettled grievance goes to a board hearing, which by statute must be fourteen days after the grievance is first referred to the board. Once the grievance reaches this adjudicative stage, the Ontario board takes much the same approach as would any other arbitrator.[1]

1. See *Electrical Power Systems Construction Assoc.*, (1978) 18 L.A.C. (2d) 205 (O.L.R.B.).

B. Review jurisdiction

790. In addition to its direct jurisdiction over grievance arbitration the British Columbia board, alone among Canadian labour boards, has been given a power to review the decisions of arbitrators.[1] This jurisdiction has not been interpreted by the board as giving it a full appellate power to overrule the arbitrator's award, but has been defined by the board as a power to review arbitration proceedings to ensure fairness of procedures and to ensure that the arbitrator has taken into account the principles established by the collective bargaining statute.[2]

1. S.108.
2. *Simon Fraser University*, [1976] 2 C.L.R.B.R. 54 (B.C.L.R.B.).

C. Concurrent jurisdiction

791. Some breaches of the collective agreement may also constitute violations of collective bargaining legislation, giving rise to an overlap of jurisdiction between the arbitrator and the labour board. While as a general rule labour boards have deferred to the jurisdiction of the arbitrator, there appears to be increasing recognition by the boards that this policy of deferral may not be appropriate in all situations. One exception to this general policy of deferral are those situations where the labour board considers that the arbitration process cannot deal effectively with the matter. Such a situation might occur where there is a direct conflict between the interests of the union and those of the grievor, or where there is some form of collusion between the union and the employer to be prejudice of the employee grievor.[1] A second exception to the general policy of deferral are those matters raising issues extending beyond the interpretation and administration of the collective agreement and affecting the general structure of collective bargaining.[2] Labour boards have indicated that they now regard it as their function to deal with the broader issues of collective bargaining, and have not been content to have this type of issue settled by grievance arbitration.

1. *Imperial Tobacco Products*, [1975] 1 C.L.R.B.R. 1 (O.L.R.B.); *Bell Canada*, [1978] 1 C.L.R.B.R. 1 (C.L.R.B.).
2. *Kodak*, [1977] 1 Can. L.R.B.R. 280 (O.L.R.B.).

Index

The numbers refer to paragraphs.

Index

British North America Act: 8, 9, 10, 224

Cabinet: 16, 17, 87, 117–118, 134
Canadian Labour Congress: 304, 305–312, 327
Captive audience speech: 381, 382, 383
Certification: see union certification
Checkoff clause: 70, 498, 499, 776
Child labour: 174
Civil law: 1, 21, 108, 109, 112, 599
Civil rights: 9, 11, 315
Civil service: 1, 17
Closed shop: 70, 330–332, 497
  (See also: Union security)
Coercion: 366, 374, 381, 382, 383, 385
Collective agreement: 49, 51, 57, 58, 62, 136–139, 140, 141, 162, 179, 190, 233, 234, 235, 257, 289, 342, 343, 354, 370, 372, 384, 397, 473, 477, 481–489, 490, 494, 501, 520–522, 525, 529, 546, 585, 586, 587, 594, 633–639, 683, 685, 686–791
  Administration and enforcement: 706–781, 782
  Compulsory provisions: 551, 683
  Contractual effect: 689–695
  Duration: 530, 549, 688, 699
  Enforceability: 316, 320, 372, 633, 661, 698, 700, 702, 705, 782
  Form: 687–688
  Grievance procedure: 707–709
  Normative effect: 689, 696
  Ratification: 687
  Termination: 481–489, 529, 699–701
Collective agreement bar: 443, 486
Collective bargaining: 42, 45, 49, 54, 58, 60, 61, 63, 69, 81, 84, 85, 86, 87, 89, 90, 103, 130, 149, 157, 161, 190, 214, 229, 258, 313, 320–323, 326, 327, 328, 340–356, 401–553
  Illegal demands: 547–550, 553
  Mandatory demands: 547–550, 551
  Notice: 526–529
  Purpose: 421–424
  Voluntary demands: 547–550
Collective bargaining policy: 119, 340–356

Collective bargaining rights: 306, 330, 332, 341, 342, 360, 384, 385, 401–489, 492–501, 521, 537, 690
  Acquisition: 401, 403–447
  Exclusive: 306–434, 443, 450, 486, 492–501, 537, 551
  Method of acquisition: 434–447
  Termination: 401, 481–489
  Transfer: 401, 480
Collective bargaining unit: 449–479
  Agreed upon: 459
  Craft v. Industrial: 54, 455–458
Collective negotiations: see collective bargaining
Commissaires: 122
Commission employee: 232
Common law: 1, 21, 50, 74, 108, 109, 112, 128–132, 137, 148, 161, 194, 199, 232, 235, 243, 280–284, 289, 295, 313–319, 330, 342–343, 363, 405, 598–605
Communication: 5, 11, 32, 44, 92
Compensatory damages: see damages
'Comply-now, grieve-later' rule: 755, 756
Conciliation: 59, 80, 122, 124, 507–513, 515, 554, 555, 559, 629, 630
  (See also: Mediation)
Conciliation
  compulsory: 507–513, 554, 559, 629
Conciliation board: 508–509
Conciliation officer: 510–513
Confidential employees: 410
Constitution: 7, 22, 102–106, 315, 615, 616, 617
Constitutionality: 105, 315, 616
Construction industry: 1, 44, 103, 201, 427, 435, 436, 449, 469, 479, 493, 642, 787
Consumer price index: 223
  (See also: Index)
Contempt of court: 392, 394, 678, 679
Cost of living index: 220, 321
  (See also: Consumers index)
Craft unionism: 54, 455–458
Criminal code: see Criminal law
Criminal conspiracy: 74, 76, 315, 316, 318, 600, 652

Index

Index

Office holders: 144
One person company: 163
Ontario: 2, 28, 90, 113, 248, 249, 258, 285, 296, 321, 331, 332, 344, 345, 348, 349, 350, 361, 425, 433, 436, 444, 462, 465, 470, 475, 478, 485, 486, 489, 509, 530, 567, 583, 625, 659, 661, 682, 685, 715, 764, 787–789
Overtime: 770–771, 777

Paid holidays: 585, 586, 587, 772
Parliament: 14, 15, 108, 303
Participation: 419
  (See also: Economic participation)
Partnership: 153, 322
Part-time employees: 462
Peacekeeping procedures: 51, 551, 629, 630, 683
Pension: 219–231, 244, 550, 585–588
  Disability pension: 222
  Survivor's pension: 222
Pension Appeal Board: 217
Pension Plans: 219–231, 550
  Canada Pension plan: 220–224
  Old age security pension: 225–228
  Private pension plans: 229–231
  Quebec pension plan: 224, 226
Petitions: 438, 439
Picketing: 62, 66, 67, 106, 122, 129, 131, 316, 324, 342, 399, 400, 545, 554, 569–572, 593, 598–627, 641, 645, 646, 647, 648, 675, 693
  Mass—: 608
  Secondary—: 620–627
Piece-Wages: 232
Piece-Worker: 232
Placement agencies: see Employment Agencies
Political parties: 25, 30, 31, 94, 96, 97
Population: 3, 33–44
Populism: 29
Pregnancy: 210, 211, 215, 273
  (See also: Maternity leave)
Presumption of dismissal for union activity: 364, 365, 388
Presumption of yearly hiring: 165

Price control: 12, 121
Prime Minister: 14, 16
Prince Edward Island: 183, 258, 285, 322
Private sector: 1, 48, 72, 90, 95, 411, 423
Probationary employees: 144, 747, 748
Procedural rules: 114, 324, 335–338, 348, 668–671
Professional employees: 155, 412, 463
Profit sharing: 229
Promotion: 353, 585, 731, 760, 777
Provinces: 1, 10, 90
Provincial governments: 8, 89, 96, 102
Provincial premier, 14, 16
Public administration: 92, 95
Public employees: 44, 144, 221, 411, 423, 524, 576, 652
Public morality: 180
Public order: 106, 180, 334
Public sector: 43, 48, 95, 411, 423, 558
  (See also: Public Administration and Administrative Agencies)
Purchase of a business: see Sale of a business

Quantum meruit: 171, 193, 299
Quebec: 1, 2, 13, 21, 28, 29, 33, 37, 93, 116, 122, 183, 224, 248, 258, 286, 310, 322, 344, 372, 402, 436, 485, 493, 512, 520, 558, 579, 599

Rand formula: 70, 190, 330, 497, 498, 501
  (See also: Union security)
Reduction of working hours: 235
Redundancy: 365
Regional development: 38
Regionalism: 28, 38
Reinstatement: 294, 349, 351, 389, 397, 583, 584, 727, 781
Remuneration: 143, 148, 159, 192–231, 232, 233, 234, 235, 250, 296, 299
  (See also: Wages)
  Form of—: 200
  Periodical—: 194–195
Reserved rights theory: 695
  (See also: Managerial Prerogatives: 695)

288

Index

Termination of contract – *contd.*
   (See also: Discharge, dismissal)
   By bankruptcy: 270, 276, 298
   By death of one of the parties: 270, 275
   By dissolution of firm: 278, 298
   By frustration: 270–274
   By mutual consent: 148, 270
   By notice: 280–286
   (See also: Notice)
   By retirement: 270, 285
   (See also: Retirement)
   By sale of the business: 270, 279
   For cause: 287–288, 289–290, 291
   Group termination: 286
   (See also: Lay-off)
Termination notice: see Notice
Territories: 10
Test of employment status: 405
Tort: 129, 238–242, 318, 324, 343, 398,
   598–605, 628, 655, 662–665
Trade licensing: 119, 121
Trades and Labour Congress of Canada:
   78
Trade secrets: 264–268
Trade training: 119, 121
Trade union: see Union
Transfer of business: 472–479
Transportation: 5, 44, 79, 92
Travelling salesmen: see Salesmen
Trespass: 610–612
Trial courts: 111–114
Tribunal du Travail: 116, 122, 402
Truck payments: 200, 202

Unemployment: 37, 83
Unemployment insurance: 198, 207–218,
   589
Unfair labour practices: 62, 69, 86, 122,
   320, 361, 362, 363–400, 567, 578
Unincorporated associations: 321, 323,
   324, 325, 330, 331, 658, 704
Union
   Central union: 327–329, 432
   Certification: 56, 61, 62, 71, 122, 327,
   332, 384, 385, 425, 434–447, 450,
   482, 483, 486, 487, 631, 632
   Civil suits: 656–660

Constitution: 130, 325, 327, 425, 426,
   427, 428, 429, 480
Convention: 304, 307, 338
Councils: 305–312, 433, 449
Decertification: 482–483, 484, 485,
   552
Democracy: 325–356, 425
Development and expansion: 73–101,
   313, 319
Disciplinary tribunal: 335–338
Displacement: 484
Dissolution: 372, 391
Dues: 200
(See also: Dues Shop)
Facilities: 370, 420, 777
Inactivity: 485–488
Internal affairs: 122, 303, 317, 325–
   356, 429, 775
International: 83, 93, 98, 300, 303–
   304, 306, 309–312, 338, 432
Legal status: 313–356, 658–660, 702–
   704
Local–Parent relationship: 327–329,
   421, 425
Local union: 327–329
Membership and influence: 42, 43–44,
   47, 56, 82, 91, 92, 95, 300–301, 330–
   339, 365, 366, 374, 426–429, 437
Organization: 93, 98, 317, 325–356,
   425
Political activity: 94, 96, 97, 307, 309,
   424
Recognition: 56, 61, 62, 71, 84, 87,
   361, 375, 384, 385, 434, 435
(See also: Certification)
Registration: 315, 316, 318
Representativeness: 434, 436, 437–
   442, 482
Responsibility: 656–657
Size and number: 43, 82, 91, 92, 95,
   301–302
Union security: 70, 190, 330–334, 370,
   375, 426, 428, 497–501, 504, 691,
   774–776
(See also: Checkoff, Agency shop,
   Union shop, Closed shop, Dues shop,
   Rand formula)

290